Fundamentals of
Business Communication

by

Sherry J. Roberts, PhD
Jennings A. Jones College of Business
Middle Tennessee State University
Murfreesboro, TN

Publisher
The Goodheart-Willcox Company, Inc.
Tinley Park, Illinois
www.g-w.com

Library of Congress Catalog Card Number 2010040298

ISBN 978-1-60525-472-2

2 3 4 5 6 7 8 9 – 12 – 16 15 14 13 12

Library of Congress Cataloging-in-Publication Data

Roberts, Sherry J.
    Fundamentals of business communication/ by Sherry J. Roberts—1st edition
        p. cm.

    Includes index
    ISBN 978-1-60525-472-2
        1. Business communication—Juvenile literature. 2. Business writing—Juvenile literature. I. Title.

HF5718.R593 2012
    651.7—dc22   2010040298

2

Introduction

Are You a Good Communicator?

In today's fast-paced world, communication is more important than ever. As technology continues to change the world, the methods of interacting with others must be adapted to meet new challenges. *Fundamentals of Business Communication* will help you meet those challenges.

Studying this text will guide you in developing foundational knowledge and skills related to the **Common Core State Standards** of writing, reading, listening, and speaking. These four areas of study are the blocks that will help build your communication talents.

As you read the material in this book, you will learn about interacting in a global society, as well as how to effectively use technology in the communication process. A review of grammar basics will help sharpen the skills you need when creating written documents and verbal messages. Features on business ethics and protocol will provide insight on how the communication process comes together in today's workplace.

Each chapter is designed with you in mind, presenting topics in a manner that is easy to read and understand. Numerous illustrations and photos elaborate the concepts for clear understanding. Opportunities to evaluate what you have learned, as well as apply the concepts, help assure you grasp the topics that have been presented.

Fundamentals of Business Communication provides opportunity for you to maximize and refine your talents. As you explore and discover communication in this text, you will learn skills that will follow you wherever your interests may lead in life.

About the Author

Dr. Sherry J. Roberts has been teaching for over 25 years, 14 of which were as a business education teacher at the secondary level. Dr. Roberts currently teaches business communication in the Jennings A. Jones College of Business at Middle Tennessee State University. With a research focus of online communication, Dr. Roberts has published in several professional journals. She has presented on the subjects of instructional technology, personal finance, communication, and business education at the international, national, regional, and state levels. In 2004, Dr. Roberts received the Teacher Educator of the Year award from the Arkansas Business Education Association, and in 2009 she received the Collegiate Teacher of the Year award from the Southern Business Education Association. She served as the president of the Southern Business Education Association in 2010. Dr. Roberts was named the 2010–2011 Bridgestone/Firestone Distinguished Assistant Professor for the Jennings A. Jones College of Business at Middle Tennessee State University.

Excellent Organization

Student Focused

Each chapter opens with a consistent plan of learning for success.

Famous Quote

A quote about communication sets the stage for each chapter.

Go Green

Sharing best practices for the environment, Go Green gives tips on ways to wisely use resources in a business setting.

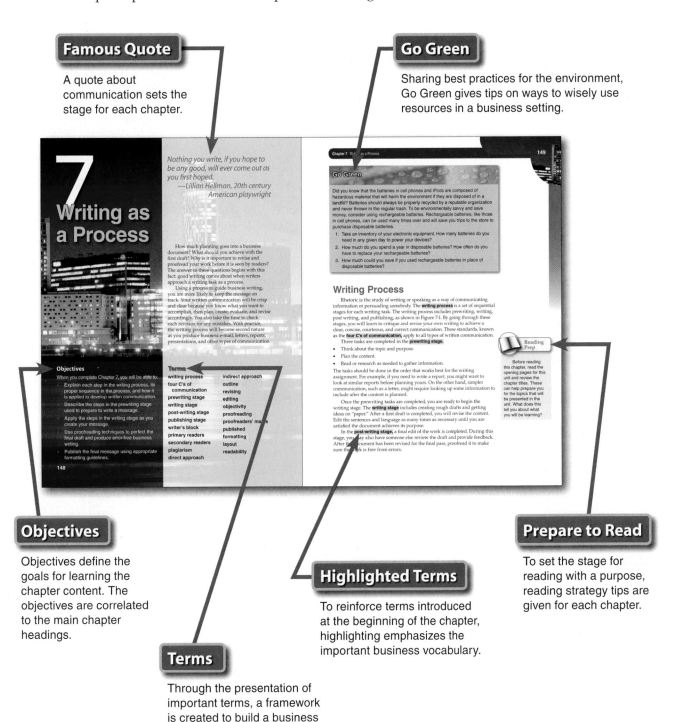

Objectives

Objectives define the goals for learning the chapter content. The objectives are correlated to the main chapter headings.

Terms

Through the presentation of important terms, a framework is created to build a business vocabulary.

Highlighted Terms

To reinforce terms introduced at the beginning of the chapter, highlighting emphasizes the important business vocabulary.

Prepare to Read

To set the stage for reading with a purpose, reading strategy tips are given for each chapter.

Ongoing Assessments

Outcome-Oriented Learning

Multiple opportunities are provided for self-assessment within the chapter, as well as at the conclusion, to check learning as the content is explored. Each activity is unique to cover the concepts and critical thinking skills that are developed in each chapter.

Chapter Summary

Detailed chapter summaries provide a quick overview and reinforcement of chapter content.

Apply Your Knowledge

Application of concepts through critical-thinking activities allows unique interpretation of content learned in the chapter.

Build Your Business Portfolio

Ongoing organizational tips guide the creation of a portfolio for job, school, or volunteer positions.

Review Your Knowledge

Questions that review basic concepts provide an opportunity to evaluate understanding of the content presented.

Practice What You Have Learned

Using data files available on the Student Companion Web Site, hands-on activities encourage real-life application of skills presented in the text.

Connections Across the Curriculum

Hands-on activities in academic areas show how communication skills are used in every discipline and walk of life.

Checkpoint

Through point-of-coverage assessment at the end of main chapter sections, understanding of content is confirmed before progressing through the remaining content. Solutions to the Checkpoint questions are located on the Student Companion Web Site at www.g-wlearning.com/Communication.

Engaging Features

Workplace Spotlighted

Special features in this book bring content to life in a way that allows the reader to understand and apply what is learned. In each chapter, emphasis is given to selected business topics that are important to building positive communication skills.

BUSINESS ETHICS

Confidential Information

As an employee of a company, you may hear confidential information about employees or the company business. It is unethical to share any confidential information you learn. Doing so may cost you your job. Repeating information is sometimes known as gossiping and some people find it harmless. Television shows present the "water cooler talk" and make the "grapevine" sound like a fun office activity. However, depending on the confidentiality of the topic, sharing information may be considered a violation of privacy laws. Always protect any confidential information you learn and respect the situation in which you learned it. This will not only promote ethical behavior in the organization, it may build your reputation as a trusted person.

Business Ethics

By presenting ethics in communication topics, real-life information is given to provide insight on issues that arise in the workplace.

Business Protocol

Focusing on topics of protocol, tips for professionals are given to outline acceptable behavior in business situations.

BUSINESS PROTOCOL

Social Networking Media

Many organizations use social networking media, such as Facebook, for marketing and sales purposes as well as to recruit and hire employees. As you use social networking media for personal use, remember that a potential employer may search the Internet and see information you thought only your friends would see. When posting photos and other information, follow acceptable protocol. Only post items that are in good taste and would not embarrass you should a potential employer or educational institution see it. Do an Internet search for "social networking media protocol" to find guidelines for posting personal information.

TEAMWORK

In the business world, teams often collaborate on written communication. Using the outline developed in the previous teamwork exercise, each team member should write a first draft of the e-mail to be sent to the realtor. See how quickly a first draft can be created in which all of the ideas are expressed in sentence form.

Teamwork

Collaborative work experiences are encouraged to develop individual team members and leadership skills.

Cases

Highlighted cases simulate real-life scenarios to give context to issues that arise in the workplace.

CASE

What Rights?

Josh Hanneken is an employee of a nationwide hardware store chain. He has been placed in charge of creating a presentation about a new set of benefits that will take effect in the coming year. Once it is ready, employees across the nation will log into the corporate intranet and view the presentation.

Josh has started planning the presentation and has done some preliminary research as well. He has found some media on the Internet that he would like to use, including sounds, graphics, and photographs. He is thinking that copyright laws would not be in effect since he is using the media for educational purposes—educating the employees.

1. Do you think that Josh has a clear understanding of copyright law?

2. Would a typical EULA allow Josh to use the media in the manner that he plans?

3. Are there any other considerations?

Engaging Features

Careers

Communication is important in every career. The careers feature gives an overview of the 16 Career Clusters and the impact of communication skills on each career.

Event Prep

As a practice activity for competitive activities for CTSOs such as FBLA, BPA, and DECA, various exercises give tips and tricks to prepare for competitions.

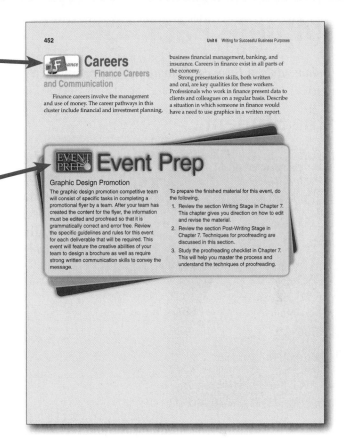

Office Documents

Model documents in Microsoft Office 2007/2010 provide direction for formatting business documents throughout the material.

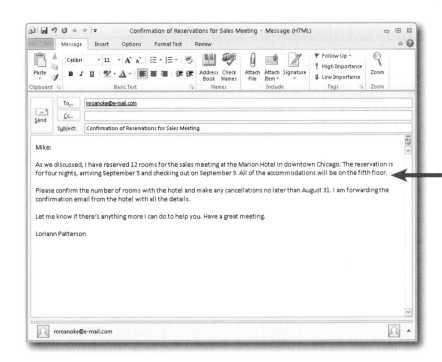

Your Complete Solution

Complete Package

Fundamentals of Business Communication provides a complete package for both the student and instructor.

For the Student...

Student Workbook

This workbook provides an extension opportunity for students to apply what they have learned in the text. Activities for each chapter include objective questions, critical thinking, and open-response opportunities so that students may apply and assess basic concepts learned in the text.

Student Companion Web Site

The free Student Companion Web Site at www.g-wlearning.com/Communication provides enrichment materials.

Contents and Activities
- E-flash cards
- Matching activities
- Crossword puzzles
- Interactive quizzes
- Chapter glossaries
- Data Files
- Checkpoint solutions
- Web links
- Resources

Your Complete Solution

For the Instructor...

Instructor Companion Web Site

Contents and Activities:
- E-flash cards
- Matching activities
- Crossword puzzles and solutions
- Interactive quizzes and solutions
- Chapter glossaries
- Data Files and solutions
- Checkpoint solutions
- Web links
- Resources

Instructor's Resource CD
- Individual lesson plans for each section of the chapter
- Pacing guide
- Correlations
- Electronic files for all instructional material
- Solutions to all end-of-chapter activities
- Solutions to the student workbook activities

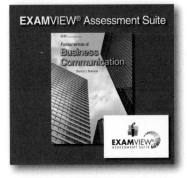

EXAMVIEW® Assessment Suite
This testing software includes the test generator and test bank for quick creation of customized assessment for your classes.

Instructor's Presentations for PowerPoint
PowerPoint slides review key concepts and terms and can be used to introduce or review the chapter.

Our Reviewers

The author and publisher would like to thank the following professionals, who provided valuable input to the development of this text.

Sarah Barras
Business Education Teacher
Hamilton Southeastern High School
Fishers, IN

Sara Black
Career and Technical Education
Green Hope High School
Carey, NC

Johanna Bodenhamer
CATE Department—Business Education
Saluda High School
Saluda, SC

Jodie S. Brown
English Teacher
GATE Coordinator
Joan F. Sparkman Alternative Education Center
Rancho Vista High School
Temecula, CA

Tim Dalton
Division Chair
Business and Math
Victor J. Andrew High School
Tinley Park, IL

Anthony L. Dillon
Education Associate
South Carolina Department of Education
Columbia, SC

Mary Flesberg
Business Education Department Chair
Moorhead High School
Moorhead, MN

Gerri M. Kimble
Business Technology Teacher
Hoover High School
Hoover, AL

Marisela López
Business Education Teacher
Thomas Jefferson High School
Dallas, TX

Cheryl Mallan
Instructor
Administrative Computer Technology
San Antonio College
San Antonio, TX

Joseph B. McFarland
Retired Business Educator
Redding, CA

Veronica Mitchell
English Teacher
Beechwood High School
Adjunct Instructor
Gateway Community and Technical College
Ft. Mitchell, KY

Frederick W. Polkinghorne, PhD
Assistant Professor
Department of Adult and Career Education
Valdosta State University
Valdosta, GA

Terry D. Roach
Professor
Business Communication
Arkansas State University
Jonesboro, AR

Judith P. Sams
Program Specialist
Business and Information Technology
Virginia Department of Education
Richmond, VA

Marcy Satterwhite
Business Instructor
Lake Land College
Mattoon, IL

Gary L. Schepf
IT Intern Coordinator
Jack E. Singley Academy
Irving, TX

Melissa Schram
Business Teacher
Millard West High School
Omaha, NE

Alice Smith
Chairperson
Department of Business
Lafayette Central Catholic Junior/Senior High School
Lafayette, IN

Debra Stein-Silberlust
Chairperson and District Coordinator
Business Education
Sewanhaka Central High School District
Floral Park, NY

Matt White
ITT Technical
Hilliard, OH

Brief Contents

Table of Contents

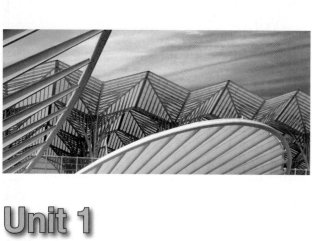

Chapter 2
Communicating in a Global Society
40

Unit 1 Communicating for Success

Chapter 1
Understanding the Communication Process

Chapter 3
Using Technology to Communicate

Chapter 12
Giving Presentations 266

it 4
eaking for
ccessful
mmunication 252

pter 11
aking Informally 254

Chapter 4
Communicating and
Working in Teams 74

Unit 2
Grammar Basics
for Successful
Communication 88

Chapter 5
Improving
Grammar Skills 90

Chapter 6
Improving
Grammar Mechanics   118

Unit 3
Writing for
Successful
Communication   146

Chapter 7
Writing as a Process   148

Chapter 8
Writing Style   172

Chapter 9
Formatting Letters,
Memos, and E-Mails   192

Chapter 10
Writing
Effective Busin
Communicatio

Unit 5
Listening and Reading for Successful Communication

Chapter 14
Listening with a Purpose

Chapter 15
Reading with a Purpose

Unit 6
Writing for Successful Business Purposes

Chapter 16
Writing and Interviewing for Employment

Chapter 17
Writing Reports

Chapter 18
Using Visual Aids

Glossary

Index

Unit 1
Communicating for Success

In This Unit

Communication is of vital importance to every business. From communicating with customers and suppliers to directing employees, the success of the business relies on the communication skills its employees have and how effectively those skills are applied.

This unit introduces the topic of communication, beginning with a discussion on the communication process. From there, you will learn about the global scale of communication in business. This unit concludes by discussing the technology of communication and how to communicate in teams. Completing this unit will help you meet college and career readiness (CCR) anchor standards for language, as outlined by the **Common Core State Standards**.

1

The art of communication is the language of leadership.
—James C. Humes,
American author and
presidential speech writer

Understanding the Communication Process

Communication plays an important role in your life, both personal and professional. Each task and situation—whether involving writing, speaking, listening, or reading—requires you to do your best. In this text, you will learn the communication skills necessary for quality communication and business success. In the process, you will improve your ability to communicate in social situations, both personal and business related.

Objectives

When you complete Chapter 1, you will be able to:

- **Describe** the state of communication today.
- **Identify** the steps in the communication process.
- **Compare** informal and formal business communication.
- **Explain** the written and verbal communication skills that are essential to successful communication in the workplace.
- **Describe** the role nonverbal communication skills play in the communication process.
- **Discuss** how to overcome common barriers to effective communication.

Terms

communication
communication process
encoding
decoding
informal communication
protocol
formal communication
peers
written communication
verbal communication
nonverbal communication
body language
context
personal space
paralanguage
barriers
sending barriers
receiving barriers

Go Green

When you go to the store to buy office supplies or other items, be sure to bring your own reusable bag. By using reusable bags to carry products home from the store, thousands of pounds of landfill waste can be eliminated every year. While there are different schools of thought on this topic, it is generally accepted that plastic bags take almost 1,000 years to degrade. Additionally, discarded plastic bags can pose threats to wildlife and the soil. Did you know store owners have to purchase the plastic or paper bags and that they pass on the cost to the consumer through higher product prices?

1. The next time you go to the store, ask if you will receive a discount for bringing your own reusable bag.

2. How many plastic bags do you think you use in a month?

Communicating Today

What does communication mean to you? Sending a text message? Using your cell phone? If you ask the question of someone a bit older than you, that person may say sending a postcard or writing a letter.

Communication is the process of sending and receiving messages that convey information, ideas, feelings, and beliefs. This process is fundamental to all human interaction. In fact, it is so basic that it can be taken for granted most of the time. You would not be able to get through the day if you stopped to plan and analyze the impact of every communication you have. On the other hand, there are many times throughout the day when you do stop to think and prepare before you communicate. Most people have a natural sense for when planning and preparation are critical to what is said and how it is stated.

Over the last decade, communication has changed more rapidly than at any other time in history. Technology allows real-time communication and has revolutionized the way personal and professional business is conducted. You no longer have to wait for "snail mail" to arrive and you can "skype" with friends and coworkers to conduct virtual meetings.

With the rapid change in the way business is conducted, it is more important than ever to remember the basics of communication—the process of sending and receiving messages that convey information, ideas, feelings, and beliefs. While the world is moving at a rapid pace, good communication skills and work ethics are still very important to being successful in the business world.

Reading Prep

Before you begin reading this chapter, try to find a quiet place with no distractions. Make sure your chair is comfortable and the lighting is adequate.

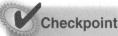

Checkpoint

1. What is communication?
2. How has technology changed communication over the past decade?

Communication Process

Why do you communicate? To share information, create relationships, persuade, and entertain others. In a typical day, you may:

- write an e-mail explaining a new company policy;
- call a colleague to say congratulations on a job well done;
- create a sales message to persuade customers to buy your product;
- design a digital media presentation for a meeting; or
- send an instant message to a friend.

Communication may involve written, verbal, or nonverbal messages. You will communicate throughout every day in your career.

Shutterstock

Before you begin to study the specific skills that will make you a better writer, speaker, listener, and reader, it is a good idea to explore the broader concept of the communication process. The **communication process** is a series of actions on the part of the sender and the receiver of the message, as shown in Figure 1-1. The six parts of the process are the sender, message, channel, receiver, translation, and feedback. Each of these parts are discussed in the next sections.

An essential element of being receptive to messages is having an open mind. Making assumptions about what someone is going to say before he or she speaks might cause you to ignore words that send a different message. The ability to openly receive a message can also be disrupted when the receiver has biases toward the sender. To have an open mind means you are willing to respectfully listen to the sender without letting negative feelings or emotions get in the way.

Sender

The sender begins the communication process. First, the sender decides there is a need to relay information to the receiver. Then, the sender assembles the information. The information takes the form of the message.

Figure 1-1. The six parts of the communication process.

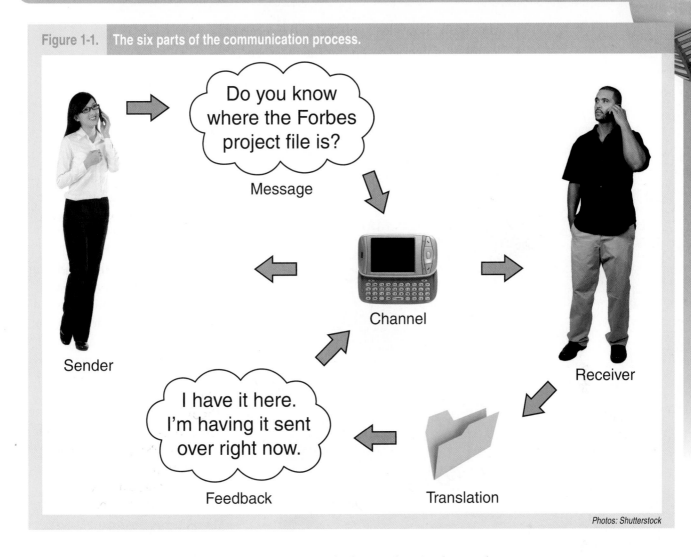

The success of the communication begins with the sender. As the sender creates the message, care must be given to make the language of the message clear, consider the audience, and formulate the message accordingly. It is the sender's responsibility to clearly state the purpose of the message and to provide relevant detail.

Message

The sender of the message decides what format the message will take. The message may be in words (written or spoken), pictures, or even video. Putting the message into the format it will be sent to the receiver in is known as **encoding.**

Channel

The sender decides the best channel through which to send the message. This may be a face-to-face conversation, telephone conversation, letter, or e-mail, among others. Factors influencing how you choose to transmit a message include the following.

- importance of having a written record of the information
- need for the receiver to have the information immediately

- proximity; how close you are to the receiver
- number of people receiving the message
- level of formality necessary
- expectations of the receiver

There are many different channels for communicating a message, from a letter or e-mail to a face-to-face conversation.

Shutterstock

Receiver

The receiver physically receives the message from the sender through whatever channel the sender selected. In turn, the receiver has a responsibility to the sender. When you are on the receiving end of the message, keep in mind that communication is a two-way process. How do you feel when you send an e-mail to which you never receive a response? Your attention to the message is essential to the communication process. Paying attention to the sender is both a matter of courtesy and necessity.

Translation

Once the receiver receives the message, it will be translated, called **decoding,** to see if the contents are understood. Keep in mind that message is not actually "received" if the receiver does not understand the content of the message.

Feedback

Feedback is the receiver's response to a message. This tells the sender if the receiver understood the message as it was intended. For example, if you choose not to respond to an e-mail, the sender has no idea of whether or not you received the message. Many businesses have their e-mail applications set up to automatically request a "read receipt." That way, at least the sender knows the e-mail got through, but it does not tell the sender if the message was understood.

Checkpoint

1. What are the six parts of the communication process?
2. What is the difference between encoding and decoding?

Informal and Formal Business Communication

Business communication may be informal or formal. **Informal communication** is casual sharing of information with no customs or rules of etiquette involved. Reporting hierarchy, or levels, is not important in informal communication. People from various levels, divisions, and positions interact with each other in a casual way. Informal communication could be text messaging, telephone calls, or just talking at the water cooler. Also known as the grapevine, a healthy dose of informal communication is necessary to build communication within an organization. But, it may or may not be a dependable source of facts.

TEAMWORK

Meet with a group of students to analyze the communication process. Take turns describing a specific situation in which you were initially the sender and one in which you were initially the receiver. Identify the other persons involved in the process.

Sometimes, there may be a **protocol** (customs or rules of etiquette) as to how certain levels of employees interact with each other. This is known as **formal communication.** For example, it may not be appropriate for a manager to bypass the vice president about an issue and go straight to the CEO. Formal communication usually happens according to level within an organization. It flows in three directions, as shown in Figure 1-2.

Figure 1-2.   There are three basic flows of communication within a business.

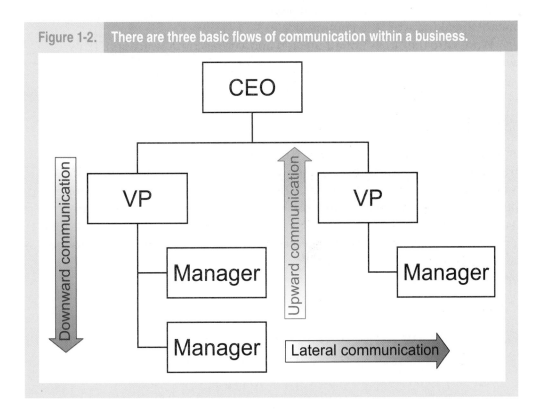

- Upward communication takes place with your supervisors, managers, and executives.
- Lateral communication takes place with **peers** (persons of equal standing or work position).
- Downward communication takes place with those over whom you have a position of authority.

Formal communication typically takes place in letters, e-mails, or other messages that are planned and put in writing or spoken. Written documents are generally used when it is necessary that information be recorded for future reference.

Checkpoint

1. What is the difference between formal and informal business communication?
2. What is a protocol?

Written and Verbal Communication

If you were to chart your daily activities, you would find that you spend most of your time communicating. Communication skills affect your basic ability to understand others, establish positive relationships, and perform in most situations. Being able to communicate skillfully, therefore, is essential to your ability to succeed in your career. **Written communication** means recording words through writing or keying to communicate. **Verbal communication** means speaking words to communicate.

Words are the "tools" of all written and verbal communication. How well you use these tools affects the success of your messages. When you send messages, you select language and construct sentences in a way that will achieve your purpose. On the receiving end of communication, your purpose is to interpret the words and provide feedback. Being aware of the responsibilities of your role at both ends of a message helps ensure that communication occurs.

TEAMWORK

Working in a group, describe where you observed (or created) a sending barrier to communication and a receiving barrier to communication. Get feedback from your teammates on what caused the barrier and what you could have done differently to avoid it.

Written Communication

Accurate written messages are vital in the business world. Business communication is written for a variety of purposes and almost always requires planning and skill in execution. Perhaps the subject is technical, requiring lists of measurements and specifications. Perhaps a written record of a decision is needed to make a record. A complex explanation may require step-by-step instructions or a situation may call for a persuasive request.

Business writing requires use of Standard English and knowledge of business style for formatting documents. This is true of important documents, such as letters to customers and clients, reports, and presentations. You should also use Standard English in e-mail; texting language is not acceptable in business. Today, e-mail is a primary means of communication in most businesses.

Written communication is used to record and convey information of varying levels of importance. It can have enormous impact on how a business functions. Business communication represents you and your company. This means that even though e-mail is often used in place of a casual verbal conversation, it is necessary to stop and think before writing. Every written communication creates a record that can be recalled in the future.

There are three basic approaches to reading written communication: skimming, scanning, and reading for detail. These approaches are discussed in detail in Chapter 15.

Verbal Communication

Speaking is also known as verbal or oral communication. In the course of a workday, most people spend at least some portion of time talking with coworkers, supervisors, managers, or customers. This communication involves a variety of situations, such as conversations about work tasks, asking and answering questions, making requests, giving information, and participating in meetings.

Planning and organizing your thoughts is an important part of verbal communication. This might be as simple as thinking before you speak or as elaborate as outlining a presentation and practicing several times before you deliver it. Planning always involves thinking about who will receive the message and what you want to accomplish. Making notes before a phone call, having an agenda for a meeting, or researching information in advance are all methods you can use

Verbal communication involves speaking words to transmit a message.

Shutterstock

to prepare before talking to people at work. This helps you clearly focus on your purpose so that you can choose the appropriate language and medium. Planning also saves time because you are less likely to need to repeat a message or have a second meeting to clarify. You will explore the methods for planning verbal communication in Unit 4.

Checkpoint
1. What is written communication?
2. What is verbal communication?

Nonverbal Communication

Nonverbal communication refers to actions, as opposed to words, that send messages. This is often called body language, but behavior is also part of nonverbal communication. Some nonverbal messages are subtle, such as posture. Others involve behavior that sends loud messages in spite of what you might say. Nonverbal communication can be so strong that it overwhelms the written or verbal message.

For example, if you visit a client's office and leave your coat on while standing near the door, the client is going to receive the message that you are in a hurry to leave. If someone stops by your office to talk and you say you are not busy, but you keep scrolling through your mailbox, the message you are sending is you are busy. Such actions as these and others, like failing to offer a handshake or arriving late for meetings, help others interpret your true message.

Body Language

When you speak, you send nonverbal messages through gestures, facial expressions, and other body actions or posture. This is your **body language.** If you smile, sneer, raise an eyebrow, shrug your shoulders, nod in agreement, cross your arms, or clench your teeth, you are communicating just as if you are talking. The receiver picks up on these cues, which become an important part of your message. This is why being aware of nonverbal communication is an essential business skill. While you have been aware of nonverbal communication all of your life and have responded to it, how often have you given it serious thought? In the business environment, you must be aware of the nonverbal messages you send and receive. Otherwise, you run the risk of sending the wrong message or feedback.

There is often not a literal meaning to a nonverbal message. Everybody knows a frown means the person is unhappy, but most nonverbal messages must be considered in the context in which they occur. **Context** is the environment or setting in which something occurs or is communicated. Context is the other words or situation that surround a word, action, or idea and helps clarify meaning. For example, a smile can mean the person finds your statement funny or it could mean they do not believe you. Context is used to determine what it actually means.

Have you ever had a facial expression betray your emotions no matter how hard you tried to hide them? This type of nonverbal message is not only unintentional, it is often uncontrollable. In fact, sending nonverbal messages without realizing it is quite common. A distracted listener may allow his or her eyes to roam the room, not realizing that the speaker interprets the wandering eyes as disinterest or disdain. Being more self-aware is the only way to prevent these kinds of unintended messages.

In American culture, *eye contact* is an important form of body language. Appropriate eye contact means looking directly at the other person while engaged in conversation, but not staring too intently. Staring may make the other person uncomfortable.

Most people have a natural tendency to look directly at the person with whom they are engaged in conversation. But what if someone approaches you while you are doing something, such as dialing a telephone or reading a document? If you do not stop what you are doing and make eye contact, you are saying, "Please go away, I'm too busy to talk to you now." If you stop and look up, the person can still read the expression on your face—is it relaxed or tense? If you look tense, you are still sending the message that you do not wish to be interrupted.

Touch and Space

Touch is another form of body language that sends strong messages. A firm handshake along with eye contact and a smile send an important message when you are introduced to someone new. These gestures convey openness and confidence. Conveying open and confident body language in business situations helps you create an impression of someone who is competent and trustworthy.

In the business environment, a handshake is about the only form of touch that is acceptable. Any other form of physical contact must be within the boundaries of correctness. These boundaries vary, depending on the nature of the business and the culture. For example, a dentist must touch your face in order to complete an examination. However, if you work in an office and somebody touched your face, you would be offended, if not very upset. In general, do not engage in any physical contact other than what is required of your work.

Personal space—the space you place between yourself and others—is another aspect of body language. How close to someone do you stand

Be very aware of personal space in the workplace. Do you feel this man is violating this worker's personal space?

Shutterstock

or sit? The personal-space boundary becomes apparent when someone gets too close. Be aware that cultural background may be a factor in defining the personal-space boundary. Americans tend to keep a slightly greater distance between themselves and others than do people from certain cultures. So, consider this when interacting with people in diverse settings.

How you identify your personal space and the judgment you apply to the space of others varies depending on your social upbringing and community norms. When you enter a business environment, be aware that the workplace has its own unwritten rules of social and community behavior. Noticing and adapting to them will help you to communicate with comfort and assure that those receiving your message are comfortable.

Behavior

Nonverbal messages can compete with verbal messages, and can even negate them. This is true of body language. It is also true when it comes to your actions. If you say one thing and do another, your verbal messages are likely to be ignored. For example, a supervisor who asks workers to stay late, but who does not do the same, probably will find few staff members willing to work late. As the saying goes, actions speak louder than words. In this example, the supervisor is saying, "the work isn't as important as I said it was."

When first entering the workforce, it is important to take behavioral cues from others with more experience, but do not make the mistake of emulating poor habits. For example, suppose the starting time is 9 a.m. and you are allotted one hour for lunch. But, several employees arrive a little later than nine and take a little longer than an hour for lunch. Do not follow this behavior.

Arriving on time and limiting your lunch to the allotted one hour let your boss know that you are dependable and willing to follow the rules.

Paralanguage

Paralanguage is the attitude you project with the tone and pitch of your voice. It is reflected in speech as a sharp or soft tone, raising or lowering of the voice, speaking quickly or slowly, and the general quality of the voice. Paralanguage is nonverbal communication that reflects the speaker's true attitude, so it is important to be aware of it. When the content of your message is contradicted by the attitude with which you are communicating, your message will be received accordingly. If you say you are not angry, but you raise your voice, the receiver will know you really are angry.

Whenever you are speaking, remember that the tone, pitch, quality of voice, and rate of speaking convey emotions that will be judged by the receiver, regardless of the content of the message. If you get critical feedback from others about any of these voice qualities, be sure to take it seriously. The voice is not just a vehicle (channel) for the message, it is part of the message. As a communicator, you should be sensitive to the influence of paralanguage on the interpretation of your message by the receiver. When your voice complements the message, there is a greater chance that your words will be received as you intended.

CASE

Routine Habit

The weekly budget meeting at Leading Edge Productions was routine: same day, time, place, and participants. Charlie Burrows made it a habit to arrive at every meeting ten minutes late. On Friday, as Charlie walked in, Harold Rankowski stopped presenting and sneered momentarily before turning back to the board and continuing with his presentation. Charlie ignored Harold's nonverbal communication signals and went to his place at the meeting table and took a seat. A few moments later, Charlie started checking e-mails on his cell phone.

1. What message is Charlie sending by arriving late to budget meetings and not paying attention to the speaker?

2. How important were the nonverbal messages the speaker was sending Charlie?

3. What could happen as a result of his behavior?

 Checkpoint

1. What is nonverbal communication?
2. Why is paralanguage considered nonverbal communication?

Barriers to Effective Communication

The six steps in the communication process can create potential barriers at the sender's end of the process, at the receiver's end, or both. **Barriers** are anything that prevents clear, effective communication. They may occur in written, verbal, and nonverbal communication.

Sending Barriers

Sending barriers can occur when the sender says or does something that causes the receiver to tune out. This can happen when the receiver simply does not understand what the sender is talking about. The words used may not be clear to the sender. Such misunderstandings cause daily problems ranging from minor events to serious, costly errors. Additional ways the sender might cause barriers include:

You may encounter many different barriers to communication without even knowing it. This man is creating a barrier to communication because he is on the phone at the same time he is trying to talk to his coworker.

Shutterstock

- using poor grammar or spelling;
- overlooking typographical and formatting errors;
- presenting visually unattractive text or inappropriate graphics;
- assuming too much or too little about what the receiver already knows; and
- using inappropriate language (slang, jargon, or too formal or informal phrasing).

Face-to-face nonverbal communication that causes barriers includes:

- distracting mannerisms;
- facial expressions that conflict with the words being said;
- inappropriate dress or demeanor;
- sarcastic or angry tone of voice; and
- speaking too softly or too loudly.

In these situations, the sender's written or verbal message may be lost or undermined by competing nonverbal messages. The sender who does not have a good grasp of the purpose for communicating is likely to relay a confused and ineffective message.

How can the sender overcome barriers? The sender has responsibilities to the receiver to make sure the message is clear and understood.

- For written documents, follow the rules of writing, grammar, and formatting documents. A well-written and properly formatted document will send a positive message.
- For face-to-face communication, maintain positive body language and behavior.
- Do not assume too much or too little about what the receiver already knows.
- Select the appropriate format for your message, such as an e-mail or a phone call, based on the situation.
- Ask for feedback from the receiver to see if your message came across clearly.

CASE

Matter of Time

Lisa Shaw returned from lunch to find an e-mail message from the executive vice president, Angela Herrera. Ms. Herrera wanted to know when Lisa's manager, Bert Winfield, would return from his trip so a meeting could be arranged. Lisa checked Mr. Winfield's itinerary and saw that his flight was scheduled to land the next day at 9:56 a.m. She informed Ms. Herrera that Bert would return "around 10 a.m." tomorrow and come straight to the office. Ms. Herrera scheduled a meeting for 10:30 the next morning; Bert arrived 40 minutes late.

1. What did Lisa neglect to think about? What should she have done differently?

2. As the receiver, what part did Ms. Herrera play in the miscommunication?

3. What part of Lisa's feedback did Ms. Herrera miss? What feedback did she fail to give?

Receiving Barriers

Receiving barriers can occur when the receiver says or does something that causes the sender's message not to be received. These barriers can be just as harmful to the communication process as sending barriers. The receiver has responsibility to give attention and respect to the sender. Most receiving barriers can be overcome with a little self-awareness.

- For written documents, make sure you read all of what has been written.

- Take responsibility for getting clarification if you do not understand the message.

- While *hearing* is an innate ability, except in the case of a physical disability, *listening* is a conscious action. For example, if you are reading while engaged in a telephone conversation, you are not actively listening. Active listening is discussed in Chapter 14.

- Give feedback. Let the sender know you received the message and ask questions or give information if needed.

Receiving barriers are the result of the receiver's actions.

Shutterstock

Although senders are responsible for sending clear messages, listeners should be ready to recognize unclear messages. A listener who is willing to accept responsibility for getting clarification will be a more effective communicator.

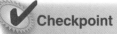

Checkpoint

1. What is a sending barrier?
2. What is a receiving barrier?

Chapter 1 Review

Chapter Summary

Communicating Today

- Communication is the process of sending and receiving messages that convey information, ideas, feelings, and beliefs.
- Communication has changed more over the past decade than at any point in history.

Communication Process

- The communication process is a series of actions on the part of the sender and the receiver of the message.
- The sender begins the communication process.
- The message is encoded by the sender.
- The message is sent through a channel.
- The receiver receives the sender's message, translates it, and provides feedback to the sender.

Informal and Formal Business Communication

- Informal business communication is casual sharing of information with no customs or rules of etiquette.
- Formal business communication is information shared with regard to accepted protocol.

Written and Verbal Communication

- Written communication means recording words through writing or keying to communicate.
- Verbal or oral communication means speaking words to communicate.

Nonverbal Communication

- Nonverbal communication includes body language and behavior.
- Body language is the gestures, facial expressions, and other actions and posture you present while communicating.

- Body language must be interpreted in context.
- Context is the environment or setting in which something occurs.
- Touch and personal space are sensitive issues in the business world, so be very aware of these.
- Paralanguage, or the tone and pitch of your voice, sends a strong nonverbal message.

Barriers to Effective Communication

- Barriers to effective communication can be sending or receiving barriers.
- Sending barriers are the result of something the sender does or says that prevents the message from being received.
- Receiving barriers occur when the receiver does or says something that prevents the sender's message from being received.

Review
Your Knowledge

1. Define communication.
2. List the six parts of the communication process.
3. What is the difference between formal and informal business communication?
4. List the three directions in which formal communication typically flows.
5. Describe the difference between written and verbal communication.
6. Why is nonverbal communication important?
7. What is the difference between body language and behavior?
8. Explain why paralanguage is considered a form of nonverbal communication even though it involves use of the voice.
9. Describe sending barriers.
10. Describe receiving barriers.

Apply
Your Knowledge

1. Many of the rules of communication applied in everyday interactions are so ingrained they are automatic. Take a few minutes to think about how your communication "behavior" is influenced by your relationship to the individual with whom you are communicating. Identify the different ways you speak and behave when in the presence of the following people.

   A. brother or sister
   B. best friend
   C. acquaintance or friend of a friend
   D. parent
   E. instructor
   F. senior citizen
   G. police officer
   H. stranger

2. Identifying appropriate channels of communication is an important business skill to learn. Sometimes it is important that a record of communication is made. Other times, documenting information is not necessary. Identify which channel of communication should be used for the following situations (letter, memo, formal e-mail, casual e-mail or text, phone call).

   A. asking a colleague where to find information about a company organization chart
   B. confirming a meeting time
   C. summary of minutes from a meeting
   D. telling someone to meet you at the front door in five minutes
   E. forwarding information to a client

3. Written communication requires the use of Standard English. Create a list of at least 20 "words" or "phrases" in texting language. For each, write out the correct form in Standard English.

4. Ask a close friend or family member to describe your nonverbal communication in the four categories mentioned in this chapter (listed below). Ask the person to be honest and give you both the positive and negative things he or she observes. Take some time to review the notes and think about the feedback; then meet with the person to discuss your viewpoint of the observations. Talk about areas of strength and where you would like to improve.

   A. body language
   B. touch and space
   C. behavior
   D. paralanguage

5. Create a list of at least ten sending barriers and ten receiving barriers, not including the examples provided in this chapter. For each barrier, identify a way to overcome the barrier.

Practice
What You Have Learned

Access the *Fundamentals of Business Communication* Student Companion Web Site at www.g-wlearning.com/Communication. Download each data file for this chapter. Follow the instructions to complete a reading, writing, and grammar activity to practice what you have learned in this chapter.

Connections
Across the Curriculum

Social Studies. Use the Internet to research the topic of body language and culture in the US. Create a table correlating the behavior or body language to what it means. For example, crossed arms usually means you are being defensive.

Science. Communication is as important in science as it is in any other aspect of life. Communication Science is a program that prepares people for roles such as communication research. Research Communication Science and write a few paragraphs explaining what is involved in the career.

Build
Your Business Portfolio

A portfolio is a selection of materials that you collect and organize to show your qualifications, skills, and talents. When you apply for a job, community service, or college, you will need a portfolio to showcase your qualifications for the opportunity for which you are applying.

There are two types of portfolios that are commonly used: print portfolio and electronic portfolio (ePortfolio). An ePortfolio is also known as a digital portfolio.

1. Use the Internet to search for "print portfolio" and "ePortfolio." Summarize each type and create an overview of how to create each one.

2. You will be creating a portfolio in this class. Which portfolio type would you prefer to create? Write several paragraphs describing the type of portfolio you would prefer and why.

Careers
Architecture and Construction Careers and Communication

People with careers in architecture and construction are involved in the design, preconstruction planning, construction, and maintenance of structures. They may design, build, restore, or maintain homes, bridges, industrial plants, dams, hospitals, highways, and shopping malls. Some careers may involve landscape architecture, urban planning, and interior design.

Careers in these professions require strong communicators, as giving direction and input is an important component of the job. People in these professions must be able to explain their expectations and ideas in order for the end result to meet their criteria. Give a scenario in which a poor communicator could cause major problems for someone in this profession.

Event Prep

Student Organizations

Professional student organizations are a valuable asset to any educational program. These organizations support student learning and the application of skills learned to real world situations. There are a variety of organizations from which to select, depending on the goals of your educational program. Competitive events may be written, oral, or a combination of both.

To prepare for any competitive event, do the following.

1. Contact the association a year before the next competition to have time to review and decide which competitive events are correct for you or your team.

2. Closely read all of the guidelines. These rules and regulations must be strictly adhered to or disqualification can occur.

3. Read about which communication skills are covered for the event you select. Communication plays a role in all the competitive events. Research and preparation are important keys to successful competition. Use this book as a guide to help you prepare the communication aspects of all competitive events.

4. Go to the organization's Web site to locate specific information for the events. Visit the site often, as information can change.

5. Pick one or two events that are of interest to you. Print the information for the events and discuss your interest with your instructor.

2

Communicating in a Global Society

We all should know that diversity makes for a rich tapestry, and we must understand that all the threads of the tapestry are equal in value no matter what their color.
—Dr. Maya Angelou,
American poet and civil rights activist

As a member of the business community, you will interact with people from different cultures. This is obvious when considering an international business. However, even if the business functions on a regional level, the workers and customers involved in the business will come from a variety of backgrounds. In this chapter, you will learn how to communicate with others from different cultures and backgrounds, as well as how to identify and embrace diversity in the workplace.

Objectives

When you complete Chapter 2, you will be able to:

- **Describe** the global society.
- **Identify** issues related to communicating in a global society.
- **Describe** barriers to communication related to a diverse workplace.
- **Identify** areas in which sensitivity is required in a diverse workplace.
- **Explain** factors to consider for ethical communication.

Terms

global society
enunciate
stereotyping
diversity
culture
intercultural differences
ethics
copyright
fair use

Go Green

The next time you need to clean the smudge marks from your LCD display, television screen, or computer monitor, remember to avoid chemical cleaners. Chemical cleaners are hard on the equipment and some are bad for the environment.

1. Search the Internet for natural products designed for cleaning screens. What are some environmentally safe ideas for cleaning screens?
2. What products or chemicals are suggested to avoid for cleaning screens?

Global Workplace

Advances in technology have changed how you think, work, and communicate. No longer are you confined to your own city or neighborhood to do business. You can communicate, in real time, with anyone in the world. The ability for worldwide communication and movement has created a **global society** in which goods and services are bought and sold both inside and outside of the country of origin.

The world today seems like a smaller place than it was just a few years ago. People of all cultures are able to travel to other countries and become part of the workforce there, creating a global workplace. As these people work side-by-side with others from a different country, customs and etiquette become important differences to understand for successful business transactions.

To expand on a global basis, however, does not just mean American companies going overseas. Global expansion includes companies based in other countries, such as an Asian or European car manufacturer, moving to the United States to open plants and hire American workers. American workers, even in their own country, must learn the culture of their employer. Just because the company's facility is on American soil does not mean the employer will assume American culture. It could be just the opposite, firmly holding on to the culture of the company's native country.

Reading Prep

Before reading this chapter, review the introductory material preceding Chapter 1. Textbooks generally provide a preview of the book and how the material is presented. Did this material help you understand how to use this book?

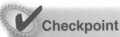
Checkpoint

1. What is a global society?
2. When would an American worker working in a business on American soil need to learn the customs of another country?

Communicating in a Global Society

Within a global society, communication can be a challenge. As you learned in Chapter 1, communication can be written, verbal (oral), or nonverbal (body language). The next sections discuss issues related to communication in a global society.

Verbal Communication

Patience is required in conversations where neither person understands the other's language well. These conversations can be frustrating. However, there are actions you can take to try to make conversations successful.

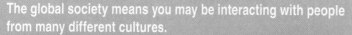

The global society means you may be interacting with people from many different cultures.

Shutterstock

- Speak slowly and clearly.
- Separate questions.
- Learn to listen.
- Avoid yes or no questions.
- Check for meaning.
- Write it down.
- Be supportive of others.
- Avoid slang.
- Check your humor.
- Be polite.

Enunciate—clearly pronounce words—and speak slowly enough to be understood. However, it is important that you do not slow down to such an extent that the person thinks you are making fun of them.

Have you ever been asked several questions at one time? By the time you answer any of the questions, it can be hard to remember the other questions. When asking a question, ask one question and wait for it to be answered before asking a second question. Try not to ask either/or questions. These may be difficult for someone who does not speak English well to answer.

It is important that you speak and then listen. Give the other person a turn to talk, and do not monopolize the discussion. This is the polite way to converse in all cultures.

If you ask a question that requires a yes or no response, the receiver of the question may misinterpret the question. In some cultures, a response of *yes* means the person agrees or is going to do what is asked. In other cultures, *yes* only means that the person heard you, not that they are in agreement with you. So, instead of asking yes/no questions, try to ask questions that require an expanded response.

Not only do you need to be a good speaker, but you need to be an active listener. Check the meaning of a question or response if you are unsure of what was said. It is also helpful to summarize what has been said. This will help you identify if the other party has understood what has been discussed.

Often, information exchanged when doing business should be documented. This is especially important in global business to make certain that topics and decisions made are indeed what were intended. When in doubt, write down the information when communicating with someone. If you later find the recorded information is not needed, simply discard it.

If you are communicating with someone whose English skills are not strong, be supportive and encouraging. This will make the situation more comfortable and increase the other person's trust in you. However, be careful not to seem condescending.

Slang or colloquialisms (informal sayings used between friends and peers) may not be understood by others outside of your circle. No matter how good someone from another culture speaks English, slang such as "put your best foot forward" or "hit the target" may not be understood. These expressions are based in the culture of English speakers. In order to understand the expression, a person may need to understand the history behind the saying.

In some cultures, it is not appropriate to use humor during business meetings or discussions. Respect and tradition are very important in some cultures, whereas in other cultures it is acceptable to be lighthearted and informal in business situations. When communicating with individuals from other cultures, it is best to keep business conversation serious and avoid jokes and other humorous comments.

Always be courteous and polite. Never forget to say *please* and *thank-you*. This shows you respect the other person and should help them feel more comfortable speaking with you. Also, avoid topics that might be sensitive, such as politics or religion. Focus on the business topics.

CASE

Quick Speech

Abby was excited about her new job at the computer store. Her responsibilities were to work the help desk on the weekends. On her first day, Carlos brought a customer, Ms. Alexander, who needed help adding her new printer to her computer. Carlos tried to explain to Abby the problem that Ms. Alexander was having. Abby was having difficulty understanding what Carlos was saying because he spoke so quickly and used so many technical terms.

Once Carlos left, Abby asked Ms. Alexander to once again explain the problems she was having adding her new printer. Ms. Alexander very slowly explained what was happening and Abby was able to walk her through the process of adding her new printer. After Ms. Alexander left, Abby talked with Carlos. She told him that sometimes when he talks, he speaks too quickly to be understood.

1. How could Carlos have handled the situation better with Ms. Alexander?

2. Why do you think Carlos was having such a hard time talking with Ms. Alexander?

3. Why was Abby more successful with Ms. Alexander?

4. How would you have handled the situation?

Always be aware of cultural differences, whether communicating face to face or via e-mail, letter, or phone.

Shutterstock

Written Communication

Written messages to those from other countries can also be challenging. Be aware that there is always a word or phrase that might translate differently and cause confusion. For example, when you see the date notation 10/5/15, you probably translate it as October 5, 2015. This is the format used in the United States: month, day, year. However, in most other countries, the common format is: day, month, year. So, 10/5/15 means May 10, 2015. A misunderstanding such as this could create problems for someone with whom you are doing business.

When creating written documents, follow the same rules outlined for verbal communication. Avoid any words that might be misinterpreted or difficult for someone of another culture to understand. Have a colleague review your message to look for items that might cause confusion or raise questions. If you know someone who is an expert in global communication or fluent in the language of the country you are communicating with, seek this person's help.

When doing business in a global society, it is important to do your research. It is not enough to know your business. You must also research the area, region, or country prior to doing business. This will help prevent misunderstandings and enhance the communication with whom you are doing business. Figure 2-1 provides tips for improving your cultural communication skills.

TEAMWORK

Working in teams, prepare a presentation that describes ways to improve communication with classmates from other countries.

Nonverbal Communication

Nonverbal communication can be an especially sensitive area when communicating with those from other cultures. In some cultures, it is acceptable to stand very close to a person, even having your face very close to the person when talking. However, in other cultures and for

Figure 2-1. Follow these tips on improving communication with other cultures.

Listening Skills

Work on improving your listening skills. Active listening skills can be helpful in understanding what is being said and interpreting the meaning of what is being said.

Speaking Skills

Work on improving your speaking skills. Speak clearly and slowly. Also, be sensitive to your audience so that you can encourage or affirm the communication.

Observation Skills

Work on improving your observation skills. Do you look at your surroundings? Do you watch for actions or reactions of others? Observation is helpful in business; learn to "read" others by their nonverbal communication.

Patience

Work on being patient with those who have differences from you. This shows respect for others.

Flexibility, Adaptability, and Open-Mindedness

Work on being flexible, adaptable, and open-minded when doing business with other cultures. This will help to keep the lines of communication open.

most Americans, this behavior would be very offensive. So, think you are safe keeping your distance and not touching the other person? In some cultures, it is a sign of friendship to hold hands with a business acquaintance, regardless of their gender, and not doing so may be viewed as an insult.

You must always be aware of the customs and traditions of those with whom you interact. Be sure to understand what is expected. It is especially important to find out what is considered offensive. For example, in some cultures, when offered a business card it is respectful to spend a few seconds studying the card before continuing and it is considered extremely offensive to put the business card in your back pocket. By understanding how nonverbal language is interpreted by other cultures, you can avoid awkward situations.

Checkpoint

1. What is enunciation?
2. What is the date format used in most countries other than the US?
3. Why is nonverbal communication an especially sensitive area when communicating with those from other countries?

Overcoming Barriers

Communication barriers may arise when cultures come together in the workplace. Not everybody has the same ideas of how to behave or the same expectations when doing business. However, by being aware of those differences and being open to other practices, communication barriers can be avoided and overcome.

Workplace practices in America generally dictate that the rules of business etiquette are followed. Meetings are expected to start on time, colleagues and peers shake hands, and business cards are exchanged with others. As the global workplace expands, it is important to be aware of communication barriers, understanding that American customs are not necessarily the same as customs in other cultures. Some of the common communication barriers include body language, spoken language, stereotypes, interpretation of time, and personal space.

Body Language

Have you ever had someone ask if you are upset and you wondered how they knew? It could be because of your nonverbal communication, which is discussed in Chapter 1. How you hold your body (walking, standing, sitting), eye contact, and even how you make gestures communicate to others.

In all cultures, body language has a specific meaning. To prevent barriers, be aware of what nonverbal communication conveys. For example, in the United States, eye contact is expected, but in other cultures it can be seen as offensive or even threatening. In American culture, it is common to shake hands when meeting someone, but in another culture, bowing may be the appropriate gesture. As you work with people from other cultures, be sure to research appropriate body language for those cultures.

TEAMWORK

In teams, research various slang and gestures that might be misinterpreted by someone from another country. Be sure these expressions and gestures are not considered rude in the United States. Present your list as a poster to the class.

Spoken Language

Many times the spoken language is a barrier to clear communication. In global business, English is commonly spoken. But, be aware that for many of these colleagues, English is a second language. It is important to be patient in conversations to make sure everyone understands what is being said. If you found yourself in a situation where you were communicating in a language that is not your native language, you would appreciate the same respect.

Keep in mind that language barriers may exist not just between cultures, but within a culture. Regional cultures may use phrases that are not accepted in other parts of a country. Being aware and sensitive of language barriers will help you be successful in the workplace.

Stereotypes

Classifying or generalizing about a group of people with a given set of characteristics is known as **stereotyping.** It is not acceptable to stereotype. Stereotyping individuals by gender, religion, ethnic group, or any other form hinders business and communication efforts. These barriers can be overcome by focusing on issues and on each individual's contribution to the job at hand.

Interpretation of Time

It is important to understand the meaning of time when communicating with other cultures and plan accordingly. For example, indicating a report must be delivered *as soon as possible* can be interpreted in many different ways. In the US, it may be interpreted as deliver it tomorrow or even by the end of today. However, another culture may have an established business tradition of only running reports once a week or once a month. To a person in that culture, the report would be delivered according to the accepted custom of his or her culture. Be aware of the differences in how cultures interpret time. Avoid miscommunication by stating exact time deadlines instead of something that may be open to interpretation.

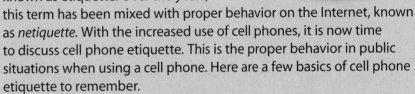

BUSINESS PROTOCOL

Cell Phone Etiquette

In everyday life and business, there is a proper way to behave. This is known as etiquette. Over the years, this term has been mixed with proper behavior on the Internet, known as *netiquette*. With the increased use of cell phones, it is now time to discuss cell phone etiquette. This is the proper behavior in public situations when using a cell phone. Here are a few basics of cell phone etiquette to remember.

- Cell phones are not fashion accessories.

- When at a meal or in a meeting, leave the cell phone on vibrate and in your pocket or purse. Do not place your cell phone on the table; it can be very disruptive to others when the phone vibrates.

- When at a meal or in a meeting, only answer the phone or text if it is an emergency. If expecting a call or text that is pertinent to the meeting, you must explain to those around that you are expecting the communication before using the cell phone.

- When in any public place, such as a movie theater, grocery store, or even walking down the sidewalk, remember that there are others around you. Nobody is interested in your conversation or the fact that you are using your phone. If you must talk in public, remember to be discrete and respectful of those around you. Talking loudly is very rude and disruptive.

- If you are taking pictures with your cell phone, get the permission of those who might be in the picture before you click. Not everyone wants their picture on your cell phone or to be sent to others.

- When you are driving, use a Bluetooth or other hands-free phone for calls. Never text or use a handheld cell phone while driving.

- Walking in public while talking on a hands-free device can make it look as though you are talking to yourself.

Personal space varies by situation and culture. Your personal space may be much smaller when talking to friends than when speaking with a business associate.

Shutterstock

Personal Space

Personal space is defined as the area around you that you feel is your own. Anyone inside of that area is seen as invading your personal space. The exact personal-space area varies from person to person and culture to culture.

All cultures have accepted personal-space requirements for talking face-to-face. In some cultures, conversations are held with each person's face only inches apart. However, in the United States, personal space for a conversation is much greater, typically about two to four feet. Respect the personal space of others and, hopefully, they will do the same for you.

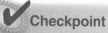

Checkpoint

1. List five areas in which barriers to communication may occur when communicating with those from other cultures.
2. What is nonverbal communication?
3. In the US, what is a typical personal space for having a conversation?

Diversity in the Workplace

America has often been called a *melting pot*, meaning many cultures have come together and combined to create what it thought of as American culture. However, Americans also celebrate their unique cultures, which is why America is also called a *salad bowl*. In a salad, the different parts combine to make the whole salad, but each individual part can still be recognized and tasted.

The American workforce is a diverse group of many different ages, ethnicities, physical abilities, mental abilities, races, spiritual practices, and more. **Diversity** means that we are all different in our own way, coming together to share and create a dynamic workplace. Workers in the United States come from different types of families, educational backgrounds, and even countries.

Diversity brings with it the challenges of communicating in a way that everyone understands. Various groups have their own ways of communicating, and those outside the group may not associate the same meaning with certain terms or behaviors. Methods of communication must evolve into acceptable terms that each person in the group can understand.

Having a diverse workforce brings advantages and challenges. With the population rapidly changing to include a wide range of cultures, ages, and other characteristics, having a diverse workforce helps guide a company in understanding the needs and wants of the customer. A diverse workforce also positions an organization as progressive and a place that people want to work, helping the effort to hire the best and brightest. However, companies must also be aware of discrimination laws. Also, employees, including managers, must be educated on tolerance and working together.

Culture

As companies continue to expand globally, it is important to understand the culture that workers may face. **Culture** is defined as shared beliefs, customs, practices, and social behavior of a particular group or nation. As workers interact with other companies on a global scale, awareness of these cultures is necessary as business communication takes place. Shaking hands, exchanging business cards, and dining together are examples of important communication that can have a positive or negative impact on an international business meeting. Knowing what is acceptable to a coworker from another culture will help facilitate positive interaction.

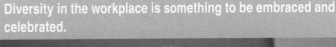
Diversity in the workplace is something to be embraced and celebrated.

Shutterstock

Intercultural Differences

The United States is made up of people from various cultures. Many people keep their culture as they move into the workplace. This mix of various cultures brings with it differences in values, attitudes, and perceptions. These differences are called **intercultural differences.** Intercultural differences are seen not only in what people from other countries bring, but also in what people from different areas of the US bring. People from different regions of the country may have their own sets of values, behaviors, ideas, and even variations in language (known as dialect). Knowing what coworkers value can help communication efforts in the workplace.

Gender

Women and men are not limited in career choices. Roughly half of the American workforce is female. Women and men may have different styles of communication. This creates a need for negotiating ways of working together.

The number of older workers is expected to increase over the next several years. Be aware of differences in communication between your generation and other generations.

Shutterstock

Age

The Bureau of Labor Statistics reports that in 2010 about 20 percent of the workforce in the United States is 55 years of age or older, and by 2019 that figure will rise to about 25 percent. Each generation has its own style of communication, which can lead to communication barriers. The age diversity in the workplace requires sensitivity to differing issues along with the need to find ways of effectively communicating across the generations.

Disabilities

A diverse workplace may include people with disabilities related to hearing, vision, speech, physical movement, or cognitive development. Often, communication must be adapted to meet the needs of these individuals. The goal of communication is to deliver a message that is understood by the receiver. In some cases, technology may be used to assist in communication. For example, text-to-speech software can be used to communicate a written message to a worker with a vision-related disability. A worker who has a physical disability related to the arms or hands may use an alternative keyboard or input device to write documents and e-mails. Successful communication involves sending a message that is understood, so adapt the communication to the situation in order to achieve this goal.

Checkpoint

1. What is the difference between America as a melting pot and America as a salad bowl?
2. Define diversity.
3. What is culture?

Ethical Communication

Ethics are the principles of what is right and wrong that help people make decisions. Ethical communication is applying ethics to messages and other documents to make sure all communication is honest in every way. Many companies have a code of ethics that dictates how business should be conducted. In order to make sure these codes are honored, both leaders and individual workers must set examples for acceptable behavior.

It may be tempting for those writing messages or representing the business to get caught up in exaggerations or inaccurate claims about the company products or services. However, misrepresenting information, intentionally or unintentionally, can lead to lawsuits, loss of customers, or employees losing jobs. When creating documents that represent your organization, ask the following questions to make sure the information is ethical.

Be aware of any disabilities that may require adjusting the communication process to ensure successful communication.

Shutterstock

- Has confidentiality been honored?
- Has privacy of the company been protected?
- Is the information presented factual and honest?
- Has appropriate credit been given to contributors of the communication?
- Has copyrighted material been used appropriately?

Confidentiality in communication means that specific information about a company or its employees is never shared except with those who have clearance to receive it. Not only should trade secrets be kept confidential, but personal employee information should never be shared. Always check company policies before sharing any company information that is requested from you.

Any information stored on company computer systems belongs to the company and should be protected. This also applies to company passwords, which should never be shared with anyone who does not have proper clearance.

Business communication should be accurate and facts or figures should not be exaggerated or embellished. Make certain that information presented in the communication gives an honest picture of the business.

Taking credit for someone else's work is known as plagiarism. Do not take credit for work that is not your own. Taking credit for someone else's work in an oral presentation is still plagiarism, even though you are doing so verbally. Always cite the source of information, but never copy the information without permission.

Copyright is the exclusive rights awarded to the author or creator of an original work. This means that you may not copy the work without the permission of the author or creator of the work. **Fair use** is a doctrine related to copyright law that allows for limited use of copyrighted material, such as for teaching or research, without requiring permission from the author or creator of an original work. Figure 2-2 lists important facts about copyrights.

Creating ethical documents is an important part of communication in the global workplace. However, ethical behavior is also important in day-to-day activities. To discourage unethical behavior in the workplace, these suggestions may be considered as a part of a code of ethics.

- Office equipment should not be used for personal tasks. Personal e-mailing, using the photocopier to copy documents, etc., should not be done with company property.

- If you need to take care of personal business, request time off. Performing personal activities on work time takes away from work you are being paid to accomplish.

- Making negative comments about the company or those with whom you work is not professional behavior.

Professionalism should be the number one priority as you conduct business, whether at home or in the office. When there are situations where business communication does not seem to be ethical, ask the leaders in the company for guidance.

 Checkpoint

1. What are ethics?
2. What is the difference between copyright and fair use?

Figure 2-2.	It is important to be aware of copyright law.

- Did you know every original work is automatically copyrighted and protected as soon as it is in tangible form? A copyright notice is not required.

- Did you know it is a copyright violation to copy something without permission and give it away? Even though no money has been exchanged, this is still illegal.

- Did you know e-mails are copyrighted? E-mail is an original work in tangible form, so it is automatically copyrighted.

Chapter 2 Review

Chapter Summary

Global Workplace

- In a global society, goods and services are bought and sold both inside and outside the country of origin.
- Global business means not only American companies expanding in other countries, but companies from other countries expanding in the United States.

Communicating in a Global Society

- When communicating in a global society, it is important to be aware of written, verbal, and nonverbal communication.
- Patience is required when verbally communicating with somebody whose native language is not the same as yours.
- When writing messages for those from other cultures, be as clear as possible and be aware of potential differences in how words and phrases are interpreted.
- Nonverbal communication can be an especially sensitive area when communicating with those from other cultures, so be sure to research customs and traditions.

Overcoming Barriers

- Workers and managers must learn to handle barriers to communication that might arise so they can effectively communicate in the workplace.
- Some of the common communication barriers may include body language, spoken language, stereotypes, interpretation of time, and personal space.

Diversity in the Workplace

- America has been described as both a melting pot and a salad bowl when referring to culture.
- Diversity means that we are all different in our own way, coming together to share and create a dynamic workplace.
- Intercultural differences are the varying values, attitudes, and perceptions of different cultures.
- Effective communication requires sensitivity to issues related to culture, gender, age, and disabilities.

Ethical Communication

- Ethics are the principle of what is right and wrong that help people make decisions.
- Some considerations for ethical communication are confidentiality, privacy, honesty, plagiarism, copyright law, and fair use doctrine.

Review
Your Knowledge

1. Describe a global society.
2. List ten tips for effective verbal communication in the global workplace.
3. Define enunciation.
4. How may something as simple as a written date result in miscommunication?
5. Describe how body language can result in miscommunication in the global workplace.
6. How is personal space determined?
7. How is American culture like a salad bowl?
8. Define culture.
9. What are ethics?
10. How does fair use doctrine relate to copyright law?

Apply
Your Knowledge

1. Research the global workplace. Write a report of at least two pages discussing your findings. Then, prepare and deliver an oral report.

2. You have applied to study abroad. Select a country where you wish to study. Then, research the culture of that country. Pay particular attention to nonverbal communication in that country. For example, is it expected to shake hands or to bow when greeting somebody? Create a table comparing nonverbal communication in the United States to that in the country you selected.

3. Make a list of possible barriers to written, verbal, and nonverbal communication when communicating with somebody from another culture. For each possible barrier, describe how you would remove the barrier.

4. Over the course of one day, make a list of all elements of diversity you observe in your school. To respect each individual's privacy, do not list any names. Then, for each element of diversity, describe any way in which communication may need to be altered to accommodate the diversity.

5. You are part of a team putting together a history of your community. You have interviewed many members of the community to gather some of the data. Describe why you would or would not need to cite the information gathered from interviews.

Practice
What You Have Learned

Access the *Fundamentals of Business Communication* Student Companion Web Site at www.g-wlearning.com/Communication. Download each data file for this chapter. Follow the instructions to complete a reading, writing, and grammar activity to practice what you have learned in this chapter.

Connections
Across the Curriculum

Social Studies. Research a country that interests you. Focus on the cultural aspects of that country, finding out information on how business is transacted. How does this country handle gift giving? Are there specifics for seating at meetings or dinners? Do body language, personal space, and interpretation of time differ from that in the United States? What other information would be important to know when doing business in this country?

Language Arts. Using the data you collected in the previous activity about a country and its culture, put together a presentation of the information. Present your research in the form of a chart or other graphic organizer.

Build
Your Business Portfolio

It is helpful to have a checklist of components that should be included in your portfolio. Your instructor may provide you with a checklist. If not, create a checklist that works best for you.

1. Decide on the purpose of the portfolio you are creating: temporary or short-term employment, career, application for college.

2. Research your chosen purpose to find suggested items to include that will help you create a professional portfolio.

3. Create a checklist to use as an ongoing reference as you create your portfolio throughout this class.

Careers
Government and Public Administration Careers and Communication

Government and public administrations career areas involve working in a governmental position or on issues related to government matters. Seven pathways make up this cluster.

These pathways include government, national security, foreign service, planning, revenue and taxation, regulation, and public management and administration. Places of work range from nonprofit organizations to overseas locations or local, state, or federal governments.

Government jobs sometimes deal with the global workplace, so strong communication skills are essential. Why is it important for government workers to recognize diversity and cultural differences in the workplace?

Event Prep

Ethics

There are many competitive events that participants may enter as a member of various student organizations. Review the events offered by your organization and the rules and regulations that apply to each activity. The ethics event is a competition in which teams participate to defend an ethical dilemma or topic.

To prepare for the ethics event, do the following.

1. Review the ethics section in this chapter.

2. Read each of the special Business Ethics features that appear throughout this book.

3. Put together a team of others also interested in this event.

4. Work collaboratively with your team to review and discuss each Business Ethics feature in this book.

5. Use the Internet to find more information about ethics and business communication. Print this information for future study material.

6. Look ahead and review Chapter 12 on giving presentations. That chapter will help you organize your thoughts and approach to taking your stand on the issue that is assigned to you or your team.

3 Using Technology to Communicate

Anytime we have new forms of communication, it changes behavior whether it is political or business or any type of behavior. Radio and TV did that. The PC will be classed as big or bigger an advancement in communications than those devices were.

—*Bill Gates, American entrepreneur and computer innovator*

Today, no discussion about communication would be complete without a conversation on how technology has made everyday life and the workplace more efficient and effective. It is possible to communicate 24 hours a day, seven days a week, reaching others in the community, office, or around the world. Technology has allowed communicators to be better by opening up new ways in which to communicate.

Objectives

When you complete Chapter 3, you will be able to:

- **Describe** how computers can be a communication tool for everyone.
- **Compare** various methods of conducting a remote meeting.
- **Explain** how to overcome barriers to communication in remote meetings.
- **Describe** how social media can be used as a means of communication.
- **Identify** ways in which to overcome barriers to communication associated with social media.
- **List** established technology that can be used for communication.
- **Describe** how wireless technology is used for communication.
- **Identify** security issues related to using technology to communicate.

Terms

downloading

uploading

compressed files

self-extracting compressed files

shareware

freeware

for-purchase software

Web 2.0

instant messaging (IM)

text messaging

texting

teleconferencing

conference calling

podcast

Web seminars

online meetings

social media

blogs

social bookmarking

social networking sites

professional networking sites

cell phones

smartphones

voice mail

pagers

wireless technology

malware

identity theft

Go Green

At school and in the office, paper helps people communicate. Paper is used to take notes, write reports, and for countless other tasks. A "paperless society" still creates many reasons to print rather than to save information digitally. According to the EPA, the average office worker in the US will use approximately 10,000 sheets of paper in a year. Considering how much paper is used each year and how much ink or toner is needed to print those pages, resources can be conserved by planning printing needs.

1. Talk with the person in your school who purchases paper. How much paper does your school use each year?
2. How can you reduce the number of pages you print and still keep the important information you need?
3. How can the amount of ink or toner be conserved?
4. Where can you recycle ink or toner cartridges in your community?

Communicating Using Computers

You may or may not know much about the early computer and its journey to influencing the way people communicate. When the first general-purpose, electronic computer came on the scene, it was very large. It weighed 30 tons and was about three feet thick, by eight and one-half feet tall, by 80 feet long. It had to be kept in a cool space so it would not overheat. The temperature in the room was so cold that often workers required a sweater even in the summer months. But, evolving technology has changed all of that. The average computer no longer needs special indoor temperatures to function. Also, computers are easily portable and an essential part of the business environment, as well as for everyday life, as shown in Figure 3-1.

Computers can do a lot, but they cannot think for you. You still need communication and decision-making skills to create business documents that are professional and express a clear message. The spelling checker only verifies if the word is in the dictionary and does not know you meant to write *two* instead of *tow*. The computer will see *tow* as a word and not suggest a correction. A grammar checker may identify the error, but you must still make the decision to accept or reject the suggested change. The key to using technology to communicate is to know how to use the tools that are available and to use good proofreading and editing skills.

Computers can be a communication tool for everyone. Rapidly changing technology, both hardware and software, means new communication tools are being quickly brought to market.

- Translation software converts messages from one language to another, allowing communication between people who do not speak the same language.
- Speech-recognition software allows the user to record spoken words in a document, and can also be used to enter computer commands.

Reading Prep

Before reading this chapter, look at the chapter title. What can you predict will be presented?

Figure 3-1. Advances in computer technology have dramatically changed the way in which communication takes place.

Personal Computers (PCs)

Apple, Inc.

Personal computers are smaller than mainframe computers. They include desktops, laptops, tablet PCs, netbooks, and iPads. Technology continues to change rapidly and PCs are constantly being refined.

Peripherals

Input and output devices connected to the computer to perform activities like printing, scanning, or keyboarding. Wireless peripherals, such as a keyboard and mouse, allow work without being tied to the computer. The list of peripherals is becoming endless.

Communicating Using Computers

Computers have redefined how people communicate. Computers are used to produce written communication as well as for spoken and visual communication. The media capabilities of the computer can be used to listen to music, watch videos, make phone calls, and attend virtual meetings. Computers have changed the way business is conducted and will continue to evolve.

Storage Devices

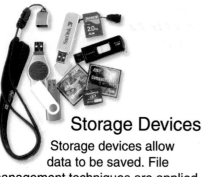

Storage devices allow data to be saved. File management techniques are applied to organize the information. Information can be saved on internal hard drives, external hard drives, CDs/DVDs, and flash drives (as well as on cloud sites).

Software

Software makes the computer work. Operating system software controls the functioning of the computer. Application software, such as word processing, database, and spreadsheet software, allows the user to produce documents. Other application software is used to create videos, play games, and so on. Utility software helps configure and maintain the computer as well as provides virus protection. Compression software is used to reduce the amount of storage space consumed by a data file.

- Alternative input devices are available for people with visual, physical, and cognitive disabilities to make communication possible. Alternative keyboards/mice, touch-screen displays, screen enlargers, and text-to-speech software are widely available assistive technologies.

- To communicate with a person who has a hearing disability, video translators make sign language available. Simply key in a word and the hearing impaired person can view the sign language on the video translator.

These are just a few examples of how technology continues to advance communication capabilities.

The Internet is an important part of using computer technology to communicate. In the process of using the Internet, you will often engage in downloading and uploading. **Downloading** is the process of saving files from a Web site or file transfer protocol (FTP) site. **Uploading** is the reverse, saving files to a Web or FTP site. The files you download and upload may be compressed. There are several popular formats of compressed files, including ZIP and RAR. **Compressed files** may contain multiple native-format files, such as documents or photographs, and are much smaller in size than the uncompressed versions. Compressed files must be decompressed using extraction utility software to access the data they contain. Some compressed files are created as **self-extracting compressed files,** which can be decompressed by simply double-clicking on the file.

For most types of software, there are shareware, freeware, and for-purchase options. **Shareware** is software that can be installed and used, then purchased if you decide to continue using it. Shareware usually has a notice screen, time-delayed startup, or reduced features. Purchasing the software removes these restrictions. **Freeware** is fully functional software that can be used forever without purchasing it. To be considered freeware, the software should not be a restricted version of for-purchase software. If it does, the software is considered shareware. **For-purchase software** is software you must buy to use, although you can often download a timed or limited-use demo. The difference between a demo of for-purchase software and shareware is subtle. Typically, shareware software is not time limited, meaning that the software remains functional forever with the restrictions in place. Shareware is based on the honor system where those who continue to use the software purchase the software. A demo of for-purchase software, however, typically stops working after a period of time. In the case of a limited-feature demo, the best features are either not functional or functional for a limited time.

Checkpoint

1. What does speech-recognition software allow?
2. What is the difference between downloading and uploading?
3. What is the difference between shareware, freeware, and for-purchase software?

Communicating in Remote Meetings

As business has become more global, workers have become members of teams that may be in different locations. **Web 2.0** is a term associated with

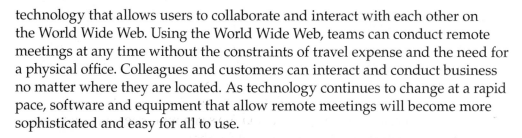

technology that allows users to collaborate and interact with each other on the World Wide Web. Using the World Wide Web, teams can conduct remote meetings at any time without the constraints of travel expense and the need for a physical office. Colleagues and customers can interact and conduct business no matter where they are located. As technology continues to change at a rapid pace, software and equipment that allow remote meetings will become more sophisticated and easy for all to use.

Instant Messaging and Text Messaging

Instant messaging (IM) and the similar **text messaging** (more commonly called **texting**) are used for the most basic type of remote meeting. Participants conduct a conversation by keying and sending responses, rather than talking or using video. The conversation usually takes place in real time, but the messages can be stored and retrieved at a later time. Using an IM service, multiple people can participate in a live conversation.

Use of instant messaging and texting should be cleared through your organization's technology team before using. There are issues related to security, just as with e-mail.

In addition to using instant messaging and texting to conduct remote meetings, many businesses use these as customer-support tools. Customers can IM or text the customer-support staff with questions and received answers in return in the form of an IM or text.

CASE

Sales Texting

Jim, the sales manager for a regional company, received a text message from a customer inquiring about a product. Jim texted the customer back.

Thx 4 ur msg. R u ready 2 ordr? 800.555.4523

Minutes later, the customer called Jim on the phone and asked several questions about the product. Jim offered to e-mail some literature to the customer, which the customer indicated would be very helpful.

1. Was this an example of a remote meeting?

2. Did Jim act appropriately when first contacted by the customer?

3. What could Jim have done differently to improve communication?

Teleconferencing

Teleconferencing, commonly called **conference calling,** is another basic type of remote meeting. There is no video, just verbal communication with three or more people on a telephone call. Most business phone systems allow conference calling. In some cases, several people will be in one location using a speaker phone to speak with one or more individuals in other locations.

Podcasts, Web Seminars, and Online Meetings

A web broadcast (webcast), more commonly called a **podcast,** is a series of digital media files, released at regular intervals, that contain information related to a specific topic. The files may be audio or video and can be retrieved by a user at their convenience. A podcast is a way to post new information for business associates who may not be on the same schedule, since each can access the information at a time convenient for them.

Web seminars are similar to teleconferencing, but with the added element of a video display. Software such as GoToMeeting and WebEx are used to host the Web seminar. One computer display is shared over the Internet and the others attending the meeting can view the action onscreen. A Web seminar may consist of video, text, and voice communication. To allow voice communication, an attendee typically calls a phone number and is connected to a conference call. The visual part of the web seminar is viewed by using a Web browser to access the link provided by the person conducting the seminar.

Online meetings allow participants to take teleconferencing and web seminars one step further and actually collaborate on documents being presented. The leader of the meeting can give participants control of the computer so others can contribute and change the presentation in real time. Through desktop sharing and markup tools, each person can physically make suggestions while others watch and wait for a turn.

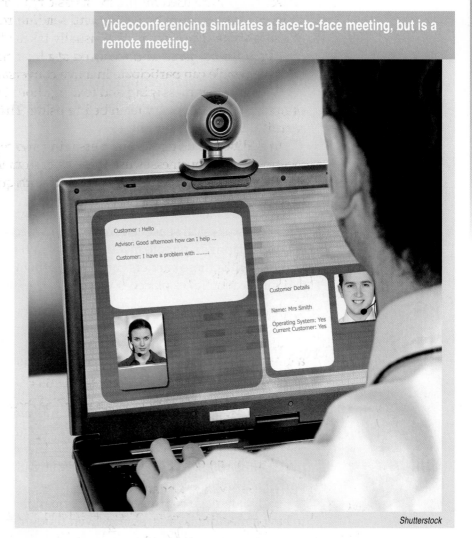

Videoconferencing simulates a face-to-face meeting, but is a remote meeting.

Shutterstock

Videoconferencing

Videoconferencing allows team members in different locations to talk to and see each other. Through the use of an Internet connection and a computer equipped with a Web camera and communication software, meetings can be conducted and members can talk "face-to-face," even though the team is in different locations. There are many videoconferencing services that make it easy to set up a live conference.

Virtual Whiteboards

A virtual whiteboard is another example of a method to conduct a remote meeting. You are probably familiar with a whiteboard in meetings and classrooms where notes are written as the meeting or class is being conducted. When finished, the whiteboard is then wiped clean for the next user. A virtual whiteboard is very similar, except the participants are not in the same room. A Web application on the computer allows participation in the meeting and use of the whiteboard. The only equipment that is necessary is the computer, Internet connection, and the Web-based application. This technology is gaining popularity with many businesses who regularly conduct remote meetings.

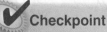

Checkpoint

1. What is Web 2.0?
2. How is a remote meeting conducted using instant messaging or texting?
3. What is the difference between a podcast and a Web seminar?

Overcoming Communication Barriers of Remote Meetings

There are barriers to working with colleagues and customers who are not in your physical space. However, many people think that the positives of communicating in remote meetings outweigh the negatives. Organizations that recognize these barriers can address them and ensure that smooth communication takes place.

- lack of attention
- lack of eye contact and body language
- transmission delays
- technology glitches

When you cannot see the person on the other end of the meeting, it may be difficult to remain attentive. Participants may be distracted by an activity, such as reading e-mail, and have a negative impact on the meeting. When participating in remote meetings, behave in a manner as if you were physically in the same room. It is important to pay attention to the presentation and participate in the event.

Body language conveys much information to meeting participants related to how a meeting is progressing. Even though you may be using a Web camera, much of the body language will be lost due to the sampling rate of the camera. It is important to have very clear verbal communication in remote meetings because the nonverbal language may not be evident. Additionally, there is an intrinsic element of being in the same room as the person with whom you are communicating that is not achieved during a remote meeting. Video conferencing can help overcome this barrier, but the communication will not be the same as if you are in the same room.

When multiple people are on a call, there is always the chance that you will hear a voice delay from participants. This may cause others to start talking over each other. Be aware that voice delays are probable. Leave pauses between sentences so others can hear you or comment without cutting off others.

When communicating with somebody in a remote meeting, you may not be able to interpret any nonverbal language.

Shutterstock

No matter how up-to-date the equipment and software, there will always be glitches that creep into the meeting, such as an inoperable Internet connection or a software issue. When planning remote meetings, be prepared by having a backup plan in case one part of the presentation cannot be used due to a technical issue.

Checkpoint

1. List four barriers to communication in a remote meeting.
2. How can the lack of eye contact and body language in a remote meeting be overcome?

Communicating Using Social Media

A popular communication method that has developed in the last few years is social media. **Social media** is an Internet-based tool that allows users to share information within a group. Some social media sites are password protected and members are approved by owners of the site before being accepted. Other social media sites are open for anyone to use. Businesses, as well as individuals, can take advantage of using social media sites to discuss and share ideas, thoughts, and interests. Some social media tools include:

- Web logs (blogs);
- social bookmarking;
- social networking; and
- professional networking.

Web logs, or **blogs** as they are known, are Web sites maintained by an individual who posts topics or opinions. Users do not need a password to access the blog. A blog typically provides information or news about subjects that the owner of the Web site chooses to discuss. Individuals sometimes use blogs as personal diaries to share information with friends. Business blogs are generally used to share information with customers or potential customers.

Social bookmarking is a method of saving bookmarks to a public Web site so others may have access to them. Some creators of social bookmarks add keywords or metadata so that the user can read the description of the bookmark before opening it. When you bookmark (save a Web address) to your personal computer, you cannot access it from any other computer. However, when you post the bookmark as a social bookmark, it is saved on a Web site where you can share it with others. By using social bookmarking, you can share useful Web sites with friends or customers.

Social networking sites are Web sites that allow users to share information for the purpose of building relationships within their individual networks. These networking sites are password protected and usually include personal profiles of the users. Caution should be used when posting personal information that you would not want someone outside of your network to have. Even though these sites are password protected, outsiders may still gain access to your information. Employers may use social networking sites to research potential candidates and universities may use these sites to screen applicants. Some of the most popular social networking sites include the following.

TEAMWORK

Working with one or two classmates, brainstorm a list of social media. Discuss how each form can be used for business. Present your conclusions to the class.

- Facebook
- Twitter
- MySpace
- YouTube
- Flickr

Professional networking sites are similar to social networking sites in their setup and operation. However, professional networking sites are used for professionals seeking to expand their career networks. One of the most popular professional networking sites is LinkedIn.

Checkpoint

1. What is a blog?
2. How does a social networking site differ from a professional networking site?

Overcoming Communication Barriers of Social Media

Social media is a useful tool when used correctly. Like any form of communication, there are barriers to be overcome when using social media. Both individuals and businesses can benefit or suffer harm when social media is abused.

Blogs

When others are posting information, it is difficult to manage the story being recorded. Sometimes, negative information can be posted about an individual or business, and there may not be recourse to set the record straight. This can be prevented by setting up a blog with a review process for posts by users.

Social Networking Sites

Users must be careful of the types of personal information and photos that are posted to social networking sites. This information can be shared with others without your permission, including potential employers or business associates. To overcome this barrier, only post information that is related to the business. Personal information should never be posted on a social network that is used for business.

Professional Networking Sites

Users must also be aware of what is being posted to a professional networking site. Employers use these sites to gain information about potential employees, so keep this in mind when you are sharing information with your network. Also, be aware that you are a representative of your company. Therefore, keep the postings professional and related to your business or career.

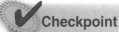

Checkpoint
1. How can the barriers to communication be overcome on a blog?
2. How can the barriers to communication be overcome on a social networking site?

Communicating Using Established Technology

With all of the available advanced technology, there are still the basic tools of communication. All too often, technology users in the 21st century take these basic tools for granted or overlook them.

Smartphones have become an important part of business communication.

Shutterstock

The first **cell phones** were basic telephones that allowed the user to move around and communicate without a landline. Now, most cell phones are advanced computerized devices called **smartphones** that can be used to check e-mail, surf the Web, take pictures, *and* talk on the phone.

In the past, an answering machine was used to record voice messages when somebody was not available to answer the telephone. Now, **voice mail,** which is the modern version of the answering machine, is readily available with any landline or cell phone subscription. For your business voice mail greeting, use a professional message that states your name, directions for leaving a message, and any other details a customer or colleague may need to know. For your personal voice mail greeting, keep your message brief and also be professional. There is always the possibility that an important contact, such as a potential employer, may access your personal voice mail.

Pagers are devices that let the user know there is a message waiting. These were once popular for communicating with others outside of the office before cell phones became an economical option. Pagers are still used where cell phones cannot get service, as well as where cell phones are banned. Some hospitals use pagers because cell phones may interfere with the operation of some medical equipment. Additionally, many restaurants use pagers to notify waitstaff when orders are ready to serve.

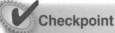

Checkpoint

1. List three things that can be done with a smartphone.
2. What is voice mail?
3. Give two examples of how pagers may still be in use today.

Communicating Using Wireless Technology

To the user, technology connections are generally invisible. Most people do not think about how the technology works, or even why it works, until it stops working. Wireless technology is an important part of digital communication, as shown in Figure 3-2. **Wireless technology** is used to connect devices without the use of lines, cables, or other type of physical connection.

- Voice over Internet Protocol (VoIP or Voice over IP) is a technology that allows for voice and digital media communication over the Internet or any other network using Internet protocols.

- A wireless personal area network (WPAN) connects devices in a given, relatively small workspace. For example, Bluetooth technology provides a wireless connection between a smartphone and its headset or earpiece.

- A wireless local area network (WLAN) connects devices in a defined area, which is larger than the area covered by a WPAN, using radio technology. For example, in your building, a WLAN can provide wireless connections between the computers and the printers.

- A wireless wide area network (WWAN) uses cellular telephone technology to connect devices throughout a geographic area. For example, a WWAN can provide a connection between a laptop computer and an Internet provider in any location where the provider's cellular telecommunication network provides coverage.

Checkpoint

1. How does a wireless personal area network differ from a wireless local area network?

2. How does a wireless local area network differ from a wireless wide area network?

Security Issues When Using Technology to Communicate

Using technology to communicate has changed the way individuals interact, both on a personal level and in business settings. However, the ease of access to digital information and communication brings with it issues of security. Companies must be aware of the security of data transmitted during communication. In addition, both companies and individuals must be concerned with the issue of identity theft.

Data Security

Companies are concerned with maintaining security over any data that is transmitted. This is required for reasons of privacy and controlling proprietary information. In many cases, it is also important to protect documents and other types of data from unauthorized changes. Firewalls and passwords are two ways in which users can be restricted from accessing data on a computer system.

Viruses are computer programs that can replicate and spread across computer systems. Most viruses are **malware,** which is a program intended to damage, destroy, or steal the data on a computer system. For that reason, it is necessary to have antivirus programs to prevent malicious software (malware) from infecting computer systems.

Figure 3-2.   Virtual communication involves communicating with others who are not physically located in the same place.

Intranet/Extranet

Intranet sites allow members of an organization to post files, download files, upload files, and share other information without going outside of the local network. Extranet sites provide sites for customers to check on orders and other services and are often password protected. An extranet is a network that can be accessed from outside an organization, while an intranet is a network within an organization. Both an intranet and an extranet are based on Internet technologies.

Remote Meetings

Remote meetings are used for teams within organizations as well as communicating with customers. Technologies that may be used for remote meetings include instant messaging, texting, teleconferencing, podcasts, web seminars, online meetings, video conferencing, and virtual whiteboards.

Virtual Communication

Technology has made working as a team effective when each team member cannot be physically located in the same place. This is called virtual communication. With virtual communication processes, colleagues are able to meet, collaborate, and share information anytime, anywhere. Remote meetings are an important part of virtual communication.

Wikis

Wikis are collaborative Web sites that contain information about an organization or subject. Wikis allow team members to update or create Web pages when changes are needed. One of the principles of a wiki is that anybody accessing the site can make changes. The Web site Wikipedia is a good example of a wiki. Companies can use that site to distribute information about the business and it is an easy way to keep the information up to date.

World Wide Web

Web sites serve as marketing, sales, and customer service tools. With live chatting, frequently asked questions (FAQs) pages, and contact pages, customers and potential customers can find information about products and services, place orders, and learn how to use a product. Podcasts posted on Web sites can deliver lessons, news, and countless other forms of information. Users can download the audio and/or visual presentations and listen at their convenience. Museums, schools, and companies post podcasts as a way to connect with users.

Identity Theft

Identity theft is a form of fraud that occurs when somebody takes your personal information and pretends to be you in order to make credit card purchases, withdraw funds from your accounts, or obtain other benefits to which you are entitled. It is important to protect your identity when communicating on the Internet or through other digital means.

BUSINESS ETHICS

Biased Behavior

As you go to work or school each day, you may encounter others who categorize people using biased words and comments. Using age, gender, race, disability, or ethnicity as a way to describe others is unethical and sometimes illegal. Use bias-free language in all of your communication, whether verbal, printed, or digital, to show respect for those with whom you come in contact. For more information on unbiased communication, search the Internet to find out the latest information on the topic.

Never give your social security number to someone you do not know. When entering passwords or personal information on Web sites, make sure the site is secure. Secure sites have a URL that starts with *https* instead of the standard *http*. The *s* indicates the site is a secure site. Secure sites may also display an icon somewhere in the browser to indicate the communication is secure. In Internet Explorer, a closed-padlock icon is displayed next to the URL text box to indicate a site is secure. There are also vendors who will secure a site for an organization. These vendors may display a seal or certificate to indicate the site is secure.

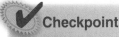

Checkpoint

1. What is malware?
2. What is identity theft?

Chapter 3 Review

Chapter Summary

Communicating Using Computers

- Computers are an essential part of business and everyday life.
- Computers cannot think for you.
- Computers can be a communication tool for everybody.
- When using the Internet, you will likely be downloading and uploading files.
- Most types of software are available as shareware, freeware, and for-purchase software.

Communicating in Remote Meetings

- Instant messaging and text messaging are used to conduct the most basic form of remote meeting.
- Teleconferencing is a type of remote meeting in which three or more people are on a telephone call.
- Podcasts, web seminars, online meetings, videoconferencing, and virtual whiteboards are all means of conducting remote meetings.

Overcoming Communication Barriers of Remote Meetings

- Four barriers to communication in remote meetings are lack of attention, lack of eye contact and body language, transmission delays, and technology glitches.
- When participating in a remote meeting, behave just as you would if you were in the same room.
- It is important to have very clear verbal communication in a remote meeting because nonverbal communication may be limited.
- Always have a backup plan in case of glitches in the technology used for a remote meeting.

Communicating Using Social Media

- Social media is an Internet-based tool that allows users to share information within a group.
- Blogs, social bookmarking, social networking, and professional networking are common types of social media.

Overcoming Communication Barriers of Social Media

- A blog with a review process for posts is a way to manage the story being recorded.
- When using a social or professional networking site for business, never post personal information or photos.

Communicating Using Established Technology

- Do not overlook using established technology for communication.
- Cell phones without Internet access, voice mail, and even pagers are all established technologies still valid for communication.

Communicating Using Wireless Technology

- Wireless technology is used to connect devices without the use of lines, cables, or other physical connections.
- Voice over Internet Protocol, wireless personal area networks, wireless local area networks, and wireless wide area networks are examples of wireless technology used in communication.

Security Issues When Using Technology to Communicate

- Companies must be aware of the security of data transmitted during communication.
- Firewalls and passwords can be used to restrict access to computer systems.
- Users must take precautions when communicating on the Internet to protect against identity theft.

Review
Your Knowledge

1. Describe uploading and downloading.
2. What is the term associated with technology that allows users to collaborate and interact with each other on the World Wide Web?
3. What is the difference between a Web seminar and a teleconference?
4. Why is lack of eye contact and body language a barrier to communication in a remote meeting?
5. What information is typically provided on a blog?
6. List five popular social networking sites.
7. When using social or professional networking sites for business, what general rule should you follow?
8. Provide two examples in which the established technology of pagers is in use today.
9. Describe wireless technology.
10. Define malware.

Apply
Your Knowledge

1. Research the various ways in which it is possible to communicate with computers. Do not forget that many devices, such as cell phones, use computer technology. For each way of communicating that you identify, write at least two paragraphs describing the method, its advantages, and its disadvantages.

2. Research the term Web 2.0. Write a paper describing Web 2.0 and how it differs from prior Web technologies (you may find some controversy on this topic). Include in your paper how Web 2.0 has advanced communication, especially as it relates to business.

3. For each of the four barriers to communication in remote meetings listed in the chapter, identify ways in which to overcome the barrier. Try to identify at least two other barriers to communication in remote meetings and identify ways in which to overcome those barriers.

4. Identify two forms of social media. Then, write a plan for setting up a business presence on each. Include a description of the type of business and what product or service is sold. Also include a detailed description of how you would leverage the social media to improve the business (such as improved customer service or increased global reach).

5. Write a set of guidelines for how to use a social media site such as Facebook for business. The guidelines should be something a new employee can be given to indicate proper behavior and information for the site. Include with the guidelines a brief description of why the guidelines are needed.

6. Identify a local business that uses pagers as part of its communication process. If possible, conduct an interview with a manager at the business to find out why pagers are used. If you cannot identify a local business that uses pagers, locate a company that sells pagers and ask a sales representative how pagers can be used in business communication.

7. Research the three types of area networks described in this chapter. Write a paper describing the advantages and disadvantages of each.

8. Go to the Web site www.idtheft.gov and research ways in which to prevent identity theft. Describe the rights that victims of identity theft have.

Practice
What You Have Learned

Access the *Fundamentals of Business Communication* Student Companion Web Site at www.g-wlearning.com/Communication. Download each data file for this chapter. Follow the instructions to complete a reading, writing, and grammar activity to practice what you have learned in this chapter.

Connections
Across the Curriculum

Social Studies. Research how assistive technology is used by people with disabilities. Write a description of assistive technology. Make a list of the various types of technology you found for assisting those with visual, audio, speech, or physical disabilities.

Math. Create a spreadsheet to show the various types of assistive technology devices that are available today. On the Y axis, list the names of available devices. On the X axis, list visual, audio, speech, and physical. Place check marks in the appropriate columns so that you may visually see each device and what assistance it provides.

Build
Your Business Portfolio

Before collecting information for your portfolio, write an objective. Are you creating this for a job interview, college application, or volunteer position in the community? You should have answered these questions in the previous chapter. Now, write an objective based on those answers. Writing an objective will help you focus on the task of creating appropriate documents to accomplish your goal.

1. Do research on how to write an objective. Your instructor can assist you in locating research.
2. Write an objective to guide you through this portfolio project.

Careers
Transportation, Distribution, and Logistics Careers and Communication

Transportation by road, rail, water, and air offers many employment options. These careers focus on effective planning, efficient management, and safe movement of products and people. Related careers focus on planning, managing, and maintaining the equipment, facilities, and systems used.

Strong interpersonal and communication skills are key qualities for these workers. One skill that is necessary for careers in this cluster is the ability to communicate with clients and business associates. Describe a situation in which someone pursuing a career in this cluster must be able to communicate in a clear and concise manner.

Event Prep

Computer Applications

Some student organizations have competitive events that feature computer applications. These events include knowledge of computer terminology and concepts, as well as production competencies. Review such events offered by your organization and the rules and regulations that apply to each activity.

To prepare for the computer applications event, do the following.

1. Review the terminology and concepts presented in this chapter.

2. Create your own glossary of terms and concepts to review prior to taking the event exam.

3. Search the Internet for computer tests that are free to use and complete these as practice.

4. Ask you instructor to provide you with sample practice tests for review prior to the competition.

4
Communicating and Working in Teams

Coming together is a beginning.
Keeping together is progress.
Working together is success.
—Henry Ford,
American businessman
and automotive innovator

Teamwork is an important part of business. In order to be an effective member of a team, you first need to understand how a team is constructed and how it functions. As you might expect, communication plays a key role in an effective team. This chapter discusses how teams function and the communication that occurs in teams.

Objectives

When you complete Chapter 4, you will be able to:

- **List** common characteristics of effective team members.
- **Explain** important things to do when planning and conducting a team meeting.
- **Describe** how written, verbal, and nonverbal communication is used in a team.
- **Discuss** leadership styles and characteristics of an effective leader.
- **List** ways of overcoming communication barriers.

Terms

team
formal team
virtual team
informal team
facilitator
recorder
timekeeper
encourager
skeptic

parliamentary procedures
leadership
leadership style
laissez-faire
democratic
autocratic
leader

Go Green

The next time your home printer needs ink or toner cartridges, take the empty cartridge to a local office supply and see if they will refill it. This is an important way to decrease the amount of materials that go into landfills while saving you money.

1. Does your school or work recycle ink and toner cartridges? If so, ask the person who does the purchasing how much money can be saved for each refill.
2. Go to the Web site of an office supply store and find out how much it costs to buy a new ink cartridge versus the cost of a refill.
3. Visit a local office supply store. What is the store policy for recycling cartridges? Is there a trade-in allowance on new cartridges for old ones brought in?

Teams

Positive communication skills are necessary at all levels within an organization. Your role as an employee within an organization will be defined. You will have specific duties to perform and specific reporting relationships. It will be important to exercise positive communication with your manager so that you have clear direction on how to complete your job tasks each day and your manager has a clear understanding of what has been completed. As an employee, you will probably also be a member of a team. As a member of a team, you will need to use positive communication skills so that you may successfully interact with those who are working with you.

A **team** is two or more people working together to reach a goal. Working together can create a better or different outcome than working as an individual to solve a problem or perform a task. A formal team may be the department in which you work, such as a customer service team or accounting team. An informal team may be the recycling committee or entertainment committee. The word *team* has become an important part of both business and social vocabulary.

Working in teams can be very effective at promoting ownership and commitment by team members. One of the biggest advantages of a team is that individuals come together to work for a focused purpose or objective. The talents and skills of the team's members can evolve into a productive and creative environment that produces a positive outcome. However, a team without a strong leader will probably not be successful. A team without strong individual team members, likewise, will not be successful. If team members are not cooperative and do not take responsibilities seriously, the task at hand will not be accomplished effectively, if at all.

Reading Prep

Before reading this chapter, look at the quote on the chapter opening page. How does this quote relate to what is being presented in the content?

Teamwork is very important in business. You will need to work on teams with many different people.

Shutterstock

In order for a team to be effective, team members must develop positive communication skills. When a team is working toward a solution for a problem, effective team members display common characteristics that make reaching goals possible.

- Cooperation. Successful team members learn to work with others, focusing on a common goal rather than an individual goal.

- Politeness. Manners are important in any situation, and exhibiting courtesy and consideration to others is important in a team.

- Patience. Working in teams can be stressful at times, so it is important to remain calm and listen to ideas of others without criticism.

- Enthusiasm. Demonstrating a positive attitude toward the task and fellow team members goes a long way to accomplishing a goal.

- Dependability. Etiquette is important; being punctual for meetings or handing in assignments is important when working with others.

- Loyalty. Commitment to your team and organization are expected.

- Building of self-esteem of others. Giving positive comments to each other and supporting ideas is important for good team relationships.

Types of Teams

Generally, there are two types of teams: formal and informal. **Formal teams** are those teams created for a specific and organized purpose. Formal teams have an appointed leader and members are chosen based on talents and skills. For example, in a business, a team may be created to take on a specific project. Individual team members may be selected from the same department or different departments within the company. In formal teams, the number of team members is generally an odd number, such as three or five. The odd number helps when voting on issues so there is not a tie when making decisions. Limiting the number of members in a team makes it more manageable for individuals to work together efficiently.

Virtual teams are made up of members who are in different locations. These teams are examples of formal teams. People do not always live or work in the town where their job is located. Through the use of technology, some employees work from home or while traveling. Team members can use telephone, video, Internet, or any other communication technology to connect to other team members. Virtual teams have become a cost-effective option for business because there are no travel expenses and team members' time can be used more efficiently.

Informal teams are teams that come together usually for a social purpose, like a softball or bowling team. Individual team members generally participate as a member of the team by choice, as opposed to a formal team where participation is usually required. The leader of an informal team may be voted on by team members or the natural leader may step up to the task of leading the team.

Team Development

Once the team is in place, the team will eventually evolve and grow as a unit. Becoming a working team takes time, and there are phases that the team will go through as it becomes a cohesive unit. The group dynamics will evolve as the team matures, but there are basic steps that each team will take.

1. Getting to know each other.
2. Learning to work together.
3. Working together.
4. Being successful.

BUSINESS PROTOCOL

Team Protocol

In teams, there is a protocol, or set of rules, that dictates behavior. Team protocol says that a team:

- states a clear unity of purpose;
- has a clear set of performance goals;
- creates an atmosphere that is informal, comfortable, and relaxed;
- encourages everyone to participate and be free to express ideas and feelings;
- leads members to a general consensus through discussion; and
- has members each carrying the appropriate workload.

Team protocol says that an effective team member:

- communicates;
- avoids blaming others;
- supports group member's ideas, considering all ideas without immediate dismissal;
- does not brag or try to be the superstar, but is a team player;
- listens actively; and
- gets involved.

Team members get acquainted with each other as the team is created. During this stage, team members discover the abilities and attitudes of the others on the team. Each member will also try to determine how and where he or she fits into the group.

During the second stage, team members work through the task at hand. This is a time for everyone to speak up and give their ideas so that a solution can be found. Brainstorming takes place, where everyone presents their ideas with no criticism or rejection of any idea.

After various solutions have been proposed, in the third stage team members learn how to work together to select the most appropriate solution to the task. There is a lot of give and take at this point because the focus is the goal of the team, not the goal of individuals.

Team members progressed through the stages of team development and reach the fourth stage. In the fourth stage, everything comes together and an agreement of the proposed solution is reached.

As the team is developing, it is important to have guidelines for moving through the process of completing the task. Suggestions for these guidelines are as follows.

- Identify the team's purpose, goals, and objectives.
- Identify ways to successfully achieve the team's goals.
- Identify each team member's responsibility in completing the task.
- Identify ways to effectively communicate with team members while working on the project.

Team Member Roles

Individual members take on various roles in every team. Some of the roles will be appointed, while others will be informal. However, every team needs the variety and balance that the various roles bring to the situation. Positive group dynamics can be created when team members have specific roles: facilitator, recorder, timekeeper, encourager, and skeptic.

Each member of a team should serve a role, and each team should have a leader.

Shutterstock

Facilitator

Acting as the leader for the group, the **facilitator** helps the team work through each step of completing a task to come up with a solution. Responsibilities may include preparing the agenda for each meeting, keeping the group members on task, staying focused on the team purpose or goal, and reporting the progress of the group to others.

Recorder

The **recorder** is responsible for creating minutes, which is a written record of the meeting that can be used as reference for progress of completing the task. This person records the discussion during brainstorming, attends to the agenda and records each item as it is addressed, and quotes group members, but does not edit or evaluate group member thoughts.

Timekeeper

A **timekeeper** is mindful of time as the team works through the task at hand. It is easy to get sidetracked while discussing issues. The timekeeper watches the clock to make sure meetings start and end on time.

Encourager

The **encourager** is an informal role who is positive and influences others to be positive when challenges occur. Teams can benefit from someone who is always positive. This role is sometimes referred to as the *optimist*.

Skeptic

Most people tend to think that a skeptic is a bad thing. But, the **skeptic** challenges the team to prove the solution is correct. Teams can benefit from this informal role, which looks at all the solutions for possible issues.

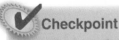**Checkpoint**

1. What are the two types of teams?
2. What are the four steps of team development?
3. List five roles that individual team members may play.

Meeting as a Team

Time is important to everyone in business. Attending meetings that are unproductive or unorganized is not a good use of anyone's time. It is important that meetings be held when discussion is warranted, not for a topic that could be handled through e-mail or other communication. When planning a meeting:

- reserve a meeting place;
- send an invitation to those who need to attend the meeting; and
- create and send an agenda before the meeting so participants can be prepared.

When conducting a meeting:

- start the meeting on time;
- preview the agenda so everyone is clear on the purpose of the meeting;
- encourage participation from the attendees;
- keep the discussion on topic;
- summarize the information at the conclusion of the meeting; and
- end on time.

TEAMWORK

Create a team and select a facilitator to lead a brainstorming session, a timekeeper to monitor the time, and a recorder to take notes. Select a topic about teams, such as how to recognize team performance, and brainstorm suggestions for team member recognition. Summarize your ideas in the form of a list and present the information to the class.

Many teams use parliamentary procedures to make sure that team meetings stay on track. **Parliamentary procedures** are rules for conducting a meeting, where the majority rules, but the minority is respected.

Checkpoint

1. When should a meeting not be held?
2. What are parliamentary procedures?

Communicating as a Team

As teams come together and accomplish their goals, communication plays an important role as solutions are presented for reviews and approvals. This is true both within the team and outside of the team.

When a team meets, parliamentary procedures can be used to maintain order and keep the meeting on track and on time.

Shutterstock

Written Communication

A team often creates written reports on its findings and how it has reached its goals. In order to create these reports, team members must work together to decide how to put the documents together. Successful teams know that well-written messages reflect competence and professionalism for the team as well as the individual contributors.

Leaders know that well-written messages reflect competence and professionalism. Leaders and team members are often asked to write letters, reports, presentations, and other documents that need to be thoughtfully written and correctly formatted. You will learn more about written communication in Unit 3.

Verbal Communication

Teams are often called on to make presentations on the activities and accomplishments of the team. Team members must be able to work together to create presentations and select the person who bests represents the group as a speaker. In some cases, more than one team member will make the presentation. Real teamwork is required to put the needs of the team before personal preferences and to make the best decision for the whole team.

Leaders and team members are often called on to make presentations or to talk in other situations in front of others. To be a good speaker, you must learn how to present yourself in a professional manner. You will learn more about making presentations in Chapter 12.

Nonverbal Communication

Team members must be respectful of fellow team members when working together and making presentations. Team members must be aware that the way in which a person walks, sits, and listens to others sends nonverbal communication signals. Nonverbal communication can send positive signals, such as agreement or interest. Nonverbal communication can also send the wrong signals to others, implying lack of interest or respect.

All effective members of a team, including the leader, lead by example. Sitting erect and watching the speaker show you are attentive and interested. Poor posture, lack of eye contact, and other nonverbal signals show you are not interested in the other person. Chapter 1 discusses nonverbal communication.

✔ Checkpoint

1. What do successful teams know about well-written messages?
2. What positive messages can nonverbal communication send?

Leadership in Teams

Strong leaders are important for a successful team. What does leadership mean to you? Think about an instructor who helped you and your classmates achieve academic goals. Consider a person in your student organization whose excitement and enthusiasm for the group motivates everyone to raise money for activities. Do you think of these people as leaders? A leader is not always a person in charge. **Leadership** can be defined as the ability to motivate or guide others. A title does not make a leader, but the willingness to motivate others makes a leader. A leader is one who motivates others to reach goals or work through challenges, whether that person is in front of the group or a part of a group. Leadership qualities can be found in most people at some point in their personal or professional careers.

Leadership Styles

Leadership style is the way in which a manager or team leader leads employees or team members. There are three basic leadership styles: laissez-faire, democratic (or participatory), and autocratic. In your career, you will meet managers, team leaders, and team members who demonstrate one or more of these leadership styles.

The **laissez-faire** leadership style means the leader lets someone complete a task on his or her own. Laissez-faire (pronounced lah-zay fare) is French for "let do" or "let it be." A leader who uses this leadership style gives responsibility for completing a task to the group. This type of leader expects the task to be completed with little or no direction or supervision.

The **democratic** (participatory) leader encourages team members

Every successful team needs a good leader. A team without a good leader will likely not be successful.

Shutterstock

or employees to participate in the leadership process. Team members or employees are encouraged to be a part of the decision-making process. This may include determining policy, procedure, task, and sometimes even the roles members will assume within the team.

The **autocratic** style of leadership is distinct because there is no question who is in charge and who are followers. The autocratic leader determines policy, procedures, tasks, and responsibility of each team member or employee within the company. This is also known as top-down style of management.

Characteristics of an Effective Leader

There are two schools of thought on leaders. Some people think a person is born a leader, while others think a person can be made into a leader. Neither position is incorrect. But, what really is important is the fact that leaders have specific characteristics enabling them to lead.

TEAMWORK

Using a flipchart or whiteboard, develop a chart with three columns. Label each column to reflect the three leadership styles: laissez-faire, democratic, and autocratic. Have the team decide which leadership style each team member has. Write each team member's name in the appropriate column. What did you learn from this?

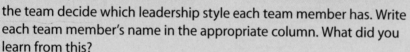

How would you describe a good leader? Think about people you have known who never express an opinion, never volunteer for a task, and never seem to take on any extra responsibilities. Would you consider these people leaders or followers? These are followers, not leaders.

Leaders are people who can motivate and direct others and who can improve a process or situation. Leaders are good communicators, are trusted by others, take risks, and lead by example. Have you ever known someone who always had a plan or solution for any situation? This person may make a good leader. There are many characteristics of good leaders. A leader:

* is self motivated;
* does not have to be asked for help, but sees a situation that can be improved and takes action;
* has integrity and tries to do the right thing for the team;
* is organized and can identify the steps needed to successfully accomplish the task at hand;
* is a motivator, someone who can move others to take action;
* can manage conflict in a team and guide others to build consensus;
* is confident, positive, and sees the glass half full;
* does not feel he or she has to do everything; and
* allows others to participate in the work required to accomplish the task at hand.

Additionally, an effective leader:

- guides or directs team members or employees through a task;
- motivates team members or employees through a task;
- creates understanding and trust between team members and the leader; and
- identifies outstanding team members and acknowledges contributions they make.

Good leaders are aware that they must work on developing their skills and constantly look for ways to improve professionally. By attending seminars, taking classes, and networking with peers, new leadership skills can be learned and developed.

Checkpoint

1. What is leadership?
2. List the three styles of leadership.
3. What are four characteristics of a good leader?

CASE

Leadership Case

Samantha Tillay started her first job working at a local restaurant. Her manager, Roland, assigned her to the line making hamburgers her first week. Roland gave her a training manual on how to properly assemble the hamburgers and gave her an hour to go over the manual. After the hour, he returned and asked her if she had any questions.

Samantha asked Roland if he would demonstrate hamburger assembly so that she would not make any mistakes. Roland told her he did not have time and all the information was in the manual. She was then introduced to Terrance, who was working on the line making hamburgers.

Terrance asked Samantha if she had questions. Samantha asked if he would show her the proper procedure for assembling a hamburger. He first told her the steps, then proceeded to show her how to assemble a hamburger according to the manual.

1. Who demonstrated leadership characteristics?

2. What leadership style was Roland demonstrating?

3. How would you have handled the situation?

4. Was Roland demonstrating effective communication skills?

Overcoming Communication Barriers in Teams

When working in teams, internal and external communication barriers may arise if the team has not clearly defined its purpose. Good leaders help the team overcome communication barriers by guiding the processes and procedures for working together.

- Identify the team's purpose, goal, and objective for the task at hand. By establishing a clear picture of what is expected, the team can create a plan of action. Be sure the plan is communicated to each team member and that each understands the plan.

A team may face many barriers to communication, such as a member who is not fully focused on the task. Be aware of possible barriers to communication and work to overcome them.

Shutterstock

- Identify each team member's responsibility for completing the task. By assigning roles and responsibilities, the end solution can be approached in an orderly way. When each team member knows his or her role, communication barriers are less likely to occur.

- Identify ways to effectively communicate with all team members while working on the project. Set boundaries for brainstorming, resolving issues, and other topics that may cause anxiety within the team.

- Identify processes that will be required as the solution for the task takes place. Determine who needs to sign approvals and what format the solution must take, such as a presentation or written summary. This reduces the chance for communication barriers to occur.

- Identify conflicts as they happen and resolve them so that progress is not delayed. Unresolved conflicts can be great barriers to communication.

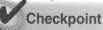

Checkpoint

1. How does a good leader help the team overcome communication barriers?
2. Why is it important to assign roles to each team member?

Chapter 4 Review

Chapter Summary

Teams

- A team is two or more people working together to reach a goal.

- Effective teams display cooperation, politeness, patience, enthusiasm, dependability, loyalty, and building of self-esteem in others.

- The two types of teams are formal and informal.

- Teams develop in steps: getting to know each other, learning to work together, working together, and success.

- Team member roles include facilitator, recorder, timekeeper, encourager, and skeptic.

Meeting as a Team

- Teams should meet only when needed, not when the topic can be handled through e-mail or other communication.

- Parliamentary procedures can be used to conduct a team meeting and keep it on track.

Communicating as a Team

- Communication plays an important role as the team presents solutions for review.

- Communication in the team may be written, verbal, or nonverbal.

Leadership in Teams

- Leadership can be defined as the ability to motivate or guide others.

- The three styles of leadership are laissez-faire, democratic, and autocratic.

- Leaders are people who can motivate and direct others and who can improve a process or situation.

Overcoming Communication Barriers in Teams

- Internal and external communication barriers may arise if the team has not clearly defined its purpose.

- Good leaders help the team overcome communication barriers by guiding the process and procedures for working together.

Review
Your Knowledge

1. Describe a team.
2. List seven characteristics of effective team members.
3. What are the two types of teams?
4. List the steps of team development.
5. What are five roles that team members may have?
6. What are parliamentary procedures?
7. Define leadership.
8. Describe the three basic leadership styles.
9. What is a leader?
10. In a team, who must be good communicators?

Apply
Your Knowledge

1. Working in the team assigned by your instructor, discuss the four stages of team development. Write a paragraph explaining each step. As you work through this activity, pay attention to how your team develops and include examples in the explanation of the stages of team development.

2. Working in the team assigned by your instructor, research parliamentary procedure. Write a report describing different types of parliamentary procedure. Include a recommendation on how to implement parliamentary procedure for a student organization.

3. Working in the team assigned by your instructor, make a list of five people the team considers a leader. These leaders do not need to be famous or public figures. Beside each name, list at least three characteristics the team feels make the person a leader. The team will also make an oral presentation to the class.

4. You are the president of student government. A local charity has asked if your team will participate in a walk to raise money for the organization.

   A. As president, define your style of leadership. Is it laissez-faire, democratic, or autocratic?

   B. Using that style, write a message to your team asking them to participate.

5. You are the team leader for a project in science class. The task is to find the unknown chemical. Because the team has been arguing about every point, nothing has been accomplished. Write a short report describing how you would overcome this barrier to communication. First, select a leadership style, then describe how you would lead the team through this crisis.

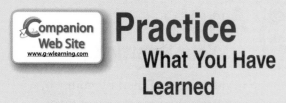

Practice
What You Have Learned

Access the *Fundamentals of Business Communication* Student Companion Web Site at www.g-wlearning.com/Communication. Download each data file for this chapter. Follow the instructions to complete a reading, writing, and grammar activity to practice what you have learned in this chapter.

Connections
Across the Curriculum

Social Studies. Research the history of parliamentary procedures. Where did these rules of order originate? Investigate other aspects of this topic.

Language Arts. Using your findings from your research on parliamentary procedures, write several paragraphs about the history of parliamentary procedures.

Build
Your Business Portfolio

As you are collecting items for your portfolio, you will need a method to keep the components in a clean, safe way for assembly at the end of this class. A large manila envelope works well to keep your documents, photos, awards, etc., in a safe place. Three-ring binders with sleeves are another good way to store your information. If you have a box large enough for full-size documents, that will work also.

1. Select a place to store items you will be collecting to assemble your portfolio.

2. Decide where the portfolio materials will be stored. Will your collection be in an envelope in your classroom, locker, or home?

Careers
Arts, A/V
Technology, and Communication
Careers and Communication

If you have creative talents along with strong communication, math, and science skills, this may be the career pathway for you. This diverse pathway includes visual and performing arts, audio-video (A/V) technology, and film.

Journalism, broadcasting, telecommunication, and printing technology are other careers in this cluster.

There are many important communication skills that are needed by people who enter a career involving creative energy. A strong outgoing personality, good communication skills, and the ability to be a team player are key qualities for these workers. Give examples of situations in which people in this career cluster would apply team-building skills.

Event Prep

Career Portfolio

Presentation of a career portfolio may be a competitive event for your student organization. A well-developed portfolio demonstrates your understanding of the job-application process and showcases your talents. You may be required to submit a print portfolio or an ePortfolio. In this book, you will create a business portfolio and understand the characteristics and process necessary to create a well-received portfolio. To prepare your career portfolio, do the following.

1. Read the guidelines provided by your organization.

2. Review the Build Your Business Portfolio activities at the end of each chapter in this book to make sure you have covered all elements of a completed portfolio.

3. Go through each step and create your portfolio as you progress through this book. This will be an on-going process.

4. When you are finished at the end of the term or in preparation for the competitive event, solicit feedback from peers and teachers.

5. Make certain that the portfolio is complete and free of errors.

Unit 2

Grammar Basics for Successful Communication

In This Unit

Communication is based on language. This is true for letters, e-mail, reports, verbal conversations, and any other type of communication. To be an effective and professional communicator, you must understand the rules of the English language. If you use language that is not correct English, your message may be misunderstood. Even worse, you may be viewed as lacking professionalism. It is very important to learn proper English.

Unit 2 presents English grammar rules. You will learn the different parts of speech and how to correctly form sentences. Completing this unit will help you meet college and career readiness (CCR) anchor standards for language, as outlined by the **Common Core State Standards**.

Chapter 5: Grammar and Writing
Sentence Parts
Nouns and Pronouns
Verbs
Adjectives and Adverbs
Conjunctions, Prepositions, and Interjections

Chapter 6: Improving Grammar Mechanics
Punctuation
Capitalization
Number Expression
Parallel Structure
Misused Words and Terms

5
Improving Grammar Skills

I never made a mistake in grammar but one in my life and as soon as I done it I seen it.
—*Carl Sandburg,*
American poet and author

Grammar is a set of rules for using language properly. Carl Sandburg, the famous American poet and writer, pokes fun at grammar mistakes in the quote above. While grammar mistakes can sometimes be amusing, they have no place in business communication. When speaking or writing, using correct grammar helps you send a clear message that can be easily understood by the receiver.

Objectives

When you complete Chapter 5, you will be able to:

- **Identify** the parts of a sentence.
- **Use** nouns and pronouns correctly.
- **Use** verbs correctly.
- **Use** adjectives and adverbs correctly.
- **Identify** conjunctions, prepositions, and interjections.

Terms

sentence	noun
subject	pronoun
predicate	verb
direct object	adjective
indirect object	adverb
subject complement	conjunction
phrase	preposition
clause	interjection

Go Green

Recycling is important so that landfills do not become overloaded. Paper and cans are often recycled, but communication tools should also be recycled. Cell phones, printers, monitors, computers, and other office equipment are considered electronic waste. Electronic waste should be properly disposed of, not just placed in the trash, due to components that may be toxic, such as the materials in a battery. Electronic equipment can be donated to charities to refurbish. However, if the equipment is beyond repair, locate a reputable electronic manufacturer, reseller, or community service center that will make sure the equipment is properly recycled.

1. Survey your community and contact organizations that participate in electronic recycling. Talk to someone at the location and get information as to where they send the equipment for recycling.
2. Where can you properly dispose of a cell phone?
3. What organizations in your area will take electronic equipment as a donation?

Sentence Parts

Words in the English language are classified as one of eight different parts of speech. The rules of English grammar relate to how these parts of speech are used to form the sentences with which people communicate. The brief definitions of the parts of speech in Figure 5-1 will help you understand the following discussion of sentence parts. You will learn more about each part of speech later in this chapter.

A **sentence** is a group of words that expresses a complete thought. Consider the two examples shown below. Are these sentences?

Under the desk.

The book is under the desk.

The first example does not give a complete thought. More information is needed to understand how *under the desk* relates to an action, person, or thing. The second example is a sentence because it provides enough information for a complete thought.

Subjects and Predicates

A sentence has two main parts, a subject and a predicate. The **subject** is the person speaking or the person, place, or thing the sentence describes. The **predicate** describes an action or state of being for the subject.

Reading Prep

Before reading this chapter, review the objectives. Based on this information, write down two or three items that you think are important to note while you are reading.

Figure 5-1.	These are the eight parts of speech.	
Part	**Definition**	**Examples**
Noun	A word naming a person, place, or thing.	girl school book
Pronoun	A word taking the place of a noun.	she it they
Verb	A word showing action or state of being.	run sing is
Adjective	A word describing a noun or pronoun.	tall young round
Adverb	A word describing a verb, adjective, or another adverb.	quickly very nearby
Conjunction	A word connecting words, phrases, or sentences.	and but or
Preposition	A word relating nouns or pronouns to other words in a sentence.	under to for
Interjection	A word expressing strong emotion.	wow oh hey

Subjects

Nouns and pronouns are discussed in detail later in this chapter. Both nouns and pronouns can serve as the subject of a sentence. Consider this sentence.

❏   Kim will sing.

What person, place, or thing does the sentence describe? The sentence gives information about Kim, who is the subject of the sentence. In the examples below, the subjects are shown in italics.

Elena writes beautiful poems.

They left the party before midnight.

The *school* has nine classrooms.

The *dog* has a white house in the backyard.

When a sentence discusses more than one noun or pronoun, it has a compound subject. In the examples below, the compound subjects are shown in italics.

Mario and *Chin* play video games after school.

The *cars* and *trucks* were parked behind the building.

In some sentences the subject is not stated, but it is understood. This form is often used when speaking directly to a person. In the examples below, *you* is the understood subject of each sentence.

The black and brown dog is running. What is the simple subject and the complete subject of this sentence?

Shutterstock

> Run home and tell your mother about the accident.
>
> Read all of the instructions before answering the questions on the test.

Each subject in the earlier examples is called a simple subject. A **simple subject** is just the nouns or pronouns about which the sentence gives information. The simple subject and other words that describe it make the **complete subject.** In the examples below, the complete subjects are shown in italics.

> *The fresh, hot bread* has a wonderful smell.
>
> *The payment for admission* includes snacks.

Predicates

The **simple predicate** of a sentence includes only the verbs that show action or state of being. In the examples below, the simple predicates are shown in italics.

> My brother *cleaned* his room.
>
> Julia and I *will attend* a concert at the park.
>
> Ms. Chung *is* the principal.

A **compound predicate** contains two or more verbs joined by *and* or some other conjunction. Both verbs describe action or state of being for the subject. In the examples below, the compound predicates are shown in italics.

> Mr. Romero *rose* to his feet *and addressed* the audience.
>
> The shipping clerk *wrapped* the package *and mailed* it.

The **complete predicate** of a sentence includes the verb and other information that tells what the subject is or does. In the examples below, the complete predicates are shown in italics.

> Ms. Chung *is the principal.*
>
> My brother *cleaned his room.*
>
> Julia and I *attended a concert at the park.*

Objects and Complements

Sentence predicates often contain objects. A **direct object** is someone or something that receives the action of the verb. In the first example below,

Mr. Rosenbaum is the person who performs the action. *Read*s is the action performed (the verb). *Story* is the direct object—the thing that receives the action of the verb. In the following examples, the objects are shown in italics.

> Mr. Rosenbaum reads a *story* to his class every Monday.
>
> The little boy threw the *ball*.
>
> The cows ate the *hay*.

A predicate that contains a direct object can also contain an indirect object. An **indirect object** names something or someone for whom the action of the verb is performed. It often comes before the direct object in the sentence. In the first example below, *gave* is the action (the verb). *Present* is the direct object. *Me* is the indirect object. In the following examples, the indirect objects are shown in italics.

> Grandmother gave *me* a birthday present.
>
> The teacher gave the *students* instructions for the test.
>
> The boy gave the *dog* a biscuit.

A predicate with a verb that shows a state of being may contain a subject complement. A **subject complement** is an adjective that describes the subject or a noun that renames or tells what the subject is. In the first example below, *beautiful* (an adjective) is a subject complement that describes *dress* (the subject of the sentence). In the second example, *captain* is a subject complement that renames *Jamal*.

> Your new dress is *beautiful*.
>
> Jamal is *captain* of the team.

Phrases and Clauses

Sentences can be very short, such as *He is*. Longer sentences can contain phrases and clauses that add more information to the sentences. Correctly structuring phrases and clauses will convey the meaning you intend listeners and readers to receive.

Phrases

A **phrase** is a group of words that act together to convey meaning in a sentence. Both complete subjects and complete predicates can contain phrases. Phrases can be short or long; however, a phrase does not contain both a subject and a predicate. Some examples of phrases are shown in Figure 5-2.

Figure 5-2. The words in a phrase act together to convey meaning.

Type of Phrase	Examples
Noun	*Watching movies* is my favorite hobby.
Verb	The sale *has been running* all week.
Adjective	The rookie is a *quick, strong* player.
Adverb	He climbed the ladder *very quickly*.
Preposition	She made uniforms *for the team*.

Clauses

A **clause** is a group of words within a sentence that has a subject and a predicate. When a clause gives a complete thought and could stand alone as a separate sentence, it is called an **independent clause.** In the following examples, the independent clauses are shown in italics. Note that the third example has two independent clauses.

> *Jane will head the team* because she has the most experience.
>
> Since we arrived late, *we missed the opening speech.*
>
> *I read a novel*, and *she watched a movie.*

The woman who is wearing the yellow scarf will give the presentation. Are there any restrictive clauses in this sentence?

Shutterstock

A clause that requires the rest of the sentence to provide a complete thought is called a **dependent clause.** A dependent clause used alone is a writing error and is often called a **sentence fragment.** Subordinating clauses, restrictive clauses, and nonrestrictive clauses are types of dependent clauses.

A **subordinating clause** is joined to the rest of the sentence with a subordinating conjunction, such as *since, because, when, if,* or *though.* In the following examples, the subordinating clauses are shown in italics.

> I cannot attend the meeting, *though I am interested in the topic.*
>
> *When we land*, everyone will leave the plane.
>
> *Because the rain was very heavy*, a flash flood warning was issued.

A **restrictive clause** is a type of dependent clause that is essential to the meaning of the sentence. The clause identifies a particular person or thing. In the following examples, the restrictive clauses are shown in italics. In the first example, the clause identifies one particular boy on the team. In the second example, the clause identifies a particular group of students. In the third example, the clause identifies a particular vase.

> The little boy on the team *who has a broken arm* will not play.
>
> Students *who do not follow the rules* will be banned from participation.
>
> The vase *that you dropped* was very valuable.

A **nonrestrictive clause** provides information that is not essential to the meaning of the sentence. The clause provides information that may be helpful. However, the receiver can understand the message without that information. In the following examples, the nonrestrictive clauses are shown in italics.

> Mark West, *who loves to swim*, is the only boy on the team.
>
> The bicycle, *which is dirty and rusty*, is an antique.

Sentence Structure

Sentences are structured as simple sentences, compound sentences, or complex sentences. A **simple sentence** has one independent clause and no dependent clauses. It often contains one or more phrases. Examples of simple sentences are shown below. The subject or predicate of a simple sentence can be compound. The first example has a compound subject. The second example has a compound predicate.

> Paula and Jan ate lunch in the cafeteria.
>
> Alberto will ride his bike this afternoon and swim tomorrow.
>
> The cart rolled down the narrow, winding road.
>
> Julie is an administrative assistant.

A **compound sentence** has two independent clauses joined by a conjunction, such as *and* or *but*. Examples of compound sentences are shown below.

> Paula ate lunch in the cafeteria, and Kim ate lunch in the park.
>
> Aman invited me to study with him, but I had other plans.
>
> A heavy rain fell, and the game was delayed.

Complex sentences have an independent clause and one or more dependent clauses. Examples of complex sentences are shown below. The first example has one independent clause (shown in italics) and one dependent clause. The second example has one independent clause (shown in italics) and two dependent clauses.

> When you write a business letter, *you should use clear and concise language.*
>
> *Mrs. Parsons,* who lives on Maple Street, *complained about the noise,* which was keeping her awake at night.

A sentence that has two independent clauses and one or more dependent clauses is called a **compound-complex sentence** (or a complex-compound sentence). Examples of compound-complex sentences are shown below.

> Mrs. Parsons complained about the noise, which was keeping her awake at night, but the police officer did not file a report.
>
> Whenever she dines at a restaurant, she orders a salad and this helps her stay healthy.

When writing business documents, varying the type and length of the sentences you use can make the message more interesting. Your goal is to make the message flow smoothly from one thought to the next and be easy to understand. Using too many short sentences can make the message seem choppy with disconnected thoughts. Using too many long, complex sentences can make the message difficult to understand.

Reading level is a measure of the difficulty of a written message. You can use the spelling- and grammar-checking features of popular word-processing programs to see the readability statistics of a passage, as shown in Figure 5-3. In this example, one paragraph contains four sentences. The reading level is grade 8.5 based on the Flesch-Kincaid model.

Figure 5-3. You can use a built-in feature of Microsoft Word to show readability statistics for a selected passage or the entire document.

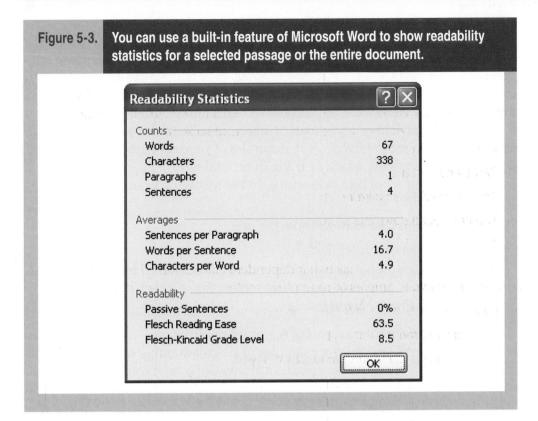

Checkpoint

1. What is a sentence?
2. What are the two main parts of a sentence?
3. What are the five types of clauses?
4. List the four types of sentences.

Nouns and Pronouns

As you learned earlier, nouns and pronouns are used as the simple subject in sentences. They can also serve as a direct object, an indirect object, and the object in a prepositional phrase. Pronouns should properly relate to the nouns they replace.

BUSINESS ETHICS

Plagiarism

Plagiarism is a form of theft where you copy somebody else's material without permission. Under copyright law, as soon as something is in tangible form, it is automatically copyrighted. A copyright protects the creator from others using the material without permission. Just about everything you see in print, all the music you listen to, any images you see on television or movie screens, and almost all information on the Internet is copyrighted. This means if you copy any of this material without the permission of the copyright holder, you have committed theft.

Nouns

A **noun** is a word that names a person, place, or thing. Nouns help you point out your best friend, tell someone about your hometown, or ask your brother to pass the potatoes. Without nouns, communicating would be very difficult. *Maria, Chesterfield Park,* and *potatoes* are examples of nouns.

A **proper noun** names a particular person, place, or thing. *Mr. Thomas, Atlanta,* and *Empire State Building* are examples of proper nouns. A **common noun** describes a person, place, or thing in general terms. *Teacher, city,* and *building* are examples of common nouns. In the following examples, the nouns are shown in italics.

The *boy* and his *bike* were wet from the *rain.*

Central Park has a soccer *field.*

Carrots are my favorite *vegetable.*

Singular and Plural Nouns

Nouns can be singular or plural. A singular noun names one person, place, or thing. *Girl, carrot,* and *bus* are examples of singular nouns. A plural noun indicates more than one person, place, or thing. *Girls, carrots,* and *buses* are examples of plural nouns. The plural form of a noun is created in one of several ways, as shown in Figure 5-4.

Figure 5-4. These guidelines outline how to make singular nouns plural.

Guidelines	Singular	Plural
For most nouns, add *s* to the singular form to create the plural form.	cat	cats
	rock	rocks
	football	footballs
For nouns that end in *sh, ch, s, x, z,* or similar sounds, add *es* to the singular form.	bush	bushes
	box	boxes
	class	classes
	blitz	blitzes
For nouns that end in a consonant and a *y,* change the *y* to *i* and add *es.*	city	cities
	baby	babies
For nouns that end in *o* preceded by a vowel, add *s* to the singular form. For most nouns that end in *o* preceded by a consonant, add *s* to form the plural. For some exceptions, add *es.*	stereo	stereos
	radio	radios
	memo	memos
	piano	pianos
	potato	potatoes
For many nouns that end in *f* or *fe,* change the *f* sound to a *v* and add *s* or *es* to the singular form. For others, keep the *f* and add an *s.*	life	lives
	knife	knives
	roof	roofs

Irregular nouns are those that do not follow the guidelines described in Figure 5-4 for making plurals. Rather than adding *s* or *es* to the singular form, the plural form often has a different spelling from the singular form. In other cases, the singular and plural forms are spelled the same. Examples of irregular nouns are shown below.

Singular	Plural
child	children
man	men
woman	women
goose	geese
person	people
deer	deer
barracks	barracks

A **collective noun** refers to a group or unit that contains more than one person, place, or thing. *Army, class, committee,* and *team* are examples of collective nouns. Although a collective noun refers to a group of people or things, these nouns can also be plural or singular. In the following examples, the collective nouns are shown in italics.

> The British *army* crossed the river; the French and Italian *armies* went by another route.
>
> The Mendoza *family* left the park, but the Chung and Olson *families* remained.
>
> During our safari, we saw one *herd* of elephants and two *herds* of zebras.

Because the way to form the plural of nouns varies, you probably will not remember the proper form for every word you want to use. When you are unsure about the plural form of a noun, check a dictionary. Dictionaries typically do not show the plural form of nouns that are formed simply by adding *s* or *es* to the singular form. However, the plural form is typically shown when the noun is irregular (tooth and teeth), ends in *o*, or ends in a consonant and a *y*. Figure 5-5 shows a sample dictionary entry that indicates the plural form of a noun. Some online dictionaries provide an icon you can click to hear the word pronounced.

Possessive Nouns

Possessive nouns indicate ownership by the noun or an attribute of the noun. For most singular nouns, the possessive form is created by adding an apostrophe and an *s* to the noun. In the first example below, *girl's* is a possessive noun indicating ownership of books by one girl. In the second example, *manager's* is a possessive noun indicating the attribute friendliness. The possessive noun can come before or after the item owned. In the third example, *Gloria's* is a possessive noun indicating ownership of a bracelet. The apostrophe and *s* are added to the final word in compounds words, as shown in the last example.

Figure 5-5. This is an example of an online dictionary entry. Notice the icon that can be clicked to hear the pronunciation of the word.

city ('si-tē)
n. pl cities
1. A population center larger than a town.
2. A municipality incorporated in the United States.
3. The inhabitants of a city as a group.

> The *girl's* books were placed in her locker.
>
> My new *manager's* friendliness was reassuring.
>
> The lost bracelet was *Gloria's*.
>
> My *sister-in-law's* garden contained many types of flowers.

For most plural nouns, an apostrophe is added to form the possessive noun. In the first example below, *girls'* is a plural possessive noun indicating the ownership of jackets by two or more girls. When a noun has an irregular plural that does not end in *s*, an apostrophe and an *s* are added to form the possessive, as in the second and third examples.

> The *girls'* jackets were neatly stacked on the bleachers.
>
> The *women's* dinner was held in James Hall.
>
> The *children's* games taught them math skills.

In some cases, adding an *s* to a word that already ends in *s* or an *s* sound results in an awkward pronunciation for the word. In those cases, the possessive is still formed using an apostrophe and an *s*. However, the extra *s* or *es* sound is not pronounced. Such words are often proper names. Examples are shown below.

Mrs. Phillips's home is located by the river.

The *Foxes's* relatives are coming to dinner.

The *Ganges's* banks were lined with trees.

Pronouns

Pronouns are words that replace nouns in a sentence. Pronouns allow messages to flow smoothly without repeating nouns or noun phrases over and over. For example, you could begin a paragraph with a sentence that refers to Mr. Joseph Patel and then use the pronoun *he* to refer to Mr. Patel in later sentences. Pronouns should properly relate to the words they replace. When pronouns are not used correctly, the meaning of the sentence will be unclear.

Pronouns and Antecedents

Pronouns can refer to people or things. The word a pronoun replaces is called its **antecedent.** Most pronouns have antecedents, but some typically do not. The pronoun *I*, which refers to the speaker, and the pronoun *you*, which refers to a person being addressed, usually do not have antecedents. In the following examples, the pronouns are shown in italics. In the second example, *girls* is the antecedent of *they*. In the third example, *ball* is the antecedent of *it*.

I am sure that *you* will win.

The girls lost the game, and *they* were very upset.

Shelia hit the ball before *it* touched the ground.

Personal Pronouns

Personal pronouns refer to specific persons or things. To correctly use pronouns, you need to consider their properties: number, gender, person, and case. The number of a pronoun indicates whether it is singular (referring to one person or thing) or plural (referring to more than one person or thing). Gender indicates whether the pronoun refers to a male, a female, or an object without gender. Always use pronouns that agree with their antecedents in number and gender. Examples are shown in Figure 5-6.

Personal pronouns can be in one of three persons. A pronoun in **first person** refers to someone who is speaking or writing. A pronoun in **second person** refers to someone who is being addressed. A pronoun in **third person** refers to someone being discussed. Examples of pronouns in first, second, and third person are shown below.

First person
I am happy to be home.
Give the information to *us*.

Figure 5-6.	Pronouns indicate number and gender.			
Pronouns	**Number**	**Gender**	**Example**	
she, her	Singular	Feminine	Monica left *her* coat by the door.	
he, him	Singular	Masculine	James arrived late and *he* missed the kickoff.	
it	Singular	Neutral	The ball was hit hard and *it* went out of the park.	
they, we	Plural	Neutral	The children played hard and *they* grew tired.	

Second person

Alicia, will *you* return on Monday or Tuesday?

Chet, *your* project is finished.

Third person

Pablo was tired, so *he* went home.

The children ate lunch and then *they* played in the park.

The case of a pronoun indicates the way it is used in a sentence. **Nominative case** pronouns are used as the subject in a sentence or as subject complements. **Objective case** pronouns are used as direct objects, indirect objects, or objects of prepositions. **Possessive case** pronouns show ownership. Examples are shown in Figure 5-7. Note that some pronouns, such as *you* and *it*, can be either nominative or objective, depending on how they are used in a sentence.

Figure 5-7.	Pronouns can be nominative, objective, or possessive case.	
Case	**Pronouns**	**Example**
Nominative	I, you, he, she, it, we, they, who	*I* am happy to be home.
		You should be careful.
		Who made this cake?
Objective	me, you, him, her, it, us, them, whom	*Whom* does Charles trust?
		Give *me* a ream of paper.
		Pass the bucket to *him*.
Possessive	my, mine, your, yours, his, her, hers, it, its, our, ours, their, theirs, whose	*My* notes were unclear.
		Bring *your* homework to school.
		Whose phone is ringing?

Other Pronouns

Other types of pronouns include interrogative pronouns, relative pronouns, demonstrative pronouns, indefinite pronouns, and adjective pronouns. These pronouns do not indicate gender, but they can indicate number. Some pronouns fall into more than one category, depending on their use in the sentence.

Interrogative pronouns, which are used to ask a question, include *what, which, who, whom,* and *whose.* Typically, these pronouns do not have a known antecedent. The pronoun represents something or someone not known. The suffix *ever* is sometimes used with interrogative pronouns to form words such as *whoever* or *whatever.* In the example below, *who* is used as an interrogative pronoun.

❑ *Who* answered the telephone?

Relative pronouns are used to begin dependent clauses in complex sentences. Relative pronouns include *who, whom, whose, which, what,* and *that.* The pronouns *who, whom,* and *whose* are used to refer to a person. *Which, what,* and *that* are used to refer to an animal or object. In the example below, *who* is used as a relative pronoun.

❑ The woman *who* came to the door asked for directions.

Demonstrative pronouns identify or direct attention to a noun or pronoun. *This, that, these,* and *those* are demonstrative pronouns. *This* and *that* refer to singular nouns or pronouns. *These* and *those* refer to plural nouns or pronouns. *This* and *these* are generally used to refer to something nearby. *That* and *those* are generally used to refer to something at a distance.

Nearby
This was damaged during shipment.

At a distance
Those will be shipped from another city.

Indefinite pronouns generally refer to an object or person that has been identified earlier or does not need specific identification. Examples of indefinite pronouns include *some, none, one, every, neither, other, both, each, any, such,* and *another.* Compound examples include *everyone, somebody, anyone, anything,* and *someone.* In the example below, *some* is used as an indefinite pronoun.

❑ *Some* will be thrown in the trash.

Some pronouns can also be used as adjectives or in adjective clauses. Examples include *some, none, all,* and *who.* In the example below, *some* is used as an **adjective pronoun.**

❑ Would you like *some* candy?

✓ Checkpoint

1. What is a noun?
2. What is a pronoun?
3. What is an antecedent?

Verbs

A **verb** is a word that shows action or state of being. Using verbs, you can recount the action in a basketball game, tell how much you dread a test, or explain that a blueberry pie tastes delicious. Verbs may be the most important of the parts of speech. Only a verb can express a complete thought by itself, having *you* as the understood subject.

Types of Verbs

A verb can be one of two basic types: those that show action or those that show a state of being. Examples of action verbs include *read, sing, run, count, laugh, go,* and *eat.* Examples of verbs that show a state of being are *be, is, are, was, were,* and *am.* In the examples below, the verbs are shown in italics.

> I *count* the money when the store closes.
>
> Sue, *eat* your vegetables.
>
> I *am* hungry.
>
> *Go*! (*you* is the understood subject)

Linking Verbs

Verbs that show a state of being are also called **linking verbs** when they relate a subject to a subject complement. In the first example below, the verb *is* links the subject (Ralph) to the subject complement (a tall boy).

> Ralph *is* a tall boy.
>
> Kendra *was* the president of the club.

Helping Verbs

Verbs that work with a main verb to show action are called **helping verbs** (or auxiliary verbs). These verbs express little meaning on their own. However, they help make the meaning of the main verb clear. Examples of helping verbs include *be, been, am, is, are, was, were, has, had, have, do, does, did, can, could, may, might, will, would, should, shall,* and *must.* In the examples below, the helping verbs are shown in italics.

> He *is* calling your name.
>
> Movies *are* shown in a dark room.
>
> She *has* walked around the track.
>
> I *should* press the fabric after sewing each seam.

TEAMWORK

Work with three classmates to complete this activity. You and one classmate will work as a team. Your other two classmates will work as a team. Each team should do the following.

- Write a paragraph that contains six or more sentences.
- Include at least one simple sentence, one compound sentence, and one complex sentence in the paragraph.
- Include at least three pronouns, with one of them being used incorrectly.
- Exchange paragraphs with the other team.
- For each sentence in the paragraph, tell the structure of the sentence: simple, compound, complex, or compound complex.
- For each sentence, indicate the simple subject and the simple predicate. If the sentence includes a direct object, indirect object, or subject complement, also indicate that.
- Identify the error in pronoun usage and tell how the error could be corrected.
- Discuss your answers with the other team.

Compound Verbs

A **compound verb** consists of two or more verbs in the same sentence. The verbs can be main verbs and helping verbs, as shown in the first example below. A compound verb can include two or more main verbs and no helping verbs, as shown in the second example.

> Jim *will climb* to the top of the hill.
>
> Pedro *ran* to the fence and *jumped* over the gate.

Properties of Verbs

Verbs can have one or more of five different properties: voice, mood, tense, person, and number. Understanding the properties of verbs can help you create messages that are free of verb errors.

Voice

An action verb can be in either active voice or passive voice. In **active voice,** the subject of the sentence performs the action. In the first example below, the subject (Alfred) performs the action (rowing). In **passive voice,** the subject of the sentence is acted upon, as in the second example.

> Alfred *rowed* the boat.
>
> The boat *was rowed* by Alfred.

Sentences written in active voice are considered to be more direct and easier to understand than those written in passive voice. Sentences in passive voice can seem wordy or awkward. However, using passive voice is appropriate in some cases. When you do not know who performed the action, use passive voice, as in the example below. Passive voice is often used in writing scientific papers to make actions or conclusions sound more objective.

> The car *was stolen.*

Mood

The mood of a verb relates to the way in which the speaker or writer wants the sentence to be understood.

The girl is running the race. What is the verb in this sentence and what type of verb is it?

Shutterstock

The **indicative mood** is most commonly used. It expresses a straightforward statement of fact or opinion or asks a question. The **imperative mood** states a command or a direct request. The **subjunctive mood** expresses an idea, suggestion, or hypothetical situation. Examples of sentences in each mood are shown below.

Indicative
The snowstorm raged for two days.
When will the new printer be delivered?

Imperative
Leave the building.
Please pass your papers to the front.

Subjunctive
I recommend that you hire three assistants.
If I were you, I would read this book.

Tense

The tense of a verb indicates when the action or state of being takes place. The **present tense** of a verb indicates that the action or state of being takes place now. The **past tense** indicates that the action or state of being has already occurred. For many verbs, the past tense is formed by adding *ed* to the present tense. Examples include *walk/walked, hunt/hunted*, and *look/looked*. For irregular verbs, the spelling of the past tense varies. Examples include *run/ran, drink/drank*, and *pay/paid*. The **future tense** indicates that the action or state of being will occur at a later time. The future tense is formed by adding *will* before the present tense of the verb. Examples of verb tense are shown below.

Present tense
The horse runs around the paddock.

Past tense
The horse ran around the paddock.

Future tense
The horse will run around the paddock.

Verb tenses can be further divided into simple and perfect tenses. The simple tenses are the present, past, and future tenses discussed above. The perfect tenses are used to express that something happens over or during a certain time. The **present perfect tense** is formed by adding *have* or *has* to the past tense. The **past perfect tense** is formed by adding *had* to the past tense. The **future perfect tense** is formed by adding *will have* to the past tense. Examples of the perfect tenses are shown below.

Present perfect tense
The horse has run around the paddock. (just now)

Past perfect tense
The horse had run around the paddock. (last week, perhaps)

Future perfect tense
The horse will have run around the paddock. (next week, perhaps)

Person

Verbs can be in one of three persons. A verb in **first person** refers to an action of someone who is speaking or writing. A verb in **second person** refers to an action of someone who is being addressed (you). A verb in **third person** refers to an action of someone being discussed. Examples are shown below.

First person
I am getting ready to go.

Second person
You are not alone.

Third person
They are waiting.

Number

A verb should agree in number with related nouns or pronouns. Verbs that relate to *I* should always be singular. Verbs that relate to *you* should always be plural, even when one person is being addressed. Verbs that relate to nouns or pronouns used in the third person (someone spoken about) should agree in number with the nouns or pronouns.

First person, singular verb
I am thirsty.

Second person, plural verb
You are late for the meeting.

Third person, singular verb
The girl runs every day.

Third person, plural verb
The girls and boys run every day.

When a sentence has two or more simple subjects connected by *and*, the verb should be plural. When a sentence has two or more singular subjects connected by *or* or *nor*, the verb should be singular.

Third person, plural verb
Tom, Roger, and Aydin *sing* every day.

Third person, singular verb
Tom or Roger *sings* tenor.

Verb Forms

Understanding verb forms, such as participles, gerunds, and infinitives, can help you write clear and creative messages. These verb forms are also called verbals.

Participles

A **present participle** is a verb form that indicates action is in progress or ongoing. It can also be used as an adjective. To create a present participle, add *ing* to the present tense. Examples include *eating, drawing,* and *working.* A **past participle** indicates that action has been completed. A past participle is the same as the past-tense form discussed earlier.

Present participle
Angie is *drawing* a picture. The *running* water makes a soothing sound.

Past participle
Angie *drew* a picture last week.

A **dangling participle** is a writing error in which a participle phrase modifies nothing or the wrong person or object. In the incorrect example below, the phrase implies that the birds were paddling down the stream. This is not likely the writer's intent.

Incorrect
Paddling down the stream, the birds were startled.

Correct
As we were paddling down the stream, the birds were startled.

The members of the family is having a picnic. Does the number of the verb in this sentence agree with the subject?

Shutterstock

Gerunds

A **gerund** is a verb form used as a noun. Gerunds are formed by adding *ing* to the present tense of a verb. Examples of gerunds include *eating, shopping, talking, playing,* and *counting.* Gerunds can serve as the subject of a sentence, a subject complement, or the object of a verb or preposition. Examples are shown below.

Shopping is my favorite hobby.

My favorite exercise is *jogging.*

She does not appreciate my *snoring.*

He was arrested for *speeding.*

Infinitives

An **infinitive** is the word *to* and a verb in its simple present form. Examples include *to eat, to read, to see, to touch,* and *to find.* An infinitive or infinitive phrase can serve as a noun, adjective, or adverb. The examples below show infinitive phrases and their uses in the sentences.

To cry over spilled milk seemed a waste of time. (noun, subject)

Her dream is *to win.* (noun, subject complement)

She intended *to buy a new car.* (noun, direct object)

He found a way *to earn more money*. (adjective)

He yelled *to get her attention*. (adverb)

A **split infinitive** occurs when an adverb is placed between the word *to* and the verb. Examples of split infinitives include *to barely see*, *to slowly read*, and *to quickly jump*. A split infinitive can be useful for emphasizing the adverb. The phrase *to boldly go* may sound more forceful or dramatic than *to go boldly*. This is largely a matter of the writer's opinion. In the past, some grammar rules deemed a split infinitive to be a writing error. However, this structure is now widely accepted as correct.

Checkpoint

1. What are the two basic types of verbs?
2. What are the five properties of verbs?
3. What are the three verb forms?

The old, red mill stands next to the river. Does this sentence contain any adjectives?

Shutterstock

Adjectives and Adverbs

Adjectives and adverbs make messages more informative, descriptive, and creative. These words allow you to discuss features or traits of a person or thing or the manner in which something is done. You can tell a friend about a beautiful sunset or describe the action in a football game thanks to adjectives and adverbs.

Adjectives

An **adjective** is a word that describes a noun or pronoun. Adjectives may provide details about the noun or pronoun that give you a better understanding of the person or thing. In the first example below, *brilliant* and *bold* are adjectives that expand the meaning of *colors*. Adjectives can also define limits. In the second example below, *two* is an adjective that limits the meaning of *students*, the word it modifies or describes. Some adjectives are made from proper names and always begin with a capital letter, as shown in the third example.

Brilliant, bold colors were used in the painting.

Two students passed the exam.

African lions live in family groups called prides.

Adjectives often come before the words they modify, as shown in the previous examples. In some cases, adjectives follow the nouns or pronouns they modify, as shown in the first example below. Adjectives that are subject complements follow a linking verb and rename or describe the subject. The second example contains an adjective used as a subject complement.

> This will not lead to anything *good*.
>
> Wilma is *tired*.

Two or more related adjectives that appear before a noun or pronoun and equally modify it are called **coordinate adjectives.** These adjectives should be separated by the word *and* or by commas. However, not all adjectives that appear in a sequence are coordinate adjectives. In the first example below, *old* and *rusty* are coordinate adjectives describing the shovel. In the second example, *new* and *soccer* describe a ball, but are not coordinate adjectives.

> The *old, rusty* shovel had a broken handle.
>
> The *new soccer* ball has a blue cover.

When the order of the adjectives before a noun can be arranged without changing the meaning of the sentence, the adjectives are typically coordinate adjectives. For example, you might say the *old, rusty shovel* or the *rusty, old shovel*. You would not, however, say *soccer new ball* instead of *new soccer ball*.

Forms of Adjectives

Most adjectives have three forms: positive, comparative, and superlative. **Positive adjectives** describe, but do not compare, people or things. **Comparative adjectives** compare two people or things. **Superlative adjectives** compare three or more people or things. Examples of adjectives are shown in Figure 5-8.

> **Positive**
> The *small* book was on top of the stack.
>
> **Comparative**
> The red book was *smaller* than the blue book.
>
> **Superlative**
> The red book was the *smallest* of the books.

Articles

The adjectives *the, a,* and *an* are called articles. An **article** is an adjective that limits the noun or pronoun it modifies. Articles come before a noun, pronoun, or noun phrase and can be definite or indefinite. The **definite article** *the* refers to a specific person or thing. The **indefinite articles** *a* and *an* typically refer to a person or thing in a general way. Use *a* before words that begin with

Figure 5-8. Adjectives can be positive, comparative, or superlative forms.

Positive	Comparative	Superlative
large	larger	largest
happy	happier	happiest
low	lower	lowest
beautiful	more beautiful	most beautiful
eager	more eager	most eager
good	better	best
less	lesser	least

a consonant sound and *an* before words that begin with a vowel sound. Articles need not be repeated before each noun in a series of nouns. In the following examples, the articles are shown in italics.

> *The* cat chased *the* mouse.
>
> *A* cat will sometimes come when called.
>
> *The* counselor has *an* open, caring attitude.
>
> *The* letter, envelope, and stamp were placed on *the* desk.

Demonstrative Adjectives

This, that, these, and *those* are demonstrative adjectives. A **demonstrative adjective** is used before a noun to indicate number and location. *This* and *that* are used with singular words. *These* and *those* are used with plural words. *This* and *these* indicate a location that is near the speaker. *That* and *those* indicate a location that is not near the speaker. Refer to the examples below.

> *This* food is delicious.
>
> *That* boat is moored at another pier.
>
> *These* children sing well.

These same words are demonstrative pronouns when they take the place of a noun. Review the section Pronouns earlier in this chapter for examples of demonstrative pronouns.

Adverbs

An **adverb** is a word that describes a verb, adjective, clause, or another adverb. Adverbs tell how, when, or where something is done. They can also limit or qualify a description. In the first example below, *beautifully* tells how Jose sang and *yesterday* tells when he sang. Both adverbs modify the verb *sang.* In the second example, *fast* tells how the girl ran. *Very* qualifies the adverb *fast.* In the third example, *perhaps* qualifies the first clause of the sentence. In the last example, *finally* modifies the rest of the sentence (an independent clause).

> Jose sang *beautifully yesterday.*
>
> The girl ran *very fast.*
>
> *Perhaps* this answer is correct, but I am not sure.
>
> *Finally,* she will finish her work.

The leaves are gently falling in the park. Does this sentence contain any adverbs?

Shutterstock

Forms of Adverbs

Like adjectives, adverbs have three forms: positive, comparative, and superlative. **Positive adverbs** describe, but do not compare, actions or qualities. **Comparative adverbs** compare two actions, conditions, or qualities. Add *er* or *more* to create the comparative form of most adverbs. **Superlative adverbs** compare three or more actions, conditions, or qualities. Add *est* or *most* to create the superlative form of most adverbs.

> **Positive**
> Aysha drives *fast.*
> The painting is *beautiful.*
>
> **Comparative**
> Aysha drives *faster* than Janet.
> Jia Li's painting is *more beautiful* than Jeanette's painting.
>
> **Superlative**
> Aysha drives *fastest* of all contestants.
> Jia Li's painting is the *most beautiful* of all the paintings.

Some adverbs do not have comparative or superlative forms. Examples of these adverbs include *almost, before, here, there, now, then, too, very,* and *never.* These adverbs express qualities or conditions that are not suitable for comparison. Some adverbs, such as *little, much, bad,* and *well,* have irregular comparative and superlative forms. Consult a dictionary when you are unsure about how to form the comparative or superlative form of an adverb.

Conjunctive Adverbs

Conjunctive adverbs, such as *however, therefore,* and *also,* connect or introduce clauses or phrases in a sentence. They help clarify the ideas in the sentence. In the first example below, *therefore* connects two independent clauses in the sentence. In the second example, *then* introduces the main clause of the sentence. In the third example, the adverb comes at the end of the sentence. Examples of conjunctive adverbs are shown in Figure 5-9.

> The snow fell heavily; *therefore,* the roads were slippery.
>
> *Then,* rearrange the numbers, beginning with the smallest one.
>
> He went to the grocery store; he did not buy anything, *however.*

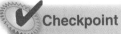

Checkpoint

1. What is an adjective?
2. How is an adverb different from an adjective?

Figure 5-9.	These are conjunctive adverbs.			
accordingly	finally	likewise	otherwise	still
again	however	meanwhile	rather	then
besides	indeed	next	similarly	therefore
certainly	instead	now	so	yet

CASE

Grammar Counts

Angela Diaz works in the Human Resources Department at a small company. She is reviewing letters and résumés from applicants for a customer service position. Angela has decided to invite four people to come in for interviews. After reading several applications, she selected three candidates to interview. Angela is debating about whom to choose for the fourth candidate. Jason Wells has the appropriate education. He has worked for several years in a customer service job. However, Angela noted several errors in grammar in Jason's letter and résumé. Connie Wong has the appropriate education, but her experience is limited. Connie's letter and résumé are clear, courteous, and concise with no grammar errors.

1. Which candidate, Jason or Connie, do you think Angela will invite for an interview? Why?

2. Are good grammar skills important for a customer service representative? Why or why not?

Conjunctions, Prepositions, and Interjections

Conjunctions and prepositions are important parts of speech because they connect words, phrases, or clauses to other elements in the sentence. Expressing a thought with clarity without using these words would often be difficult. Interjections are probably the least used of the parts of speech. However, they play an important role in expressing strong emotions.

Conjunctions

A **conjunction** is a word that connects other words, phrases, or sentences. There are three types of conjunctions: coordinating, subordinating, and correlative. Each type has a particular use in connecting elements in sentences.

Coordinating Conjunctions

Coordinating conjunctions join two or more sentence elements that are of equal importance. The elements may be words or clauses. Examples of coordinating conjunctions include *and, or, nor, but, yet, so,* and *for.* In the first example below, *and* joins the three words *coats, gloves,* and *hats.* In the second example, *but* joins two independent clauses.

The coats, gloves, *and* hats are in the closet.

He invited me to a play, *but* I did not go.

Subordinating Conjunctions

Subordinating conjunctions connect dependent clauses to independent clauses. Examples include *although, because, since,* and *unless.* Since the subordinating conjunction introduces the dependent clause, it comes at the beginning of the clause. However, the dependent clause can come before the independent clause, as in the first example below, or after it, as in the second example.

> *Because* the day was warm, I did not wear a jacket.
>
> I did not wear a jacket *because* the day was warm.

Correlative Conjunctions

Correlative conjunctions are two or more words that work together to connect elements in a sentence. Examples include *both/and, either/or, not only/but also, rather/than,* and *neither/nor.* The elements connected can be words, phrases, or clauses. Refer to the examples below.

> *Both* students *and* teachers attended the assembly.
>
> The triathlon includes *not only* running, *but also* swimming and cycling.
>
> He *neither* read the book *nor* studied for the exam.
>
> I would *rather* run in the park *than* wash the dishes.
>
> *Either* eat your broccoli *or* leave the table.

Prepositions

A **preposition** is a word that connects or relates its object to the rest of the sentence. The English language has dozens of prepositions. Examples of prepositions include *to, at, by, under, of, beside, over,* and *during.* More examples are shown in Figure 5-10. The object of a preposition can be a noun, phrase, or objective case pronoun. A prepositional phrase consists of the preposition, its object, and any related adjectives and adverbs. In the following examples, the prepositional phrases are shown in italics.

> The cards are *on the table.*
>
> The hat is *beside the very pretty dress.*
>
> She mailed the package *to him.*

Prepositional phrases often show location in space or time for the object of the phrase. In the first two examples below, the prepositional phrases show location in space. In the third example, the phrase shows location in time.

> The book is *on the floor.*
>
> The book is *underneath the stapler.*
>
> The leaves change color *in the fall.*

Prepositional phrases can serve as adverbs in a sentence. In the example below, *without pain* tells how the man ran the race.

> The man ran the race *without pain.*

Figure 5-10.	These are prepositions.					
about	at	down	inside	on	through	up
above	before	during	into	onto	to	upon
across	behind	except	like	outside	toward	versus
after	below	for	near	over	under	with
along	beneath	from	of	past	underneath	within
among	beside	in	off	since	until	without
around	by					

Interjections

An **interjection** is a word that expresses strong emotion, such as surprise, fear, anger, excitement, or shock. An interjection can also express a command. Examples of interjections include *wow, oh, hey, ouch, well,* and *hurray.* Interjections can appear at the beginning of a sentence that expresses strong emotion. The sentence can end with a period or an exclamation point, depending on how forceful the writer wants the sentence to be. In the following examples, the interjections are shown in italics.

> *No*, don't touch that!
>
> *Oh*, you surprised me.
>
> *Well*, I am insulted by that remark!

Interjections can also appear alone with an exclamation mark, with the following sentence providing more information. This makes the interjection seem more forceful. When an interjection expresses surprise, it can be followed by a question mark rather than an exclamation mark.

> *Ouch!* That hurts.
>
> *Hurray!* We won the game.
>
> *What?* You can't be serious.

Interjections should be used sparingly in formal business communication, such as letters and reports. For example, an interjection might be used when quoting someone's spoken words. Interjections can be effective in advertising materials or sales promotions. These messages are more informal and are designed to grab the reader's attention. However, still use interjections sparingly.

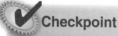

Checkpoint
1. What is a conjunction?
2. How is a preposition different from a conjunction?
3. What is an interjection?

Chapter 5 Review

Chapter Summary

Sentence Parts

- A sentence is a group of words that express a complete thought.
- A sentence has two main parts, a subject and a predicate.
- Predicates often contain objects, either direct or indirect.
- Longer sentences can contain phrases and clauses.
- A sentence may be structured as a simple, compound, or complex sentence.

Nouns and Pronouns

- Nouns and pronouns are used as the simple subjects in sentences.
- A noun is a person, place, or thing.
- A pronoun replaces nouns in the sentence.

Verbs

- A verb is a word that shows action or state of being.
- The five properties of verbs are voice, mood, tense, person, and number.
- Verb forms include participles, gerunds, and infinitives.

Adjectives and Adverbs

- Adjectives and adverbs are used to make sentences more descriptive.
- An adjective is a word that describes a noun or pronoun.
- An adverb is a word that describes a verb, adjective, clause, or another adverb.

Conjunctions, Prepositions, and Interjections

- Conjunctions and prepositions connect words, phrases, or clauses to other elements in the sentence.
- An interjection is a word that expresses strong emotion.

Review Your Knowledge

1. List the eight parts of speech.
2. What is a sentence?
3. List the two main parts of a sentence and describe each part.
4. Explain the difference between a direct and indirect object.
5. Describe the difference between a phrase and a clause.
6. What is the difference between a simple sentence, compound sentence, and complex sentence?
7. Explain the difference between a noun and pronoun.
8. Describe the two types of verbs.
9. What do adjectives and adverbs add to a sentence?
10. What do conjunctions and prepositions do in a sentence?

Apply Your Knowledge

1. Read the sentences listed below. For each sentence, write the sentence part labels and the corresponding sentence part: simple subject, complete subject, simple predicate, complete predicate, direct object, indirect object, subject complement, and prepositional phrase. Note that some sentences will not have all of these parts.

    A. The large box contains office supplies.

    > Partial example: simple subject: box; complete subject: the large box

    B. The woman went to her office and placed a call.

    C. Return the book to the library.

    D. This man is the committee chairperson.

E. The boys and girls gave the teacher their drawings.

F. The large flower arrangement of roses and lilies was beautiful.

2. Identify the nouns and pronouns in the sentences below.

A. The waiter placed a coaster under the glass.

B. The car skidded wildly and knocked down a utility pole.

C. No! I do not want to withdraw from the race!

D. She is keying quickly and accurately.

E. Certainly, I will complete the finance report.

F. What do you recommend?

G. The menu will include potatoes or rice.

H. The cars were moving slowly because the streets were covered with snow.

I. He waited patiently, but the package did not arrive.

J. Some items will be returned to the store.

3. Write a paragraph that describes an activity, sport, or hobby that interests you. Use each of the eight parts of speech at least once. Use at least one simple sentence, one compound sentence, and one complex sentence. Pay particular attention to the correct usage of verbs.

4. Write a paragraph describing what you see in your room or looking out of a window. Use each of the eight parts of speech at least once. Use at least one simple sentence, one compound sentence, and one complex sentence. Pay particular attention to the correct usage of adjectives and adverbs.

5. Identify the conjunctions, prepositions, and interjections in the sentences below.

A. The cat is hiding beneath the chair.

B. You can have either pizza or pasta.

C. Well, that book was a disappointment.

D. The rude person was using a cell phone during the movie.

E. Oh, you think you are so smart.

F. Not only will I run the race, but also I will win it.

G. The dog is running toward the ball.

Practice
What You Have Learned

Access the *Fundamentals of Business Communication* Student Companion Web Site at www.g-wlearning.com/Communication. Download each data file for this chapter. Follow the instructions to complete a reading, writing, and grammar activity to practice what you have learned in this chapter.

Connections
Across the Curriculum

Language Arts. What is the origin of the word grammar? Write several paragraphs about your findings.

Math. Grammar is used in writing, but something similar is used in math as well. What is the "grammar" of mathematics? Write several paragraphs on your findings.

Build
Your Business Portfolio

You will be creating both a print portfolio and an ePortfolio in this class. It will be necessary for you to set up a folder for the electronic files that will be in the ePortfolio.

1. Ask your instructor where to save your documents. This could be on the school's network or a flash drive of your own.

2. Create a folder on the network drive or flash drive using your name and Portfolio as the name of the folder. For example, if your name is Bob Rentz, your folder will be BRentzPortfolio.

Careers
Health Science
Careers and Communication

Healthcare is one of the fastest-growing industries in the United States, so careers in this cluster are in high demand. The career pathways include therapeutic and diagnostic services, health information, support services, and biotechnology research and development.

People who work in health sciences have a variety of responsibilities, from providing healthcare to managing data and providing support services. As a healthcare professional, good communication skills are crucial and can impact patient care.

Why do you think good communication skills are important to the health science industry? Explain why you think good writing skills are important in this profession. In what situations would a healthcare professional need to apply writing skills?

Event Prep

Business Communication

The business communication competitive event consists of an objective test that covers multiple topics. Participants are usually allowed one hour to complete the event. One of the topics that will be included in the event is written communication concepts. Effective communicators work to perfect the mechanics of written communication. By participating in the business communication event, you will have an opportunity to showcase your written communication skills.

To prepare for the objective business communication test, do the following.

1. Study the vocabulary words at the beginning of each chapter in this book. Make sure you understand each definition.

2. Study the grammar concepts presented in this chapter.

3. Review the chapter summary for each chapter in Unit 3, Writing for Successful Communication.

4. Memorize the parts of a letter and parts of a memo, as described in Chapter 9. Questions will be included covering writing of cover letters, memos, and e-mails.

5. Study the parts of a report, as presented in Chapter 17. You may be asked to identify various sections of reports and outlines.

6 Improving Grammar Mechanics

You keep using that word. I do not think it means what you think it means.

—Inigo Montoya,
from The Princess Bride
by William Goldman

Mechanics are the technical aspects of doing something. Mechanics of writing involve punctuation, capitalization, number expression, and parallel structure. The proper use of these aspects of writing help you create clear messages. Selecting the correct word or term to give the meaning you desire is also important. A message can be unclear when a speaker or writer selects the wrong word, as Inigo points out in the quote above from *The Princess Bride*.

Objectives

When you complete Chapter 6, you will be able to:

- **Punctuate** sentences correctly.
- **Use** capitalization correctly.
- **Express** numbers correctly in words or figures.
- **Use** parallel structure in sentences.
- **Select** the proper use of commonly misused words and terms.

Terms

punctuation	colon
terminal punctuation	apostrophe
period	contraction
abbreviation	hyphen
question mark	permanent compound
exclamation point	temporary compound
internal punctuation	quotation marks
comma	capitalization
dash	proper noun
parentheses	parallel structure
semicolon	homonym

Go Green

Paper manufacturers are always looking for renewable resources and new ideas to produce environmentally friendly paper products. One ecofriendly paper is made from by-products of sugarcane with no wood involved in its production. Sugarcane products degrade faster as waste than wood products and sugarcane paper is cleaner to make than wood-based paper. Many office supply companies are carrying sugarcane paper with more new product to come.

1. Visit your local office supply store or go online to research sugarcane-paper products. What type of products did you find?

2. Do a price comparison of a ream of sugarcane paper compared to a ream of "regular" wood-based paper. Is there a difference in price?

Punctuation

In writing, **punctuation** consists of marks used to show the structure of sentences. Both terminal (end-of-sentence) and internal marks indicate separations of words into sentences, clauses, and phrases. These marks guide readers and help them understand the meaning of sentences and passages.

Terminal Punctuation

Punctuation marks used at the end of a sentence are called **terminal punctuation.** Terminal punctuation marks include periods, question marks, and exclamation points.

Periods

A **period** is a punctuation mark used at the end of a declarative sentence—a sentence that makes a statement. As you learned in Chapter 5, a sentence has a subject and a predicate and expresses a complete thought. So, the period signals the reader that the expressed thought is ending. Periods provide structure to paragraphs, which can contain several sentences. The sentences in the following examples end with periods.

> The final exam will be on May 26.
>
> Alma traveled to Lexington to visit her friend.
>
> Andrew rented a car for his vacation trip.

Periods are also used to divide parts of an abbreviation or signal the end of an abbreviation. An **abbreviation** is a shortened form of a word or letters used to stand for a word or term. Examples of words and their abbreviations are shown in Figure 6-1. When an abbreviation ending in a period comes at the end of a declarative sentence, the period also serves to end the sentence. See the *company* example in Figure 6-1.

Reading Prep

Before reading this chapter, flip through the pages and make notes of the major headings. Compare these headings to the objectives. What did you discover? How will this help you prepare to read new material?

Figure 6-1.	Here are some common abbreviations along with examples of how they appear in sentences.

Word	Abbreviation	Sentence
association	assoc.	The Park Assoc. will host a picnic.
captain	Capt.	Capt. Hook was a pirate.
company	co.	Send the check to Johnson Co.
doctor	Dr.	Dr. Chung is a surgeon.
Earl Dale, John Fitzgerald Kennedy	E. D.	E. D. Ross quoted a speech by JFK.
	JFK	
Kentucky	KY	The last line of the address is: Monticello, KY 42633.
master of arts	MA	Shelia Reins, MA, teaches this class.
mister	Mr.	Mr. Diaz voted for the motion.
superintendent	supt.	The supt. of the building unlocked the door.

An initial, the first letter of a name, is a type of abbreviation followed by a period in many cases. Use a period with initials that stand for a given name. Do not use periods for initials that stand for a person's complete name, as shown in Figure 6-1. Academic degrees, such as master of arts, have traditionally been abbreviated with periods (M.A.). Such abbreviations are now typically written without periods (MA), as shown in Figure 6-1.

In addresses, use the two-letter state abbreviations with no periods, as recommended by the US Postal Service. In general writing, some authorities recommend using the traditional, three-letter abbreviation for a state name followed by a period. Other authorities recommend using the two-letter state abbreviations in all cases. Both styles are correct; however, you should be consistent in using one style or the other.

Periods are used after numbers and letters in some types of lists, such as outlines or numbered lists. In the partial outline example below, periods follow the numbers and letters.

Punctuation
I. Terminal punctuation
    A. Periods
        1. Sentences
        2. Abbreviations
    B. Question marks
    C. Exclamation points
II. Internal punctuation
    A. Commas
    B. Colons

In a vertical numbered list, each number is followed by a period, as shown in the example below. The text of each item in the list is followed by a period only if it is a complete sentence. If the item is not a complete sentence, do not use a period.

Follow these steps.
1. Carefully read the contracts.
2. Check the accuracy of all numbers.
3. Sign your name on each copy of the contract.
4. Return the contracts by overnight mail.

Question Marks

A **question mark** is punctuation used at the end of an interrogative sentence—a sentence that asks a question. As with a period, the question mark signals the reader that the expressed thought is ending. Along with periods, they provide structure to paragraphs. A question mark can be used after a word or sentence that expresses strong emotion, such as shock or doubt. The sentences in the following examples end with question marks.

Will the plane arrive on time?

Did she travel to Lexington to visit her friend?

Has he rented a car for his vacation trip?

What? Are you serious?

A question mark can be part of a sentence that contains a quote. Place the question mark inside the quotation marks when the quote asks a question. See the first example below. Place the question mark outside the quotation marks if the entire sentence asks a question. See the second example below.

Teresa asked, "Will the work be finished soon?"

Did he say, "The sale will end on Friday"?

Exclamation Points

An **exclamation point** is a punctuation mark used to express strong emotion. Exclamation points are used at the end of a sentence or after an interjection that stands alone. An exclamation point can be used at the end of a question rather than a question mark, if the writer wishes to show strong emotion.

Stop hurting me!

Hurrah! This is great.

Will you ever grow up!

As with question marks, an exclamation point can be part of a sentence that contains a quote. Place the exclamation point inside the quotation marks when the quote expresses the strong emotion. See the first example below. Place the exclamation point outside the quotation marks if the entire sentence expresses the strong emotion. See the second example below.

All of the students shouted, "Hooray!"

He said, "you are disqualified"!

Internal Punctuation

Punctuation marks used within a sentence are called **internal punctuation.** These marks include commas, dashes, parentheses, semicolons, colons, hyphens, apostrophes, and quotation marks.

Commas

A **comma** is a punctuation mark used to separate elements in a sentence. The elements can be items in a series, clauses, phrases, words of direct address, parts of dates, parts of addresses, or missing (understood) words. Commas provide breaks or pauses in a sentence. These breaks help readers more easily understand sentences.

Commas are used to separate items in a series. The items can be words, phrases, or independent clauses joined by a conjunction such as *and, or, but, so,* or *yet.* Place a comma after each item in the series that comes before the conjunction. Some style guides recommend omitting the last comma.

A comma is also used before a coordinating conjunction that joins two independent clauses. If the clauses are very short, as in the last example below, the comma can be left out.

> Apple, pears, or grapes will be on the menu.
>
> She won the game by hitting the ball, running the bases, and sliding home.
>
> Maria sang a ballad, Chin-Sun read a poem, and Henry played the piano.
>
> The sun rose, and the birds began to sing.
>
> Stand up and smile.

A dependent clause that comes at the beginning of a sentence should be followed by a comma. When a dependent clause comes at the end of a sentence, a comma is not needed.

> If you want to arrive on time, you must leave now.
>
> You must leave now if you want to arrive on time.

Commas are used to separate some words or phrases from the rest of the sentence. Place a comma after an introductory word or phrase, including a phrase that introduces a quote. Place a comma before and after an adverb, such as *however* or *indeed,* when it comes in the middle of a sentence.

> Yes, I will attend the meeting.
>
> After reading story, the students wrote answers to the questions.
>
> He answered, "I am not hungry."
>
> To Carla, Shane seemed depressed.
>
> Preparing a delicious dessert, however, requires using fresh ingredients.

Some explanatory phrases are restrictive, providing information that is essential to the meaning of the sentence. Restrictive phrases are not separated by commas, as shown in the examples that follow. Commas are used to separate a nonrestrictive explanatory word or phrase from the rest of the sentence.

Restrictive

The game that was cancelled has been rescheduled.
The famous poet Carl Sandburg gave a presentation.

Nonrestrictive

The game, which we lost, was exciting.
Gloria's husband, Jorge, drove the car.

When an adjective phrase contains coordinate adjectives, use commas to separate the coordinate adjectives. As discussed in Chapter 5, coordinate adjectives equally modify a noun or pronoun. Remember, not all adjectives that appear in a sequence are coordinate adjectives.

Coordinate adjectives

The *long, hot* summer was finally over.

Not coordinate adjectives

The *tall brick* building has a black roof.

Commas are used to separate words used in direct address. The words can be proper nouns (as in the first example below), the pronoun *you*, or common nouns (as in the second example). When the nouns of direct address come within the sentence (rather than at the beginning), a comma is placed before and after the nouns of direct address. See the third example below.

Quon, please answer the next question.

Everyone, please sit down.

After lunch, boys and girls, I will read a story.

Commas are used to separate elements in dates and addresses. When a date is expressed in the month-day-year format, commas are used to separate the year. When only the month and year or a holiday and year are used, a comma is not needed.

On December 7, 1941, Japan attacked Pearl Harbor.

In January 2010 she retired from her job.

The race took place on Labor Day 2011.

A comma is used after the street address and after the city when an address or location appears in general text.

Mail the item to 123 Maple Drive, Columbus, OH 43085.

He arrived in Boise, Idaho, yesterday.

The sky was painted with blue; yellow; and orange. Is this sentence punctuated correctly?

Shutterstock

A comma is used to indicate missing words that can be understood without being repeated. In the example below, *I have relatives* is understood rather than stated each time.

⨼ In Oregon I have six relatives; in Kansas, eight; in Maine, two.

Dashes and Parentheses

A **dash** is a punctuation mark that separates elements in a sentence or signals an abrupt change in thought. The dash is more properly called an em dash. This name comes from its width, which is the same as the uppercase letter M. A dash (em dash) is not a hyphen or en dash. Hyphens are discussed later in this chapter.

A dash provides a stronger break than a comma. To give a break mild emphasis, use a comma. To give a break strong emphasis, use a dash.

⨼ My history teacher, an avid reader, visits the library every week.

⨼ My history teacher—an avid reader—visits the library every week.

Use a dash to signal an abrupt change in thought in a sentence. If the words come in the middle of a sentence, use a dash before and after them. See the examples below.

⨼ I thought you would—oh, never mind.

⨼ I need my car keys—I've lost them again—so I can drive to work.

Parentheses are punctuation marks used to enclose words or phrases that clarify meaning or give added information. They always appear as a pair. Place a period that comes at the end of a sentence inside the parentheses only when the entire sentence is enclosed in parentheses.

⨼ Deliver the materials to the meeting site (the Polluck Building).

⨼ Please review the table. (The table is in Appendix A.)

Use parentheses to enclose numbers or letters in a list that is part of a sentence. When the words that introduce a list could be a complete sentence, use a colon before the list, as shown in the second example below.

⨼ Revise the sentences to correct errors in (1) spelling, (2) punctuation, and (3) capitalization.

⨼ Bring your sewing machine and basic sewing supplies: (a) cutting mat, (b) rotary cutter, and (c) thread.

A nonrestrictive explanatory word or phrase can be separated from the rest of the sentence by commas, dashes, or parentheses. Both dashes and parentheses provide a stronger break than commas. Note the use of these marks in the examples below.

⨼ The contributions of three students, Mark, Elena, and Hoshi, made the event a success.

   The contributions of three students—Mark, Elena, and Hoshi—made the event a success.

   The contributions of three students (Mark, Elena, and Hoshi) made the event a success.

Semicolons

A **semicolon** in an internal punctuation mark used to separate clauses or some items in a series. A semicolon provides a stronger break than a comma.

When two independent clauses in a sentence are not joined by a coordinating conjunction, use a semicolon to separate the clauses.

Twelve students took the test; two students passed.

The bike ran over a nail; the tire went flat.

I left; however, she stayed.

Items in a series are typically separated by commas. However, when at least one item in the series already contain commas, semicolons are used to separate the items. Using semicolons makes identifying the separate elements easier.

We visited Newark, New Jersey; Portland, Maine; Concord, New Hampshire; and New York, New York.

The group included Mr. Roberts, an auditor; Ms. Keys, a forensic accountant; and Mr. Lopez, the company president.

Colons

A **colon** is an internal punctuation mark that introduces an element in a sentence or paragraph. The elements can be words, phrases, clauses, or sentences. The colon provides a stronger break than a comma.

The bag contains three items: a book, a pencil, and an apple.

You need to practice these activities: keying numbers quickly and proofreading carefully.

She failed the test for one reason: she did not study.

He considered several alternatives: He could keep working in a difficult situation and say nothing. He could report his boss for harassment. He could find a new job.

A colon is also used after a phrase, clause, or sentence that introduces a vertical list. See the example below.

Follow these steps.
1. Identify the problem.
2. Talk to the people involved.
3. Consider possible solutions.
4. Select the best alternative.
5. Implement the solution.

Colons are used in other situations that do not relate to the structure of a sentence. Some of these uses are shown in Figure 6-2.

Apostrophes

An **apostrophe** is a punctuation mark used to form possessive words and contractions. Possessive words show ownership. An apostrophe or an apostrophe and an *s* are added to many nouns to create the possessive

Figure 6-2. Shown here are examples of where colons may be used.

Uses	Examples
Business letter salutation	Dear Mrs. Martinez:
Introduction of a definition	note: a brief written record
Hours and minutes	Meet me at 5:45 p.m.
Title and subtitle	*Star Wars: The Force Unleashed*
Reference note between city and publisher	*Webster's New World College Dictionary.* Cleveland: Wiley Publishing Inc., 2009.

form. Note that possessive pronouns, such as *her, our, mine,* and *their,* do not use an apostrophe. Examples of possessive nouns with apostrophes are shown in the sentences below. To review more information about possessive words, see Chapter 5.

> Akeno's dress was red.
>
> The boys' bikes were parked by the building.
>
> This year's crop was poor.

A **contraction** is a shortened form of a word or term. It is formed by omitting letters from one or more words and replacing them with an apostrophe to create one word—the contraction. Examples of contractions and the words they represent are shown in Figure 6-3.

Apostrophes can be used to indicate that letters are omitted from words for brevity or writing style. For example, in a poem the final *g* might be omitted from words ending in *ing.* Note that these uses are not preferred for business writing.

> Leisure suits were in style in the '60s. (1960s)
>
> The candidates will meet to discuss activities of the gov't. (government)
>
> Rock 'n' roll will never die. (and)
>
> The bells were ringin', and the choir was singin'. (ringing and singing)

Figure 6-3. These are common contractions along with examples of how they appear in sentences.

Words	Contractions	Sentences
do not	don't	Don't leave until after dinner.
does not	doesn't	He doesn't want to go to the movies.
you are	you're	While you're reading, I will listen to music.
I am	I'm	I'm sorry I'm late.
is not	isn't	She isn't ready to go.
he has	he's	He's playing golf today.
I have	I've	I've read three books this week.
I will	I'll	I'll let you know later.
will not	won't	She won't finish the work on time.
I would	I'd	I'd be happy to oblige.

Apostrophes are used in forming the plural of single lowercase letters. The apostrophe helps the reader avoid misunderstanding the sentence. For example, without the apostrophe, *a's* would be read *as*. Apostrophes are not used to form the plural of capital letters unless the meaning would be unclear without an apostrophe.

The word *Mississippi* has four s's and two p's.

She got all Bs on her progress report.

Hyphens

A **hyphen** is a punctuation mark used to separate parts of compound words, numbers, or ranges. Compound words that always have a hyphen are called **permanent compounds. Temporary compounds** are created as needed by the writer. Hyphens are also used in word division.

Many compound words have a hyphen between elements. Examples include *close-up, mother-in-law,* and *voice-over.* These nouns always have hyphens. Some adverbs, such as *out-of-doors,* always have hyphens. A dictionary can be used to find permanent compound words.

The close-up was blurry.

My mother-in-law made dinner.

The wedding was held out-of-doors.

In many cases, the writer must decide whether to use hyphens in compound words based on how they are used in a sentence. Compound adjectives typically have hyphens when they come before the words they modify, but not when they come after them. See the examples below.

The well-done pot roast was delicious.

The delicious pot roast was well done.

These out-of-date books should be thrown away.

Throw away the books that are out of date.

In some words that have prefixes, a hyphen is used between the prefix and the rest of the word. Examples of prefixes include *all, ex, pre,* and *self.* Words with these prefixes are used in the following examples.

The all-inclusive report was presented at the meeting.

My ex-wife has custody of our children.

These quilt patterns are from the pre-Civil War era.

My self-imposed discipline helped me reach my goals.

Hyphens are used in numbers that are expressed as words and number or letter ranges. Figure 6-4 describes some of these uses and gives examples.

When a word is divided at the end of a line of text, a hyphen is used between parts of the word. See Figure 6-5 for guidelines for dividing words.

Figure 6-4. Hyphens may be used in numbers and ranges.

Uses	Examples
Fractions expressed in words	one-half, two-thirds
Numbers less than 100 that have two words	twenty-one, forty-three
Numbers or letters in a range	20-25, A-Z
Social Security numbers, telephone numbers, or serial numbers	987-65-4325, 1-800-555-0124
Between letters of a word that is spelled out, as when writing dialogue	That's spelled T-w-y-f-o-r-d-s.

Figure 6-5. Use these guidelines for dividing words.

Word Division Guidelines

- Do not divide a word that has one syllable or is a contraction.
- Divide words only between syllables.
- When a word already contains a hyphen, divide it only at the existing hyphen.

    Example:
    self-
    assured

- Divide solid compound words between the two base words.

    Example:
    down-
    town

- Do not place a single letter of a word at the end of a line.

    Incorrect:
    a-
    gain

- Do not place only one or two letters of a word at the beginning of a new line.

    Incorrect:
    quick-
    ly

- Divide between two single-letter syllables that come together in a word.

    Example:
    situ-
    ation

- Avoid dividing proper names.

Quotation Marks

Quotation marks are used to enclose short, direct quotes and titles of some artistic or written works. (Long quotes are set apart from the paragraph and are not enclosed in quotation marks.) Quotation marks can also be used to show irony or nonstandard use of words. A direct quote is a restatement of someone's exact words, as shown in the first example below. A general statement that relays a similar thought does not use quotation marks, as shown in the second example.

> "Which color do you want," he asked.
>
> He asked which color you want.

A sentence with a direct quote often has an explanatory phrase, such as *he said* or *she replied,* that refers to the person speaking. The phrase is followed by a comma (or a colon in more formal situations) when it comes before the quote. A comma comes before the phrase when the phrase follows the quote. The quoted words can also be split, with the phrase coming between them. The words quoted are enclosed in double quotation marks, as shown in the examples below.

> Martin replied, "Sales have increased by 50 percent during the last quarter."
>
> "It's time to go home, children," said the teacher.
>
> "Now that everyone is here," Susan said, "we can begin."

A quote need not be a complete sentence; it can be a word or a phrase as spoken or written by someone. See the examples below.

> When the mayor refers to "charitable giving," does that include gifts to all nonprofit organizations?
>
> The announcer mentioned that the news about the economy "has been positive for two months."

When a quote contains another quote, the quote within a quote is enclosed in single quotation marks. See the first example below. Notice the placement of the period in the first example. Periods and commas always go inside closing quotation marks. The placement of a question mark in relation to quotation marks varies. When the entire sentence is a question, place the question mark outside a closing quotation mark. When only the quote is a question, place the question mark inside a closing quotation mark. The same logic applies to the use of an exclamation point with quotation marks.

> He answered, "Niran said, 'Order shirts for everyone on the team.'"
>
> Did he say, "The project will be delayed"?
>
> He asked, "Who will work on Saturday?"
>
> The cheerleaders shouted, "Go team!"

When writing a dialogue, the words of each speaker are enclosed in quotation marks. The speakers are often identified at the beginning of the dialogue, but not with each statement that follows. Begin a new paragraph each time the speaker changes. When the words of one speaker require two or more paragraphs (with no interruptions), place an opening quotation mark at the beginning of each paragraph. Place a closing quotation mark at the end of the last paragraph.

> Anna arrived at the office and greeted her coworker, Joan. "Good morning. You're getting an early start today."
> "Yes, I have some reports I need to finish this morning."
> "I will be in a meeting until around one o'clock. Would you like to go to Strong's Deli for a late lunch?"
> "That sound's great. See you later."

BUSINESS PROTOCOL

Respecting Space

Space can mean how far or how close you are when conversing or it can indicate differences in status. For example, some work groups have unwritten rules about who sits where in meetings. The leader might typically sit at the end of the table or in the middle, so other team members know not to take the leader's chair. At large meetings, people in lower-level jobs might be expected to stand if the room gets so crowded there are not enough chairs.

If you have an appointment with someone in his or her office, do you walk through the door or wait to be invited in? What is the correct protocol? If the person is a high-ranking officer of the company, you might choose to stand in the doorway until invited in to take a seat. If it is a colleague you work with every day, you might walk in and sit down at the appointed time, even if the person is talking on the telephone when you arrive. Doing this with your boss or someone higher, however, would be an invasion of space. It is important to know what your employer expects from you before you act.

Titles of complete books, movies, and other artistic works are typically shown in italics (or underlined). Titles of shorter works, which may also be part of a larger work, are shown in quotation marks. Examples include articles in magazines, chapters in a book, short poems, episodes of a television or radio show, sections or special features of a Web site, and titles of songs.

> "Books and Journals" is the first chapter in *The Chicago Manual of Style.*
>
> "When and Where" is a favorite episode of *Warehouse 13* fans.

Quotation marks are used to enclose words that are meant to show irony. In the first example below, the writer is implying that Connie was not really busy. Quotations marks are also used to enclose words used in a nonstandard way. In the second example, the term *sinking ship* is used to describe a failing business—not a real ship.

> Although Connie had the afternoon off, she was too "busy" to help me.
>
> In a survey of small businesses, one in five managers said their companies are "sinking ships."

Grammar Checker

Use the grammar checker in your word processing software to help you locate possible errors in punctuation, capitalization, and word usage in your documents. Figure 6-6 shows the spelling and grammar checker in Microsoft Word.

Be aware, however, that a grammar checker is not perfect. Some things the grammar checker raises as possible errors may not be errors. You need to carefully proofread and evaluate suggestions given by the grammar checker before accepting the changes. In Figure 6-6, the program has identified

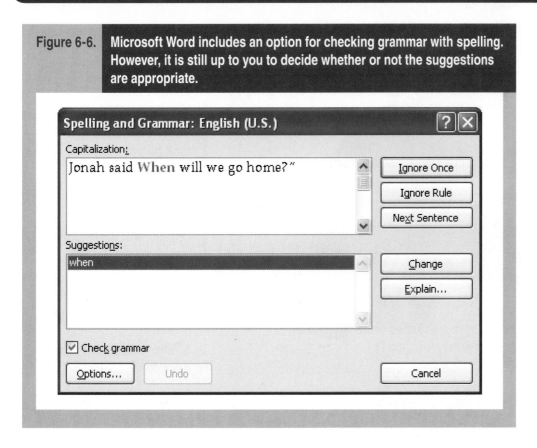

Figure 6-6. Microsoft Word includes an option for checking grammar with spelling. However, it is still up to you to decide whether or not the suggestions are appropriate.

an error. The comma and quotations marks are missing before the quote. However, the suggested solution is not appropriate.

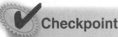

Checkpoint

1. What is the difference between terminal punctuation and internal punctuation?
2. List three types of terminal punctuation.
3. List seven types of internal punctuation.

Capitalization

As it relates to writing, **capitalization** means writing a letter in uppercase (B) rather than lowercase (b). Capital letters signal the beginning of a new sentence and identify important words in titles and headings. This helps readers see the structure of paragraphs, reports, articles, and other messages. Capital letters are also used for proper nouns, for some abbreviations, in personal and professional titles, and for parts of business letters.

Sentences

A sentence begins with a capital letter. Numbers that begin a sentence should be spelled as words, and the first word should be capitalized. If the number is very long, consider revising the sentence so the number is not at

A great pediatrician is caring and gentle, like Dr. Ramirez is. Is the capitalization in this sentence correct?

Shutterstock

the beginning. The first word in a quote within a sentence should be capitalized if the quote is a complete sentence.

] He was elected mayor.

Thirty-three students took part in the graduation ceremony.

He said, "Wait for me by the door."

"What," she asked, "do you want me to do?"

Headings, Titles, and Documents

Capital letters are used in headings for reports, articles, newsletters, and other documents. They are also used for titles of books, magazines, movies, and other works. Follow the guidelines below for headline style capitalization.

- Capitalize the first word and the last word in a heading or title.

  ] *Gone with the Wind*

- Capitalize all other important words in a heading or title.

  ] *The Adventure of the Hansom Cabs*
  Softly He Goes into the Night

- For numbers with hyphens in a heading or title, capitalize both words.

  ] *Twenty-One Candles*

- Do not capitalize articles or prepositions within a heading or title. When a title and subtitle are written together, the first word of the subtitle is capitalized regardless of the part of speech. Note that the title and subtitle are often separated by a colon.

  ] *The Finest Story in the World*
  Tales of Troy: Ulysses the Sacker of Cities

- Do not capitalize coordinating conjunctions (*yet, and, but, for, or,* and *nor*) in a heading or title.

  ] *Pride and Prejudice*
  Never Marry but for Love

- Do not capitalize parts of names that normally appear in lowercase (Hans von Luck).

  ⌐ *Panzer Commander: The Memoirs of Colonel Hans von Luck*

Business documents, such as letters and memos, use capital letters to begin certain document parts. Capitalize the first word in the salutation and the complimentary close for a letter. Capitalize the heading words (To, From, Date, and Subject) in a memo. Some style guides recommend using all capitals for these words.

Dear Mrs. Stockton:

Sincerely yours,

Proper Nouns

Proper nouns begin with a capital letter. A **proper noun** is a word that identifies a specific person, place, or thing. Examples include names of people, pets, nationalities, schools, cities, regions, and buildings. Directional words (north, south, and east) are capitalized when they refer to a region. Proper nouns are capitalized in the examples below.

Joe Wong is the principal of George Rogers Clark High School.

My dog, Susie, is three years old.

We live in Columbus, Ohio.

The family drove west as they traveled through the South during their vacation.

This is my favorite Chinese restaurant.

The meeting will be held in the Fountain Square Room.

Abbreviations and Titles

Some abbreviations use capital letters. Titles that come before a name and some that come after a name use capital letters. Follow the guidelines below for using capital letters with abbreviations and titles.

- Capitalize initials used in place of names.

  E. J. Roberts is on the committee.

  UCLA won the football game.

- Capitalize abbreviations that are made up of the first letters of words.

  HTML stands for hypertext markup language.

  FAA stands for Federal Aviation Administration.

- Capitalize the name of months and days and their abbreviations.

  Mon. is the abbreviation for Monday.

  Jan., Feb., and Mar. are in the first quarter of the year.

- Capitalize abbreviations for names of states and countries.

  NY is a state in the United States.

  The price is given in US dollars.

- Capitalize abbreviations for directional terms and location terms in street addresses.

    ❑ She lives at 123 NW Cedar Ave.

- Capitalize call letters of a broadcasting company.

    ] My favorite television show is on CBS.
    ] Radio station WFLW plays easy-listening music.

- Capitalize abbreviations that note an era in time.

    ❑ The article included a map of Europe for the year 1200 CE.

- Capitalize titles that come before personal names.

    ] Sen. Carl Rogers called Mr. Juarez and Dr. Wang.
    ] Sister Catherine sings in the choir.

- Capitalize seniority titles (Jr., Sr.) after names.

    ❑ Mr. Thomas O'Malley, Jr., spoke at the ceremony.

- Capitalize abbreviations for academic degrees and other professional designations that follow names.

    ] Carlos Herrera, MD, testified in the court case.
    ] Jane Patel, LPN, was on duty at the hospital.

Checkpoint

1. What does it mean to capitalize a letter?
2. Which words should not be capitalized in a heading or title?
3. What is a proper noun?

Number Expression

Numbers can be expressed as figures or as words. In some cases, as in legal documents and on bank checks, numbers are written in both figures and words. When the two expressions of a number do not agree, readers are alerted to ask for clarification.

Number expression guidelines are not as widely agreed upon as rules for punctuation and capitalization. Follow the guidelines in this section for general writing. If you are writing a research report or an article for a particular group or publication, ask whether there are number expression guidelines you should follow for that item.

Numbers Expressed as Words

Follow the guidelines below for expressing numbers as words.

- In general writing, use words for numbers one through nine. (See other style guides for exceptions to this guideline.)

    ❑ One dog and three cats sat on the porch.

- Use words for numbers that are indefinite or approximate amounts.

  ] About fifty people signed the petition.

- Use words for numbers one through nine followed by *million, billion,* and so forth. For numbers 10 or greater followed by *million, billion,* and so forth, use a figure and the word.

  ] Two million people live in this region.

  The relief organization serves 12 million people.

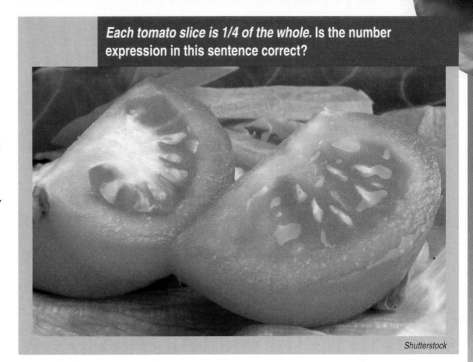

Each tomato slice is 1/4 of the whole. Is the number expression in this sentence correct?

Shutterstock

- Use words for a number that begins a sentence. If the number is long when written as words, consider revising the sentence so it does not begin with a number.

  ] Twenty copies of the report were prepared.

- When two numbers come together in a sentence, use words for one of the numbers.

  ] On the bus, there were 15 ten-year-olds.

- Use words for fractions. Note that a hyphen comes between the words.

  ] Place one-half of the mixture in the pan.

- Use words for numbers with *o'clock* to express time.

  ] Come to dinner at six o'clock.

Numbers Expressed as Figures

Numbers in table format are typically expressed as figures. Follow the guidelines below for expressing numbers as figures in general writing.

- In general writing, use figures for numbers 10 and greater. (See other style guides for exceptions to this guideline.)

  ] She placed an order for 125 blue ink pens.

- When some numbers in a sentence are 9 or less and some are 10 or greater, write all the numbers as figures.

  ] The box contains 5 books, 10 folders, and 15 pads of paper.

- Use figures with a dollar sign to express amounts of money. Do not use a decimal and two zeros when all dollar amounts in a sentence are even amounts.

  ] The total amount is $18,395.40.

  The charges were $5, $312, and $89.

- For an isolated amount less than $1, use figures and the word *cents*. When an amount less than $1 appears with other amounts greater than $1, use figures and dollar signs for all of the numbers.

  ] Buy a cup of lemonade for 75 cents.

  ] The prices were $12.50, $0.89, and $12.45.

- For a large, even dollar amount, use the dollar sign, a figure, and a word, such as *million* or *billion*.

  ] The profits for last year were $5 million.

- Use figures for days and years in dates.

  ] On February 12, 2011, the court was not in session.

- Use figures for mixed numbers (a whole number and a fraction) and for decimals.

  ] I bought 3 1/2 yards of red fabric.

  ] The measurements are 1.358 and 0.878.

- Use figures with *a.m.* and *p.m.* to express time. However, use *noon* and *midnight* to express these two times.

  ] The assembly will begin at 9:30 a.m.

  ] The baby was born at noon on June 15.

  ] The restaurant closes at midnight.

- Use figures in measurements, such as for distance, weight, and percentages.

  ] We drove 258 miles today.

  ] The winning pumpkin weighs 50 pounds.

  ] Sales have increased 20 percent in the last year.

- Use figures to refer to pages, chapters, figures, or parts in a book.

  ] Open your book to chapter 3, page 125.

  ] Refer to figure 6 on page 72 for an example.

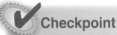

Checkpoint

1. How should the numbers one through nine be written?
2. Words are used for fractions. What else is needed?
3. How should numbers 10 and greater be written?

Parallel Structure

Parallel structure is a method of writing in which similar elements are expressed in a consistent way or using the same pattern. The elements can be words, phrases, or clauses. Using parallel structure in sentences, paragraphs, and lists makes messages easier for readers to understand.

CASE

Accuracy Counts

Kim Park works as an administrative assistant at a small company. His supervisor asked Kim to order T-shirts printed with the company name. Employees will wear the T-shirts at the company picnic. Kim prepared a letter requesting one dozen T-shirts printed with the company name. When reading over the letter, Kim thought, "Maybe I should be perfectly clear and request 12 T-shirts." A paragraph from Kim's letter appears below.

> Please send me 12 dozen T-shirts, style 345, all in size large for $10.95 each. Print this name on all the T-shirts: Jackson's Realty.

Kim was shocked and dismayed when 144 T-shirts arrived at his office two weeks later. Since the T-shirts have custom printing, they cannot be returned.

1. What mistake did Kim make that caused this problem?

2. What additional information could he have included in the order that would have caused the company to question the number of T-shirts he wanted?

Words and Phrases

To create parallel structure, use the same word or phrase form for all items in a series of words or phrases. The first example below, in which the structure is not parallel, is awkward. Gerunds and infinitives are mixed in the series. The second example uses infinitives to create a parallel structure. Note that *to* can be used before each word in the infinitive series or just before the first word. In the last example, gerunds are used to form the series.

> **Not parallel**
> She likes swimming, to read, and painting.

> **Parallel**
> She likes to swim, to read, and to paint.
> He wants to hike, swim, and ride his bicycle.
> She likes swimming, reading, and painting.

Verb forms and tenses should be constructed in a parallel pattern. Compare the two examples below. The first sentence uses verbs in the present and past tense, creating a structure that is not parallel.

> **Not parallel**
> She *waits* until the last day to begin her work, *caused* problems in the lab, and her commitment to the project *was lacking*.

> **Parallel**
> She *waits* until the last day to begin her work, *causes* problems in the lab, and *lacks* commitment to the project.

In the first example on the next page, adverbs and verbs are mixed, creating a structure that is not parallel. In the second example, only adverbs are used to express the message. Thus, the structure is parallel.

The two dogs like running, jumping, and to wrestle over a stick. Does this sentence have parallel structure?

Shutterstock

Not parallel

He was asked to do his work very fast, keep it quiet, and be accurate.

Parallel

He was asked to do his work quickly, quietly, and accurately.

In a series of prepositional phrases, it is acceptable to include the preposition only before the first object if all items in the series use the same preposition. If not, include the preposition before each object. See the examples below.

Incorrect

She placed air fresheners *in* the living room, the bedroom, the bathroom, and *under* the sink.

Correct

She placed air fresheners *in* the living room, *in* the bedroom, *in* the bathroom, and *under* the sink.

Clauses

Clauses in a series should be written in a parallel pattern. Do not change the form of one clause in the series or change the voice of the verb. In the first example below, the series has two clauses and an infinitive phrase. The second example has three parallel clauses.

Not parallel

The teacher told the students that they should read the chapter, they should answer the review questions, and to do some practice drills.

Parallel

The teacher told the students that they should read the chapter, answer the review questions, and do some practice drills.

In the first example below, two items in the series use active voice and one uses passive voice. The second example has three parallel clauses each using active voice.

Not parallel

We will review the report, read the recommendation, and a decision will be made.

Parallel

We will review the report, read the recommendation, and make a decision.

In a vertical list of numbered or bulleted items, use the same pattern for all items. For example, use all complete sentences or all single words or phrases.

Not parallel

For the camping trip you will need several items:

- towels
- swimsuits
- Bring hiking shoes.
- Sunscreen and insect-repellant spray are a must.
- birder's handbook
- A compass would be helpful.

Parallel

For the camping trip you will need several items:

- towels;
- swimsuits;
- hiking shoes;
- sunscreen;
- insect-repellant spray;
- birder's handbook; and
- compass.

Checkpoint

1. What is parallel structure?
2. How can you create a parallel structure of words or phrases?
3. How can you create a parallel structure of clauses?

Misused Words and Terms

Many words in the English language are often confused with other words or simply misused. These words may be homonyms or other words that people find confusing. Selecting the correct words helps writers and speakers convey messages that will be understood in the way they intend. Several homonyms and other words that are often confused or misused are discussed in this section. Many more exist. Consult a dictionary whenever you are not sure about the meaning or proper use of a word.

Homonyms

A **homonym** is a word that sounds the same as another word. However, the meaning and spelling are different from the other word. Several examples of homonyms and their meanings are shown in Figure 6-7.

TEAMWORK

While many confused or misused words are discussed in this chapter, many more are waiting to confuse the unwary writer. Work with a classmate to complete the steps below.

- Search the Internet and other sources to find five pairs of words or terms that are often confused or misused (other than ones listed in this chapter).
- Write the definition of each word.
- Write a sentence that uses each word correctly.
- Work with the other teams in your class to compile a list that includes the words and definitions found by each team.

Figure 6-7. Here are some homonyms along with examples of how they appear in sentences.

Words	Meaning	Example
aid	To help	I appreciate your aid in completing this project.
aide	An assistant	The senator's aide returned my call.
brake	A mechanism to slow a vehicle	Step on the brake when you want to stop.
break	To separate into pieces	Break the candy bar into four pieces.
complement	Something that completes or improves	This fruit sauce will complement the cake.
compliment	To praise or flatter	I must compliment you on your performance.
ensure	To guarantee	He will ensure that the job is done well.
insure	To buy an insurance policy	I will insure my new car.
fare	Fee	The fare to ride the ferry is $5.
	Get along	How did you fare in the contest?
fair	An exhibition like a carnival	We went to the county fair.
	Just or pleasing	The rules of the game are fair.
hear	To detect a sound	I hear a bird singing.
here	At this place	Sign your name here.
hole	An opening or tear	The dog dug a hole in the yard.
whole	Complete	She ate the whole cake.
know	To understand or be aware	I know how to solve this problem.
no	Negative or none	No, I refuse to go with you.
led	Guided or showed the way	She led the search party.
lead	A metallic element	The lead in my pencil is broken.
male	Gender	Three puppies are male and one is female.
mail	A letter or package	Collect your mail from the mailbox.
passed	To have gone by or beyond	I passed you on the road.
past	At a previous time	Different methods were used in the past.
there	At a particular place	Put the book there.
their	A plural pronoun showing ownership	Their dog ran away.
they're	A contraction for *they are*	They're upset about the accident.
to	Toward the direction of	The boys walked to the park.
too	Also	She wants an ice cream cone, too.
two	A number	Two birds flew over the lake.

Other Misused Words

Many other words are also misused or confused, even if they are not homonyms. Several examples of frequently misused words and their meanings are shown in Figure 6-8. Again, consult a dictionary when you are unsure of the meaning of a word.

Checkpoint

1. What is a homonym?
2. What should you do if you are uncertain of the meaning or correct usage of a word?

Figure 6-8. Here are some frequently misused words along with examples of how they appear in sentences.

Words	Meaning	Example
advice	Guidance or suggestion given	My advice is to leave it here.
advise	To give guidance or warn	I advise you to wait until tomorrow.
affect	To influence	Will this error affect my grade?
effect	A result or outcome	His speeches have a positive effect on the voters.
	To cause	Can the group effect a change in policy?
all together	Everyone or everything in one place	The students are all together at the school.
altogether	Completely, wholly	He was altogether convinced of her innocence.
concurrent	Happening at the same time	The concurrent meetings begin at noon.
consecutive	Following one after the other	The consecutive meetings will take all afternoon.
continual	Repeated quickly	The continual interruptions were annoying.
continuous	Without pause or interruption	The continuous noise of the engine kept me awake.
farther	At a more distant place	We will walk one mile farther today.
further	To a greater extent, more	He will evaluate the possible solution further.
less	Not as great (for something that cannot be counted)	He is less enthusiastic than she is.
fewer	Not as great (for things that can be counted)	She has fewer books than he does.
imply	To suggest indirectly	He implied that I was ignorant.
infer	To conclude or reason	I inferred from his tone that he was angry.
lie	To recline or rest	I will lie down for a nap after lunch.
lay	To put or place	Lay the watch on your dresser.
precede	To come before	The teacher will precede the students into the room.
proceed	To move forward, take action	I will proceed with the operation.
raise	To lift, grow, build, or increase	Please raise my salary.
rise	To get up	I will rise from my chair and take a walk.
set	To place or put	Set the pizza on the table.
sit	To be seated	Please sit in the front row.

Chapter 6 Review

Chapter Summary

Punctuation

- Punctuation consists of marks used to show the structure of sentences.
- Terminal punctuation signals the end of a sentence.
- Terminal punctuation includes periods, question marks, and exclamation points.
- Internal punctuation separates a sentence into phrases and clauses.
- Internal punctuation includes commas, dashes, parentheses, semicolons, colons, apostrophes, hyphens, and quotation marks.

Capitalization

- Capitalization means writing a letter in uppercase instead of lowercase.
- Sentences begin with a capital letter, even if a number begins the sentence.
- The important words in a heading or title are usually capitalized.
- Proper nouns are capitalized.
- Some abbreviations are capitalized.

Number Expression

- Numbers may be expressed as figures or words.
- Numbers one through nine are spelled out, for 10 and greater use figures.

Parallel Structure

- To create parallel structure, express similar elements in similar ways.
- Using the same word or phrase form in a series of words or phrases creates parallel structure.
- Using one form of a clause or voice of a verb in a series creates parallel structure.

Misused Words and Terms

- Homonyms are two words that sound the same, but have different meanings.
- Consult a dictionary if you are unsure of the meaning or correct usage for a word.

Review Your Knowledge

1. How is terminal punctuation different from internal punctuation?
2. When is a dash used in a sentence?
3. What is the rule for using a semicolon?
4. Give two uses of an apostrophe and explain how each is used.
5. When is a hyphen used in a sentence?
6. What is a permanent compound? Give an example.
7. What is a proper noun?
8. What is the general rule for using numbers expressed as words and expressed as figures?
9. Explain the meaning of parallel structure and why is it important.
10. What is a homonym?

Apply Your Knowledge

1. Write the following sentences, revising each to correct errors in punctuation.
   A. How many records are in the filing cabinet.
   B. She said, The restaurant serves delicious cheeseburgers; spicy pasta; and decadent desserts."
   C. When the project is finished; send an invoice to our office.
   D. She yelled frantically, "Get out of the way."
   E. I will; indeed, practice playing the piano every day.
   F. This answer is not oh, I understand now.
   G. Use a pointed stick (a pencil works well, to reach into the corner.

    H. The womans' horse raced around the track, the jockey urged him on.

    I. The service begins at 10.45 a.m.

    J. His self assured smile was charming.

2. Write the following sentences, revising each to correct errors in capitalization.

    A. I have an appointment to discuss my taxes with ms. schiller from the irs on monday.

    B. The store clerk said, "this sweater is on sale."

    C. The nights are very cold in the north during january.

    D. eight cars were involved in an accident near chicago, il.

    E. His favorite book is *A guide to birds in north America*.

    F. I met mr. chen at the philadelphia museum of art to view paintings by italian artists.

    G. the History class begins at 9:30 A.M.

    H. The hit movie, *skating on thin ice*, will be shown on nbc.

    I. miriam samuels, md, performed the operation.

    J. eduardo works at the homeless shelter with sister elizabeth.

3. Write the following sentences, revising each to correct errors in number expression.

    A. Please purchase six soccer balls, 12 softballs, and five basketballs for use on the playground.

    B. For mowing this small lawn, I will pay you twenty-five dollars.

    C. Approximately 100 people attended the event.

    D. The company was sold for twenty million dollars.

    E. She was born on March twenty.

    F. The runner fell 5 feet from the finish line.

    G. Of the shoppers who were surveyed, only fifty percent liked the product.

    H. The bell rings to signal lunchtime at 12 p.m.

    I. 25 paintings are on display at the small gallery.

    J. She was awakened from a sound sleep at 5 o'clock this morning.

4. Write the following sentences, revising each to make the items in a series have parallel structure.

    A. To prepare for a presentation, you should study the material you will discuss, writing an outline, and practicing the delivery.

    B. The park provides a perfect place for hiking, to ride a bike, to play tennis, and having a picnic.

    C. When mixing the ingredients, proceed slowly, be careful, and use caution.

    D. He placed signs announcing the garage sale at the corner, the end of the street, the end of the driveway, and near the house.

    E. The students will gather in the gym, the teacher will announce the contest winners, and prizes will be awarded by the principal.

5. Write the following sentences, selecting the word that correctly completes each sentence.

    A. Can you (advise, advice) me on how to handle this issue?

    B. Let's plan to discuss this policy (farther, further) at our next meeting.

    C. The girls' basketball team has five (less, fewer) players than the boys' basketball team.

    D. How do you wish to (precede, proceed)?

    E. Did his comment (imply, infer) that I am at fault?

    F. Have you had this illness in the (passed, past)?

    G. The grocer will (ensure, insure) that the produce is fresh.

    H. Let me (know, no) when you arrive in our city.

I. He liked the food and (complemented, complimented) her on her cooking.

J. The suspect (led, lead) the police on a long, dangerous chase.

Practice
What You Have Learned

Access the *Fundamentals of Business Communication* Student Companion Web Site at www.g-wlearning.com/Communication. Download each data file for this chapter. Follow the instructions to complete a reading, writing, and grammar activity to practice what you have learned in this chapter.

Connections
Across the Curriculum

Social Studies. Use the Internet to research the origin of punctuation. Who first used punctuation? Write several paragraphs describing what you learned.

Math. Punctuation marks are used in writing, but they are also used in math formulas. Make a list of punctuation marks that you might use in math class.

Build
Your Business Portfolio

Your portfolio is a collection of items that will be an ongoing project throughout this class. This is a living project and will grow and change until you are ready to present your finished portfolio. At this stage, locate copies of certificates of accomplishment that show your talents. These certificates can be any documentation of your reliability, participation in organizations, or other recognition that a potential interviewer may look on as important.

1. Scan these documents for the ePortfolio. In your ePortfolio folder, create a subfolder named Achievements. Save each certificate in the subfolder with the file names Achievements01, Achievements02, etc.

2. Place the printed certificates in your container for your print portfolio.

Careers
Education and Training Careers and Communication

Do you have the ability to inspire and motivate others? Are you sensitive to the needs of others? If so, a career in education and training may be an option for you. This area includes teaching, training, professional support services, administration, and administrative support.

Good speaking, writing, listening and reading skills are crucial because these people direct others as well as counsel and educate. Give several examples of when a teacher or trainer would use basic communication skills.

Event Prep

Business Communication

The business communication competitive event consists of an objective test that covers multiple topics. Participants are usually allowed one hour to complete the event. Some of the topics that will be included on the test cover capitalization, punctuation, spelling, and grammar. Effective communicators work to perfect the mechanics of good writing. By participating in the business communication event, you will have an opportunity to showcase your writing skills.

To prepare for the objective business communication test, do the following.

1. Study the vocabulary words at the beginning of each chapter in this book. Make sure you understanding each definition. Practice spelling the vocabulary words.

2. Review the rules of punctuation and capitalization in this chapter.

3. Ask your instructor to give you practice tests from each chapter of this book. It is important that you are also familiar with answering multiple choice and T/F questions. Have someone time you as you take a practice test.

Unit 3
Writing for Successful Communication

In This Unit

Writing is required in business for many purposes and in diverse forms. Yet, there is one common aspect to all business writing: it is focused on a particular purpose to achieve a specific result. Think about it; business is all about action. So, more than any other form of writing, the primary function of business writing is to produce action—to get someone to buy, sell, agree, or respond in a desired way.

Unit 3 presents techniques for writing various types of communication for specific business purposes. The chapters in this unit help you develop the habit of following a process for preparing business documents and developing a writing style that is concise, effective, and professional. You will also learn how to design and format documents for readability and visual appeal, as well as how to write for specific business purposes, such as getting a job interview and landing a job. Completing this unit will help you meet college and career readiness (CCR) anchor standards for writing, as outlined by the **Common Core State Standards**.

7
Writing as a Process

Nothing you write, if you hope to be any good, will ever come out as you first hoped.
—Lillian Hellman, 20th century American playwright

How much planning goes into a business document? What should you achieve with the first draft? Why is it important to revise and proofread your work before it is seen by readers? The answer to these questions begins with this fact: good writing comes about when writers approach a writing task as a process.

Using a process to guide business writing, you are more likely to keep the message on track. Your written communication will be crisp and clear because you know what you want to accomplish, then plan, create, evaluate, and revise accordingly. You also take the time to check each revision for any mistakes. With practice, the writing process will become second nature as you produce business e-mail, letters, reports, presentations, and other types of communication.

Objectives

When you complete Chapter 7, you will be able to:

- **Explain** each step in the writing process, its proper sequence in the process, and how it is applied to develop written communication.
- **Describe** the steps in the prewriting stage used to prepare to write a message.
- **Apply** the steps in the writing stage as you create your message.
- **Use** proofreading techniques to perfect the final draft and produce error-free business writing.
- **Publish** the final message using appropriate formatting guidelines.

Terms

writing process
four C's of communication
prewriting stage
writing stage
post-writing stage
publishing stage
writer's block
primary readers
secondary readers
plagiarism
direct approach

indirect approach
outline
revising
editing
objectivity
proofreading
proofreaders' marks
published
formatting
layout
readability

Go Green

Did you know that the batteries in cell phones and iPods are composed of hazardous material that will harm the environment if they are disposed of in a landfill? Batteries should always be properly recycled by a reputable organization and never thrown in the regular trash. To be environmentally savvy and save money, consider using rechargeable batteries. Rechargeable batteries, like those in cell phones, can be used many times over and will save you trips to the store to purchase disposable batteries.

1. Take an inventory of your electronic equipment. How many batteries do you need in any given day to power your devices?

2. How much do you spend a year in disposable batteries? How often do you have to replace your rechargeable batteries?

3. How much could you save if you used rechargeable batteries in place of disposable batteries?

Writing Process

Rhetoric is the study of writing or speaking as a way of communicating information or persuading somebody. The **writing process** is a set of sequential stages for each writing task. The writing process includes prewriting, writing, post writing, and publishing, as shown in Figure 7-1. By going through these stages, you will learn to critique and revise your own writing to achieve a clear, concise, courteous, and correct communication. These standards, known as the **four C's of communication,** apply to all types of written communication.

Three tasks are completed in the **prewriting stage.**

- Think about the topic and purpose.

- Plan the content.

- Read or research as needed to gather information.

The tasks should be done in the order that works best for the writing assignment. For example, if you need to write a report, you might want to look at similar reports before planning yours. On the other hand, simpler communication, such as a letter, might require looking up some information to include after the content is planned.

Once the prewriting tasks are completed, you are ready to begin the writing stage. The **writing stage** includes creating rough drafts and getting ideas on "paper." After a first draft is completed, you will revise the content. Edit the sentences and language as many times as necessary until you are satisfied the document achieves its purpose.

In the **post-writing stage,** a final edit of the work is completed. During this stage, you may also have someone else review the draft and provide feedback. After the document has been revised for the final pass, proofread it to make sure the work is free from errors.

Reading Prep

Before reading this chapter, read the opening pages for this unit and review the chapter titles. These can help prepare you for the topics that will be presented in the unit. What does this tell you about what you will be learning?

Next is the **publishing stage.** It is time now to print your work on good-quality paper or prepare it for electronic submission. The message is now ready to publish or send to the reader.

You probably already use the writing process, whether or not consciously thinking about it. Taking the time to break down the stages of the process and analyze how you approach each one will help you become a better and more efficient writer. The writing process relieves the stress of writing because it turns each task into a series of manageable activities. Writing begins with the knowledge that you will be your own first critic. It is polished until you are ready to publish or share the work with a reviewer. Putting this process into action helps lead down the path to a satisfactory finished product.

As you read about the writing process, consider that this process is also useful when preparing presentations. Planning and researching are useful in preparing to discuss a topic and are critical when you are preparing a formal presentation.

Checkpoint

1. What are the four stages of the writing process?
2. List the three tasks in the prewriting stage.

Prewriting Stage

Before you write, there is some homework to do. The extent of this homework varies, depending on the importance and complexity of the topic. If you put in the time at the beginning to completely explore the topic, you are less likely to backtrack. Approaching a blank piece of paper without a plan can be very intimidating and often causes writer's block. **Writer's block** is a psychological condition that prevents a writer from proceeding with the writing process. The writer feels unable to begin the writing task. Certainly, it is easier to write when you have a good grasp of the purpose and all of the relevant information at your fingertips.

Plan for the prewriting by completing the checklist in Figure 7-2. With this information determined, you can go about the *how* of the prewriting stage. Gather your information, research ideas, organize your thoughts, and choose

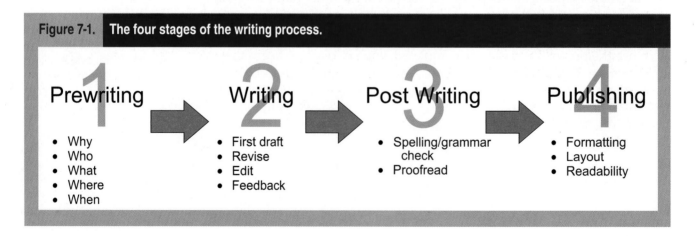

Figure 7-1.   The four stages of the writing process.

Figure 7-2.	Use this checklist in the prewriting stage.

Prewriting Checklist

This checklist summarizes the steps for successful prewriting. Use it as a guide each time you begin the prewriting stage of the writing process.

- ❑ Decide *why* you are writing (the purpose of the document).
- ❑ Identify *who* the audience will be.
- ❑ Determine *what* ideas you want to communicate.
- ❑ Research *where* can you find the information you need.
- ❑ Know *when* the document needs to be finished.
- ❑ Decide *how* the information should be organized and the best approach to use.

a medium. The medium may be a note, chart, brochure, memo, letter, report, or other form. The illustration in Figure 7-3 shows the checklist applied to a writing task.

Why You are Writing

When you write, there is a specific purpose or reason for doing so. The purpose will usually fall into one of these broad categories:

- pass on information
- respond to questions and requests
- make a request
- direct others
- persuade

For example, if you are writing to a coworker who will help complete projects in your absence, the general purpose is to direct. The specific purpose is to provide a list of the projects that must be completed and details about what needs to be done on each one. Identifying both the general and the specific purposes for writing will help you to write appropriately.

Good business writing has a clearly defined purpose for the intended audience.

Shutterstock

Figure 7-3. The prewriting checklist was used to develop this information.

Answering the Prewriting Questions

Al Ferris, a recruiter in Human Resources, has a writing assignment. To plan his message, he completed the checklist in the prewriting stage. This is the information he developed based on the checklist.

Purpose: To pass on information about the status of our search for a new research department administrative assistant. Want HR manager to see we are moving forward and approve our activities.

Audience: Colette DeNanares, HR manager.

Content: What has been done to date; plans for continuing search.

Sources: Talk to coworkers in HR to confirm activities related to search. How many applicants do we have? How many interviews have been conducted? Which advertisements are yielding the best candidates?

Deadline: Tomorrow (2/7) noon.

Organization: Description of current activities; approach to continuing the search; estimated time frame for identifying five final candidates for research managers to interview.

Who Your Audience Is

Written business communication may have one or more primary readers. **Primary readers** are those directly involved in the purpose for writing. These readers are the ones who will act on the content of the message. After reading the written document, primary readers should be satisfied that you considered their points of view and addressed their concerns.

Often, there are also secondary readers. **Secondary readers** are those who need to know the communication took place. These readers receive copies of the document and, typically, do not have to do anything other than read the information.

How do you determine the point of view for a reader? In business, you often personally know the readers. You can anticipate their reactions because you know the background knowledge they have about the topic. If you do not personally know the readers, you should still have some general knowledge about them. For example, if you are communicating with someone who has a scientific background, this person will probably be responsive to facts and figures. An individual in public relations may be concerned with how a business activity is perceived by others and may judge the communication from this perspective. Use these insights to guide your writing.

The audience should also be considered. Is the communication internal or external to the organization? Are you writing to a superior, subordinate, or peer? Your answers to these questions will influence the format and tone of your document.

What You Want the Reader to Think and Do

Asking what ideas you want to communicate helps focus on the essence of the message. What message do you want the reader to take from the communication? Ideas can be general. For example, the message may be, "we are very interested in supporting your organization at the upcoming convention." The message can also be specific, such as, "we would like to host a barbecue on the beach on the evening of your choice." The list of ideas helps you identify where specific data are needed to support the purpose. As you read and research to find the information, new ideas may surface. Always consider the proper scope of the content for the message. Keeping ideas focused on the main purpose is an important aspect of this stage of the writing process.

When you want the reader to do something in response to the message, be specific about the expectations. Clearly state what actions you are requesting in a polite, firm tone. In some cases, the message itself clarifies for the reader the reasons for the requested action. In other instances, you might also need to explain the benefits of taking the action or the reasons for a request. For example, suppose you are writing to inform fellow employees of a company blood donation drive. One purpose of the communication is to tell them where and when the event will take place. However, another purpose is get them to volunteer. By volunteering, employees will be helping others and ensuring that blood is available for themselves and their families if ever in need. In this case, mentioning the benefits of participating is as important as requesting the specific action.

It is important to remember to communicate in a clear, concise, courteous, and correct manner (the four C's of communication). The style in which you write reflects not only your personality, but also your company. Communication that contains typographical errors or poor language usage negatively

It is important in business writing that the reader receives the intended message.

Shutterstock

reflects both on you and on your company. Using abbreviations and spelling common to text messaging is *not* acceptable in most business organizations. In the final stage of the writing process, you will make sure usage, grammar, and spelling are correct.

CASE

Difficult Decision

Calvin Smith works in the graphics department of a marketing firm. He wanted to propose a new brochure for a client's large chain of fitness centers. He thought a large brochure with colorful photos featuring the luxurious spa, pool, and snack bar, as well as the gym and classes, would attract new customers for the client. Earlier, he conducted market research, which supported his idea that users of fitness centers are looking for more than just a place for a sweaty workout. Users want a place offering the opportunity for social and professional networking and to relax with friends as well.

Although Calvin believed that the target market would respond if the company changed its promotion to the new, more expensive format, he needed to convince his manager and the client that the new brochure was a good idea. His manager had a goal of winning an award for the company at the next marketing awards ceremony. The client was working with tightening the budget. Calvin had two e-mails to write: one to his boss and one to the client, the marketing director for WorkOUT Gyms.

Before writing, Calvin jotted down the features of the new brochure and the marketing data he had accumulated. He also did a cost comparison between the brochure he is proposing and the one the client had requested. Next, he organized the ideas in the order he thought would be best. As he did this, Calvin realized both documents share the same purpose. First, he had to convince the reader that the new brochure design was worth the added expense because it would achieve the goal of attracting new clients. Secondly, the brochure would be a part of an award-winning campaign that would give both companies publicity. Calvin completed the draft and revised, edited, and proofread the copy. He then attached samples of the old brochure and a rough layout of his new idea. He felt satisfied both readers had adequate information to judge for themselves the merit of his idea.

1. Do you think writing one proposal was a wise decision? Why or why not?

2. If Calvin had written two separate proposals, how might they have been different? Would the same information be necessary for each? Explain your answers.

Where You Can Find the Needed Information

The topic dictates where you must look for source material. For example, if writing about a competitive product, you may need to obtain brochures and other literature from the manufacturer. Other sources of information may include colleagues, existing correspondence and reports, databases, searches on the Internet, and print or online newspapers and trade journals. Be prepared to track down what you need in a timely manner so that you can write a message with substance, while meeting the deadline.

As you gather information, always check the facts to be sure the data are accurate. Are names, dates, prices, and statements accurate? If you have a question about any information, be sure to verify the facts. Review the findings to distinguish fact from opinion. Determine if your idea agrees with company policies and procedures. Locate any explanatory material that should be attached.

Always properly credit any information used from any source. As soon as information is in tangible form, it is protected by copyright laws. Using someone else's information and calling it your own is called **plagiarism.** It is both illegal and unethical. If you have any questions on the proper procedure for referencing a source, consult an appropriate style guide, such as *The Chicago Manual of Style*, Modern Language Association *MLA Handbook,* American Psychological Association (APA) publication manual, or other accepted style manual.

When You Need the Document Finished

In business, deadlines are an important consideration. A letter that is poorly timed may not accomplish what you thought it would. A late proposal, no matter how brilliant, is essentially worthless. Establishing priorities and managing your time to accommodate all stages of the writing process help meet deadlines.

Use deadlines to help determine what you can accomplish given the specific circumstances. If you need to respond to a message in several hours, you obviously do not have time to complete extensive research. On the other hand, if you have a month to assemble a report, you can thoroughly study the topic.

In business, good writing is critical. It is very important to plan the extra time good writing requires. If you are not given a specific deadline, set one for yourself.

Gathering information takes time and patience. Sometimes, long hours are needed to meet a deadline.

Shutterstock

How the Information Should Be Organized

Once you have the needed information, determine the approach of the document as well as the order of information within the document. Determining the order of information requires planning which piece of information comes first and the order of the remaining details. The "approach" of the document is how the information is presented, diving into the topic or subtly providing it to the reader. Most houses have a front door and a back door. This provides a good analogy for the two ways in which you can approach a topic. You can either come in through the front door by using a direct approach or the back door by using an indirect approach.

Direct Approach

With the **direct approach,** the topic is followed by descriptive details. The direct approach is desirable for most written communication, particularly when the reader is expecting a straightforward message. To use a direct approach, organize and present the information in the clearest and most logical way, beginning with a statement of the main idea and moving on to support it. Note in the following three examples how the individuals use the direct approach to organize information.

To train new customer service representatives and teach them the steps in assisting a client, Joe Fernandez organizes a training manual in step-by-step sequence. The manual lists each possible problem a customer might encounter and the questions to ask. The manual also has the suggested responses from start to finish, beginning with answering the call (step 1) and ending with asking the customer if there is anything else he or she needs assistance with today (step 12).

Ikumi Wantanabe writes a proposal of her one-year plan for increasing sales. She decides to organize her materials chronologically. This shows how the plan will unfold month by month.

Alexandra Ford prepares a report summarizing staff changes and key events in her company's branch offices. She organizes the information alphabetically by city—first Albuquerque, then Atlanta, followed by Birmingham, and so on.

In each of the three examples above, the main idea is presented first. Then, the supporting information is presented.

Business reports are an example of written communication. Writing should be organized in a logical manner.

Shutterstock

Indirect Approach

With the **indirect approach,** details come before the main idea of the paragraph. The indirect approach can work well when the message is harsh or the writer needs to prepare the reader for bad news. Examples of negative information include informing the reader a service cannot be provided, an idea cannot be implemented, or a deadline cannot be extended. Also use the indirect approach when you need to persuade the reader with a request such as to extend a deadline, accept less money, or change a decision.

With an indirect approach, begin with information that prepares the reader to respond in the way you want them to respond. The next three situations call for an indirect approach. Note how information is presented.

Cameron Smith has to tell her production team that everyone must work overtime for the next two months. She decides to begin the message to the team by emphasizing the benefits everyone will realize from the overtime: bonus pay and higher profit sharing. Then she goes on to detail the long hours it will take to meet a difficult production deadline.

To announce the new employee safety program in the company newsletter, Chris DeLorenzo begins his article by citing the current accident rate. Then he explains how the new program has been developed to curb the frequency of accidents and to conform to federal regulations. At the end, Chris lists each new safety procedure, mentioning first those that offer the most protection to workers.

> **TEAMWORK**
>
>
>
> Working with your team, read the following situation and complete the exercise. As the team agrees on the items requested, make a list on a flip chart, dry-erase board, or paper.
>
> You have been promoted and must move from Denver, Colorado, to Toledo, Ohio. Your company's human resources department has given you a relocation plan that includes the names and addresses of real estate agents in the Toledo area. You decide to contact one of these agents to help you in your house hunting.
>
> A. Define the purpose and audience.
>
> B. Brainstorm a list of all information that must be included in the letter. Ask yourself what will help a realtor select the best places for you to view.
>
> C. Organize the list into an outline.

To more efficiently handle customer accounts, Dave Feinberg has ordered a sophisticated new software program for use by the office staff. To learn the program, the staff must attend training seminars held on four consecutive Saturdays. To get the staff excited about the program and willing to forfeit several weekends for the training, Dave starts his message by emphasizing the time-saving features of the software. After he has convinced the staff that the program will benefit them, he explains the training schedule.

In each of the three examples above, the main message is considered bad or negative. For example, employees having to follow the new safety procedures is deemed to be the negative message. Since the main message is negative, it is presented last after the benefits are presented.

CASE

Positively Put

Carla Cohen wanted to persuade the executive committee of a telemarketing firm to expand its staff, a cost of an unbudgeted $125,000. The committee chair agreed to review her written proposal. Carla knew the chair and the committee would not be excited about spending more money. Her proposal had to be very convincing.

Carla sat down to prepare her proposal. She listed statistics and background data that supported her stand. Once she had identified the information to include, Carla began her document:

> This proposal will convince you we need to hire three additional telemarketing representatives as soon as possible. The cost to our organization will be about $125,000 annually. However, once you consider our needs and weigh the benefits, there will be no doubt this action is desirable.

1. What approach did Carla choose to take for her proposal?

2. Do you think it was likely to work? Why or why not?

3. What would you have done if you were in her place?

Developing an Outline

The purpose of an **outline** is to help identify the information you want to present and the proper sequence and to ensure related ideas are covered in the same section. Not every writing task requires a formal outline. However, any communication that is not strictly routine can be improved by taking the time to jot down the two or three points you want to make.

For complex communication, such as reports and presentations, a formal outline helps organize and clarify the relationship between ideas and sections of content. Start by selecting the key points—the information that will help you achieve the purpose for writing. Under each key point, list its supporting points and any necessary details under those. Then, consider the approach and the order in which you want to present the information.

One way to produce an outline is to make a numbered list of the main points. Initially, record the items in the order in which you think of them. Then, move the items around until they reflect the order in which you will present the information, as shown in Figure 7-4. Remember, the outline is a tool, a temporary list that allows you to organize the document, find the direction, and start writing.

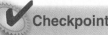

Checkpoint

1. What are the five categories of reasons for writing?
2. List the two types of readers for a message.
3. What is plagiarism?
4. List the two types of approaches that can be used for writing.
5. Describe the purpose of an outline.

Figure 7-4. **A formal outline for the information shown in Figure 7-3.**

Outline:
Status of Search for New Human Resources Administrative Assistant

I. Position is still open
   - A. No new hire to date
   - B. Five candidates interviewed, but none met criteria
   - C. No further response from advertisement

II. HR staff has stayed on top of the situation
   - A. Contacting search firms for referrals
   - B. Evaluating wage/compensation package
   - C. Contracting with a temporary agency

III. HR staff has a plan for filling the position
   - A. Continue an aggressive search
   - B. Evaluate job description—is the job bigger than its title?

Writing Stage

With notes or outline in hand, you are ready to write. You know the purpose of the message and the action desired from the reader. You have the facts that support each idea and know the order in which the information will be presented. The goal of the writing stage is simple: get your ideas on paper in sentence form. Following the writing checklist in Figure 7-5 will help guide you through the process.

Creating the First Draft

To begin the writing stage, start by creating a first draft. Since the reader will not see the first draft, it does not matter where you begin. You can begin at the top of the outline and work to the bottom. Or, you may decide to start somewhere in between. In many cases, opening and closing paragraphs are easier to write once the main sections of the content are drafted.

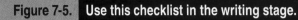

Figure 7-5.   **Use this checklist in the writing stage.**

Writing Checklist

This checklist summarizes the steps for successful writing. Use this as a guide each time you begin the writing stage of the overall writing process.

❑   Create the first draft of the document.

❑   Improve the message by revising the first draft.

❑   Edit the draft for correct grammar, mechanics, spelling, and word usage.

❑   Solicit feedback from others to help perfect the final document.

Resist the urge to revise as you write. Plan to revise after the whole draft is completed. Knowing that you will revise as many times as needed to get a final draft allows you to move quickly.

As you write, do not worry too much about the organization of the material. Move things around if the flow is out of order, but organizational problems can often be more clearly seen when you read the whole document. Include more information, rather than less. It is usually easier and quicker to delete content than to backtrack to determine how to add missing content.

While writing the first draft, do not worry about format precision. If writing a letter or a report with headings, for example, where heads are placed and spacing can be left for the revision stage. Also, how sentences sound is not important in the first draft. Do not stop to wonder whether a certain sentence could be improved, a word changed, or if some grammatical aspect of the sentence is correct. There will be time to evaluate and polish in the revision stage. Just maintain your train of thought and get all information down on "paper." The more you get sidetracked making revisions while writing the first draft, the longer it will take to get all of the information on paper and the harder it is to get back on track after each pause.

By just writing without stopping to make decisions about effectiveness, you can quickly complete a first draft of a short document. A first draft based on the outline in Figure 7-5 is shown in Figure 7-6. This first draft needs revising and proofreading, but the writer has successfully put all of the ideas of the outline in sentence form.

Revising

Once you have all of your ideas in draft form, the next step is to improve the quality of the message by revising. **Revising** means rewriting paragraphs and sentences to improve organization and content. It also involves checking the structure of the document as a whole.

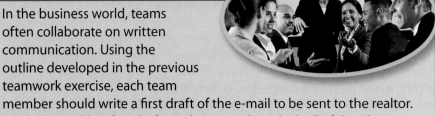

TEAMWORK

In the business world, teams often collaborate on written communication. Using the outline developed in the previous teamwork exercise, each team member should write a first draft of the e-mail to be sent to the realtor. See how quickly a first draft can be created in which all of the ideas are expressed in sentence form.

Figure 7-6. Here, the revised document is shown in Microsoft® Word. Word's track changes feature has been used to keep track of alterations.

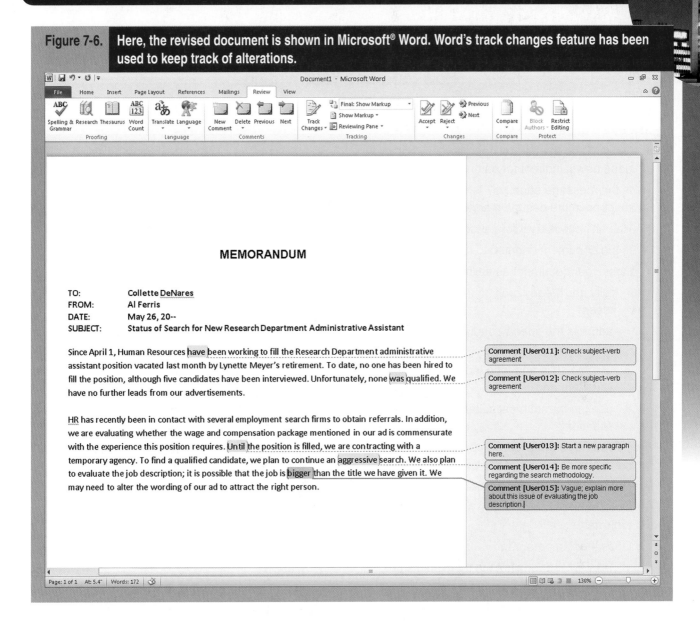

Start the revision step by considering aspects that affect the whole piece: content, organization, and formatting. Once those aspects are sound, work from the next-largest units to the smallest units—from paragraphs to sentences, words, and, finally, punctuation. After all, it makes no sense to struggle finding just the right word for a sentence when you might later remove the entire paragraph. You will learn more about style at the sentence and word levels in Chapter 8.

Careful revision leads to good writing. Learn to ask questions about the first draft. Honestly answer those questions from the reader's point of view. Make changes whenever needed. Figure 7-7 shows how each line of questioning can help refine your writing.

In some cases, you might need to go through several revisions of the first draft before achieving an acceptable final draft. In such cases, you can see how questions at each level—whole document, paragraph, sentence, and word—help identify ways to improve the message.

Figure 7-7.   These questions can help refine the document.

How to Refine Your Writing

Once you have a first draft of the document, ask these questions.

- Did you use the correct approach? Direct for good news; indirect for bad news.
- Is the message effective? Is the reader likely to respond in the desired manner?
- Has all necessary information been included?
- Is the document oriented to the reader?
- Does your document as a whole:
  - fully and clearly present the information and ideas;
  - address the specific audience being addressed;
  - use the style and tone most suitable for the situation; and
  - use the format most suitable for the situation?

Once you have considered your document as a whole, consider each of the paragraphs.

- Do paragraphs flow logically?
- Does each paragraph have a clearly identified topic sentence?
- Does the first paragraph:
  - tell your reader what the main points are going to be; and
  - focus on the reader's point of view?
- Does the concluding paragraph:
  - briefly reinforce the main point; and
  - leave the reader with a clear view of how to react or respond?
- Does each of the middle paragraphs:
  - have a clear organizational structure so the reader can easily follow the ideas;
  - include only information that supports the main points;
  - include only information that causes the reader to respond in the desired way;
  - consider and respond to possible objections the reader might make to the main points; and
  - clearly relate to the paragraphs before and after it?

Once you are satisfied with each paragraph, consider each sentence.

- Do sentences flow logically?
- Have you eliminated needless repetitions?
- Does each sentence:
  - clearly and completely state its point;
  - support the main idea;
  - work with the sentence before and after it to form a smooth, easy-to-read paragraph;
  - contain strong nouns and verbs when possible instead of too many modifiers;
  - contain modifiers placed next to the words they modify;
  - express agreement between sentence parts, such as subjects and verbs;
  - express ideas in parallel construction;
  - avoid unnecessary words and phrases; and
  - have a style and tone consistent with the rest of the document?

Once you are satisfied with each sentence, consider the words.

- Is each word the best choice, considering the:
  - reader's knowledge of the topic;
  - situation's level of formality;
  - level of specificity you are trying to achieve;
  - tone you are trying to achieve; and
  - emotional impact you are trying to make or trying to avoid?

Editing

Editing is a more-refined form of revising. It is focused on sentence construction, wording, and clarity of ideas. Where revising focuses on constructing the content, editing is polishing the document until it is in finished form.

For example, in a document with headings, the wording of each head must be checked to ensure it adequately reflects the content within the section. Heads also need to be checked for consistency and adherence to style. Sentences must also be edited and checked for correct grammar, mechanics, spelling, and word usage.

Editing for correct grammar and usage demands that you have a good command of the English language. If your skills are lacking in this area, take time to review the rules of grammar. Consult a reference manual to ensure that grammar and usage are correct. For word usage, variety, and clarity, keep a dictionary and thesaurus on hand. Printed or online versions can be used, depending on personal preference.

One way to help read your own writing from the reader's point of view is to distance yourself as much as possible from it. After the first draft is done, perhaps along with some revisions, take a break from writing. Go to lunch, go to a meeting, or do some other work and let the draft sit overnight. Better still, let it sit over the weekend. The longer you stay away from the draft, the newer it will seem when you finally look at it again. Taking a break from the writing allows you to consider it with a little more **objectivity**— free of personal feelings, prejudices, or interpretations.

Feedback

As part of the writing stage, during revisions, you might have someone review the document. It is always helpful to have a reviewer who understands the reader's point of view. A friend or coworker can read a letter, for example, to help judge whether or not it will have the intended impact on the reader. In business, it is common for important documents to be reviewed by several people, even by a committee, before distribution. This suggests that business people know the importance and impact of good writing, as well as the cost of poor writing.

Attention to detail is important in writing. A document may be revised several times before it is edited and then published.

Shutterstock

When individuals are willing to review your writing, help them provide the feedback you need. Make sure they understand the situation for which the document is written or the problem it is intended to solve. Also, do not hesitate to direct the review by asking questions. For example, ask, "what do you think of the tone of this memo?" or, "are you able to follow my directions in the third paragraph?"

Finally, be a good listener. When a reviewer suggests a change, many writers feel offended and immediately leap to defend what was written. This is unproductive. If a reviewer suggests a change or has difficulty with something, try to understand why. Ask questions to help solve the problem. It is even okay to ask for revision suggestions. In short, recognize that the reviewer is providing a critique of the writing, not criticizing the writer. Being defensive will make it difficult to convince people to review your work.

Checkpoint

1. What is the first step in the writing stage?
2. Describe the difference between revising and editing.
3. Why is it important to obtain feedback on what you have written?

Post-Writing Stage

Your written work will often be judged by its correctness and appearance. Errors distract from the message and suggest you were careless in preparing the communication. For this reason, proofreading is an important last step in the post-writing stage.

Proofreading is the process of checking the final copy for correct spelling, punctuation, and formatting and for typographical errors. The first step in proofreading is to use your software's grammar and spelling checker. However, this does *not* relieve you of the task of proofreading. Depending on the software, it may not pick up errors that occur when you key the wrong word, but spell it correctly. For example, when *you* is keyed instead of *your* or *is* instead of *as*, the software may not catch these errors because the incorrect words are spelled correctly.

Use the following guidelines for proofreading. Not every point will need to be used on every writing task. Your judgment will indicate how much attention is needed.

- Proofread for content by slowly reading the copy, concentrating on the accuracy of the message.
- First use the grammar/spelling checker, then proofread on the computer screen.
- Print a copy and proofread it again; mark errors on the printout.
- Read the copy aloud.
- Enlist a coworker to be a proofreading partner. Read aloud from the printed copy while your partner checks against the final document on screen. It is easier to catch subtle mistakes with another set of eyes.

Try to put some time between the tasks of revising/proofreading and making final changes. Again, you will be more objective if you have allowed some time to elapse between readings of the document. As you proofread, be on the lookout for these types of mistakes:

- incorrect word usage that changes the meaning of the sentence

  ❏ The courts have ruled that this type of business activity is <u>now legal</u>.

  The intended meaning: The activity is not legal. Change *now* to *not* or *legal* to *illegal*.

- errors in names, titles, addresses, dates, numbers, amounts of money, time

  ❏ Project costs have exceeded the <u>$10,000.000</u> budget.

  The period in the number should be a comma if the number is ten million or the last zero should be deleted if the number is ten thousand.

- errors of transposition

  ❏ The meeting <u>be will</u> held next Friday.

- errors in fact or logic

  ❏ The company's fiscal year runs from <u>December through January</u>.

- errors or problems in formatting (see Chapter 9)

Figure 7-8 shows standard **proofreaders' marks** universally used by writers and editors to note errors and changes. It is a good idea to learn this standardized system and use it when proofreading printed material. The marks can be understood by anyone in the event someone else is reviewing or keying the changes. When marking the printout, use a red pen so the notations are easy to spot. If another reviewer has used red, select a different color.

The checklist in Figure 7-9 summarizes the revision and proofreading steps. Use this checklist as a guide each time you evaluate your work.

Checkpoint

1. Describe proofreading.
2. What are proofreaders' marks?

BUSINESS ETHICS

Computer Ethics

While you are at work or school, it is important to be respectful in your use of computer equipment. The computer is available for your use as a tool for research or to accomplish a task. It is unethical to use the computer, without permission, for personal means such as playing games, shopping, or other activities that are outside of your assignments. It is also unethical to access confidential information, download copyrighted material, or harass others. Unapproved use of computers may open up the computer network to viruses and other issues that may jeopardize the integrity of the network as well as have legal implications. Many organizations monitor users to make certain that the computer activity is ethical and legal. Users may also be required to sign an agreement that the computer will only be used for specific purposes. To learn more about ethical use of company or school computer equipment, talk to a network administrator at the school or a business to see what his or her experiences have been regarding unethical use of equipment by students or employees.

Figure 7-8.   Standard proofreaders' marks should be used when editing a document in printed form.

Proofreaders' Mark	Original	Revised
Insert space	Letter tothe	letter to the
Delete	the commands is	the command is
Lowercase	he is Branch Manager	he is branch manager
Capitalize	Margaret simpson	Margaret Simpson
New paragraph	The new product	The new product
No paragraph/run in	the meeting. Bring the	the meeting. Bring the
Insert	pens, clips	pens, and clips
Insert period	A global search	A global search.
Move right	With the papers	With the papers
Move left	Access the data	Access the data
Center	Chapter 6	Chapter 6
Transpose	is it reasonable	it is reasonable
Spell out	475 Mill Ave	475 Mill Avenue
Stet—do not delete	I am very pleased	I am very pleased
Close up	Regret fully	Regretfully
Boldface	Boldface type	**Boldface** type
Italics	Use italics for emphasis	Use *italics* for emphasis

Publishing Stage

The final stage in the writing process is publishing. When a document is **published,** it is sent or made available to the receiver. If you are writing a letter, the letter is made available to the receiver by mailing it to that person. A report may be posted to a Web site or printed and distributed to the appropriate parties. A marketing piece may be printed and mailed to customers. There are many forms a message can take depending on the message being conveyed.

Figure 7-9. Use this checklist in the post-writing stage.

Proofreading Checklist

This checklist summarizes the revision and proofreading steps. Use it as a guide each time you evaluate your work.

- ❏ Are all sentences complete?
- ❏ Do subjects and verbs agree?
- ❏ Is the verb tense consistent?
- ❏ Are terms defined where necessary?
- ❏ Have you eliminated jargon, clichés, and pompous words?
- ❏ Have you verified dates, amounts, numbers, and other data?
- ❏ Is punctuation correct?
- ❏ Is spelling of proper names correct?
- ❏ Have you eliminated all errors in spelling and word usage?
- ❏ Are any words left out or unnecessary words left in?
- ❏ Does formatting enhance readability?
- ❏ Does formatting conform to business standards appropriate for the document?

Once the message is finalized, it is necessary to format the document for publishing. **Formatting** is the placement and style of the type on the page. Formatting is important because it is how the message is presented to the reader. Considerations in formatting include the typeface (font), font size, and the layout. **Layout** is the relationship of the text to white space. A good layout is essential to readability. **Readability** is a measure of whether or not the document is easy to read.

Typical business documents that require formatting include letters, memos, reports, and proposals. E-mail may also need formatting. For example, you may decide for an e-mail that a numbered or bulleted list, boldface, or underlining is needed to show emphasis.

When sending formal business documents, it is imperative that standard formatting guidelines are followed. These guidelines are covered in detail in Chapter 9. The memo shown in Figure 7-10 is revised, formatted, and ready for publishing.

Checkpoint

1. What is formatting?
2. Define readability.

Figure 7-10.   **The final document based on the information shown in Figures 7-3 and 7-4.**

MEMORANDUM

TO: **Collette DeNares**
FROM: **Al Ferris**
DATE: **May 26, 20--**
SUBJECT: **Status of Search for New Research Department Administrative Assistant**

Since April 1, Human Resources staff members have been working to fill the Research Department administrative assistant position vacated last month by Lynette Meyer's retirement. To date, no one has been hired to fill the position, although five candidates have been interviewed. Unfortunately, none of these candidates met the specific criteria for the job. We have no further leads from our advertisements.

HR has recently been in contact with several employment search firms to obtain referrals. In addition, we are evaluating whether the wage and compensation package mentioned in our ad is commensurate with the experience this position requires.

Until the position is filled, we are contracting with a temporary agency. To find a qualified candidate, we plan to continue an aggressive search. We also plan to evaluate the job description; it is possible that the job is bigger than the title we have given it. We may need to alter the wording of our ad to attract the right person.

Chapter 7 Review

Chapter Summary

Writing Process

- Good writing is achieved by following the four stages of the writing process: prewriting, writing, post writing, and publishing.

- The goal of the writing process is to produce a well-written document that effectively achieves your purpose.

- Following the four C's of communication—clear, concise, courteous, and correct—leads to a well-written document.

Prewriting Stage

- The prewriting stage involves thinking about, planning, and researching your goals in an orderly fashion.

- You need to determine why you are writing, who your audience is, what you want the reader to think and do, where you can find the needed information, when you need the document finished, and how the information should be organized.

- The purpose for writing usually falls into one of five broad categories.

- The audience is primary readers, but may include secondary readers.

- The essence of the message is what you want the reader to take from it.

- Information for the document can be obtained from various sources, but must not be plagiarized.

- The document must be completed by the given deadline.

- Information can be organized using a direct or indirect approach.

Writing Stage

- The initial task in the writing stage is to create a first draft.

- During the writing stage, you will revise and edit drafts of the document.

- The final draft of the document can be reviewed by peers or teachers who will provide feedback to help you perfect your work.

Post-Writing Stage

- The post-writing stage is where you proofread the document.

- Proofreading involves checking for grammar and spelling errors, as well as checking other mechanics of writing.

- It is good practice to use the spelling/grammar checking function in the word processing software to find errors in your work.

- You should complete a final proofread on screen or on a printout of the document.

- When proofreading a printout of the document, use proofreaders' marks so others can understand the revisions, if necessary.

Publishing Stage

- The publishing stage is where the completed document is sent or made available to the reader.

- Before sending the document to the reader, it must be properly formatted.

- Layout and readability are also important considerations before publishing the document.

 **Review**
Your Knowledge

1. What does it mean to publish a document?
2. An audience will be one of two types of readers. What are the types?
3. What is plagiarism?
4. When is the direct approach for writing generally used? When is the indirect approach for writing used?
5. Describe the outlining process.

6. Why is it a good idea to seek feedback on the final draft?

7. How should the process of revising be approached?

8. Describe the editing process and why it is important when creating a document.

9. Why should standard proofreaders' marks be used when editing a document?

10. What does it mean to format a document? Why is it important?

Apply
Your Knowledge

1. Using the writing process described in this chapter, produce the documents described below.

   A. Read an opinion piece in a newspaper or magazine. Write a letter to the editor supporting or disputing the editorial position.

   B. Write an opinion piece that expresses the opinions of you and your peers regarding a current event. Conduct an informal survey to obtain the opinions from your peers.

   C. Research current job opportunities and general qualifications in a career field that interests you. Write a one-page report about the job prospects for other students who might be thinking of entering this field. Include data from your research in the report.

2. Phillip Jenkins, public information director for a public utility, must write a press release regarding an accident at one of the utility's plants. Three men and one woman received minor injuries, were treated at the local hospital, and are in good condition. They will return to work in two days. The utility company for which Phillip works has been criticized in the past for allowing unsafe working conditions. However, these are the first injuries reported in many years. Consider what information Phillip needs to include in the press release in an effort to address the feelings of other plant workers and their families, company executives, the community, and the press. Outline Phillip's announcement following the steps of prewriting.

3. Using the outline created in #2, write a draft of the announcement applying the steps of writing. Which approach would you use to send this message to the readers; why?

4. On the draft created in #3, use appropriate proofreading and editing techniques to finalize the document.

5. How would you publish the announcement created in #2 through #4? Explain why.

Practice
What You Have Learned

Access the *Fundamentals of Business Communication* Student Companion Web Site at www.g-wlearning.com/Communication. Download each data file for this chapter. Follow the instructions to complete a reading, writing, and grammar activity to practice what you have learned in this chapter.

Connections
Across the Curriculum

Social Studies. Research the history of writing. What is some of the oldest evidence of writing? What did people write on and with? What other information can you find about the history of writing? Apply the writing process you learned in this chapter to write a report on your findings.

Math. Graphic organizers are helpful when preparing to write. Create a Venn diagram or other chart to show how you organized your information for the previous activity.

Build
Your Business Portfolio

Community service is an important quality that interviewers expect in a candidate. Serving the community shows that the candidate is well rounded and socially aware. In this activity, you will create a list of your contributions to community organizations. Remember that this is a living project, so you will continue to update this list until your portfolio is completed.

1. List the community service projects in which you have played a part. Give the organization, date, and activities that you performed. This is the time to showcase your contributions. Format the page so that it is attractive and free from errors.

2. Name the file as ComService and save in your ePortfolio folder.

3. Place a printed copy in your container for your print portfolio.

Careers
Law, Public Safety, Corrections, and
Security Careers and Communication

With strong interest in public safety and national security, careers in law, public safety, and corrections are increasingly in demand. Keeping citizens and the country safe is the core mission of careers in this cluster. Career pathways include working in corrections, emergency and fire management, security, and protection, law enforcement, and legal services.

Good communication skills are crucial for someone pursuing a career in this cluster. One important communication skill is the art of conveying information through reports. Explain the consequences for a person in this field of not being able to clearly convey information in an accurate and grammatically correct format.

Event Prep

Business Communication

The business communication competitive event consists of an objective test that covers multiple topics. Participants are usually allowed one hour to complete the event. Two topics that will be included are editing and proofreading. For this event, you will answer questions, rather than actually demonstrate your editing and proofreading skills.

To prepare for the objective business communication test, do the following.

1. Review the section Writing Stage in this chapter. This chapter provides direction on how to edit and revise a document.

2. Review the section Post-Writing Stage in this chapter. In this section, techniques for proofreading are discussed.

3. Study the proofreading checklist in this chapter. This will help you master the process and understand the techniques of proofreading.

4. Review the proofreaders' marks in this chapter. These proofreading marks are commonly used and you should feel comfortable if requested to proofread and mark corrections on a document.

5. Use the editing practices in the data files on the Companion Web site to help you prepare for the event.

6. Ask your instructor for additional practice exercises for proofreading.

8
Writing Style

A collection of good sentences resembles a string of pearls.
—Chinese proverb

This chapter teaches how to critically examine your writing in order to achieve a writing style that reflects the standards of today's business environment. In the past, the accepted tone and style for business writing was formal. Business writing tended to sound different from the way people talk and wordy phrases were the norm. For example, when sending materials, writers would start with, "Enclosed, please find the information you requested." Today, a writer is more likely to phrase it as, "The information you requested is enclosed."

Objectives

When you complete Chapter 8, you will be able to:

- **Define** the terms writing style and tone.
- **Select** appropriate words to convey a meaning while reflecting sensitivity to the audience.
- **Create** structured sentences to achieve variety and clarity in writing style.
- **Develop** paragraphs that convey ideas through appropriate logic, length, and use of transitions.

Terms

writing style	redundancy
Standard English	cliché
tone	industry language
bias-free words	active voice
euphemism	passive voice
condescending	transitions
context	direct approach
connotation	indirect approach

Go Green

The physical letter is still valued, but today much "written" communication is in the form of e-mail. By sending an e-mail, the message can still be communicated, but paper, ink, and other costs associated with mailing a physical letter are saved.

1. Estimate how much it would cost to send a one-page letter to a friend in another state. Take in consideration the cost of the paper, ink, postage, travel costs of going to the store to purchase supplies, and travel costs of going to the post office.

2. Do you think sending an e-mail rather than a letter is appropriate? Give examples of appropriate messages that could be in an e-mail and those messages that should be in a formal letter.

Writing Style and Tone

Writing style refers to the way in which a writer uses language to convey an idea. It reflects the numerous decisions the writer must make regarding word choice and construction of sentences and paragraphs.

In the world of business writing, Standard English is the norm. **Standard English** means that word choice, sentence structure, paragraphs, and the layout or format of communication follow standard, accepted conventions used by those who speak English. "Texting" language is *not* acceptable in business writing. Business writing must be clear and specific, as opposed to vague, pretentious, or possibly unfamiliar to the reader.

The style you use creates a **tone**—an impression of the overall content of the message. Is it friendly or hostile? Demanding or courteous? Sensitive or insensitive? Ask yourself or a reviewer if the writing has a style and tone that are both professional and friendly.

Judge your writing based on the four C's of communication. A clear, concise, courteous, and correct writing style that also shows respect and sensitivity will leave on the reader a positive impression of you and your company. That is the style to aim for in business writing.

Reading Prep

Before reading this chapter, review the highlighted terms and definitions to preview the new content. Building a business vocabulary is an important activity to broadening your understanding of new material.

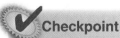

Checkpoint

1. What is a writing style?
2. Describe why "texting" language is not acceptable in business writing.

Choosing the Right Words

The world is diverse. Various groups—social, age, ethnic, and even work groups within various businesses and industries—have unique ways of communicating. Words and phrases can have different meanings in these diverse communities.

In business writing, it is important to carefully think about the words you use. This means being sensitive not only to the intended meaning, but also to the meaning the words might have in the mind of the receiver. There are word choices you can make that will increase the likelihood readers will respond in the desired way.

Precise Language

Some words are more precise than others in a given situation. When precise language is used, the readers will be better able to understand the message and respond in the desired way. For example, this phrase is vague:

"I would like to receive your feedback on this proposal *as soon as possible.*"

On the other hand, giving a specific date is clear and specific:

"I would like to receive your feedback on this proposal *no later than Friday, March 25.*"

This makes it more likely the information will be delivered when it is needed. Precise words also make writing more interesting to read, as shown in Figure 8-1. Notice how much easier it is to create a mental picture when precise words are used, as opposed to generalized or vague terms.

Always keep in mind, however, that writing style is not about formulas. Sometimes you will find it makes more sense to write in general terms before getting specific. For example, if you are writing to describe a new service offered by a spa franchise, it might be best to first describe it in general terms as *a new personal service* before specifically stating the service is a *Dead Sea Salt Scrub.*

Sensitive Language

When writing a business message, it is important to use language free of biases related to gender, age, race, culture, disabilities, or other groups. **Bias-free words** are neutral, imparting neither a positive nor negative message.

Figure 8-1   The more specific the word, the easier it is to create a mental image.

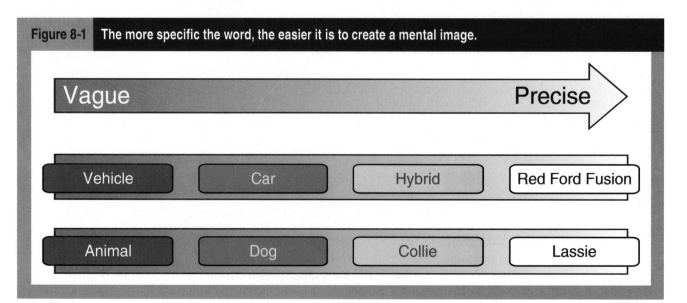

Gender, age, race, etc., cannot be inferred from a bias-free word. Using gender neutral words, such as *server* rather than *waiter or waitress,* focuses the reader on the job or the individual's qualifications instead of the gender of the individual. Rather than saying, "we hired a *young man* for the manager job," state, "we hired a *new manager."* When a disability must be referenced, use a specific term such as *hearing impaired* or *physically disabled.* Do not use outdated terms that are now considered offensive.

Some words may sound acceptable in conversation, but may come across as harsh in writing. For those words, you may need to find a euphemism. A **euphemism** is a word that expresses unpleasant ideas in more pleasant terms. For example, instead of saying, "this phone system is *cheaper,"* the preferred business language is *less expensive.* In another example, what is now commonly called the *customer service department* used to be commonly called the *customer complaint office.* This reflects a desire by the business to service a customer's needs. Some businesses even use the term *customer care* to communicate greater sensitivity to the customer's needs.

Use euphemisms when needed, but use them wisely. Some euphemisms go too far. For example, using *vertically challenged* instead of *short* to describe someone's height is transparent and sounds silly. However, you can say, "he is not very tall" without offending most people.

Another aspect of sensitivity is to avoid language that is condescending. To be **condescending** means to assume an air of superiority. Use words that the reader will understand, but not interpret to mean the writer feels superior in status to the reader. For example, giving an explanation that is too basic or oversimplified to make sure the reader understands may sound condescending to the reader. It is important to know the audience. It is important to estimate what level of knowledge the reader should have on the topic to avoid insulting the reader's intelligence.

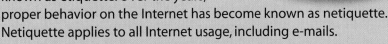

BUSINESS PROTOCOL

E-mail Netiquette

In everyday life and in business, there is a proper way to behave. This is known as etiquette. Over the years, proper behavior on the Internet has become known as netiquette. Netiquette applies to all Internet usage, including e-mails.

- Use a tone that is appropriate to your relationship and to the writing situation.
- Do not use emotion icons, or emoticons, in a business e-mail.
- Let the reader know if you are sending an attachment by mentioning it in the message.
- Do not send or forward personal messages, jokes, chain letters, or spam.
- Never use profanity or any other type of derogatory language.
- Never respond in anger to an e-mail. Wait until you are calm enough to respond in a professional manner.
- Avoid overuse of e-mail. Stop to think whether a phone call or personal visit would be more productive.
- Use the blind copy option for large external mailings to protect the privacy of each recipient.
- Do not use all caps in your message; this is considered shouting.

Personal Pronouns

Business writing style is now friendlier and more casual than in the past. One way you can achieve this tone is by making liberal use of personal pronouns. *I, me, my, you, your, he, she, it, we, they* are examples of personal pronouns. Personal pronouns come naturally in speech but sometimes writers adopt a style that avoids them. Writing that does not use personal pronouns may sound formal. Written messages will sound normal—personal, helpful, and friendly—when personal pronouns are used. Notice how the personal pronouns make the following message sound friendly and sincere:

Dear Mr. Stephenson:

I have enclosed the agreement we discussed last week for your services on the sales conference video. If the terms meet with your approval, please sign both copies of the agreement and return them to me for my signature. I will promptly return your copy so that we can begin our collaboration on the video.

All of us on the conference-planning committee look forward to working with you.

Sincerely,

Positive or Neutral Words

In business writing, it is easier to influence people and get results with words expressing a positive tone than with words expressing a negative tone. For example, it is always better to emphasize what you *can* do rather than what you *cannot* do. Notice how these two sentences create different feelings when you read them:

Negative
We cannot mail your package by overnight express mail.

Positive
You can choose to have the package sent by two-day air or three-day ground service.

Many words tend to automatically cause negative reactions. Similarly, there are words that generally have a positive effect on readers. The words italicized in the following sentences tend to create good feelings.

We hope you will be able to take *advantage* of this one-time offer.

Loyal customers like you *deserve* the very best.

It is our *pleasure* to offer you a free trial of this new product with no strings attached.

Of course, no business writer can make all messages sound positive. To maintain honesty and integrity, it is often impossible to avoid news and business decisions that a reader will not like to receive. Nevertheless, you can try to avoid negative language. When a message is likely to make the reader unhappy or concerned, search for neutral words to soften the reaction.

Use positive words to create a good impression of your work with the reader. Most readers look unfavorably on the use of negative language.

Shutterstock

Consider the words listed after this paragraph. Think about how a message using the words on the left will be received. The words on the right mean the same thing, but are neutral and, therefore, better accepted by the reader. Use a thesaurus or dictionary or consult a colleague when you need a neutral word or phrase to communicate a negative message.

Negative	Neutral/Positive
cannot	unable to
cheap	affordable/less expensive
defective	malfunctioning
fault	responsibility
misinformed	unaware
neglect	forget
regret	apologize
wrong	incorrect

In many cases, whole industries and professions have developed common language that presents bad news in a neutral way. The publishing business provides an example. Writers submit articles and manuscripts for publication and the dreaded "rejection letter" is legend in the publishing profession. Yet, you will never find any form of the word *reject* in a publisher's letter. A polite way to convey rejection is, "we must decline the opportunity to publish your work" or, "we find your work is not suitable for our publication." Similarly, companies very rarely tell applicants, "you are not qualified for the position." It would be honest, but might open the door to disputes and potential legal problems. The more sensitive and preferred way to communicate this message is to say, "we have selected another candidate who more closely suits our needs."

Shades of Meaning

Good writers look for fresh, clear words to describe and express ideas. They are also always aware that words should be handled with care. Words have an exact meaning or meanings according to the dictionary, but sometimes words convey even more meaning outside of their definition. A word's meaning can vary according to the context in which it is used. **Context** is the words or paragraphs surrounding a word that can explain the meaning.

In some cases, however, context is not enough. The real meaning of some words resides in the mind of the user or the listener, not in the word itself or in its dictionary definition. This is what is known as the **connotation** of a word— its meaning apart from what it explicitly names or describes. This is where the shades of meaning become a concern for the writer.

Be aware that many words have shades of meaning in different cultures and even different areas of the country.

Shutterstock

An example of connotation is the word *foreign*. In spite of its basic meaning of simply referring to something outside of one's own country, the word may have a negative connotation to some people. The word foreign can be associated with the idea of *other*, meaning *not one of us* or *not like us*. Thus, in the business world, you will find the word *international* is most often used in place of the word *foreign*.

With careful attention to shades of meaning among similar words, consider the audience's interpretation of a word's meaning when editing your writing. This will help you avoid the common problems of misunderstanding or misinterpretation in communication. For example, if you describe an office facility as *adequate for our needs*, one reader may interpret *adequate* as *sufficient*. Another reader may interpret *adequate* to mean *close to the lower limit of quality or acceptability*. Each of these readers has a different impression of the facility.

Consider the words *defective* and *broken*. Both are used to describe something that does not work properly. But, when a customer claims a product is defective and the manufacturer claims it is broken, the shades of meaning between the two words clash. After all, *defective* implies manufacturer responsibility, whereas *broken* implies user responsibility.

Use the dictionary, thesaurus, and your own experience to distinguish shades of meaning and choose the most appropriate words. If you are concerned that the message may be misunderstood, add context to explain the intended meaning. By doing this, there will be no confusion regarding the true meaning.

Achieving Four C's of Communication

When editing a written draft, look for places where you can make the writing clear, concise, courteous, and correct. Remember, these are the four C's of communication. Avoiding redundancies, clichés, and trendy words and using familiar words are ways to achieve the four C's of communication.

Avoid Redundancies

A **redundancy** is repeating a message or saying the same thing more than once. Two or more words may have the same meaning or two or more sentences may say essentially the same thing. This can confuse or irritate the reader. In the following example, a manager is asking a staff member to follow up on an issue after a meeting. After reading the draft, try to identify the redundancy. Then, look at the revision to see how the repetition has been eliminated. Also notice the changes add clarity, conciseness, and precision to the writing.

Draft

At Monday's status meeting, you mentioned there is a potential for cost overruns on the Jamison Park project. If you feel there could be cost overruns, I need an itemized list of what specific items are likely to incur additional costs so that we can discuss these with the team.

Would you please send me a summary listing areas of potential overruns and the reason that is causing each item to run over budget? I would like to have this before next Monday's status meeting so we can discuss the details with the team.

Revision

At Monday's status meeting, you mentioned potential cost overruns on the Jamison Park project. Please send me a summary listing the items that may run over budget and the cause of each overrun. I would like to have this by Friday so we can discuss the details with the team at next Monday's meeting.

Avoid Clichés

To make your writing concise, be on the lookout for clichés. **Clichés** are overused, commonplace, or trite phrases. Often, clichés are not well received by the reader because it seems the writer is not being original. However, a cliché might be appropriate in some situations as a shortcut. Being aware of your audience helps determine whether using such a shortcut is acceptable or if it will negatively affect the reader's attention and trust level.

Some examples of clichés from everyday speech are:

- easy as pie
- like finding a needle in a haystack
- it's not rocket science

There are also clichés that show up almost exclusively in business writing:

- Dear valued customer:
- Enclosed, please find…
- Per your request…
- We are hereby requesting…

Because clichés are, by definition, commonplace, they will not necessarily compel the reader to act. In fact, readers may not even understand a message with clichés since they are likely to skip over or block out clichés as they read. With a little imagination, it is possible to find new ways to express old ideas. Instead of the cliché, "We appreciate your business," you might consider ending a letter with the more personal remark, "As one of our best customers, you have helped Jetson Markets reach our sales goal for the year. Thank-you!"

Use Familiar Words

A businesslike tone and vocabulary may be used when writing for business communication. However, simple, everyday words, rather than long words, will help attract and hold the reader's attention. Long words look difficult to the reader and may actually be difficult to read. Long words and long sentences will make the reader wonder what you are trying to say. In contrast, short, familiar words have more force and clarity. This has to do with the readability of the sentences. Words of three syllables or more and long sentences generally count against readability scores.

As you edit drafts, make an effort to eliminate long or less familiar words. Read the sentences aloud to check whether or not the words will quickly and clearly convey the message. This is especially important if the message will be delivered to the public. In general, always aim to create a document that is easy to read and understand.

Long/Unfamiliar	Familiar
utilize	use
terminate	end
endeavor	try
demonstrate	show
ascertain	find out
query	ask
initiate	begin
procure	get
peruse	review/read
converse	talk

Some documents need to be written using **industry language,** or jargon, which is language usually specific to a line of work or area of expertise. Various professions and industries have specific words and phrases that are familiar to those who work in that field, but may not be understood by those outside of the field. For example, used-car dealers categorize vehicles according to condition and describe them as *mint* or *near-mint.* Similarly, stockbrokers talk about *bull* and *bear* markets. Retailers talk about *retail, wholesale,* and *markup/ markdown prices.* These are examples of industry language.

The challenge, however, is not to use jargon that will be unfamiliar to the reader. Think carefully, because unfamiliar words will distract readers. Jargon speeds up the communication process *only* if the reader shares your area of expertise. However, if readers are unfamiliar with the technical terms used, they will feel left out and may not understand the message. Even if your readers know the words, they may feel as though you are trying too hard to impress them with insider vocabulary.

TEAMWORK

List each of the following words and phrases on a dry-erase board or flip chart. As a team, work together to think of simpler words or phrases to replace the word on the list. Use a thesaurus if one is available.

A. Acquiesce

B. Aggregate

C. Ascertain

D. Commensurate with

E. Disseminate

F. Equitable

G. Preclude

H. Predisposed

I. Subsequent to

J. Verification

Watch Out for Trendy Words

Trendy words are acceptable if you work in a trendy business or industry. This is where knowing your audience comes in. Think before using trendy words like *awesome* or *tweet.* Be aware of whether or not trendy words are still current and if they are appropriate for the audience. Trends can very quickly disappear. Using an outdated trendy word makes your writing sound out of touch or not current.

Like jargon, using trendy words can make it look as though you are trying to impress the reader. There also is a chance that a reader will not be familiar with a trendy word or phrase. This can result in a communication breakdown.

Checkpoint

1. Why is it good to use precise language?

2. What are bias-free words?

3. List three ways to achieve the four C's of communication.

Be sure the words you choose are appropriate for your audience. Young, trendy businesspeople may understand trendy language, but in the future, will others?

Shutterstock

Structuring Clear and Concise Sentences

As a business writer, you must arrange words so sentences convey a meaningful unit of thought. Being aware of techniques for writing sentences helps improve your writing style. You can make your writing not only clearer, but also more interesting to read.

Balance Sentence Length

Short, simple sentences are more understandable than long, complex ones. However, too many short, simple sentences are boring and, in some cases, make the entire text hard to read. To judge the best length of a sentence, consider if the reader can immediately identify the main idea without having to wade through unnecessary words.

Aim to make sentences short enough to be clear, but avoid writing a series of short sentences that make the text sound choppy. Joining clauses and adding phrases will make sentences flow smoothly and add variety to your writing. These are the keys to achieving balance and keeping the reader's interest. Notice the difference in the following examples.

Draft
The company hopes the plant will open next spring. The plant will cover 200 acres. It will house 700 people. These employees are currently spread around the city in four different offices.

Revision
With much anticipation, the company plans to open the new plant next spring. The 200-acre campus will house 700 employees who are currently spread around the city in four different offices.

During the revising and editing stages of the writing process, read sentences aloud to gain a different perspective on the sentence structure. When you find several short sentences in succession, decide if combining some of them into slightly longer sentences will help the flow and clarity. When you lengthen sentences, always reread to make sure the writing is still crisp and clean. Learning to critically read your own writing takes practice. At first, it will take longer to reread and hear or see the flaws. However, as you continue to practice revising and editing, this discipline will help improve your writing.

Choose Active or Passive Voice

Verbs show the action in a sentence and either directly or indirectly tell the reader what the subject is doing or has done. You could say that verbs are the heart of the sentence. When a verb is in the **active voice,** the subject (the noun) is doing the action. In the **passive voice,** the subject receives the action.

> **Active voice**
> He explained the policy.
> The company approved the plan.
>
> **Passive voice**
> The policy was explained.
> The plan was approved.

The following sentences are written in active voice. The subject is shown in bold and the verb is underlined.

> The **company** hired her in 1989.
>
> **First Mutual, Inc.** offers financial planning services.
>
> The **union members** rejected the proposal for nonunion hiring.

All of these sentences are clear and concise. Each one precisely tells what action the subject took. Notice the lessening of the verb's impact when it is written in the passive voice:

> She was hired by the **company** in 1989.
>
> Financial planning services are offered by **First Mutual, Inc.**
>
> The proposal for nonunion hiring was rejected by the **union members.**

When you use the active voice in writing, the message comes across in a stronger tone. Active voice is best when you need to be direct and have no reason to soften the tone of a sentence. Therefore, to downplay the union's objection in the above example, the passive-voice version of the sentence would be the correct one to use.

Passive voice is perfectly acceptable in writing. However, it should be used with thought given to the purpose it serves. Here are some appropriate uses of the passive voice:

> **When the doer is unknown**
> The building was constructed in 1984.
> (Who constructed the building is unknown.)
>
> **When the doer is unimportant**
> Your order was shipped on Thursday.
> (The shipper is unimportant.)

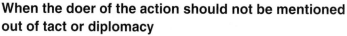
When the doer of the action should not be mentioned out of tact or diplomacy

An error was made in the computation of your taxes.
(The person who made the error is not identified.)

When the action is more important than the doer, as in formal reports

Forty charge-account customers were surveyed regarding their spending habits.
(The customers are more important than who conducted the survey.)

In these situations, passive voice is effective. In other situations, you will need to choose active voice. Keep in mind, active voice emphasizes immediacy and adds vitality to your writing.

Being concise is one of the four C's of communication. Some readers have limited time to read your communication, so they do not want to wade through extra words.

Shutterstock

Write Concise Sentences

Good business writing has *no* frills. When you write for business, it is your job to get the point across as concisely as possible. Every sentence and every word within the sentence should contribute to the overall message in a meaningful way. Businesspeople have a lot to do and want anything they read to quickly get to the point. The reader does not want to stop and think about what you are trying to communicate. Instead, the reader wants to immediately identify the issue so that a productive decision can be made.

Consider the following examples. Notice how frills in the first example detract from the message. On the other hand, the second example is stated in a more concise manner.

Draft

While I was away from my desk for a few short moments today, your package arrived from a messenger service. It was shortly before lunch. Imagine my surprise when I opened it to find the CD of photographs for the meeting I attended at 9:00 a.m.! Now it is too late to include your photos for consideration in the brochure.

Revision

The CD you sent by messenger arrived today at 11:30 a.m. Unfortunately, the meeting to discuss photography for the brochure was at 9:00 a.m., so I was not able to present your photos for consideration in the brochure.

When your writing is concise, you do not waste time explaining every detail of the situation. Subsequently, the reader does not waste time either.

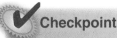

Checkpoint

1. Why should you avoid a series of short sentences?
2. In which voice is the subject doing the action?
3. What role do frills play in business writing?

CASE

The Price Is Right

Dane Kravitz is a self-published author whose book *Modern Home Renovation* is for sale on his Web site. On Monday, he received an e-mail from Dorothy Greco, a customer who had purchased the book online. Ms. Greco had been charged $28.45 on her credit card statement and was questioning the price of the book. She said she had expected to be charged $24.95, the price advertised on the Web site. Dane knew why the price was higher—the Web site had neglected to list the shipping cost that the customer would be charged. This is the copy that was on the Web site:

Modern Home Renovation is a book that every homeowner should have on the shelf. This book will help you learn all the angles to not only remodel your home but make it a showplace. Your friends and neighbors will think you are awesome and wonder how you learned to be so creative without a contractor. For a limited time, you can buy this book for only $24.95. Don't waste time— order today.

1. Did Dane use the right words when writing the Web copy?
2. Did Dane use the four C's of communication while writing this Web copy? Why or why not?
3. Rewrite the copy to make it more clear and concise. Be sure it includes the shipping cost.

Writing Effective Paragraphs

Effective paragraphs are a series of well-written, coherent sentences arranged in a meaningful order. Think of a paragraph as having three main parts: introduction or topic sentence, developmental sentences, and closing or summarizing sentence. Good paragraphs:

- use general statements to introduce and summarize main ideas
- provide specific statements that support the main idea

- identify each new main idea and supporting ideas so that the reader can follow the logic of the message
- break up text copy to make the communication appear more inviting to the reader

Apply Logic

Writing is logical when you have presented and connected ideas so that they make sense to the reader. Logic is tied to the order in which your thoughts are arranged in the writing, whether on paper or in digital form. Ask yourself these questions.

- Does the first paragraph introduce the topic?
- Are the points made in a logical sequence?
- Does each paragraph build on the previous one?

Following the writing process of prewriting, writing, and post writing will help you establish a logical flow in each paragraph.

Remember that when you write the first draft, your goal is to get all your thoughts down without stopping to revise and edit. The revision stage is the time to check the organization of your work. Does the order make sense to the reader? Is a technical term used in paragraph two, but not defined until paragraph four? Does the piece jump from point A to point C without covering point B? It is not uncommon to find that paragraphs need to be moved around to tighten the logical flow. Taking the time to do this will ensure that the work makes sense to the reader.

Control Paragraph Length

There is no standard for how many sentences a paragraph should contain. Paragraph length will vary according to subject matter and sentence construction. Sometimes a paragraph may consist of only one sentence, although these are generally avoided. The one-sentence paragraph is often used effectively as the opening or closing of a message.

Always keep the reader in mind as you write. Generally, as with sentences, business readers want paragraphs to be short and clear. Shorter paragraphs help readers to skim and scan, techniques you will learn in Chapter 15 for reading and absorbing information in the business setting. When you revise a draft, notice if there are long paragraphs. If so, look for places where it makes sense to begin a new paragraph. Do not force a break if the thoughts are so closely connected it would not be logical to have a break between them. In most cases, however, you will find that long paragraphs have points where a break can be made.

Use Transitions

The key to connecting thoughts between sentences and paragraphs is the use of transitions. **Transitions** are words, phrases, and sentences that connect ideas and clarify the relationship between sentences and paragraphs. Consider the following examples. The transitions are shown in bold.

> The promotion will begin on September 15. **Consequently,** sales should be brisk during October.
>
> Your account is seriously past due. **As a result,** your charge privileges are temporarily suspended.
>
> Let's examine the reasons for the new procedure. **First,** we need a process that is more efficient.

Transitions prepare the reader for what is coming and move the reader from one idea or set of ideas to another. This aids the reader's understanding of the message. Transitional words and phrases also add balance to sentence length when used to connect two short sentences.

Notice how paragraph two below reads more smoothly than the paragraph one, while paragraph three overuses transitions. The transition words are shown in bold.

> **Paragraph 1**
> We are increasing the price of the new merchandise. Regular customers will still get a discount on large-volume purchases. They will be able to take advantage of this discount only if they place orders every 60 days or less.
>
> **Paragraph 2**
> We are increasing the price of the new merchandise, **but** regular customers will still get a discount on large-volume purchases. **However,** they will be able to take advantage of this discount only if they place orders every 60 days or less.
>
> **Paragraph 3**
> We are increasing the price of the new merchandise, **but, on the other hand,** we will still give a discount to our regular large-volume purchasers. **Accordingly,** these purchasers will be able to take advantage of this discount only if they place orders every 60 days or less.

Without transitions, your writing will sound choppy, the relationship among ideas will be unclear, and readers may be confused. But, when these connectors are overused, your writing will sound overly wordy as in paragraph three. Choosing the right transitions and moderate use of transitions will help you achieve a smooth and readable writing style.

The English language has many useful transitional words and phrases that serve various purposes in sentences. To use them appropriately, you need to be aware of when and where these words and phrases add meaning and make the writing more effective. Figure 8-2 lists commonly used transitions and their purpose.

Choose Direct or Indirect Approach

Paragraphs may be constructed using a direct or indirect approach. These topics are discussed in Chapter 7. With the **direct approach,** the topic sentence is followed by descriptive details. The direct approach is a very readable format and is most often used in business writing. With the **indirect approach,** details precede the main idea of the paragraph. The indirect approach is useful when you must give the reader bad news. Such an arrangement allows you to present reasons before directly stating the bad news. Consider the following examples.

Figure 8-2   Useful transitions help improve your writing and lead the reader through the message.

Purpose	Transitions	Purpose	Transitions	Purpose	Transitions
Introduce a topic	first in addition besides	Provide contrast	however on the other hand but yet in contrast on the contrary	Guide a reader through time	after again eventually earlier later next now ultimately
Review a point	in other words that is in conclusion to summarize	Show cause	consequently because therefore accordingly as a result	Guide a reader through space	above below nearby
Compare items	likewise in the same way similarly in contrast				
Introduce examples	for example for instance namely including	Concede a point	granted of course to be sure certainly	Conclude	overall finally in conclusion to summarize

Direct

We are pleased to inform you that your application for membership in the Writer's Association of America has been accepted. As a member, you will have access to all of the benefits described in the attached brochure. To begin taking advantage of your WAA membership, please click on the link below to complete the online member registration form.

Indirect

Thank-you for your application for membership in the Writer's Association of America. Each year we receive applications from several thousand published writers such as yourself who have excellent credentials and writing samples. Regrettably, we are able to admit only a few new members each year and must decline your application. We hope you will continue to enjoy the nonmember benefits we offer.

By using the indirect approach, the reader is prepared for the bad news. The writer is able to state the bad news in words that do not offend.

Checkpoint

1. List the three parts of a paragraph.
2. When ideas are presented and connected so they make sense to the reader, what is the writing said to be?
3. What determines paragraph length?
4. Describe the purpose of transitions.
5. What are the two approaches that can be used to present the topic in a paragraph?

Chapter 8 Review

Chapter Summary

Writing Style and Tone

- Writing style refers to the way in which a writer uses language to convey an idea.
- Standard English is the norm in business writing.
- Tone is an overall impression of the writing.

Choosing the Right Words

- Precise language adds clarity to the message.
- Sensitive language is neutral and free from bias.
- Personal pronouns, particularly *you* and *your*, make the message more reader friendly.
- Positive or neutral words help to soften the reader's reaction to a negative message.
- Some words have shades of meaning or connotations that the writer must be aware of in order to avoid confusing or offending the reader.
- The four C's of communication can be achieved by avoiding redundancies, avoiding clichés, and using familiar words.
- Avoid trendy words that might make the message sound dated or inappropriate.

Structuring Clear and Concise Sentences

- Short, simple sentences are more understandable than long, complex ones.
- Active voice is best when you need to be direct and have no reason to soften the tone of a sentence.
- Passive voice is used to downplay a situation and soften the tone.
- Good business writing has *no* frills.

Writing Effective Paragraphs

- Paragraphs have an introduction, body, and a closing sentence.
- Effective paragraphs have logical development, are short in length, and use transitions to connect ideas.
- A direct or indirect approach can be used to present the ideas in a message.

 ## Review
Your Knowledge

1. What is Standard English?
2. Explain the term *bias free* and why bias-free language is important.
3. Why use personal pronouns in writing?
4. Give an example of a positive/neutral word or phrase and a negative word it can replace.
5. What does connotation mean?
6. What is a redundancy?
7. Give an example of a cliché in business writing.
8. What advantage is offered by short sentences compared to long sentences?
9. Describe the difference between active and passive voice.
10. What are transitions?

 ## Apply
Your Knowledge

1. Print an article from an online newspaper or magazine. Determine the writing style and tone of the article. Critique the writing regarding word choice and sentence and paragraph construction. Make a list of what is good and bad about the writer's style and briefly note why you came to that conclusion.

2. Select one of the following themes and prepare a 50-word paragraph. Pay attention to word choice and sensitivity toward the reader. After you have written the paragraph, describe how you applied the four C's of communication to the message.

   A. Personalize your writing.

   B. Words have the power to influence people.

   C. Today's media provides too much information.

   D. Disappearance of the art of personal handwritten notes, letters, and invitations.

   E. Why I would choose a career in _____. (*fill in the blank*)

3. Identify which of the following sentences are written in passive voice. Rewrite those sentences that would be better in the active voice. Also, rewrite any sentences that you feel could be clearer.

   A. The site for the new company headquarters was selected by the committee.

   B. Our chemist tested the perfume samples.

   C. The quota was not met by the sales department last month.

   D. The amendment was approved by a majority of the board members.

   E. Last week, the Department of Health inspected the restaurant.

   F. Several steps are being taken by our staff to improve customer service.

   G. Smoking is prohibited in the entire building.

   H. This shipment should be examined for damage.

   I. For some reason, the manager believed that we had left our job early.

4. Rewrite the following draft of an e-mail to improve word choice and sentence and paragraph construction.

   > We received an order of 50 luminescent bulbs yesterday from your outfit. Needless to say, we cannot ship it until we receive a cashier's check because of your questionable credit rating.

> We want your business. We're sure you have a good excuse for your credit history, but a bird in the hand is worth two in the bush. In other words, we need the greenbacks before we release the goods.
>
> No hard feelings, just send the check in the enclosed envelope.
>
> Have a grand day!
>
> Sincerely,

Practice
What You Have Learned

Access the *Fundamentals of Business Communication* Student Companion Web Site at www.g-wlearning.com/Communication. Download each data file for this chapter. Follow the instructions to complete a reading, writing, and grammar activity to practice what you have learned in this chapter.

Connections
Across the Curriculum

Math. In column one of a spreadsheet, list the trendy words that you and your friends use. In column two, translate what each word or phrase actually means. For example, "I am down with it" means "I agree". In column three, list words your parents or instructors considered trendy. Translate their meanings in column four.

Language Arts. Write a few paragraphs to describe what you learned from your chart on trendy words created in the previous activity.

Build
Your Business Portfolio

Another addition to your portfolio should be evidence of academic accomplishments such as report cards, honor roll certificates, etc. These certificates not only show your grades, but will show accomplishments in specific subject areas that may guide your future interests in college or a career.

1. For the ePortfolio, scan these documents. In your ePortfolio folder, create a subfolder named Academics. Save each certificate in the subfolder with the file names Academics01, Academics02, etc.

2. Place a printed copy in your container for your print portfolio.

Careers
Science, Technology, Engineering, and Mathematics
Careers and Communication

Workers in this career cluster use math and the scientific processes in laboratory and testing services and also conduct research. Often their work leads to discoveries that have the potential to improve life. Careers in this cluster are available in two areas: science/mathematics and engineering/technology.

Writing must be presented in a professional manner. Careers in this field require good writing skills in order to present research and sell ideas. Give an example of a situation in which someone in this field might need to write a document to persuade.

Event Prep

Desktop Publishing

The desktop publishing competitive event may consist of an objective test and production test completed as a team. After your team has created the content, the information must be edited and proofread so that it is grammatically correct and error free. Review the specific guidelines and rules for this event for each deliverable that will be required. This event will feature the creative abilities of your team to create a well-designed document as well as strong written communication skills to convey the message.

To prepare the finished materials for this event, do the following.

1. Review this chapter as it will help you develop a style of writing that will be appropriate for documents that you may be assigned.

2. Take note of the section on sensitive language, trendy words, and redundancies. This will be important information as you create copy.

3. Look ahead to Chapter 18 on creating graphics. Remember to keep your graphics clear and easy to understand. Fonts are important as well as the overall design.

4. Ask your instructor for assignments that you and your team can use as practice.

9

Formatting Letters, Memos, and E-Mails

The more elaborate our means of communication, the less we communicate.
—Joseph Priestly, 18th-century English theologian

A standard book has a title page, chapter titles, page numbers, margins, and paragraphs to organize the topics. Readers expect publishers to have this formatting in books. Similarly, readers of business documents have expectations about how those documents should appear. In this chapter, you will learn the standards of formatting for routine documents used in business communication: letters, memos, and e-mails.

Objectives

When you complete Chapter 9, you will be able to:

- **Increase** the readability of your writing by applying standard formatting.
- **Format** letters using standard elements and styles appropriate for business letters.
- **Format** memos using standard elements and styles appropriate for business memos.
- **Use** netiquette when creating and formatting e-mails.

Terms

standard formatting
visual cue
white space
readability
headings
parallel structure
block-style letter
modified-block-style letter
date
inside address
salutation
mixed punctuation
open punctuation
body

complimentary close
signature
signature block
reference initials
enclosure notation
copy notation
postscript
memos
templates
guide words
notations
blind copy
e-mail
netiquette

Go Green

The USB flash drive is becoming a popular alternative to rewritable CDs (CD-RWs). Even though CD-RWs are reusable, they can be easily damaged and may end up in a landfill after just a few uses. USB drives, on the other hand, are more durable, reusable, and easy to carry and store. Have you seen the new ecofriendly bamboo USB drives? Bamboo is one of the fastest growing woody plants on the planet, so this renewable resource is a good choice for the case of a USB drive.

1. Visit your local office supply store or go online to research bamboo flash drives. What did you find out about how bamboo is being used for office products?

2. Do a price comparison of a standard flash drive compared to a bamboo flash drive. Is there a price difference?

Formatting

Business readers expect documents to be set up in a certain way. **Standard formatting** is a generally accepted way to set up a document so its appearance follows a convention. Writers use standard formatting so their business documents are consistent in appearance with what the reader expects. Letters, reports, graphics, headings, and other elements are visual cues that make it easy for the reader to locate and understand information. A **visual cue** is an element the reader sees and interprets to have a particular meaning. For example, a red octagonal sign is a visual cue to a driver to stop at the intersection.

The appearance of a document is the first impression your writing makes on the reader. That first glance at your message should be an open invitation to the receiver. *Format* refers to how written information is presented on the printed page or screen. Another term for format is *layout*. The arrangement of text and graphics in relation to the white space on the page determines the visual appeal to the reader. **White space** includes margins, space between paragraphs, and any other blank space on the page. Without properly formatted elements, the reader can easily become lost or distracted. If your message lacks visual appeal, it may be discarded even before it is read.

Readability is a measure of how easy it is for the reader to understand your writing and locate information within a document. Readability is achieved through a combination of clear writing and effective formatting. Together, these elements help obtain the response you need from the reader.

Writing is most readable when it is presented in small segments with adequate white space. Information presented in long paragraphs is uncomfortable for the reader and physically tiring to read, since the eyes are given few breaks. Putting all of these points together, you can use the following techniques to enhance readability.

- Introduce the message with a short paragraph.
- Use headings.

Reading Prep

As you read this chapter, stop at the checkpoints and take time to answer the questions. Were you able to answer these without referring to the chapter content?

- Use standard fonts and sizes.
- Vary font style.
- Use parallel structure.
- Use formatting and organizational symbols.
- Use high quality paper.

A well-formatted document appears open and inviting. Figure 9-1 shows a poorly formatted document. Figure 9-2 shows an example of how that document can be properly formatted. Always refer to a style manual, such as the *Chicago Manual of Style* or the *MLA Handbook*.

Use an Introductory Paragraph

No one likes to sort through a long paragraph right at the beginning of a document. Write a short opening for the message that concisely introduces the main idea. This paragraph should set up the reader for the information to follow.

Figure 9-1. This excerpt from a style manual is a mass of text without formatting elements to aid readability.

Figures must have captions that explain the content. It is not necessary to start by saying, "This figure shows…" or "The graph contains…" Simply begin by stating the significance of what the reader will see. In most circumstances, the caption appears below rather than above the illustration. The list of figures, which appears on the preliminary pages of the document, must contain each figure's number and the caption as it appears on the figure. With figure captions, always use Arabic numerals. In addition, it is standard to capitalize the first letter of all words except prepositions or articles appearing in the middle of a title. Follow the rules of punctuation as with narrative text.

Figure 9-2. The addition of formatting—a heading, paragraphs, and a bulleted list—makes this version of the document shown in Figure 9-2 much easier to read.

Figure Captions

Figures must have captions that explain the content. It is not necessary to start by saying, "This figure shows…" or "The graph contains…" Simply begin by stating the significance of what the reader will see.

In most circumstances, the caption appears below rather than above the illustration. The list of figures, which appears on the preliminary pages of the document, must contain each figure's number and the caption as it appears on the figure.

These guidelines apply to the format of figure captions.

- Always use Arabic numerals.
- Capitalize the first letter of all words except prepositions or articles appearing in the middle of a title.
- Follow the rules of punctuation as with narrative text.

Use Headings

Headings are words and phrases that introduce sections of text. They organize blocks of information in a document. For example, the heading for this section is Use Headings.

Headings can be used effectively in both short and long documents. When the topic covers more than one key point or important issue, consider using headings. They serve as guideposts to alert the reader to what is coming.

Use Standard Fonts and Sizes

The font, also called the typeface, is the definition of the characters that make up a set of letters, numbers, and symbols. Standard fonts and sizes vary by organization or business. Often, the default font of the word processing application used by a business determines the preferred standard.

The default font and size for body text in Microsoft Word 2007/2010 is 11-point Calibri. Many organizations have adopted this as the standard. However, the traditional standard is 12-point Times Roman (or Times New Roman). Always follow the standard set by your instructor or organization.

For e-mails, it is often accepted to use the default font in e-mail software. Many e-mail–reader applications strip out all formatting. This leaves the reader with "plain text," so any applied formatting is lost.

Use Varying Heading Font Styles

Vary the font size and style in headings to clarify organizational structure. Main headings, which divide long topics into sections, should have the largest font size. Use a smaller font size for subsections or paragraph headings. Bold, italic, and underlining can also be used to show difference in headings.

Too much variation in font size and style within a document is distracting to the reader. A single font is usually sufficient for most business documents. It is rarely necessary or desirable to use more than two or three different fonts in one document.

Readability of a message is important. In business, often a reader has only a brief time to read the message. It must be clear and concise.

Shutterstock

Use Parallel Structure

Parallel structure occurs when similar sections or elements contain similar patterns of words to show they are of equal level. For example, look at the subheads in this main section (Formatting). Each head begins with the word *use.* Parallel structure is easily created when similar words are used in writing in similar ways. Therefore, words in headings, lists, and other elements that form a pattern should be worded in a consistent manner.

When dividing a topic with headings, use the same structure for wording of each. For example, you can begin each heading with an action verb, or *ing* word. Parallel structure will help the reader quickly and easily see how the document is organized.

Use Formatting and Organizational Symbols

Highlight important information or set off related items by using bulleted lists, numbered lists, asterisks, underlining, or boldface type. Numbered lists should be used only when the order of the items is important, such as sequential steps. If the order of the items is not important, use a bulleted list. Always treat lists consistently throughout a document.

Use High-Quality Paper

When publishing letters for hardcopy distribution, make sure you use high-quality paper. This will help the presentation of your information look professional. Photocopier paper may not be the best quality for a business letter. It is a good idea to keep a supply of higher-grade paper to use for important correspondence.

Checkpoint

1. What is another term for layout?
2. What function do headings serve?
3. What is another term for typeface?
4. What is the maximum number of fonts that should be used in a document?
5. What is the purpose of a parallel structure?

Formatting Letters

In business, document types are characterized not only by different purposes, but also by different formats. By using the appropriate format, you immediately tell the reader what type of document is being received.

Most businesses have established guidelines for formatting letters, memos, reports, and other documents. Letters are messages printed on stationery and should conform to workplace standards. Businesses generally use one of two standardized letter formats: block or modified block.

The **block-style letter,** as shown in Figure 9-3, is formatted so all lines are flush with the left margin. No indentions are used. Appropriate guidelines for spacing between the date, inside address, greeting, letter body, and signature block need to be followed.

The **modified-block-style letter** places the date, complimentary close, and signature to the right of the center point of the letter. All other elements of the letter are flush with the left margin. Figure 9-4 shows a letter formatted in the modified-block style. The decision to indent the paragraphs needs to be considered, depending on the guidelines of the workplace.

CASE

Policy Change

Drew Fitzgerald, the manager of a restaurant, needs to have his employees follow the policies established by company headquarters. Recently, he was informed of several changes in the hygiene policy. To relay the information to his employees, Drew reviewed each policy change at an employee meeting. He also planned to write a letter to the employees and post it on the employee bulletin board. Drew drafted the following notice.

NOTICE: CHANGES IN HYGIENE POLICY

Effective August 15, all employees will use a new hand-washing procedure prior to the start of a shift and following any breaks. Workers are to use the new disposable scrub brushes along with antibacterial soap for no less than five minutes of washing. Use the foot-operated sinks and air dryers for washing and drying, respectively. For those whose hands are sensitive to repeated scrubbing, use the antibacterial lotion in the wall dispenser. Also, food handlers must wear disposable gloves for all stages and phases of food handling. This includes preparing soft drinks, which formerly was handled by cashiers. These new procedures will increase our overall level of cleanliness and the safety of our food products. We appreciate your compliance.

1. What format would you recommend that Drew use for his letter, block or modified-block style?

2. Revise and format the letter to improve the readability of this message.

Standard Letter Elements

Block-style and modified-block-style letters have the same line spacing and top, bottom, and side margins. Both also contain the same standard letter elements:

- date
- inside address
- salutation
- body
- complimentary close
- signature
- notations

Figure 9-3. This letter is formatted in block style with mixed punctuation.

WESTERN DISTRIBUTION, INC.
740 North Main Street • Santa Ana, CA 92701
(310) 555-1600 • Fax (310) 555-1699
www.westerndistrb.com

Date → November 12, 20--

Inside address → Ms. Rochelle Andia
800 Susquehanna Lane
Bryn Mawr, PA 15221

Dear Ms. Andia: ← Salutation

Body → You are right! The correspondence your firm prepares sends a message to the reader. For this reason, you will want to send a clear message of efficiency, as illustrated by this block style letter with mixed punctuation.

This letter has been keyed using the default font of Word 2010. Notice the placement of each part of the letter is flush left. By placing each part of the letter at the left margin, you save time and create a professional-looking document.

The letter will have a complimentary close and signature line, also positioned at the left margin. If someone keyed the letter for you, that person's initials will appear below the signature line. If there are any enclosures or notations, an indication of such will appear after the signature line.

By following these simple rules, you will be able to create a letter that will make a good impression for your company.

Complimentary close
Sincerely,

Teresa Gomez

Signature block → Teresa Gomez
Account Executive
Accounting Department

Initials → urs

Enclosure ← Enclosure notation

Figure 9-4. This is the same letter shown in Figure 9-3, but formatted in modified-block style. It also uses open punctuation.

WESTERN DISTRIBUTION, INC.

740 North Main Street • Santa Ana, CA 92701
(310) 555-1600 • Fax (310) 555-1699
www.westerndistrb.com

Date ➜ November 12, 20--

Inside address ➜ Ms. Rochelle Andia
800 Susquehanna Lane
Bryn Mawr, PA 15221

Dear Ms. Andia ◀— Salutation

You are right! The correspondence your firm prepares sends a message to the reader. For this reason, you will want to send a clear message of efficiency as illustrated by this modified block style letter with open punctuation.

This letter has been keyed using the default settings of *Word 2010*. A modified block letter can have indented paragraphs, but this example uses block paragraphs with all lines beginning at the left margin.

Body ➜ Notice the placement of the date, complimentary close, and signature lines. Each of these lines has been keyed at the center point of the page. However, the initials of the person who keyed the letter and any enclosures or notations will appear flush left.

By following these simple rules, you will be able to create a letter that will make a good impression for your company.

Complimentary close

Sincerely ◀—

Teresa Gomez

Signature block ➜ Teresa Gomez
Account Executive
Accounting Department

Initials ➜ urs

Enclosure ◀——— Enclosure notation

Date Line

The **date** consists of the month, day, and year. The month is spelled in full. The day is written in figures and followed by a comma. The year is written in full and consists of numbers. For example:

December 18, 20--

Inside Address

The **inside address** is the name, title, and address of the recipient. The two examples that follow show how to format an inside address.

Mr. Angelo Costanzo, Manager
Griffin Plumbing Supply Co.
1987 Susquehanna Avenue
Wilkes-Barre, PA 18701

Ms. Denise Rodriquez
President & CEO
Urban Development Council
150 Grosvenor Avenue
Washington, DC 30005

Note that the state abbreviation is always two letters and in all capitals (all caps).

Salutation

The **salutation** is the greeting in a letter and always begins with *Dear*. This is followed by the recipient's first name or, according to your relationship, title and last name.

There are two types of punctuation used in letters. **Mixed punctuation** is a style in which a colon is placed after the salutation and a comma after the complimentary close. **Open punctuation** is a style in which there is no punctuation after the salutation or complimentary close.

Mixed Punctuation
Dear Perry:
Dear Mr. Fisher:
Dear Katherine:
Dear Ms. Randall:

Open Punctuation
Dear Perry
Dear Mr. Fisher
Dear Katherine
Dear Ms. Randall

Always address a letter to a specific person, unless you are intentionally directing it to an organization. It may take a phone call or Internet search to get the correct name, but it is worth the effort to personalize business messages. Also, make sure you correctly spell the receiver's name and use the appropriate title: Dr., Mr., or Ms. (Mrs. is rarely used in business writing). Spell out and capitalize titles such as Professor and Reverend. If you are unsure of a person's gender, use the full name:

Dear Pat Cashin:
Dear Ryan Gulati:

If you need to write a letter without the name of a specific person, do not use traditional greetings, such as *Dear Sir or Gentlemen*. You may use *Ladies and Gentlemen;* however, the best course is to use words that describe the role of the person:

Dear Customer:

Dear Circulation Manager:

Dear Editor:

Body

The **body** of the letter is the message. Format the body according to the block or modified-block style. Most businesses use the block style. Single-spaced letters are standard; however, some businesses prefer the default setting of the word-processing software used. In Microsoft Word 2007/2010, the default line spacing is 1.15.

Complimentary Close

The **complimentary close** is the sign-off for the letter. Only the first word is capitalized. Mixed or open punctuation is used in the complimentary close, but be consistent with the style you used in the salutation. The complimentary close follows the body of the letter and is appropriately spaced, as shown in Figure 9-3 and Figure 9-4. The most commonly used closings are:

When creating a business letter, be sure to follow an accepted format. Readers will expect the letter to have certain elements to guide them through the letter.

Shutterstock

Mixed Punctuation
Sincerely,
Sincerely yours,
Cordially,
Cordially yours,

Open Punctuation
Sincerely
Sincerely yours
Cordially
Cordially yours

Signature

The writer's name and title are called the **signature** or **signature block**. The writer's job title and department appear beneath the name, unless a letterhead is used that contains this information. Begin the signature block below the body of the letter. The blank lines of space are used for the handwritten signature.

Sincerely,

Margaret Shaw
Coordinator
Business Development

When the message writer is designated as the company as a whole, the company name may appear in all-capital letters below the complimentary close. The letter is not signed by the writer in this case.

Sincerely,

JIMENEZ-BRADFORD REALTY

Notations

Letters may include **reference initials.** These indicate who keyed the letter. If the writer keyed the letter, initials are not included. Reference initials are lowercase letters.

Cordially yours,

Margaret Shaw
Senior Vice President

smb

If the person keying the letter is not the person who wrote it, initials are included at the bottom of the letter to indicate who keyed it.

An **enclosure notation** alerts the reader to materials that are included in the mailing along with the letter. Spell out and capitalize the word *Enclosure*. If there is more than one enclosure, you may indicate the number of items included or list them. The word *Attachment* may be used instead of the word *Enclosure*.

Enclosures

Enclosures: 3

Enclosures: Statement
            Check
            Letter

Shutterstock

A **copy notation** is needed when others are being sent a copy of the letter. The notation appears below the signature, as shown in Figure 9-3 and Figure 9-4. If there are enclosure notations or reference initials, it appears below these. Use *c* (for copy) or *cc* (for carbon copy or courtesy copy) followed by a colon and a list of the full names of individuals receiving copies.

] cc: Tina Ricco
       Gary Kowalski

Additional Letter Elements

There are three additional letter elements that are sometimes used in business letters: attention line, subject line, and postscript. These elements may also appear in personal letters. The following sections discuss these elements.

Attention Line

There is a wealth of resources available to the writer—telephone, Internet, company databases—that make it largely unnecessary to address correspondence without an individual's name. However, if this circumstance does occur, substituting a position or department title for a specific name is a good solution. For example, you may know the marketing manager is to receive the letter, but cannot find the name of the manager. In this situation, it is appropriate to include an attention line that says *Attention Marketing Manager.* This line is positioned as part of the inside address:

] Attention Marketing Manager
   Urban Development Council
   150 Grosvenor Avenue
   Washington, DC 30005

Subject Line

A subject line in a letter is used like a subject line in an e-mail. It helps the reader know the content of the message before reading. The subject line may be in all caps or initial caps and the word *subject* is optional. The subject line appears after the salutation and before the body of the letter.

] Dear Mr. Ramito:

   SUBJECT: MINUTES OF SUMMER MEETING

   Thank you for attending the summer meeting of the *Green Entrepreneur* that was held last month in Orlando. We appreciate your attendance and your contribution to this meeting…

Postscript

A **postscript** means *after writing* and is information included after the signature. In business letters, the postscript is no longer used to represent an afterthought. For example, in the past a writer may have included an omission as a postscript, such as:

] P.S. I forgot to tell you we're moving. After June 1, you can reach us at our new address.

With the advent of word-processing software, the need for postscripts disappeared. If you discover that something important was omitted from the body of a letter, simply edit the letter and include it.

Occasionally, however, a writer uses a postscript to emphasize or personalize a point. Sales letters often use postscripts for special effect.

> P.S. Remember, our sale ends this Thursday. Don't miss the wonderful savings in store for you!

Use postscripts sparingly. Frequent use of postscripts may suggest to the reader that you did not plan your message.

Envelopes

If you are physically mailing a letter, it is necessary to address an envelope. Most businesses generally use a standard size 10 envelope, which is 4 1/8″ × 9 1/2″. The US Postal Service recommends the address be in all capital letters with no punctuation as shown in Figure 9-5.

To properly fold and insert the letter into the envelope, fold the bottom third up, then the top third down. Place the folded letter in the envelope so the dateline is facing up toward the flap of the envelope. The last fold will be at the bottom of the envelope.

Checkpoint

1. What style of letter formatting has all elements flush with the left margin?
2. Whose initials are the reference initials?
3. If cc appears at the bottom of a letter, what does this mean?
4. For what is a postscript generally used?

Figure 9-5.   **When addressing a standard size 10 envelope, use the spacing shown here.**

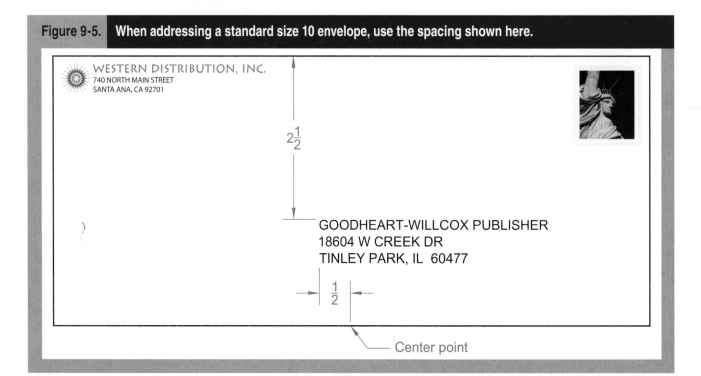

WESTERN DISTRIBUTION, INC.
740 NORTH MAIN STREET
SANTA ANA, CA 92701

$2\frac{1}{2}$

GOODHEART-WILLCOX PUBLISHER
18604 W CREEK DR
TINLEY PARK, IL 60477

$\frac{1}{2}$

Center point

Formatting Memos

Memorandums, more commonly called **memos,** are hardcopies used for intra-office communication. Memos are similar to e-mails in purpose and design, but are more effective when the writer wants a printed communication or assumes the reader will want a hardcopy for his or her records. Executives and departments that issue policies and other formal messages often use memos attached to e-mails as a means of communicating with employees.

Memos are usually created and printed on forms with the company name and logo at the top. You may also create memos using **templates,** which are predesigned forms supplied in word processing software. The word *memorandum* or *memo* is in large letters at the top and the **guide words** *to, from, date,* and *subject* appear at the top, as shown in Figure 9-6. These words often appear in all caps.

TEAMWORK

Working in the team assigned by your instructor, research the various standard sizes of envelopes used for business mailings. Make a list outlining each size, an example of its use, and if the standard postage rate can be used to mail it.

Memo Parts

A memo contains certain elements. The next sections discuss the parts of a memo and how they are formatted.

To Line

The name of the recipient(s) appears in the TO: line. Omit courtesy titles (Mr., Ms.). Names may be in list format or on a single line separated with commas.

Figure 9-6. A preprinted memo form may contain this information.

J. WRIGHT & ASSOCIATES

MEMORANDUM

TO:

FROM:

DATE:

SUBJECT :

    TO: Tyler A. Dembowsky
         Edward Josi
         Jeannette Loria

    TO: Tyler A. Dembowsky, Edward Josi, Jeannette Loria

If the list of recipients is very long, you may choose to key the word *Distribution* in the TO: line and list the names at the bottom. The names should be in alphabetic order or in order of position (from highest to lowest) in the company or department.

    Distribution:
    Tyler A. Dembowsky
    Edward Josi
    Jeannette Loria
    Ann Peabody
    David Horowitz

If a memo is being sent to a group of employees, use the name of the group instead of listing all the individual names.

    TO: Customer Care Associates

From Line

In the FROM: line, fill in your full name or the name of the person for whom you are keying the memo. It is optional for the sender to initial the typed name before the memo is sent.

    FROM: Jose Ortez

The writer may choose to include his or her job title:

    FROM: Jose Ortez, Marketing Director

Date Line

The DATE: line contains the date that the memo is being sent. Spell out the name of the month. Include the full year in numbers.

    DATE: August 1, 20--

Subject Line

In the SUBJECT: line, indicate the subject in language that clearly states the topic. Be concise. Also, capitalize the main words in the subject line.

    SUBJECT: Merit Increases

Body

When keying a memo, begin the message below the subject line, as shown in Figure 9-7. The paragraphs are positioned flush left. Key the message in a single-spaced format with a double space between paragraphs. As in letters, your business may prefer to use line spacing of 1.15, which is the default of Word 2007/2010.

Figure 9-7.   **This sample memo is properly formatted.**

MEMORANDUM

Guide words →

TO: Patricia Lorenzo

FROM: Jeremy Ornstein

DATE: May 22, 20--

SUBJECT: New Catalog

Body →

We are preparing the fall catalog and I would like to get your opinion on the attached cover designs. Will you please look over these designs and share them with your staff?

I'd like to meet with you on Friday morning to go over them and decide which one we want to use. Let me know if 9 a.m. on Friday is free on your calendar.

Special notations →

jkl

Attachments (5)

bc: Jared Arnette

Special Notations

Notations at the bottom of the memo are used to indicate specific things to the reader. For example, *c* or *cc* indicates copies are being sent. Another notation is *bc* for **blind copy,** which is used when you are sending a copy of the memo to someone without the recipient's knowledge.

If copies are being sent to others, add the notation cc (for carbon copy or courtesy copy) line and the list of names at the bottom of the memo. The blind copy notation appears at the bottom of the file copy and the copy for the recipient who is blind copied, but not on the copy for the primary recipient.

> cc: Tyler A. Dembowsky
>   Edward Josi
>   Jeannette Loria

Other notations include confidential, attachments, and enclosures. It is traditional to also include the preparer's initials in lowercase when someone other than the writer keys the memo. These notations follow the same formatting guidelines as letters and are shown in Figure 9-7.

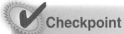

Checkpoint

1. What guide words appear at the beginning of a memo?
2. List the five elements of a memo.
3. In addition to the standard elements, what else may appear on a memo?

Formatting E-Mail

E-mail, which is short for electronic mail, is a major vehicle for business communication. **E-mail** is a message that is created, sent, and received digitally (electronically).

The following sections discuss standards for business e-mails. Businesses generally have policies for using e-mail as well as disclaimers and other guidelines for sending e-mail correspondence. Figure 9-8 shows an example of e-mail completed in business style. E-mail is formatted similarly to a printed memo.

Header

In the TO: line, key the names of the recipients from whom you want a response or who have a primary interest in the topic. Use the COPY: line for names of those who are receiving the information as secondary recipients. Normally, a reply is not expected from those who are copied.

TEAMWORK

Working in the team assigned by your instructor, research e-mail reader software. Make a chart showing at least five options, the system requirements, and the cost to purchase. One of the software options should be freeware. Write a memo to your supervisor (your teacher) listing the options and recommending an e-mail reader.

Figure 9-8. This e-mail is properly formatted.

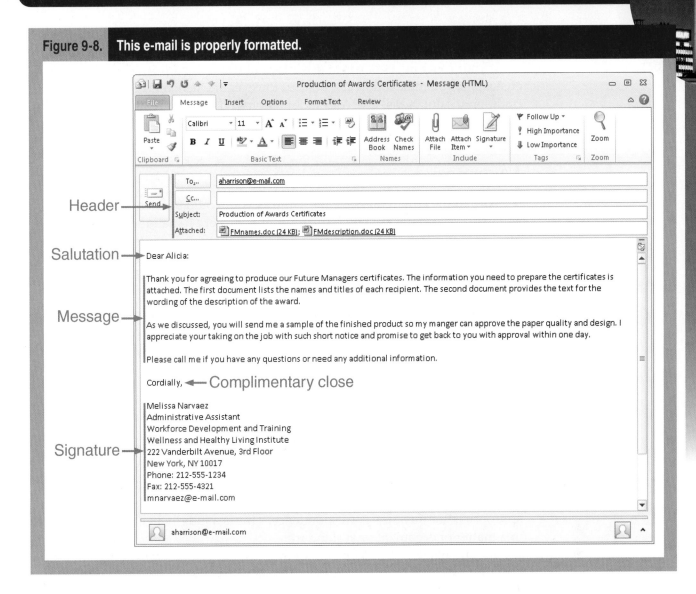

You may opt to send blind copies, but use this option sparingly. In most business situations, it is courteous to let the reader know all who are receiving the e-mail. However, for an e-mail sent to a large number of people outside of an organization, it is courteous to use the blind copy function to ensure the e-mail addresses of the recipients remain private. If all recipients are listed in the BLIND COPY: line, the only e-mail address each recipient can see is the sender's address.

Limit the subject of each e-mail to one topic and clearly and concisely state the subject. For example, a subject of "Hello" is not suitable, but "Business Report 8-14" may be appropriate. By focusing the topic and the content of the e-mail, readers can more easily keep track of subsequent replies.

Salutation

E-mail tends to be more informal than letters. In most businesses and organizations, people address each other by their first names in e-mails. You may use the salutation "Dear" as in a letter, depending on whether you are writing a formal or informal e-mail. Some companies have adopted the style of using very informal salutations, such as addressing customers by first name.

If your company policy is to use informal forms of address, even to outside customers, you must follow the policy. However, the general rule is to use traditional salutations. Use your judgment based on your relationship with the recipient and the rules of your organization. If you address the recipient by first name in person, it is usually correct to do the same in written communication.

Message

Format the e-mail message the same as you would a letter or memo. Use appropriate spacing, as shown in Figure 9-8. Adhere to netiquette when writing both personal and business e-mails. **Netiquette,** or Internet etiquette, is a set of guidelines for appropriate behavior on the Internet, including e-mail, and should always be followed. These rules include the accepted standards within the organization as well as general standards that apply externally. When you are sending e-mail as a representative of your business, use Standard English—correct grammar, punctuation, spelling, and usage—and the spelling check feature before sending. Remember, you are in a business environment and your e-mail could be forwarded to others who might make judgments about what you have written.

Complimentary Close and Signature

E-mails often take the place of routine phone calls and face-to-face conversations with colleagues and external business associates. Writers often forego including a closing and formal signature in these kinds of messages. However, a courteous *Thanks* or *Thank you* at the end of the message is usually appropriate for business correspondence. This is a judgment call for the writer or a matter of organizational standards.

For e-mails that are used in place of a letter, it is important to include a complimentary close just as you would in a printed letter. It is standard to include your full name and contact information at the bottom of the e-mail for the convenience of the reader.

E-mail programs allow you to set up the signature to be automatically inserted. In the signature block, include your name, job title, department, and contact information. It is customary to include the e-mail address in the signature, since many e-mail–reader programs display the sender's full name instead of the e-mail address.

Attachments

Take care when sending attachments to ensure the recipient can handle the size and type of file. Many e-mail servers have limits on the size of files that can be received. Also, because viruses can be spread through attachments, you might want to check to make sure the recipient is comfortable receiving attachments or to notify them that an e-mail you will be sending will contain an attachment. It is standard practice in business to delete, without reading, any e-mail that has an attachment unless the attachment is expected.

CASE

Is the Meeting On?

Jeanine Flanders is the assistant manager of Greenway West, a resort in Tampa, Florida. Jeanine regularly corresponds with clients who plan to visit Greenway West for both business and pleasure.

In September, Corey Bingham inquired about holding a meeting at the resort in December. By mid-October, Mr. Bingham had not responded to the letter and information packet that Jeanine mailed the day after receiving the inquiry. As of October 16, the December dates she had discussed with Mr. Bingham were still open. Jeanine decided to write to Mr. Bingham to encourage him to make his decision. Here is the message she wrote:

> When you called me in September about accommodations for your December 3–7 meeting, I tentatively reserved a block of meeting and residence rooms for your group. Although you did not ask me to do so, I wanted to make certain I had rooms for you in case you decided to choose Greenway West for your conference.
>
> If you are still thinking about having us host your conference (and I certainly hope you are), I will need to hear from you by October 25. This is the latest date on which I can guarantee accommodations for the dates you requested.
>
> Since we last spoke, the resort has added a solarium with an indoor pool plus a very spacious sauna. I've enclosed a colorful brochure to let you see for yourself. I hope yours is one of the first groups to use these new facilities!

1. Should Jeanine send this message as a letter, memo, or e-mail? Why?
2. Format this message to create a final document. Use your choice of letter, e-mail, or memo.

E-Mail Replies

Respond as quickly as possible to e-mails. Stay with the original topic in your reply. If you want to bring up a new topic, send a new e-mail and note the topic in the subject line. Creating a new e-mail with a new subject line makes it easier to keep the information flow understandable. Additionally, it allows both the sender and recipient of the e-mail to electronically file and organize the e-mail.

When you are out of the office, use the automated reply feature to send a message stating when you will return. This is a professional courtesy so the sender knows you are unavailable and not being careless about responding.

Useful E-Mail Features

Use of e-mail can be made more efficient by taking advantage of the many convenient features that most systems provide. The following sections discuss productivity tools common to most e-mail software that help you manage e-mail.

E-mail is an important part of business communication. Always use netiquette when composing e-mail.

Shutterstock

Address Book

The contacts or address book lists the names of all employees on the system and inserts the name when you key a few letters. Many similar names might be in the system, so always check to make sure the correct names are listed before clicking the Send button. Address books also have search features to help you find names and other information, such as employee job title, location, and phone number.

Send Options

Send options let you set criteria before you send an e-mail. Some of the criteria that can be set include level of urgency, confidentiality, and being notified when the e-mail is opened or deleted.

Reply Options

The reply options allow you to determine who receives the reply. You can choose to reply only to the sender or to all recipients of the e-mail. Most e-mail readers also have a setting for including the original message beneath the reply. The e-mail subject line is usually given the prefix RE: to indicate it is a reply.

Forward

The forward option allows you to send a message you receive to a new recipient. The e-mail subject line is usually given the prefix FW: to indicate it is forwarded message. Once you click the Forward button, you can add multiple e-mail addresses to the TO: line.

Folders

Folders are used to store e-mails you have sent or received. You can also store drafts of e-mails you are planning to send. Folders can be set up by topics, names, or any other filing system you prefer. If your organization has a standard filing system, be sure to use it.

Views

The view feature allows you to sort e-mails in various views. For example, you can choose to sort by names, topics, dates, size, or other criteria. Sorting by name is a quick way to see all e-mails you have received from a particular coworker.

Trash

E-mails that you delete are sent to the trash folder. Depending on how your e-mail software is set up, e-mails in the trash folder may be immediately discarded or kept until you manually empty the folder. Be sure to check the settings for emptying the trash as some e-mail readers have an automatic emptying setting. Once an e-mail is removed from the trash folder, it cannot be retrieved.

BUSINESS ETHICS

Ethical Messages

There will be instances when it is necessary to write a sales message or other type of documents for your organization. Even though it may be tempting to focus on sales "hype" or other persuasive techniques to convey a message, remember to keep the information honest. Embellishing a message about a product or service or intentionally misrepresenting a product or service is unethical and may be illegal. There are truth-in-advertising laws that must be followed. Focus on the truths of the message and use your communication skills in a positive manner to create interest or demand for the product or service. Search the Internet to find out more about truth-in-advertising laws.

Calendars and Planning Tools

Many e-mail systems include tools that help you plan and organize your work. These tools are like a handheld daily planner. You can schedule meetings, set reminder alarms, and schedule reoccurring tasks.

Checkpoint

1. What does the header of an e-mail contain?
2. What is the general rule used to determine if you can address somebody by their first name in an e-mail?
3. Why should you alert a recipient that an e-mail you will be sending will contain an attachment?
4. In addition to following netiquette, what should you do in an e-mail?

Chapter 9 Review

Chapter Summary

Formatting

- Making a professional impression with your written correspondence is important in any business situation.

- The use of white space and graphics will make the information easy to read.

- Readability is a measure of how easy it is for a reader to understand your writing and locate information within the document.

Formatting Letters

- Letters may be block style or modified-block style and either open or mixed punctuation can be used.

- Business letters have standard elements that include date, inside address, salutation, body, complimentary close, and signature.

- Additional elements in a business letter may include an attention line, subject line, and notations.

Formatting Memos

- Memos are generally used for interoffice communication.

- Memos have a heading that consists of the guide words TO, FROM, DATE, and SUBJECT.

- There is no salutation or closing for a memo, but special notations may be used.

Formatting E-Mail

- E-mails are commonly used in business and are formatted similarly to a memo.

- Business e-mails should have a salutation and closing.

- Use good business judgment when sending e-mail and observe the rules of netiquette.

- Take advantage of the productivity tools offered by most e-mail software.

Review
Your Knowledge

1. Explain standard formatting.
2. What is parallel structure?
3. How does a block-style letter differ from modified-block-style letter?
4. List the seven common elements of letters.
5. What is the difference between open punctuation and mixed punctuation?
6. List the three additional elements that may be used in a business letter.
7. What is a postscript?
8. Describe a memo and its purpose.
9. Related to formatting, what is an e-mail similar to?
10. Explain netiquette.

Apply
Your Knowledge

1. Rewrite the following draft of a business letter so that it is properly formatted to increase its readability. Use a block format with open punctuation.

Ms. Genevieve LeMond 7214 Mulberry Street DeKalb, IL 61616 June 20, 20--

Dear Genevieve. I am sorry I cannot be at the PER meeting for the final, official goodbye to you as a fellow pollution-control champion. I personally want to communicate how strongly I feel about you as a mentor. No one can prepare better waste-containment strategies, rally support for earth-friendly activities, or use her knowledge more effectively to make changes at the community level! I've also admired your ability to communicate with officials at large corporations and persuade them to support our grassroots efforts. Now, as you enter a new life phase of your career, I hope you find new challenges to attack with your talents. And whatever you choose to pursue next, may it bring you satisfaction. Sincerely. Minerva Harvet Executive Director

2. Write a suitable subject line for the following memos. Create the memos and format them using accepted standards.

A. You need to ask your supervisor for approval to take two personal days to attend your sister's graduation in another state.

B. A vice president of sales is asking the sales staff to work overtime to complete the end-of-year inventory.

C. You are a marketing coordinator asking your manager's staff members for their April expense reports by May 25 because you will be on vacation May 29–June 5.

D. You are a supervisor asking members of the accounting department to attend a seminar on a new accounting system for payroll production.

3. You work at the Woodlake History Center. Each year the center hosts an employee family picnic. This year you are the picnic committee chair. Write an e-mail to your committee members to tell them the date, time, menu, and activities planned for the picnic (supply your own details). Use formatting such as bullets, asterisks, numbers, underlining, and boldface type to emphasize important information.

4. What type of written communication—letter, memo, e-mail—would you select in each of the following situations? Explain your answers.

A. You need to convince your supervisor to increase the advertising budget by 10 percent.

B. You want to tell your customers about a new credit policy.

C. The company's stockholders want a detailed analysis of last quarter's income statement.

D. The manufacturing arm of the Tyler Company in New York City wants to tell the marketing division, located in Boston, the specifications of a new product.

E. You want to congratulate a recently promoted coworker.

Practice
What You Have Learned

Access the *Fundamentals of Business Communication* Student Companion Web Site at www.g-wlearning.com/Communication. Download each data file for this chapter. Follow the instructions to complete a reading, writing, and grammar activity to practice what you have learned in this chapter.

Connections
Across the Curriculum

Math. Create a grid with the words *letters*, *e-mail*, and *memos* on the X axis. On the Y axis, write the elements of a letter, memo, and e-mail. Put check marks in the columns to show which parts the three have in common. Write a paragraph to explain how each is different from, yet the same as, the others.

Language Arts. How is texting or instant messaging used in business today? Write several paragraphs describing how it is used, why it is used, and the pros and cons of using texting in businesses.

Build
Your Business Portfolio

Your portfolio should showcase samples of work you have completed that demonstrate your talents. Whether it is writing, photography, or other activity, you should showcase the best examples. Now is the time to start collecting items, which you can edit later. Go through past assignments where you wrote a research paper, book report, or similar project that demonstrates your writing talents.

1. Save document files of your best work in your ePortfolio folder. Create a subfolder named Talents. Save each report in the subfolder with the file names Talents01, Talents02, etc.

2. Place a printed copy in your container for your print portfolio.

Careers
Human Services
Careers and Communication

Careers in human services relate to family and personal needs. If you like to help others, one of these careers may be for you. People who enter careers in this cluster often desire to protect, nurture, or provide services for others in need. Career pathways include services in early childhood development, counseling and mental health, family and community, personal care, and consumer services.

Careers in human services require correspondence to clients, both verbally and in written communication. Give examples where letters, e-mails, or memos might be used in a career in human services.

Word Processing

Competitive events for word processing will be a timed activity in which documents will be produced. This event will demonstrate not only your ability to key documents, but your technology and communication skills. As a part of this event, it will be necessary to proofread and edit your documents before submitting them for grading.

To prepare for the word processing test, do the following.

1. Review formatting rules in this chapter and parts of letters, e-mails, and memos.

2. Study the proofreading checklist in Chapter 7. This will help you master the process and understand the techniques of proofreading.

3. Review the proofreader marks in Chapter 7. These proofreading marks are commonly used and you should feel comfortable if requested to proofread and mark corrections on a document.

4. Practice keying, proofreading, and editing actual documents. Ask your instructor to give you feedback.

A career in human services requires strong communication skills.

10
Writing Effective Business Communication

The limits of my language means the limits of my world.

—Ludwig Wittgenstein, 20th century philosopher and leader of Philosophy of Language movement

With e-mail, text messages, and instant messaging, thousands of business messages are communicated to customers, clients, and colleagues every hour of the day. Being able to transmit a message instantly once it is composed does not mean that messages should be sent without the requisite preparation. Consider your purpose and the reader. This chapter explains the common purposes for writing business communication. You will also learn writing techniques for developing messages that inform, request, respond, and persuade. These guiding principles will help you organize and develop content to ensure you get the result you need.

Objectives

When you complete Chapter 10, you will be able to:

- **Write** positive- and negative-informational messages using direct and indirect approaches.
- **Write** requests that display courtesy and reasonableness to elicit a favorable response.
- **Write** simple and complex responses that promote the goodwill of an organization.
- **Write** an effective message to persuade that has a positive tone and is reader oriented.
- **Write** an effective message to sell that has a positive tone and is reader oriented.

Terms

confirmation message
transmittal message
instructions
directions
technical message
technical document
requests
routine requests

special requests
diplomacy
frequently asked questions (FAQ)
boilerplate
courtesy response
persuasive message
sales message

Go Green

What kind of lightbulb is in the lamp on your desk? If you are using a compact fluorescent lamp (CFL), you are saving 80 percent of the energy used by a regular incandescent lightbulb. A CFL will last up to 10 times longer than an incandescent bulb. However, these CFLs do contain mercury, so they must be disposed of properly. Do some research on the compact fluorescent lamps.

1. How do CFLs compare in price to a regular incandescent lightbulb?
2. What makes a CFL different in appearance from a regular lightbulb?
3. Where can you properly dispose of a CFL in your community?

Planning

Writing effective business documents is a process that begins with planning. In the planning stage, consider your purpose and the reader. To begin planning, ask yourself these questions.

- Why are you writing?
- Who is your audience?
- What do you want the reader to think and do?
- What ideas do you want to communicate?

The answers to these questions will help guide you through the writing process. The end result will be a message that is clear, concise, courteous, and correct.

Checkpoint

1. What begins the process of writing an effective business document?
2. What are the four C's of communication?

Providing Information

Probably the most common reason for writing business messages is to provide information to customers, colleagues, or supervisors. Putting information in writing avoids miscommunication, making it more likely that you will get the result you want. In addition, written documents provide a record that can be used later for reference to remind yourself or others what has transpired on a project or business issue.

There are two general approaches to writing a message: direct and indirect. You will write many different kinds of business messages that inform. Although each writing situation is unique, selecting which approach is used should be the first decision you make. Which approach you select is based on whether the information will be received positively or negatively by the reader.

Reading Prep

Before reading this chapter, go to the end of the chapter and read the summary. The chapter summary highlights important information that was presented in the chapter. Did this help you prepare to understand the content?

Positive and Neutral Messages

When you write messages that contain positive news or straightforward information that is neutral, a direct approach is usually the best choice. The following order is a sound organizational plan for a positive message.

1. **State your reason for writing.** Since you know the reader wants the information or will welcome the positive news, a simple statement that introduces the topic is enough. If the subject line in an e-mail message can achieve this, you can go directly to number 2.

2. **Provide the information.** Using active voice, write simple, clear sentences that convey the information. Use formatting devices (see Chapter 9) that clarify, such as dividing the topic into paragraphs, using numbered or bulleted list, or using headings.

3. **Close courteously.** The final paragraph of your message should be courteous and businesslike. If you want the reader to do something, make the request in direct, clear language.

The e-mail in Figure 10-1 shows how a direct, positive message flows smoothly and logically.

Figure 10-1.	This is a positive informational message.

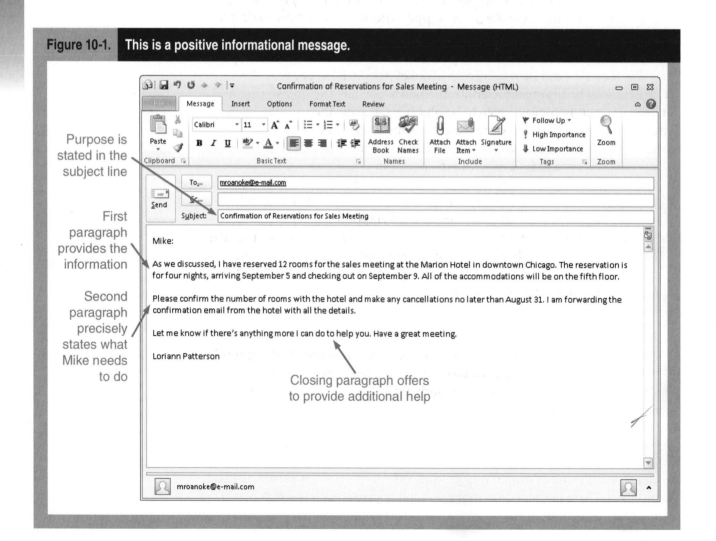

Purpose is stated in the subject line

First paragraph provides the information

Second paragraph precisely states what Mike needs to do

Closing paragraph offers to provide additional help

Negative Messages

If the direct approach is used to inform someone of bad news, the reader may get the impression that you are uncaring. It is better to use the indirect approach when the reader will not be happy to receive the information. An indirect approach uses a variation of the positive-message organizational plan. Rather than inform first and then explain, give the explanation first to buffer the negative part of your message. An indirect organizational plan might use these steps.

1. **Begin with an explanation.** Show that you understand the reader's point of view. Make statements that show empathy and anticipate the reader's response by addressing possible objections or concerns up front.

2. **State the negative information in positive language.** Be honest, but choose words that are tactful and respectful. For example, instead of saying, "the museum *does not offer* a group discount to nonmembers," say, "our group discount policy *applies only to* members of the museum."

3. **Close courteously.** Be as positive as possible, but only offer hope for a different response in the future if this is realistic. Otherwise, be firm, but not harsh. From the example in number 2, the closing might invite the reader to become a member and supply information on how to do so.

In the e-mail shown in Figure 10-2, Georgette Andrews explains to Mike Roanoke that he is not the chosen speaker for a sales conference. Georgette uses the indirect approach to inform Mike of her decision because she knows he will be disappointed with the news. She has used reasoning and sincere, courteous compliments to bolster her decision and buffer Mike's disappointment. However, to be too complimentary could be seen as patronizing. Note also that Georgette's tone is firm. Nothing she said would open the door to negotiations about the decision.

When choosing between the direct and indirect approach, consider things other than whether the content is positive or negative. For example, when the matter is routine and may not seriously disappoint the reader, the direct approach might be a better choice even when the news is not good. It is also usually a better choice when communicating an urgent message to which the reader must immediately respond. As always, the specifics of the situation must be your guide when you write.

Routine Informational Messages

Business writers frequently send informational messages that are routine in nature. As with other types of written communication, the level of formality in a routine message depends on the audience. However, a casual, friendly tone is usually appropriate.

A typical routine informational message is one written to confirm a verbal agreement made with a customer, client, or colleague. This is called a **confirmation message.** A manager writing to coworkers to confirm a meeting would write a short, informal e-mail message. On the other hand, a message written to a customer to confirm the terms of an agreement for services would be written more formally.

CASE

Problem Solved

Last month Charlotte Lopez, the writer of a popular blog devoted to women's career success, agreed to serve as the luncheon speaker at the annual meeting of the Women in Business Association (WBA) on January 15. While on a skiing vacation during the December holidays, she had an accident and will be unable to travel for at least a month. Late December is too late for the organization to get another speaker. She drafted the following message to Vicki Crawford, president of the WBA.

Thank you again for your invitation to speak at the Women in Management meeting on January 15. Because of the influence your group has on the business community, particularly in mentoring young men and women, I consider your invitation an honor.

Unfortunately, I have just had an accident while skiing on vacation. A broken leg will have me incapacitated for at least a month, so I am unable to travel to your meeting. Please accept my apology. I know the frustration these kinds of scheduling changes can cause.

Rita Short, one of the most popular bloggers on our Web site, is available to take my place. I have forwarded all of the information to her and she will call you this afternoon. Rita is a dynamic speaker and has a huge following on Facebook and Twitter. She will bring an in-depth understanding of your audience. Please ask Rita for whatever you need.

Again, I regret that I cannot fulfill my commitment. I was looking forward to meeting you and your colleagues in person. I know you will have a great meeting.

1. What approach did Charlotte use to deliver her news? Did she use it effectively?

2. Can you identify the statements that explain and those that inform?

3. How did Charlotte buffer the bad news in this message?

4. Did she do the right thing by assuming Vicki would want her to pick her replacement?

Figure 10-2. This is a negative informational message.

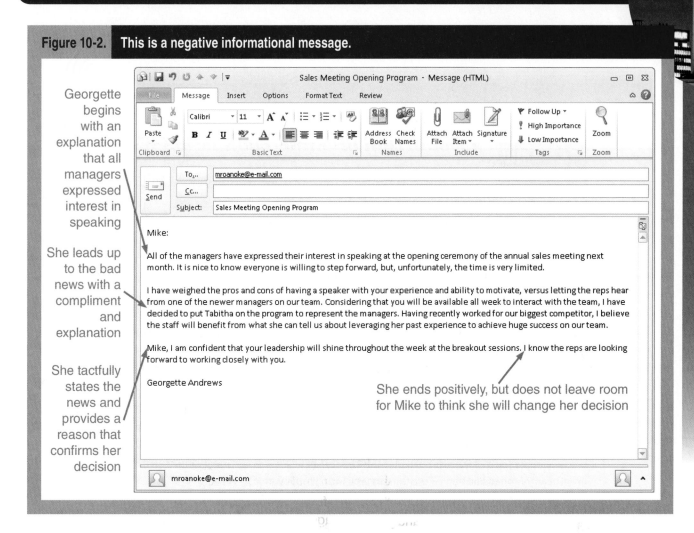

Georgette begins with an explanation that all managers expressed interest in speaking

She leads up to the bad news with a compliment and explanation

She tactfully states the news and provides a reason that confirms her decision

She ends positively, but does not leave room for Mike to think she will change her decision

(Email message contents:)

To: mroanoke@e-mail.com

Subject: Sales Meeting Opening Program

Mike:

All of the managers have expressed their interest in speaking at the opening ceremony of the annual sales meeting next month. It is nice to know everyone is willing to step forward, but, unfortunately, the time is very limited.

I have weighed the pros and cons of having a speaker with your experience and ability to motivate, versus letting the reps hear from one of the newer managers on our team. Considering that you will be available all week to interact with the team, I have decided to put Tabitha on the program to represent the managers. Having recently worked for our biggest competitor, I believe the staff will benefit from what she can tell us about leveraging her past experience to achieve huge success on our team.

Mike, I am confident that your leadership will shine throughout the week at the breakout sessions. I know the reps are looking forward to working closely with you.

Georgette Andrews

Confirmation messages are a guard against miscommunication. This is especially important when dealing with customers because miscommunication can lead to anger and frustration. Confirming correct dates, times of events, and addresses or other location information prevents mistakes that destroy customer goodwill. Following up on oral agreements or information given in meetings or telephone calls provides a record for future reference and shows your professionalism. Confirmation messages are also useful when you want to verify something you indirectly learned. Checking with a colleague or customer before acting on secondhand information you have received shows common sense and respect.

The letter in Figure 10-3 does a good job of confirming a verbal agreement. The letter is both detailed and congenial and follows the guidelines given in Figure 10-4.

Figure 10-3.   This is a letter of confirmation.

ASSOCIATION OF RARE BOOK DEALERS

1200 First Street
Austin, TX 73221
Phone (512) 555-1499   Toll Free (800) 555-0080   Fax (512) 555-1752
www.RareBookDealers.org

October, 20--

Mr. Phillip Paxton
The Bookfinders
17 East Arden Street West
Lafayette, IN 47907

Dear Mr. Paxton:

As agreed in our telephone conversation yesterday, I have reserved exhibit space K for you at the national convention of the Association of Rare Book Dealers, which will be held in Austin, Texas, on December 2–4.

The enclosed diagram shows the exhibit area layout. Your space is highlighted so that you will know precisely where you are located in relation to the other exhibits. This is an excellent location—in the mainstream of convention traffic—and I am sure you will be happy with it.

Details concerning electrical outlets and other facilities in the exhibit area are described on the back of the exhibit-area layout. If you have any additional needs or questions, please do not hesitate to contact me. We will do everything possible to accommodate your needs.

The cost for the four days is $2,400. We will need payment for half that amount ($1,200) by November 15 to hold your space. The remainder is to be paid when you arrive at the convention.

I extend a warm welcome to Austin and hope the convention will be a very successful occasion for you and your company.

Sincerely yours,

Audrey Mix
Exhibit Manager

Enclosure

Transmittal Messages

A **transmittal message** is routine communication accompanying documents or other materials attached to e-mails or sent by a delivery service. One of the main purposes of the message is as a record of when was something sent. The message may also include a description of the materials or any relevant information that the reader needs. This additional information might be something you would tell the reader if you were to deliver the materials by hand.

Figure 10-4. Follow these guidelines when writing a confirmation message.

Guidelines for Writing a Confirmation Message

- Clearly and specifically state the circumstances to which you are referring.
- Make every effort to provide complete and accurate information that reflects your best notes or memory.
- Ask questions, rather than making assumptions, if any part of the agreement is not clear in your mind.
- Ask the reader to confirm that the information is correct. If necessary, invite additional feedback to ensure that you and the reader have a mutual understanding and agreement.

The level of formality of a transmittal message depends on the reader and the situation. Letters to customers or e-mails and memos to colleagues are often cordial, informal messages adding little important information. On the other hand, a report writer might include a formal message in a transmittal letter to introduce the report to the reader. In this case, the report writer can opt to include the transmittal as part of the formal report. Transmittals that accompany official business documents (proposals, bids, contracts, formal reports, etc.) may have legal implications and, therefore, must be carefully worded.

The informally written transmittal document in Figure 10-5 identifies the attached documents and explains relevant information. This document is both brief and congenial, provides the needed information, and follows the guidelines in Figure 10-6.

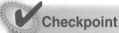

Checkpoint

1. When should the direct approach be used?
2. Which approach should be used to deliver a negative message?
3. What is the purpose of a confirmation message?
4. How is a transmittal message used?

Instructions and Directions

Instructions and directions are routine business messages very similar in nature. The main difference is that **instructions** usually can be carried out in any order, while **directions,** whether simple or complex, usually must be followed in sequence. If the sequence of directions is not followed, the reader may not be able to successfully complete the goal. Both are best written in list format and require clear, precise language. The key to achieving your purpose is clarity.

Figure 10-5.   This e-mail is a transmittal message.

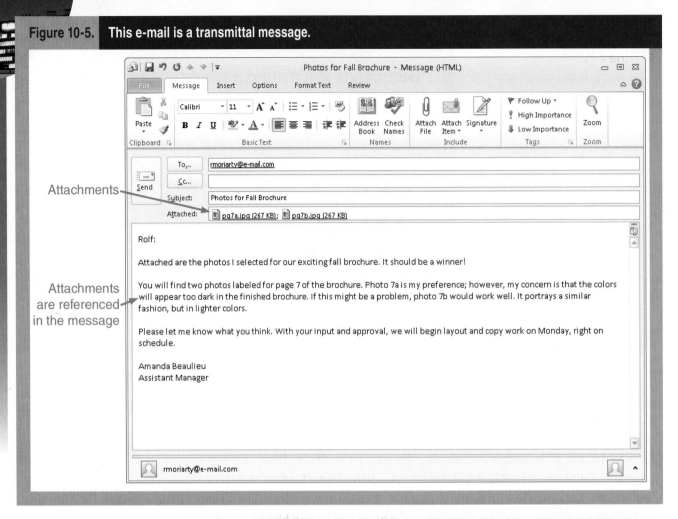

Attachments

Attachments are referenced in the message

Rolf:

Attached are the photos I selected for our exciting fall brochure. It should be a winner!

You will find two photos labeled for page 7 of the brochure. Photo 7a is my preference; however, my concern is that the colors will appear too dark in the finished brochure. If this might be a problem, photo 7b would work well. It portrays a similar fashion, but in lighter colors.

Please let me know what you think. With your input and approval, we will begin layout and copy work on Monday, right on schedule.

Amanda Beaulieu
Assistant Manager

Figure 10-6.   Follow these guidelines when writing a transmittal message.

Guidelines for Writing a Transmittal Message

- Identify or describe what is being sent. Make the message brief, unless you need to provide full details about what you are sending.
- State why the item is being sent if you think that the recipient will be puzzled.
- Explain anything about the contents of the transmitted item that you think is important for the recipient to know.

Begin by thinking about whether the reason for the message is self explanatory. Can the message be conveyed through the subject line of an e-mail, for example, or does it require a few sentences at the beginning of the message? As with all written documents, planning is important. Take time to think through exactly what you want the reader to do. Write your first draft, put it aside for a while, and then read it objectively. Revise and edit to eliminate unnecessary words and substitute precise terms for vague ones. Unclear instructions and directions cause frustration at the very least, but, in the worst case, can cause things to go terribly wrong.

Compare the first and second draft of an instruction for using a recording device:

> **Unclear**
> The amber-colored button on the back panel activates the recording option when moved from left to right.

> **Clear**
> Slide the orange switch on the back from left to right to begin recording.

Notice that the revised version starts with a verb. This construction is better because the sentence identifies the action for the reader. The revised instruction also uses clearer language: *orange* instead of *amber, begin* instead of *activate,* and *back* instead of *back panel.*

Following is an example of well-written instructions. Since each item is independent of the others, the instructions can be completed in any order. The writer begins with a brief explanation of the purpose for the instructions.

> Thanks for filling in for me on Friday. Here are the items that need your attention:
>
> 1. If Philip Otero calls about the status of his contract, tell him it is on the vice president's desk for signature and will be forwarded to him early next week.
>
> 2. An order of office supplies will be delivered around noon. Just sign for them and have the delivery person place the boxes in the supply room. I'll unpack the supplies on Monday.
>
> 3. The flyer for our annual diversity luncheon needs to be e-mailed to the staff. Jeannie in Graphics will forward it to you as soon as she finishes the final corrections. I have proofread the flyer, but please give it one more review and work with Jeannie if there are any errors to fix before you send the e-mail.

Sometimes, it may seem easier to give verbal instructions rather than writing long explanations. Consider, however, that instructions need not be lengthy. Take the time to revise and edit written instructions until sentences are short and clear. Why take this extra time? Consider what could happen if the previous instructions were provided verbally instead of as written instructions. This scenario leaves the burden on the coworker to get it right. The coworker would either rely on memory or would need to take notes. Conversations are not easy to remember when people are very busy. Often, notes jotted down in a hurry are unreadable or inaccurate. How many times have you heard someone say, "I can't read my own writing?" With written instructions, the coworker can focus on each task as the need arises. The writer has taken responsibility for ensuring the reader has a clear understanding of what needs to be done and is able to carry out the instructions with ease. The e-mail shown in Figure 10-7 provides an example of clear directions written in a logical sequence.

Checkpoint

1. What is the difference between instructions and directions?
2. Which format is best for instructions and directions?

Writing a Technical Message

A **technical message** or **technical document** is one in which the reader is provided with technical information. Technical documents inform the reader and are often instructions or directions. User manuals, installations instructions, software documentation and help files, and service sheets are all examples of technical documents.

Figure 10-7.   **This is an example of directions.**

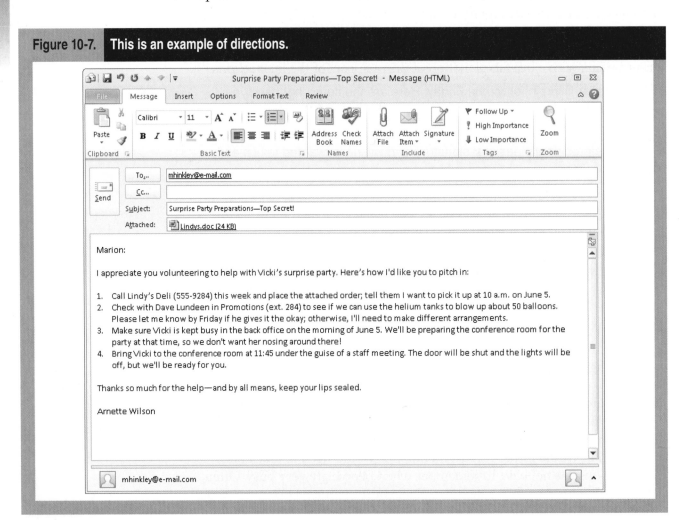

While precise language is important for all messages, it is especially important in technical documents. In many cases, incorrect information in a technical document may lead to injury to the reader attempting to use the information. For example, if a service procedure for a lawnmower is missing a step related to safety, somebody using that procedure could be injured by a belt, blade, or other item on the mower. In addition to the injury to user, there may be an issue of liability for the company that published the incorrect information.

It is very important when writing technical documents to understand the knowledge level of the reader. The language you choose must be accessible to the reader. For example, suppose you are writing a service manual for an industrial-grade hydraulic valve. Most likely, the person reading the service manual will be a professional technician seeking information on repairing the valve. This means you can assume a certain level of knowledge regarding hydraulic systems. On the other hand, an owner's manual for a refrigerator is intended for homeowners. The average homeowner will likely not know what an electroservo motor is, so you need to explain how to identify that component.

Be aware of any terminology the reader may not know or understand. Explain terms when needed, but remember not to talk down to the reader. Also, you cannot use vague or ambiguous language. Technical documents must be very precise.

Many technical documents contain illustrations. Consider a typical owner's manual for a cell phone. The writer must explain how to program and use the phone. Almost every owner's manual for a cell phone will have at least an illustration of the buttons on the phone. Usually, callouts identify the different parts of the phone. Callouts are lines pointing to part of an illustration with text that identifies or explains the part.

Often, when you write a technical document, you will need to work with a technical illustrator. In some cases, the writer may be responsible for the illustrations. In either case, it is important to remember that you are informing the reader of precise information. The ultimate goal is to have the reader fully understand the information you are presenting.

Checkpoint

1. What is the purpose of a technical document?
2. Why is it important to understand the knowledge of the reader when creating a technical document?

Making Requests

Requests ask the reader for some type of action or response. Business workers regularly send and receive routine requests. **Routine requests** are expected by the receiver. Examples of routine requests include requests for materials, information, and services.

Other requests are not routine in nature. They are more complex and require explanation. These are considered **special requests.** Special requests require planning an approach that will create a positive response.

For example, consider a request that will inconvenience the reader because it requires extra work or a change in the way something is normally done. You need to convince the reader to accept the special request. Choose the indirect approach and start with an explanation of your reasons for making the special request. The words you use should show courtesy and diplomacy. **Diplomacy** is the tactful handling of a situation to avoid offending the reader or arousing hostility. Diplomacy goes beyond saying *please* and *thank you.*

Read the letter in Figure 10-8. Notice how the writer is careful to explain the situation. He expresses willingness to pay for the services provided, if necessary. The writer also offers to share information with Mr. Lipscomb as a courtesy.

Balance is the key to writing effective requests. Avoid including too much or too little information. Think about what the recipient needs to know and write accordingly. See the examples in Figure 10-9. The messages progress from too little information, to more than enough information, to just the right amount of information.

The e-mail message in Figure 10-10 contains a request for an appointment. Note how the writer provides sufficient information, but no unnecessary details.

Be Clear, Specific, and Accurate

When you make a request, the most important thing is to put yourself in the reader's place. Analyze what you write to make sure the reader will not have to struggle to determine your request. Plainly state what you want and be as specific as possible. If you have more than one item or question, use bullets to list them.

If you are requesting information about a previous transaction or project, consider if the reader might be confused about the project to which you are referring. Is there a specific title, number, or other identifying feature that will help? Make sure you have included all of the necessary information and double-check to make sure it is accurate. While it may take more time to prepare the message when you have to verify information, ultimately you will save time (yours and the reader's) by being accurate. This is the best way to ensure a timely and accurate response.

Provide Adequate Information for a Response

When making requests, think about what the reader will have to consider. Are there any decisions to be made? If so, you might need to include information to ensure you get what you want, as opposed to what the reader decides to give you. For example, if someone is making airline reservations for you, state your preferences, such as which airline and preferred seating. Include the times you want to arrive and depart and consider other questions that might arise. Does the region have more than one airport? Do you want the best price or is it more important to have a nonstop flight? If you fail to think through the details in advance, you might not be happy with what you get in return.

Figure 10-8. This is a request for a special favor.

Basserette Industries

3370 St. Charles Avenue
New Desert, NV 89772
702.555.6612 Fax 702.555.7157
www.Basserette.com

July 17, 20--

Mr. Elmer Lipscomb
Lipscomb Advanced Laboratories
2732 Trabajo Nuevo Road
Miami, FL 33003

Dear Mr. Lipscomb:

I am the Office Manager for our company and have been given the task to research ways in which we can expand and modernize our laboratory. Our lab was organized many years ago when we were a very small company. Over the years, we have been fortunate to expand our business and greatly increase the number of staff we employ. Our engineers, chemists, scientists, and executives need a modern space with brand new technology at their fingertips.

I am inquiring to see if you have sample model layouts and recommendations for equipment and materials to create a new lab. We are very interested in reviewing any resources that you may have to share with us.

Also, I visited your Web site and noticed that you have a virtual tour of labs you have helped create for other customers. If you could give me a password to log into the demo site, I would appreciate it.

If your department is not the correct contact for new lab purchases, I would appreciate it if you could direct me to the appropriate division of your company.

Thank you very much, Mr. Lipscomb. If we are successful in our lab redesign, we would be happy to serve as a reviewer of your services.

Cordially,

Kenneth Rodriguez
Office Manager

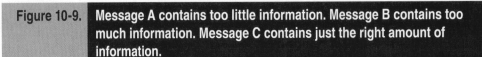

Figure 10-9. Message A contains too little information. Message B contains too much information. Message C contains just the right amount of information.

A Please send me information on the products we can order.
Thanks.

B I recently discovered that I do not have the latest catalogs, price lists, or other information concerning the products and companies from which we order supplies. I have some materials, of course, but they are out of date.

I have just been promoted to the position of administrative assistant to the General Counsel's office. I want to make sure our staff can select appropriate equipment, materials, and supplies. For this reason, I would like to request that you send me the latest catalogs, price lists, and other product information as soon as possible.

Thank You.

C Please send me the latest catalogs and price lists from our office suppliers. I would appreciate any other information about ordering office supplies and equipment.

I am the new administrative assistant for the General Counsel's office. Any guidance you can give me on keeping our staff equipped with the appropriate materials and supplies would be greatly appreciated.

Thank you and I look forward to working with you.

Also, let the reader know exactly when you need to have the request fulfilled. Plan your request in advance to allow enough time for the reader to fulfill the request without being pressured. When the request must be fulfilled in a hurry, it might be wise to phone or e-mail before sending the request and ask if the response can be expedited.

When your request requires something be sent to you, include all information needed by the reader. Include your name, address, phone number, fax number, and e-mail address on any correspondence.

Provide Background Information

Sometimes you need to provide background information for the reader. Always explain why you are making a request unless you are sure the reader knows. You might receive a negative response or no response if the reader does not feel comfortable about fulfilling your request. For example, a human resources department may have restrictions on sharing certain types of employee information. Explaining why you need such information is critical to the decision about whether or not to release the information.

| Figure 10-10. | This e-mail is a request for an appointment. |

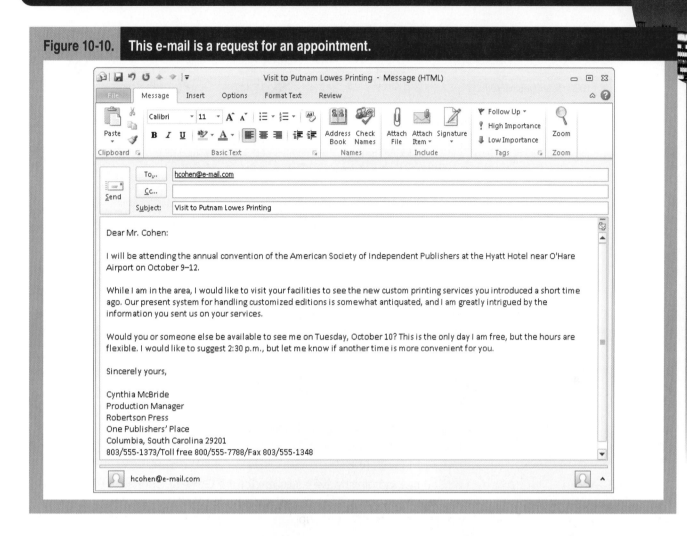

When you supply background information, the reader can be more helpful. He or she might be able to anticipate other needs that you may not realize you have. For example, you ask the information technology department to purchase a software program for your use. However, you are unaware the program will not run on the equipment in your office. By explaining how you plan to use the program, the IT person can suggest an alternative.

Figure 10-11 shows a request that provides background information, allowing the reader to quickly and completely respond. Readers will appreciate it when you use this approach.

Be Courteous

Be courteous when making a request. The words *please* and *thank you* are always in style. Even when you are a customer and the reader has solicited a request from you, it is more effective to ask rather than to demand. People tend to be more helpful when they are treated with respect.

Your courtesy should be sincere, but avoid going to an extreme. When you come on too strong, your words might be perceived by the reader as insincere. Better to say, "the entire department is grateful for your contribution to this project," than to say, "words cannot express how grateful the entire department is for your contribution to this project."

Figure 10-11. This brief letter is a request for information.

Dear Order Department:

Last March, we ordered several cases of 100 percent cotton rag stock from your paper division. We were very pleased with the quality of this paper and would like to place another order. Unfortunately, we have disposed of the boxes and cannot locate the exact stock number of the paper. Your catalog describes over ten varieties of cotton rag stock and we are not certain which one we ordered.

Can you help me by checking your records to find the exact product ordered by Print Co. in March of this year? We ordered the stock in both white and cream. I would appreciate a confirmation of the product numbers, paper weight, and price so that we might place a new order as soon as possible.

Thank you for your help.

Sincerely,

Requests can be written for many different reasons. Whatever the reason, be sure to follow proper writing procedures to create an effective request.

Shutterstock

When you feel a simple thank you will not suffice, it may be appropriate to offer to return a courtesy or favor. For example, if you are conducting a survey, offer to share the results. If you are assembling a proposal, let readers know their contributions will be acknowledged.

Be Reasonable

Make sure that your request is reasonable. It is improper to ask someone to do something that is unethical. It is also unfair to ask someone to do something outside of normal job functions or that requires an extreme sacrifice. You are more likely to get cooperation when your reader does not feel pressured or exploited.

When requesting something that creates work for the reader, find a way to make the task easier. Perhaps you need a speaker on short notice. Maybe you want the reader to complete a lengthy questionnaire. In these situations, you can use an indirect approach. Explain why you are making the request and acknowledge that it might be inconvenient. Balancing your request with courtesy and background information will help you get the response you need.

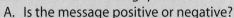

TEAMWORK

Bring a letter that you or your family may have received in the mail. Discuss each example with the group and find support for your answers to the following questions.

A. Is the message positive or negative?

B. Is the message reader oriented?

C. Does the letter appear to be a form letter?

CASE

The Play Is the Thing

Reginald Cornish is in charge of the student activity program at a small college in Brattleboro, Vermont. In the summer he will be hosting a group of international students who are studying English.

Reginald wants to provide the students with cultural activities during their stay. He sees a newspaper listing for a play that he believes the students will enjoy. He wants to write the New London Barn Theater to request rates for group attendance (20 students, one in a wheelchair) at a matinée performance. He hopes to get tickets for one of two Saturdays in August. He wants to make this a fun learning experience, so he decides to inquire about a backstage tour as well. Reginald drafted the following message to the theater manager.

> I would like to arrange for a group of international students to attend a performance of *Meet Me in St. Louis.* Do you have a large block of seats available either Saturday, August 4 or 11? Also, do you offer a student or group discount? Do you offer backstage tours? We would like to stay after the performance and get a short informational tour if possible.
>
> I need this information from you by June 15. Thank you very much.

1. Did Reginald include all of the information the theater manager will need to respond?

2. Rewrite his message to improve the writing style and format.

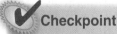

Checkpoint

1. What is the difference between a routine request and a special request?

2. What is diplomacy?

3. Why would you need to provide background information?

Responding to Requests

Like requests, responses to customers, colleagues, and supervisors deal with both routine and special matters. Some requests might require you to confer with others, such as when an exception to a policy or practice of the organization is involved. Other requests might require you to retrieve information from sources inside or outside of the company. In some cases, you might need to organize information in a form that will be most helpful to the person making the request.

Every employee needs to build goodwill with colleagues, customers, and clients. Companies build goodwill through providing consistent, quality service. To build goodwill, consider how you would respond to a request from a supervisor or top executive and then apply the same amount of attention to other requests. Every request is a prospect for a new or continued relationship. Ultimately, these relationships have an impact on your future success within an organization. Your attitude toward working with others and responding to their needs is an important aspect of building a successful career.

Form Response

Businesses that sell a product or service receive routine inquiries and requests from customers and write routine responses in return. The company Web site and social networking pages anticipate these questions by providing extensive information on products and services. The company Web site may also have a **frequently asked questions (FAQ)** page that provides answers to common customer questions. Nevertheless, business workers often have to respond individually to unique customer situations and to answer recurring questions or comments. Companies balance the need to provide quick, accessible answers to customers with the need to build goodwill by showing individual attention.

It is customary for companies to develop form-type responses for correspondence as well as scripts for verbal communication by customer service departments. Form-type responses use standard language, often referred to as **boilerplate** information. Having a standard response ensures consistency and helps avoid problems or confusion about a product or service. Form letters contain standard language for recurring questions, issues, and problems, but can be customized when a special situation demands a specific response.

Be sure to take the time to formulate a response to a request. Carefully think through what you want to say before writing the response.

Shutterstock

Some form-type responses are sent by e-mail. Others are printed on company stationery or postcards. Technology allows for customization of responses that go out to large numbers of customers. Instead of *Dear Customer,* each greeting or salutation addresses the customer by name.

When sending form responses, you need to know whether or not you are allowed to change any of the language and if any additional information should be sent. These decisions are based on the practices of a particular work situation. A good form letter or e-mail:

- uses language that expresses warmth and friendliness, regardless of the positive or negative nature of the original message;
- is addressed to each individual recipient by name;
- communicates that the request is important and welcome; and
- tells the reader how to get additional information or assistance.

The form e-mail in Figure 10-12 was prepared as an automatic response to customers who write to a company about its environmental policies.

Companies also prepare special booklets and brochures that accompany answers to reoccurring questions. These pieces of communication may be sent to a customer with or without a transmittal message.

Figure 10-12. **This e-mail is a form response.**

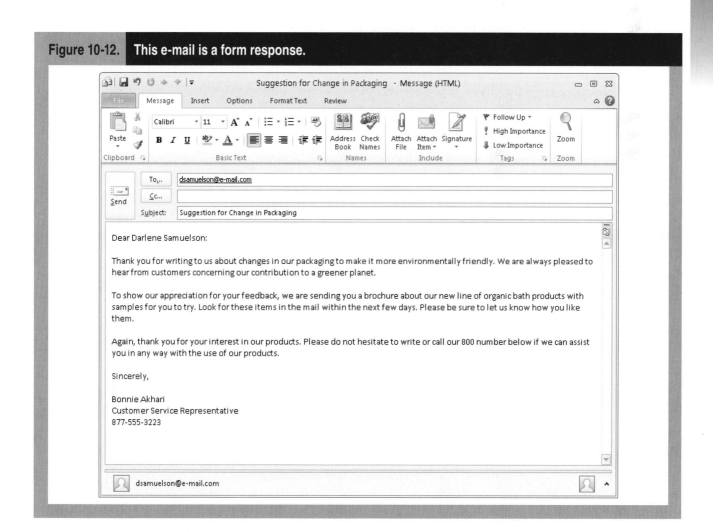

Courtesy Response

The **courtesy response** is written to confirm that a message was received and action was taken. A common courtesy response is to thank a colleague for information or for fulfilling your request. You might also send a quick response to let someone know you received a request and will need some additional time to respond.

Courtesy responses to customers provide businesses with opportunities to build trust and are a gesture of goodwill. For example, a business often sends an e-mail message to a customer who ordered online to confirm that the order has been received and will be shipped. The message shown in Figure 10-13 is an example of this type of response.

Nonroutine Response

Many business situations require responses that do not fit a set pattern. These are classified as nonroutine responses. Here are some guidelines for preparing a response to an inquiry, order, request, question, or comment when you are writing a nonroutine response.

* Open with a positive comment.

* If you cannot respond positively, use the indirect approach.

* Be complete and specific.

* Consider readability.

Whether you are using the direct or indirect approach, begin with a friendly or courteous statement, depending on your relationship with the writer. If your response is unfavorable, begin with an explanation and work your way to the less favorable responses.

Use language that is clear, concise, and specific. Completely answer each question or comment, even when responding to several. If possible, provide answers in the same order that the writer used.

Avoid long paragraphs and too many details. If the response is lengthy, look for ways to break up the text with lists or headings.

Build goodwill. When responding to a negative message, if possible, offer to do something extra as a special gesture of friendliness.

Read the product inquiry in Figure 10-14 and the detailed response in Figure 10-15. Notice how the response meets the guidelines presented here.

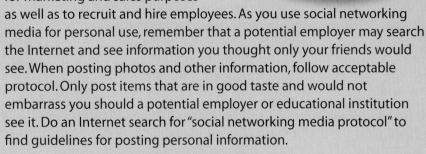

BUSINESS PROTOCOL

Social Networking Media

Many organizations use social networking media, such as Facebook, for marketing and sales purposes as well as to recruit and hire employees. As you use social networking media for personal use, remember that a potential employer may search the Internet and see information you thought only your friends would see. When posting photos and other information, follow acceptable protocol. Only post items that are in good taste and would not embarrass you should a potential employer or educational institution see it. Do an Internet search for "social networking media protocol" to find guidelines for posting personal information.

Figure 10-13. This e-mail is a courtesy response.

Dear Jonathan Douglas:

This e-mail is to inform you that your BuyBooks Account has been successfully created. Your account is immediately active and you may now submit online orders. Should you have any questions, do not hesitate to e-mail us at Buybooks@e-mail.com. We also appreciate any feedback you have for us, so please feel free to send us comments to the same e-mail address.

Please take a moment to review our privacy policy at the following URL: http://buyback.e-mail.com.

We look forward to serving you!

BUYBOOKS CUSTOMER SERVICE

Checkpoint

1. What does FAQ stand for?
2. What is the purpose of a courtesy response?
3. Describe a nonroutine response.

Writing Business Messages to Persuade

Suppose you want to sell your boss on a great idea that will boost sales or maybe you have to write a letter to a customer to persuade them to pay an overdue account. Whenever the primary goal of a message is to convince the reader to take a certain course of action, a **persuasive message** must be crafted.

Figure 10-14. This letter is an inquiry for product information.

Max Products Corporation
3224 Pautuset Avenue
Providence, RI 02933
401.555.2200

May 23, 20--

Ms. Deanna Priazai
American Plastics
1257 Reedson Road
Worcester, MA 01601

Dear Ms. Priazai:

My company is studying the potential use of shrink-wrap packaging in our operations. We are a diversified manufacturer that produces electrical components, automobile parts, plumbing supplies, and canned food as our major products.

I would appreciate it if you would send me technical specifications and pricing information on your shrink-wrap-packaging machinery. Also, any recommendations for the application of this machinery to our operations would be helpful.

Once we have a chance to review this information, we will contact you for any additional information that will aid us in making a purchasing decision.

Thank you for your time and consideration.

Sincerely,

Constance Kennedy

Constance Kennedy
Purchasing Assistant

Figure 10-15. This letter is a response to the inquiry letter shown in Figure 10-14.

 **AMERICAN PLASTICS**

1257 Reedson Road
Worcester, MA 01601
617-555-4400/Fax 617-555-4432

May 29, 20--

Ms. Constance Kennedy
Max Products Corporation
3224 Pautuset Avenue
Providence, RI 02933

Dear Ms. Kennedy:

Thank you for your letter of May 23 requesting information on our shrink-wrap, multiple-packaging equipment.

The enclosed fact sheets list the technical data and the price information you requested. In addition to packaging equipment, our company also manufactures other products that would be beneficial to your operations, particularly your canned foods division. Fact sheets for those products are also enclosed.

I would be pleased to visit your location and make a formal presentation of our product line at a time that works for you. Just let me know when you wish to schedule a meeting.

Thank you for the opportunity to introduce our company line of products to you. You may call me at 617-555-4400 if you have further questions or if you wish additional information.

Sincerely yours,

Deanna Priazai
Product Manager

Enclosure

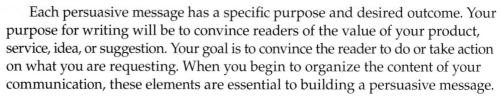

Each persuasive message has a specific purpose and desired outcome. Your purpose for writing will be to convince readers of the value of your product, service, idea, or suggestion. Your goal is to convince the reader to do or take action on what you are requesting. When you begin to organize the content of your communication, these elements are essential to building a persuasive message.

- Attract the reader's attention.
- Build the reader's interest.
- Create desire for the product or service.
- Anticipate questions and objections.
- Encourage the reader to take action.

Attract the Reader's Attention

A persuasive message needs to catch the reader's interest in the opening paragraph. It is important to know your target audience and what will grab attention. Start your message with a strong introduction and keep the information brief and to the point. Your goal is to capture the reader's interest so that the message is read in its entirety, not discarded or deleted.

Build the Reader's Interest

Once you have the reader's attention, hold it with a writing style and tone that will build interest. It takes a skillful writer to capitalize on the interest the opening sentences create. Keep the message alive by using language and a style that is easy to read and understand. Lead the reader to think, *this sounds interesting, and I want to know more about your idea.* Your message will hold the reader's interest if you can give evidence that your suggestions or ideas will help the reader to achieve, have, or do something that he or she wants.

Create Desire for the Product or Service

You can use either of two basic appeals to make people desire things: appeal to emotions through descriptive words or appeal to reason through rational argument. Appealing to emotions may be appropriate for requests such as donating to charity or volunteering for after-work events. A rational argument may be used to show the leaders of a company how becoming more green will improve the bottom line. Your target audience will dictate which approach you use based on your prior experiences with the reader.

Anticipate Questions and Objections

Think about all of the possible objections and questions the reader might have. Anticipate reasons for delaying a decision to respond and provide alternative courses of action. This is especially important if you want the reader to immediately respond to the message.

Encourage the Reader to Take Action

If you want the reader to respond, you must ask them to do something. To encourage action, emphasize the positive points of your ideas, service, product, or company. If you do not ask the reader to take action, do not expect any action to be taken.

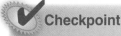

Checkpoint

1. What is the purpose of a persuasive message?
2. List the five elements critical to an effective persuasive message.

CASE

Top Forty

Regina Romano is the assistant manager of the Golden State Coastal Inn, a conference facility and hotel in Oceanside, California. Regina wants to sell local small business owners on using her company's conference facilities. Review Regina's sales message and then answer the following questions.

"Thank you for helping us put on the best conference we have ever had. Your superb facilities, service, knowhow, and helpful attitude all add up to one word: professionalism."

We wanted to share the above message from the vice president of one of our region's leading small businesses. We are happy to say that this is a typical response we get from top executives who choose Golden State Coastal Inn as their host for meetings, conferences, and seminars.

At Golden State, your meetings are our business. Making your meetings successful is our number one priority. Golden State Coastal Inn is not just another magnificent resort center that offers everything any meeting attendee could ask for. Of course, we do offer all sports, including a championship golf course and tennis courts; outstanding cuisine; an almost-ideal climate; nearby shopping malls; and a stunning view of the Pacific Ocean. We are all those things, of course. But, we are more.

By *more,* we mean that we really are professionals when it comes to accommodating your specific needs. At Golden State you will find a staff that is dedicated to personal and friendly hospitality. We provide every service you require to conduct outstanding meetings and conferences.

Skeptical? Let me prove what I have said. Please look over the enclosed colorful folder, which shows our spectacular setting and elegant facilities. Then, to learn more about our professional side, mail the enclosed card for your free copy of *So You're Having a Meeting!*

1. Does this message contain the essential elements of a sales message?
2. How would you revise the message?

Writing a Sales Message

Nearly every persuasive message sells something, even if it is only a point of view, idea, or goodwill. But, the true **sales message** must persuade the reader to spend money for a product or service, either immediately or later. An effective sales message attracts the attention of the reader, while selling the features and benefits of the product or service.

Businesses are very conscientious of effective sales strategies and the costs involved. It is important to target the correct audience for a product or service and present the information in a way the customer can understand and relate it to personal needs and wants.

Many businesses take advantage of the Internet and use e-mail blasts to reach customers. E-mail blasts are targeted mass e-mails sent to users who have expressed interest in receiving updates. E-mail blasts are an inexpensive way for businesses of all sizes to reach current and potential customers. Keep in mind, however, that e-mail blasts are *not* spam. Spam is untargeted, unwanted mass e-mail.

Print campaigns are popular, but the price tag for this medium is expensive. Companies use brochures, catalogs, and other print pieces sparingly due to the cost of printing, paper, and postage.

Social networking Web sites, such as YouTube, Facebook, Twitter, and LinkedIn, provide inexpensive opportunities for businesses to sell their product and services. In order to post on these sites, businesses spend money to create the message, but the posting is generally free.

Attract the Reader's Attention

Ask a question that makes a strong point about the need for what you are selling, the unique feature of the product, or an opportunity that is too hot to pass up.

> Do you remember last winter when we had twelve inches of snow and the stores ran out of shovels?

> Get more for your money—buy our long distance plan for your cell phone.

A lot of mail-order businesses rely on strong sales messages sent to potential customers.

Shutterstock

Think of something that the reader needs or wants and explain why your product or service will meet those needs or wants. Use a provocative statement to get the reader's attention.

> You, too, can be a millionaire.

Make a special offer or the opportunity to get a free sample.

> Discover a new and better way to stay healthy by having fresh fruit delivered directly to your door each month. Without any cost to you, we will send you a sample of our citrus fruits if you sign up for our newsletter on our Web site.

Build the Reader's Interest

Remember, an effective sales message has a positive tone that is reader oriented and captures the attention of the reader. A positive tone stresses the favorable and plays down the unfavorable.

> **Unfavorable**
> It takes up to a month to receive the product from the factory. We appreciate your patience.
>
> **Favorable**
> Once you place your order, you will receive the product directly from the factory in about 30 days.

A good sales message only promises what the company can deliver. It does not rely on exaggeration to make a sale. You are more likely to win the respect and allegiance of readers if you make reasonable, sound offers of products or services.

> **Exaggerated**
> We will never, ever miss your call because our operators are standing by at all times.
>
> **Balanced**
> We do our best to keep our customer service operators available to you 24 hours a day, seven days a week.

Convey that you value your own dignity as well as that of the reader. Talking down, lecturing, or accusing can kill any attempts at persuasion.

> **Talking down**
> Although we are very large and successful, Conover-Crane makes no distinction between small businesses like yours and giant corporations.
>
> **Building up**
> Family-run businesses like yours are important to Conover-Crane.

Create Desire for the Product or Service

To create desire, you can appeal to emotions or reason. The approach you take will depend on the situation, your knowledge of the reader, and your experience regarding what works best.

> **Appeal to emotions**
> You will sleep better, feel better, and look better after you spend a night on a Support Rest mattress.

Appeal to reason
Because of its superior construction, the Support Rest mattress conforms to your body so you sleep in optimum physical comfort that promotes energy and vigor throughout the day.

TEAMWORK

Bring several advertisements or sales brochures to class. Discuss each with your team and find examples of the following points.

1. Attract the reader's attention.
2. Build the reader's interest.
3. Create desire for the product or service.
4. Anticipate questions and objections.
5. Encourage the reader to take action.

Anticipate Questions and Objections

Anticipate questions and objections the reader may have. Then, provide information to answer those questions or overcome those objections. Readers may have questions regarding detailed product/service information, prices, how long a special offer will be valid, how to use a coupon or take advantage of a special offer, available colors/styles/options, placing an order or accessing a service, or contact information. Objections may be related to evidence backing up your statements and claims, proof that your offer is sincere, lack of an included sample, or no trial use of the product with a money-back guarantee.

Encourage the Reader to Take Action

All good sales messages close with a call to action, as shown in Figure 10-16. Remember to do these three things in your messages to increase reader response: 1) make a specific request or call for action, 2) make it easy for the reader to respond, and 3) motivate the reader to respond promptly by giving some reason or incentive.

Make a specific request or call for action
Please call our toll-free number today to receive your free copy of *The Complete Gourmet* cookbook.

Make it easy for the reader to respond
Just complete the attached order form and receive free shipping within the next 14 days. Or, call 1-877-555-2442 or visit our Web site to order.

Provide a reason or incentive to respond
The first 500 callers will receive an original lithograph from the esteemed artist Jorgen Hansford.

Checkpoint

1. What is the key difference between a sales message and other persuasive messages?
2. What are the five elements critical to an effective sales message?

Figure 10-16. **The six steps for writing an effective persuasive or sales message are illustrated in this letter.**

435 South Ironwood Drive
South Bend, Indiana 46675
219-555-5667 Fax 219-555-1234

«Date»

«Name»
«Street»
«City, State, ZIP»

Dear «Name»:

Pancho Gonzales…Rod Laver…Fred Perry…Margaret Court…Billie Jean King…John Newcombe…Arthur Ashe…John McEnroe…Chris Evert…Pete Sampras…Venus Williams…

Pardon me for name dropping, but I have exciting news about these and other all-time tennis greats that I want to share with *Tennis Monthly* readers. You know, of course, that each of these players blazed the pro circuit in one era or another, leaving an indelible imprint on tennis history. But did you know that they were also prolific writers on the subject?

Tennis Monthly has arranged to issue a series of books of major writings of twenty of the greatest names in tennis. The first is Rod Laver on *Tennis,* followed by similar books by those whose names are instantly recognized by every tennis enthusiast.

I think you will find every volume in this series immensely exciting. Each will be profusely illustrated by America's leading tennis artist, Eklund Nillsen, and will be handsomely bound in a rich-looking leather-like cover. The price of each book will be only $29.95, including postage.

Use the enclosed card to order your copy of Rod Laver on *Tennis.* I will accept your personal check or credit card now or I can bill you later. As each volume is released, I will send you advance notice. I don't think you will want to miss a single one.

SPECIAL BONUS! If your order reaches me before May 15, I will include—absolutely free—a beautifully illustrated, 24-page booklet, *Back to Fundamentals.* It could make a big difference in your game!

Sincerely,

Chris Hemby
Editor

Enclosure

Attract attention.
Those who receive *Tennis Monthly* will be familiar with these names, so reader attention captured.

Build interest.
The writer explains the reason for name dropping and gradually builds sufficient interest for the reader to want to learn.

Create desire.
The reader has become interested enough to want to own the product.

Encourage action.
Sufficient desire has been created for the reader to ask, "How do I get this series?" This question is answered and a bonus is offered as an incentive to take action.

Answer questions or objections.
Provide all information a customer will need to make a decision.

Chapter 10 Review

Chapter Summary

Planning

- Writing effective business documents is a process that begins with planning.
- Consider your purpose and the reader when planning.

Providing Information

- Putting information in writing avoids miscommunication and provides a record for all of the parties involved.
- Positive and neutral messages should be straightforward and use a direct approach.
- Negative messages should buffer the news by using the indirect approach.
- Confirmation messages should be written as follow-ups to verbal agreements.
- Transmittal messages should accompany materials to confirm the content of what is being sent.

Instructions and Directions

- Instructions can be followed in any order.
- Directions must be followed in sequence.
- Instructions should be written to confirm expectations.

Writing a Technical Message

- Technical messages and documents provide the reader with technical information.
- Technical documents are often instructions or directions.
- Precise language is especially important in technical documents.

Making Requests

- When making a request, apply the rules of communication and be clear, specific, and accurate.
- Be courteous and reasonable when asking someone to do something for you.

Responding to Requests

- When responding to a request, try to build goodwill for your organization as well as yourself.
- Many responses will be routine, such as a form response or courtesy response.
- There may be some nonroutine responses where you will apply the rules of positive communication.

Writing Business Messages to Persuade

- Writing persuasive messages requires learning how to convince someone to do something.
- By creating a well-written persuasive message, you will be able to accomplish your goal.

Writing a Sales Message

- Sales messages are also persuasive messages.
- A good sales message attracts the reader's attention, builds the reader's interest, creates desire for the product or service, and induces the reader to take action.

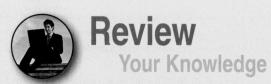

Review
Your Knowledge

1. How does the plan for writing bad news differ from writing good news?
2. Describe a confirmation message and its purpose.
3. Why would you send a transmittal message?
4. Why is sequence important in writing directions?
5. What is the purpose of a technical document?
6. What is the basic difference between a routine request and a special request?

7. What are the guidelines for preparing a response to an inquiry, order, request, question, or comment when you are writing a nonroutine response?

8. Describe the primary goal of a persuasive message.

9. How can you build the reader's interest in a persuasive message?

10. How does a sales message differ from a standard persuasive message?

 Apply
Your Knowledge

1. Write an informational message that explains the following situation to sales representatives and advises them how to act.

> You are a sales manager for Taylor, Aaron & Bache, a pharmaceutical company. Recently a report from the Food and Drug Administration started a panic among consumers regarding synthetic-insulin products. Taylor, Aaron & Bache manufactures synthetic insulin, but not any of the products identified in the FDA report. However, the information that hit the newspapers was inaccurate and could mislead customers.
>
> You want your sales representatives to provide all customers with accurate information on the FDA's findings as they pertain to your products before the customers come to you. You have created a two-page analysis of the findings for this purpose. In addition, if customers have further questions, they can be referred to Taylor, Aaron & Bache's consulting physician, Dr. Orrin Linhouse.
>
> Since this is a sensitive issue, advise the representatives to meet with customers in person to discuss the

> report. If a meeting is not possible, ask the sales representatives to mail the materials and follow up with a personal phone call.

2. Write a request message based on the situation described below. State your specific purpose for writing and informally outline your message before writing.

> You are the office manager for Maxwell Real Estate. One month ago, Leslie James, the president, scheduled a meeting of branch managers to discuss the slump in the real estate market and ways to boost sales. Ms. James wants you to send an e-mail to the five branch managers requesting that they attend this meeting, which will be held after normal business hours. She says this will be a brainstorming session and wants the staff to come prepared with ideas for reversing the downward trend.

3. Write a form letter in response to the following situation.

> A customer makes a request for a review copy of the new trade magazine WebMaster, which is published by your company, Computer Publishing, Inc. You anticipate many requests for this item and need to prepare a form response to accompany the magazine. The publisher is running behind schedule and the magazine will not be available as originally planned.

4. Write a persuasive message for the following situation.

> The national pharmaceutical convention is coming up next month. Three sales representatives from Taylor, Aaron & Bache will need to staff a booth at the convention. Attending this convention will require the reps to travel on two weekends and work on one Saturday. You need to secure a commitment from three of the sales reps to attend the convention and staff the booth.

5. Write a sales letter promoting a service you could provide for a fee. Consider your hobbies, interests, and talents. For example, if you like to take pictures or give parties, you could sell yourself as a photographer or event planner. If you like to shop, you could be a personal shopper or gift consultant. If you know a lot about cars, you could offer to assist clients by accompanying them to a showroom and helping them ask the right questions of the car sales rep.

Practice
What You Have Learned

Access the *Fundamentals of Business Communication* Student Companion Web Site at www.g-wlearning.com/Communication. Download each data file for this chapter. Follow the instructions to complete a reading, writing, and grammar activity to practice what you have learned in this chapter.

Connection
Across the Curriculum

History. Write several paragraphs describing who was the first known company or person to give product samples. Research the history of product samples as needed.

Language Arts. Research the types of social networking media available for businesses and organizations to use for advertising. Create a grid that shows the pricing, restrictions, etc., for businesses to use Facebook, Twitter, YouTube, LinkedIn, and other social networking media. Write several paragraphs to describe the advertising policies for each Web site and the similarities and differences companies should consider when advertising on these sites.

Build
Your Business Portfolio

Your portfolio should not only showcase your academic accomplishments, but the technical skills you have. Are you exceptionally good working with computers? Do you have a talent for playing a musical instrument? Technical skills are very important. Interviewers will want to know what talents and skills you have.

1. Write a paper that describes the technical skills you have acquired. Describe the skill, your level of competence, and any other information that will showcase your skill level.

2. Save the document file in your ePortfolio folder. Create a subfolder named Skills. Save each a document for each skill with the file names Skills01, Skills02, etc.

3. Place a printed copy in your container for your print portfolio.

Careers
Business, Management, and Administration
Careers and Communication

Careers in this cluster involve skills that businesses need to remain productive and run smoothly. Management, business financial management and accounting, and human resources are some career options in this cluster. Business analysis, marketing, and administration and information are also supported in this cluster. People in business also need good computer skills, common sense, decision-making skills, and problem-solving abilities.

Broad skills in planning, organizing, and evaluating business operations are essential in the business world. Describe how good writing skills are important to these broad skills.

Event Prep

Client Service

Client service is a competitive event you might enter with your organization. This event allows you to demonstrate good communication skills. You will be evaluated on your verbal and nonverbal skills as well as the tone and projection of your voice. This will be a timed event you will not be able to prepare for before the competition. The judges will present you with a customer service problem to solve and ask you to interact with them. Review the specific guidelines and rules for this event for direction as to topics and props you will be allowed to use.

To prepare for the client service event, do the following.

1. Read the guidelines provided by your organization. Make certain that you ask any questions about points you do not understand. It is important you follow each specific item that is outlined in the competition rules.

2. Review this unit to learn tips on how to become better at written communication for clients. This unit presents information on how to write for successful communication. To be a good client service representative, you must be able to listen to the customer then convey information, both written and verbal, to meet their needs.

3. Arrange to spend some time with a client service professional who can give you advice on how to effectively address customer issues.

Unit 4
Speaking for Successful Communication

In This Unit

In the business world, face-to-face communication is an important aspect of the job for many workers at all levels. Both managers and the employees who report to them spend a great deal of their workday speaking with a purpose.

Unit 4 will help you develop better speaking skills. This unit shows you how to become a better speaker through the skill of planning for informal and formal speaking situations. You will also practice and polish your presentation and everyday speaking skills. Completing this unit will help you meet college and career readiness (CCR) anchor standards for speaking and listening, as outlined by the **Common Core State Standards**.

11
Speaking Informally

Speech is power: speech is to persuade, to convert, to compel.
—Ralph Waldo Emerson,
19th century American poet

To be an effective speaker, you need to know your purpose and the purpose of the listening audience. You also need to consider what information will accomplish these purposes. Planning what you are going to say and organizing the information according to your purpose will help you decide how to best deliver the message. Each of these elements is essential when planning to speak under formal or informal circumstances in the workplace. This chapter covers informal speaking situations with specific purposes that demand immediate listener feedback.

Objectives

When you complete Chapter 11, you will be able to:

- **Prepare** for informal speaking situations.
- **Describe** appropriate etiquette for answering telephone calls and leaving voicemail messages.
- **Respond** to questions and make requests.
- **Provide** direction to others.
- **Persuade** others to action.

Terms

impromptu speaking   **direct**
etiquette   **persuade**
telephone etiquette

Go Green

Drinking water is a healthy alternative to sodas and caffeinated drinks. Americans buy thousands of bottles of water each day. However, it is expensive to buy bottled water and disposing of the container waste is adding to landfill problems. Try buying a reusable water bottle and filling it with purified tap water instead of buying a bottle of water at the store. You will save money and help the environment.

1. How many bottles of water do you typically purchase in a week?

2. If you purchased a reusable metal bottle for water, how much money would you save in a year?

Be Prepared

There are many instances during a typical business day when you will be required to speak informally. Examples include leaving voicemail messages, participating in team meetings, or providing information to a customer on the telephone. Each of these instances has a specific business objective, no matter how routine it might seem. Of course, you will not be able to plan for all of these situations. However, the habit of planning when you are able will help you have confidence and be more effective in informal speaking situations.

The primary benefit of having a plan is efficiency. In general, a plan will allow you to achieve what you set out to accomplish. The secondary benefit of having a plan is enhancing your professional image. When you are organized, you project a businesslike attitude.

Many informal situations call for impromptu speaking. An **impromptu speaking** situation is one in which you did not have advance notice. In impromptu situations, you can still take a moment to think about what you are about to say. Your goal will be to respond in a positive and intelligent manner. If someone is asking for complex information, you can decide to say, "I'll get back to you." Or, you can direct the person to a source if you are not the right person.

Sometimes you will be faced with impromptu situations that strike you emotionally. A boss might be critical, a colleague might be demanding, or a customer might be rude. This is where professionalism and poise come into play. If you maintain a positive attitude, you are more likely to speak appropriately. Remember your role as the organization's representative at all times and try to respond accordingly.

Reading Prep

Before reading this chapter, look at the illustrations in the chapter to preview the content that will be presented. Illustrations help describe the content in an easy-to-understand manner.

Handling Telephone Calls

Even though many business transactions occur over a Web site or via e-mail, personal contact is still an important part of communication with colleagues and customers. Whether you are making or receiving a telephone call, it is important to remember that you are representing your company, not just yourself.

Etiquette is the art of using good manners in any situation. When you make and receive telephone calls on the job, good **telephone etiquette** is important, which is using good manners on the telephone. You need to learn the guidelines that your organization has in place for answering the telephone.

Customer service representatives may spend most of their day on the telephone with customers. This requires professional and courteous speaking skills.

Shutterstock

Making Telephone Calls

Making telephone calls is a good example of the opportunity to plan. Whether the purpose of this communication is to pass on information, respond to questions or requests, make requests, direct, or persuade, you can improve your effectiveness and productivity by planning.

Planning begins with analyzing the situation. Ask yourself these questions.

- What is the purpose of the message?
- Who is the audience?
- What do I want to communicate?
- What information do I need?
- Has there been any misunderstanding that I need to clear up?

When you are required to relay information to someone else, the best planning technique is to make a list. Anytime you have a number of issues to discuss, questions to ask, or items of information to provide, develop a list. When making telephone calls, having a plan and written notes, if necessary, will help you clearly express yourself and stay organized. A plan will also help you remember everything you intend to cover. The goal is to be friendly and achieve your purpose in an efficient amount of time, Figure 11-1.

Leaving Voicemail Messages

There will be times when you call someone who is not able to take your call. In these situations, it is important that you leave a clear voicemail message. You need to think about what you will say if you reach voicemail instead of the person. Determine how much do you need to explain about the purpose of the call. Also, plan what will you ask the recipient of the call to do. If you want the call returned, specify a time you will be available. The guidelines in Figure 11-2 will help you prepare to leave a voicemail message.

Receiving Telephone Calls

As a worker in a business situation, you will receive calls from colleagues and customers. Try to answer the telephone on the first or second ring. Always be courteous to the caller. It is important to identify yourself when you answer the phone. Practices vary, but you might say the name of the company first and then your own name; for example, "Horton and Associates, Celeste Burrell speaking."

Figure 11-1. Good telephone etiquette is important in all situations.

Making Telephone Calls

- List each topic you plan to cover and be prepared to make notes while you talk.
- When the telephone is answered, state your name, job title, and company, unless the person already knows you.
- Speak clearly and in a normal tone of voice. Avoid using the speaker unless others are present.
- If anyone else is present or on the line, immediately inform the party you called.
- If the call will take more than a few minutes, schedule it ahead of time or ask if the timing is convenient.
- At the end of the call, summarize any important points or decisions.
- If follow-up action is required, summarize what you and the party you called will do and the timeframe.
- Thank the party you called for his or her time, information, or assistance.
- Handle any follow-up within the promised timeframe.

Figure 11-2. These are guidelines for leaving voicemail messages.

Leaving Voicemail Messages

- Speak clearly and at a pace that can be easily understood.
- Leave enough information for the person to act, such as:
  - your name, company, and your position or department;
  - your telephone number, including the area code;
  - a brief message stating the purpose of the call; and
  - when you will be available to receive the return call.
- If your call is urgent, say when you need the response.
- If your name is unfamiliar or difficult to understand, clearly spell your name.
- When you spell information, clarify letters that sound alike (t as in Tom).

You should have a plan for answering the telephone, as well as a plan for making calls. Most businesses have a script to follow if you are taking customer calls. The script helps guide you in conducting a productive conversation. If you are working in customer service, you will probably also receive training in how to deal with difficult customers. Remember, telephone etiquette is important.

You will also need to record a voicemail message for those times when you cannot answer a call. Remember to state your company name, your name, and a specific message that lets the caller know when he or she can expect a return call. Your company will probably have guidelines for recording a voicemail message.

Receiving and Making Requests

While receiving a request, whether on the telephone or in person, make notes as the speaker talks. If you are caught off guard, such as when someone stops you in the hallway, ask if the request is complex. If so, stop to retrieve paper and pen so that you can take notes rather than rely on memory when responding. Even if you have a great memory, trying to keep the facts of a request straight in your head can be challenging. Many workers carry a handheld device. This is a good way for quickly storing and retrieving information.

However, you may not be able to grant every request. If the situation requires you to refuse a request, remember to be professional. Using the indirect approach is a good way to gracefully say no. Explain why you must refuse the request, then tell the person what you can do to help.

When you are the one making a request, whether it is on the telephone or in person, be prepared to give specific directions to the listener. Routine requests are simple and direct and generally do not require much planning.

Consider Karen Von Hoffman. She was asked to prepare sales projections for her region. She recalled that Jim Doherty recently presented the findings of several studies at a planning meeting. He had presented a slideshow highlighting statistics about the characteristics of the population. Jim offered to share the slides with anyone who needed them. Is it appropriate for Karen to ask Jim if she may use his data? Certainly. How might she approach him? Even when a request is routine, it is essential to follow these rules of making requests.

- Be polite.
- Be direct.
- Be specific.
- Be informative.
- Be reasonable.
- Be grateful.

Be Polite

Business etiquette requires courtesy when making a request. Being demanding is never received well by others. Remember, everybody has a job to do, but what you are requesting may be outside of a normal task. Even if the request is related to a normal job task, you will receive better cooperation if you are polite.

Be Direct

Make the request in a straightforward manner. If an explanation is needed, make it clear and concise. Being subtle in a request can lead to misunderstanding. Be up front about what you are asking the other person to do.

Be Specific

Make sure you precisely identify your need for the request. Consider the previous example of a request from Karen to Jim regarding his presentation. Jim may frequently give presentations or he may get requests for any number of other slideshows. It is important for Karen to specify the date or title of the presentation. The person making the request must ensure that the receiver knows exactly what is needed.

Be Informative

When making a request, tell the person when the information is needed and how it is to be used. Why? There may be some reason the requested

It is important to give your undivided attention to the speaker when listening to directions.

Shutterstock

information is not suitable for your intended use. You may not know this, but the other person may. By explaining how you plan to use the material, you give the person an opportunity to share additional information with you.

Be sure to explain any deadlines. If you have a short deadline, be straightforward and polite about it. If the person cannot comply, he or she will tell you.

Be Reasonable

When making a request, be reasonable in what you are asking for and when you need it. If you are requesting 100 copies of something, do not ask the person to have them ready immediately. Make sure your request is not an imposition. Also, it is inappropriate to ask for favors or freebies from persons you do not know well.

Be Grateful

Express appreciation for the response to your request. Be explicit. Offer the listener something in return when appropriate. In the previous example, Karen might say to Jim, "By the way, I plan to add some additional slides to go with the charts. I'll send you a copy in case you might find them useful."

CASE

A Hasty Word

Pauline O'Hara was just finishing up her monthly meeting with the five sales representatives she managed. The reps were packing up their notes and discussing dinner plans when Pauline interrupted: "Oh, one last thing before we go. Miguel sent me an e-mail about a change in the electronic order form. The box for the distributor code number has been moved to the top right corner of the screen. See you next month."

Miguel Espada, vice president of sales, called Pauline two weeks later, "Remember that e-mail I sent you about the new electronic order form? I'm told that your region is the only one where the reps haven't been correctly coding their orders."

"That's funny," Pauline replied. "I told them about it at our last meeting."

1. Why do you think Pauline's reps were not correctly coding the orders?

2. What could she have done to avoid this problem?

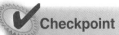

Checkpoint

1. Why should you take notes when receiving a request?

2. What are the six rules for making requests?

Giving Directions

At times you will speak to direct others. When your purpose is to **direct** others—to give instruction or guidance—you need to be sure they understand exactly what you want them to do, when it needs to be done, and why. Put yourself in the listener's place. Do not assume what people already know or predict what they will do. Err on the side of being thorough and precise. Here are a few guidelines for giving directions.

- If instructions are part of a meeting, include the topic as an item on the agenda.
- Use visuals or a handout if necessary to be clear.
- After directions are given, invite questions and feedback from your audience to make certain everyone understands.
- Listen to those you are directing. Your audience will appreciate the fact that you are an active listener and asking for feedback.
- Summarize the discussion before your listeners leave and follow up with a written statement.

 Checkpoint

1. What does it mean to direct others?
2. Why should you listen to those you are directing?

Persuading Others

Many business situations require you to persuade others. When you **persuade** someone, you convince that person to take a course of action you propose. You may want to persuade your supervisor to approve an equipment purchase, a customer to purchase your products, a coworker to help you complete a project, a supplier to speed up delivery, or your team to put in extra time on a special project.

Some of these situations, such as selling, might require specialized training. Others, such as seeking help from a coworker, might require you show the benefit the coworker will receive by helping you. Once again, good interpersonal skills are fundamental to your success.

TEAMWORK

Discuss with your group the information and arguments you might use to be persuasive in the following situation. Talk about all of the possibilities for negotiating an agreement.

You work in a small company and your job is critical to the daily operation. You have an arrangement with your colleague, Jane Wilcox. Each of you takes vacation time only when the other can be at work. On Wednesday afternoon, you find that you need to take a vacation day this Friday due to a family situation. Jane already has plans to take the day off and you have known this for weeks. When you explain the situation to Jane, she says, "I'm sorry. I've been planning this long weekend for months. I don't get enough time off as it is and I'm swamped with work right now. I won't be able to plan another day off for a long time."

If a person likes and respects you, it is much easier to persuade him or her to do what you want. If a person does not know you, his or her impression of you—your professional attitude and image—will influence the response.

Persuasion is one of the most challenging communication processes. Each situation requires a different approach or, in some cases, several different approaches. Moreover, the listener's response to one approach often forces you to take another approach, making perfect planning impossible. Nonetheless, with careful planning, you should be comfortable approaching the topic from several different angles. Being persuasive requires planning and research. The amount of planning and research depends on the situation. Figure 11-3 provides some guidelines for preparing a persuasive talk.

Checkpoint

1. What does it mean to persuade someone?
2. Why are good interpersonal skills required for persuasive speaking?

Figure 11-3.   These guidelines will help you prepare for a persuasive talk.

Keys to Preparing a Persuasive Talk

- **Understand your goals.** Know which of your goals are most important and which goals you are willing to compromise (and to what extent).

- **Understand your listener's needs and goals.** Anticipate how your listener will respond to each of your points. Make your best points first and be ready to give something in return for meeting your goals.

- **Focus on your listener's counterarguments.** Understand the reasons for accepting or not accepting your points. Use your listener's reasons to direct your own responses.

- **Be prepared.** Have all of the facts, statistics, and arguments that might persuade your listeners. Consider how you might use data to strengthen your position and address the listener's questions and concerns.

Chapter 11 Review

Chapter Summary

Be Prepared

- Efficiency is the primary benefit of having a plan for informal speaking.

- When you are prepared, you are able to achieve your goals and project professionalism.

- Being prepared helps you to have confidence and represent your organization in a positive manner.

Handling Telephone Calls

- Preparing for telephone calls will ensure you accomplish your goals and be efficient with your time as well as the receiver's time.

- Using good telephone etiquette is important to create a positive impression for your organization.

Receiving and Making Requests

- If someone makes a request of you, be certain to take notes.

- Taking notes will ensure that no details are omitted when you give your response.

- When you are making a request, be clear in the details so the listener knows exactly what you need.

Giving Directions

- When giving instruction or guidance to others, give specific details so that the listener understands what is expected of him or her.

- Always summarize and follow up to make sure the directions were clear and understandable.

Persuading Others

- You can persuade a listener by considering all of the information and points that might persuade the listener.

- Be prepared for counterarguments to those the listener might use, showing how your point of view benefits the listener.

 ## Review
Your Knowledge

1. What is an impromptu speaking situation?
2. Define etiquette.
3. Explain what is meant by telephone etiquette.
4. What are five questions to ask yourself when making a telephone call?
5. If your call is urgent, what should you do when leaving a voicemail?
6. List the guidelines you should use when making a request.
7. When your purpose is to direct others, what three things must you be sure the listener understands?
8. What is the last thing you should do when providing directions?
9. Define persuade.
10. What two things are required to be persuasive?

 ## Apply
Your Knowledge

1. Consider several situations you may encounter in a business setting that require impromptu speaking. Write one or two sentences describing a situation and turn this in to your instructor. Your instructor will then draw random situations from all of those submitted and select students to act out the situation.

2. You have received a new phone system at work and now need to record your voicemail message. Plan what you want the message to say, then write it out. Practice reading the message aloud until you are happy with how it sounds.

3. For each of the following situations, write down the information you must have to make the request and the information you must request.

   A. You need to hire an additional office assistant to lighten the workload of the other two assistants. You need to talk to someone in Human Resources about running a want ad; it is the first time you have coordinated this type of activity.

   B. You have an appointment with a benefits counselor to discuss your choice of medical and dental benefits.

4. Write notes to plan a conversation for the following situation in which you must provide direction to a new employee.

> Your new assistant came highly recommended. Shortly after he started, however, he had some personal problems that interfered with his work. As far as you know, he has his personal life back on track, but his work has not returned to the level you saw when he started. He is sometimes late for work or leaves early. He extends his breaks and lunch hour. Routine tasks such as filing and mailing seem to take longer to finish. And he seems to work less independently now, relying on you for many simple, routine decisions that he used to make. You are going to talk with him to provide direction on improving his performance.

5. Write notes to plan a conversation for the following situation in which you must persuade the IT person to write a letter for you.

> You are swamped at work and your boss asks you to respond to an unusual request made by a client. The client has numerous questions about your company's customer response management system (CRMS) because she is considering a CRMS for her business as well. Your boss hands you the client's letter and says, "Try to get a response in the mail by tomorrow afternoon." You know you are not the best person to handle this request because you

will simply have to go to the IT department to get the information. You must ask the IT director to write at least a rough draft of this letter for you.

Practice
What You Have Learned

Access the *Fundamentals of Business Communication* Student Companion Web Site at www.g-wlearning.com/Communication. Download each data file for this chapter. Follow the instructions to complete a reading, writing, and grammar activity to practice what you have learned in this chapter.

Connections
Across the Curriculum

Social Studies. Use the Internet to research the term "etiquette." Write several paragraphs describing what the term means, where it came from, and how it has evolved in the 20th and 21st centuries.

Math. Create a line graph that shows the progress of the cell phone. Use the Internet to research this topic. Start with the first year the cell phone hit the consumer market through cell phones today. Plot time versus the number of phones in use.

Language Arts. Write several paragraphs to accompany the line graph you created in the math activity. Describe the first cell phone and how it has evolved into today's most popular phones.

Build
Your Business Portfolio

An important component of any portfolio is a list of references. References can be personal (friends or relatives), people for whom you worked, or someone with whom you provided community service. Always get permission to use someone's name as a reference. You will want to adjust this list before an interview based on if the interview is for a job, college entrance, or a community service position.

1. Call several people for whom you have worked. Ask them if they are willing to serve as a reference for you. If so, ask for their contact information and verify that you have correctly written the information.

2. Call several people with whom you have done volunteer work. Ask if they will serve as a reference for you.

3. Save the document file in your ePortfolio folder. Create a subfolder named References. Save the file with the name References01.

4. Place a printed copy in your container for your print portfolio.

Careers
Information Technology Careers and Communication

Do you find the ever-changing world of computer technology fascinating? With work available in every segment of society, information technology (IT) careers are among those most in demand. The IT career pathways include network systems, information and support services, programming and software development, and interactive media.

IT professionals must be able to give and follow directions, so communication skills are crucial to their success. Give examples of situations where an IT person would give and follow directions.

Event Prep

Extemporaneous Speaking

Extemporaneous speaking is a competitive event you might enter with your organization. This event allows you to showcase your communication skills of speaking, organizing, and making an oral presentation. You will be evaluated on your verbal and nonverbal skills as well as the tone and projection of your voice. This will be a timed event for which you will not be able to prepare prior to the competition. You will be given several topics from which to choose and a time limit to create a speech as well as a time limit to deliver the speech. Review the specific guidelines and rules for this event for direction as to topics and props you will be allowed to use.

To prepare for the extemporaneous speaking event, do the following.

1. Read the guidelines provided by your organization. Make certain that you ask any questions about points you do not understand. It is important you follow each specific item that is outlined in the competition rules.

2. Ask your instructor for several practice topics so you can practice making impromptu speeches.

3. Practice, practice, practice. Your speech will be judged by a panel of professionals.

4. Ask your instructor to bring together a panel that will listen to your practice speech and provide feedback.

12
Giving Presentations

Speak clearly, if you speak at all; carve every word before you let it fall.

—Oliver Wendell Holmes, Jr., American jurist

The ability to speak with ease in front of a group is an essential skill in almost any career. Many people think of public speaking as a talent—you either have it or you do not. This is true only to a degree. Some people are naturally more at ease being in the spotlight than others, but the skills needed to make effective, informative presentations can be learned.

Like all other communication skills, being a good speaker is definitely an asset and certainly required of leaders in any field. If you possess this skill, you improve your chances of being promoted. At a minimum, you open yourself up to exciting, challenging opportunities. If you feel uncomfortable about the challenge of giving a presentation, you will get better at it with preparation and practice.

Objectives

When you complete Chapter 12, you will be able to:

Describe oral presentations.

Identify the steps to plan a successful presentation.

Prepare the content for a presentation.

List techniques for being a skilled presenter.

Terms

oral presentation

demographics

analogy

subjective

visual displays

handouts

demonstrations

presentation notes

enunciation

modulation

pitch

intonation

monotone

body language

Go Green

Turning off the power to equipment at the end of the day can save up to 25 percent on energy costs. Whenever you leave a room or if there is enough natural light to brighten the room, turn off the lights. Use a power strip for all of your equipment so that one flip of the switch turns off all of your devices. Power-down your computer and turn off the printer to save energy each evening.

1. Do you turn off all of your electronic devices at the end of each day?
2. For one month, try turning off all electric devices when they are not in use. At the end of the month, compare the electric bill with the previous month. Did your energy bill decrease?

Oral Presentations

An **oral presentation** is a speech, address, or presentation given to a group. The presentation may be a product demonstration for a few potential customers, a speech at a large convention, a report to the executive committee, or a workshop on management techniques, among other examples.

Oral presentations vary greatly in length, topic, and audience and may be formal or informal. Sometimes one speaker does all of the talking. In other presentations, two or more people share the responsibility, as in a panel discussion. Often the presentation includes a question-and-answer session, allowing the audience to participate. The audience may be coworkers, customers, professionals from other companies, or some other group with a shared interest in the topic.

Perhaps you are thinking you will not need to give presentations in your career. However, chances are that you will give presentations, if only infrequently. Presentations have become a routine part of most careers. Accountants, architects, designers, nurses, paralegals, administrative assistants all are likely to give presentations as part of their work, to provide just a few examples.

A presentation involves the same basic work as any other communication. You must plan, prepare the content, and then give the presentation. The rest of this chapter guides you through this process.

Reading Prep

Before reading this chapter, look at the illustrations in this chapter. Illustrations help the reader visualize the situations that are being presented in the content. What can you predict will be covered?

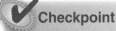

Checkpoint

1. What is an oral presentation?
2. How does an audience typically participate in a presentation?

Presentations are common in almost every career. Some presentations are very formal, while others may be very informal.

Shutterstock

Planning a Presentation

All successful presentations begin with planning. The steps for planning a presentation are similar to the steps in the writing process discussed in Unit 3. Identify the purpose, audience, situation, main ideas, organization, and materials needed (projector, whiteboard, handouts, etc.). Read, research, and think about your topic. This will help you decide how to organize the information and the level of detail to include within each main part of your topic.

Identify the Purpose

A presentation will be given to pass on information, respond to questions and requests, make a request, direct others, or persuade. These are general purposes. In addition, there will be at least one specific purpose, which is the content of the presentation. For example, the general purpose may be to persuade, while the specific purpose is to get a new software purchase authorized. Once you have identified the purpose of the presentation, write a sentence that clearly and concisely describes the purpose. You should refer to this sentence as you develop the presentation to be sure the message is meeting this objective. Remember, select the direct approach for good news and the indirect approach for news that may not be received well.

Analyze the Audience and Available Time

Think about the needs of the audience. You may need to define terms for the audience before discussing an idea. Or, you may need to describe the situation that has caused a change in policy before explaining the change. Depending on the situation, you should have some knowledge of the audience. Even if the presentation will be given at a conference to a group of people you do not know, you can assume that since they are attending the conference, they are familiar with the topic of the conference. For example, if the conference is for small business owners, you can assume the audience knows the basics of running a business. Additionally, most conferences can provide you with demographics of attendees. **Demographics** are information about a group of people (the conference attendees, in this case).

Also, determine the amount of time you will have for the presentation. You will need to fit the presentation into the available time. This may mean adjusting how much detail you provide in certain areas of your presentation. Or, you may need to provide facts and figures as handouts the audience can refer to instead of listening to you discuss the information. For example, if you are given a presentation to convince a board of directors to hire additional staff, you may provide work statistics as a handout the directors can review after the presentation. Time constraints may also impact the delivery method. For example, if you only have five minutes to speak with the board of directors, you will not have time to set up a projector and use a PowerPoint slideshow.

Gather Information

The topic determines where you look for information. You may need to consult sales figures, compare prices from competing suppliers, or obtain sales brochures or product information from manufacturers. The information may be sourced from primary research or secondary research. Primary and secondary research are discussed in detail in Chapter 17.

Remember, if you use existing material in the presentation, you need to credit the original author. You should mention the source in the oral portion of the presentation, but in any handouts or printed reports accompanying the presentation the source should be formally cited. Review Chapter 7 for more information on gathering information and citing sources.

Determine Delivery Method

Once you have gathered all of the needed information and analyzed the audience and available time, you can determine the best method for delivering the presentation. Most oral presentations are delivered live, either in person or via a Web seminar, Figure 12-1. However, in some cases, the presentation may be recorded and made available as an on-demand download or streaming video or provided on a CD/DVD.

If time and equipment allow, using a slideshow to accompany the oral presentation is an effective method of delivery. Microsoft PowerPoint is a popular choice for electronic slideshows, but there are many other programs. Some presenters use Java- or Flash-based "shows" to accompany the presentation. The slideshow is for the audience and is not your personal notes. Many of the best presenters never look at the slideshow during their presentation. Instead, they have notes on cards to refer to as needed.

Figure 12-1. This presentation is being delivered as a demonstration of using Adobe Photoshop software with the presenter explaining what is being done on screen.

Shutterstock

Often, a presentation is given as a Web seminar. This delivery method allows people in different locations to attend the presentation. In many cases, there is nobody in the same room as the presenter. Common software for Web seminars includes GoToMeeting and WebEx. The presentation can consist of video, voice, and text messaging. Usually, the video is the presenter's computer screen shared with the attendees. The presenter can talk while showing something on screen, such as a PowerPoint presentation or a software demonstration. In many cases, text messaging is used to allow attendees to ask questions of the presenter. In other cases, the attendees may call in on a phone and can speak directly to the presenter and other attendees.

Video conferencing is, in some ways, similar to a Web seminar. Video and voice are transmitted back and forth between different locations. In a video conference, a camera and microphone in each location record what is said and the action. These data are transmitted to the other location and displayed on a video screen with sound. In this way, the attendees in each location can see, hear, and interact with each other.

When determining which method is best for delivering your presentation, there are several things that need to be considered. If you are planning on using technology, such as for a Web seminar or video conferencing, make sure all attendees will be able to access the presentation. If you are using a PowerPoint slideshow or other type of show in a single location, be sure the location will have the equipment needed. If there is a reason to save the presentation, you will need to have a way to record and save the presentation. Additionally, be sure to consider the available time. Make certain that the delivery method you choose will allow the presentation to be completed in the allotted time.

CASE

Expert Words

Ray Haley is a scientist in the environmental lab of a chemical processing plant, ChemRite. He was asked by the town council to explain the company's pollution reduction activities and how these efforts conform to local, state, and national regulations. Ray is very comfortable with this topic, so he readily outlined the information he would cover in his talk. Because he was rarely called on to speak in public, he decided to write his presentation in full. Here is an excerpt:

> With regard to national regulations, I will, if you please, expound upon the exemplary record of ChemRite. No other company of similar size or stature has maintained the stringent effluent regulatory standards that are the hallmark of ChemRite's environmental policy. The polemic of certain strident environmental groups aside, we at ChemRite do care deeply about preserving our earth and our future on this planet.

1. How do you think Ray's speech was received by the town council?

2. Why do you think Ray chose to speak in this style?

3. What constructive criticism would you give him?

4. How would you rewrite the excerpt to better get the point across?

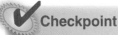

Checkpoint

1. What are five general purposes a presentation may serve?
2. What are demographics?
3. How are most oral presentations delivered?

Preparing Content for a Presentation

With the presentation planned, it is now time to prepare the content for the presentation. This includes what you will say along with any slides or other visual elements you will use. Begin by drafting the presentation.

Drafting the Presentation

When you begin to draft a presentation, develop an outline that follows the format you would use for a written document.

- Begin with an introduction.
- Identify main points.
- Identify subtopics (details) within each main point.
- End with a conclusion.

As you develop the outline, think about the situation and the most appropriate way to deliver your message. The material must be organized and presented in a logical manner. When the draft of the outline is complete, review it until you feel comfortable with the topics and order. Then you will be ready to develop the content of the presentation.

To begin drafting the presentation, write sentences, words, or phrases next to each topic on the outline to act as cues to what you want to say. If you are a beginning speaker or if the topic is complex, you might opt to draft your presentation word for word. As you write, think about how spoken language differs from written language. Aim for a less formal, more conversational delivery. Be sure to identify any words that might be unfamiliar to your audience and plan to explain them.

> When preparing the content of a presentation, be sure to include any visual aids you may need, such as slides or graphs.

Shutterstock

Introduction

The introduction of the presentation serves several purposes. It should introduce the topic of the presentation and preview the main points. In other words, "Tell them what you are going to tell them."

The introduction serves another important function, which is to draw the listener into the presentation. Include something to grab the attention of those listening to the presentation. Once you have their attention, the rest of the presentation will need to hold their attention.

Body

The body of the presentation is where you make your main points. Remember, you have introduced the audience to these points in the introduction. The main points should be presented using either the direct or indirect approach, depending on the topic. The points should appear in a logical order. As you finish each main point, briefly summarize it.

Too many main points can lead to a long, drawn-out presentation. This usually results in losing the attention of the audience. Remember, one of the four C's of communication is to be concise. Keep the number of main points to a manageable number. This will vary depending on the topic and audience.

Conclusion

The conclusion should relate to the purpose of the presentation. The conclusion should also summarize the entire presentation. In other words, "Tell them what you told them." By restating the main points and relating them to the purpose of the presentation, the audience is able to more readily retain the information. The conclusion is often where the presenter will ask for questions and answer them. This helps engage the audience with the presentation as well as allows the audience to get clarification on any points they did not understand.

Effective Presentation Techniques

Avoid reading a presentation word-for-word or trying to recall a presentation completely from memory. Reading word-for-word results in a presentation that is very boring for the audience. Also, when doing so, you cannot make eye contact with the audience. It is very important to make a lot of eye contact with the audience. It adds a personal touch and makes the audience feel connected to you. If you try to recall the presentation entirely from memory without using any notes, you run the risk of forgetting part of the presentation.

Two techniques that can enhance a presentation are the use of facts and humor. Using reliable, truly informative facts is an important part of any good presentation. Humor can also be a way to win over an audience, provided you use it correctly. Relying too much on humor or using the wrong kind of humor can detract from your message.

Facts

It is important to back up generalizations or opinions with facts and figures. Audiences want specifics, and you want to be perceived as credible. Throughout your presentation, be clear about whether you are stating a fact or an opinion.

Opinion

Our competitors are using advertising and it is working. I believe that if we invest more dollars in print and online advertising, our sales will grow over the next six months. This opinion is based on recent studies by Reliable Data Today, our standard source for consumer studies.

Fact

I have some statistics from Reliable Data Today, our standard source for consumer studies. Their numbers indicate that people who purchased new electronics over the past six months relied on print and online advertising 50 percent of the time. My conclusion is that advertising would be the best way to increase sales over the next six months.

Because statistics are so likely to influence opinion, they must be used responsibly. Consider this example.

Sales of exercise equipment rose almost 6 percent in March—that's up 18 percent over last year's sales during the same period.

What if the percentage of sales in March included purchases by fitness centers, when previous figures did not? Would the statistics cited reflect an actual difference in overall sales or just more accurate reporting? It is helpful to know how data were gathered and analyzed before using them to make a point. Cite only data that come from reliable sources. Never alter data to support your position.

If you use statistics in a presentation, keep in mind that numbers and facts can be dry and boring. Nothing puts an audience to sleep faster than a long list of data. Make the facts interesting by relating them to everyday experiences or ideas. An **analogy** is a comparison of two unlike things based on a particular aspect each have in common. Consider how the following analogy aids the listener's understanding of the facts.

Fitness experts recommend walking at least 10,000 steps per day in your daily routine. Is that really possible for the average person who works behind a desk? Does anyone know or want to guess how that translates to distance? [Let audience members answer/guess.] It's the equivalent of walking from here to downtown—about five miles.

The speaker not only used an example the audience could easily grasp, the audience was asked for participation. Doing this at the beginning of a talk is a good way to lock-in audience interest.

Humor

A short, funny story is often a good way to open a talk or provide comic relief during a presentation, Figure 12-2. However, some topics are very serious and humor should not be used in the presentation. When the topic

Figure 12-2.   Humor can be an effective way to engage the audience.

Shutterstock

will not be diminished by a touch of humor, consider how you might weave a joke or amusing anecdote related to your topic into the presentation. You can always find good jokes and stories in books and on the Internet. If you tell a personal story, make sure it is not too personal. You never want to make your audience feel uncomfortable.

When using humor, remember that humor is extremely subjective. **Subjective** means that how it is interpreted depends on personal views, experience, and background. What is funny to one person may be extremely offensive to another. Never use a joke or anecdote that could offend someone. A joke in poor taste or at the expense of someone else is in bad form and will ruin your rapport with the audience.

Also, of course, make sure the joke is actually funny. This often has as much to do with delivery and timing as it does with content.

Visual Elements

Another way to make your presentation more interesting and informative is to supplement your words with supporting visual material. Tasteful and appropriate visual displays, handouts, and demonstrations can be used to emphasize key points and add variety and interest to your presentation. See Figure 12-3. Visual elements can help your presentation achieve the four C's of communication by making the presentation more vivid and memorable.

Visual elements are strong aids in helping the audience remember what is presented. If you are not giving your audience a handout or other materials to take away, quality visuals increase the likelihood that listeners will retain key information. Figure 12-4 provides guidelines for using visuals effectively.

CASE

Lunch, Anyone?

Clarice Peters works in human resources at a transportation company. Her company is starting an employee suggestion program and she is going to make a presentation to inform employees about the program and encourage them to participate. She knows that in her audience of 500, there are workers who will be skeptical. An important idea that Clarice wants to get across is employee ownership. She believes the suggestion program is a powerful way for employees to *own* the conditions under which they work.

Clarice settled on using a humorous anecdote to amuse and inform her audience at the same time. She included this story in her talk right after her introductory remarks:

> A friend of mine told me a story about one of his coworkers. It seems that every day this fellow would bring his lunch, and every day he would complain to my friend about it. "Peanut butter again," he would groan, or, "A lousy apple…I wanted grapes." My friend usually played along, but one day it got to him. He turned to the guy and said, "If you never like your lunches, why don't you make them yourself?" "Gosh," the fellow replied, "I already do."

Clarice's audience responded with laughter. She had won them over and kept their attention and interest for the rest of her talk.

1. What made Clarice's anecdote successful?

2. Do you think it could offend anyone?

3. Why do you think it was more effective than it would have been to lecture about not grumbling and doing something?

4. What do you think Clarice might say after the anecdote to tie it into her overall message?

Visual displays are large graphic elements that accompany the presentation. These are often slideshows, but if a computer projector is not available, posters, flipcharts, or whiteboards may be used. Visual displays can show charts, graphs, photographs, or drawings. If the display is electronic, video and animation can also be displayed.

Handouts, also called leave-behinds, are printed materials that you distribute to the audience. Generally, handouts are used to help the listener understand the presentation, provide additional information, or both. They are useful for providing an outline of your key points or supplemental information that is not covered in your presentation. The nature of the material in the handout varies depending on the topic. For example, you might distribute a brochure or article written by an expert on the topic you are discussing. However, do not overload people with a large amount of reading material.

Figure 12-3.   **Visual elements can enhance your presentation.**

Visual Elements

Visual aids help your audience:

- increase understanding by presenting information graphically;
- remember information by providing visual images; and
- check understanding by relating what they hear to what they see.

Visual aids help you:

- provide a medium other than words to help you explain an idea;
- remember the order of information;
- provide a means of emphasizing and dramatizing important information;
- affect listeners even after they have left the presentation;
- maintain audience interest and enjoyment of your presentation; and
- provide variety and interest to the presentation.

Figure 12-4.   **Follow these tips if you plan on using visual elements in your presentation.**

Tips for Using Visuals

- Use only visuals that enhance the information you are presenting.
- Explain to listeners the purpose of each visual.
- Choose a medium and visuals that can be clearly seen from all parts of the room.
- Use visuals that enhance your professional image.
- Practice using the visuals so that your timing is correct.
- Make sure you know how to work technical equipment.
- Check all equipment before your presentation to ensure that it works properly.

Figure 12-5 provides some guidelines for using handouts. If listeners need the information during the presentation, distribute the materials before you begin. Place handouts on a table at the front or hand them out as people enter. For distribution after the presentation, pass them out while people are still seated.

Is there a way to show your audience exactly what you are describing? If so, work a **demonstration** into your presentation. For example, if you are explaining how to operate a piece of equipment, demonstrate its operation for your audience. If the equipment cannot be moved to where you are speaking, consider displaying a video of someone operating the equipment during your presentation.

If possible, involve the audience in the demonstration. Audience participation makes an impact on listeners and adds interest to your talk. It is a way to engage the audience with the topic of your presentation.

Figure 12-5. **Follow these tips if you plan on using handouts with your presentation.**

Tips for Using Handouts

- Do not assume audience members will read your handouts.
- Keep handouts as short as possible; be concise.
- Use a format that presents the information in a way that is visually appealing and professional.
- Include your contact information and the date of the presentation.
- If the handout or presentation is available on a Web site, include the appropriate URL.
- Before the presentation, plan when and how you will use handouts.
- Have a plan for quickly distributing materials without distraction.
- Before referring to a handout during your presentation, be sure each person has a copy.

Developing Presentation Notes

Once you have the presentation completely planned, written, and practiced, you can then convert the script to an outline with notes. **Presentation notes** are what you will use during the presentation to keep track of where you are in the presentation and to remind yourself of points should you forget anything.

Using the outline for the presentation, write down a few words for each point. The words you choose should remind you of the point, but should be brief. Remember, during the presentation you should be maintaining eye contact with the audience, not reading from notes. You can either write the words directly on your outline or you can use a note card for each point.

If you are using PowerPoint to create a slideshow for your presentation, you can make use of the notes feature. For each slide, add a few words in the notes area. Then, when you print the presentation, you can choose to print the notes. See Figure 12-6. You can then use these sheets as your presentation notes.

If you want to share your presentation with the audience, consider posting it on a Web site. In this way, the audience can access the presentation at a later date. If you post your presentation on a Web site, be sure to include the URL on a handout or include it on a visual aid and point it out.

TEAMWORK

Select one of the following as a small group activity.

A. Each group member will use a fact or statistic to create an analogy that would help a listening audience understand an idea. Each person will give a short (no more than two minutes) presentation of the analogy and get feedback from the group. Was the analogy logical? Was it effective? Was it interesting? Are there any suggestions for improvement?

B. Identify a cartoon, joke, or anecdote that could be applied to a business situation. Explain the idea or situation and provide feedback to each other based on the questions above.

Figure 12-6. You can print any notes you have added to the PowerPoint presentation. This is an easy way to create presentation notes.

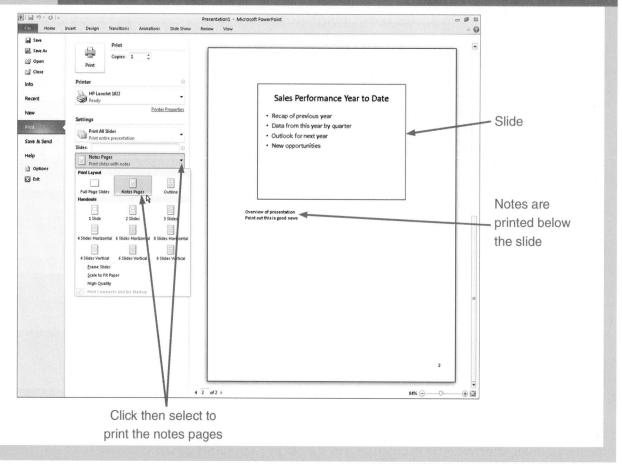

Click then select to print the notes pages

Checkpoint

1. What are the three basic parts of a presentation that need to be drafted?
2. What is an analogy?
3. What are visual elements in a presentation?

Giving a Presentation

Some people enjoy giving presentations; others approach presentations with fear. The average person probably feels nervous toward speaking in front of an audience. The idea is to conquer your nerves through planning and preparation.

Presentation skills include speaking ability (your voice quality, tone, and enunciation); body language, including eye contact and hand gestures; your comfort level with the material; your ease in using visuals and notes; and remembering what you want to say. Another important skill is your ability to plan for and handle problems that may arise during a talk.

By analyzing and adjusting how you use your voice, words, and body language, you can improve the delivery of your message. The checklist in Figure 12-7 will help guide you through the steps of becoming a skilled presenter. The benefits of sharpening your skills extend beyond formal speaking situations. You will also become more effective in the daily interactions that require you to speak.

Once you develop a presentation, practice is essential. When you are relaxed and confident, you will put your audience at ease. Good planning and sufficient practice are the best ways to become relaxed and confident with your presentation.

BUSINESS PROTOCOL
Cultural Awareness

When you are communicating with others on a global scale, make sure that you have done your homework and learned the appropriate protocol for the culture of that person. Find out if it is appropriate to shake hands or offer a business card. How should each individual be addressed—by first name or with a title? Is eye contact appropriate or offensive? Is certain attire preferred? What is acceptable body language, such as crossed arms or hands on the hips? Always do your research before a meeting so that you are comfortable and represent your organization well.

Control Your Voice

Naturally, your voice is your most important tool in speaking situations. The first step toward improving your voice is to become aware of how you sound to others. Only then will you know what, if anything, needs

Figure 12-7.   Use this speaking checklist to evaluate a presentation.

Speaking Checklist

Preparing for presentations, you:
- ❑ know the purpose of the presentation
- ❑ know the audience
- ❑ know the message you want to communicate
- ❑ organize information according to your selected approach (direct or indirect)
- ❑ outline the presentation
- ❑ check facts
- ❑ use humor wisely and appropriately
- ❑ prepare appropriate visual elements
- ❑ practice

Polishing your presentation skills, you:
- ❑ adjust your speaking volume as needed
- ❑ adjust your speaking rate as needed
- ❑ pronounce words correctly and clearly
- ❑ provide appropriate emphasis in your speech
- ❑ control your body language
- ❑ troubleshoot the presentation before giving it

Before giving your presentation, allow enough time to practice. A well-practiced presentation will be received as professional. You can practice with placeholders for any visual aids you may be using.

Shutterstock

improvement. Fortunately, you can significantly improve your voice quality by concentrating on a few simple techniques.

Self Evaluation

If you cannot be objective in evaluating yourself, ask someone for help. Be sure to select someone who has excellent speaking skills, understands your objectives, and can give you constructive criticism.

Record yourself reading a few paragraphs from a magazine article using your normal speaking voice. Then, playback the recording. Try to listen to the voice you hear as if it were someone else speaking. Ask the following questions to determine how that voice sounds.

- Is the volume appropriate?
- Is the rate of speaking too fast or too slow?
- Are words correctly pronounced?
- Do words run together, are word endings dropped, or are syllables added?
- Are words such as "um," "you know," or "like" used frequently?
- Is emphasis used enough, too much, or too little?

Volume and Rate

When you speak too loudly or too softly, listeners will be distracted from the content of your message. The audience will quickly tune out what you are saying. Be aware that you must adjust your volume to the room and the audience.

To determine if your volume is appropriate, ask a friend or coworker to sit in the back of the room where you will be presenting and provide cues. Or, during the presentation you can ask the audience if everybody can hear you. If not, you need to speak louder.

If the room is set up for use of a microphone, practice using it before the presentation. Make sure you can use the microphone with comfort. Also, make sure the amplification is the right volume for the audience.

Be aware of the rate, or speed, at which you speak. If you are usually a very fast or very slow speaker, practice your rate of speech with someone who can help you find the right pace. In general, maintain a consistent, normal rate. This should be a speed at which the listeners can comfortably stay with you.

However, vary your rate of speech for emphasis. Slow down when you present something technical or something you know the audience will write down. This is where handouts can be helpful so the audience does not have to write. Repeat the information if necessary or ask if everyone is ready for you to move on.

Pronunciation and Enunciation

Mispronounced words are at least a distraction and may even affect your credibility with the audience. Make sure you have the correct pronunciation of any technical or unfamiliar terms in your presentation. In some cases, you might be more familiar with a word in writing than you are with saying it aloud. Regional differences in speech or English not being your first language might also contribute to different pronunciation. Your goal is to have the audience clearly understand your words. Refer to Figure 12-8 for examples of common pronunciation errors. **Enunciation,** or clearly and distinctly pronouncing syllables and sounds, is also a factor in the audience understanding what you say.

You can heighten your awareness of appropriate pronunciation and enunciation by paying attention to the speech patterns of public speakers you admire. Also, use a dictionary when a question of pronunciation arises.

Figure 12-8.	**Be sure to avoid pronunciation errors in your presentation.**

Common Errors in Pronunciation

Dropping Sounds at the End of Words

For example, do you drop the *g* in *ing* words and say *runnin', eatin',* or *workin'?* Do you drop the final *t* when you say words such as *list* and *tourist?* Do you drop the final *d* in words such as *field* and *build?*

Omitting Letters and Sounds

For example, consider the word *introduce*. The correct pronunciation is *IN-tro-duce*, not *IN-ter-duce*.

Adding Sounds

For example, do you say *ATH-a-lete?* The correct pronunciation is *ATH-lete*.

Altering Vowel Sounds

For example, do you say *GEN-you-in* (correct) or *GEN-you-ine* (incorrect)?

Stressing the Wrong Syllable

For example, you should say *in-COM-pa-ra-ble*, not *in-com-PAR-a-ble*, and *in-SUR-ance*, not *IN-sur-ance*.

Mispronouncing Words

Many people make the mistake of pronouncing words just as they appear in writing. For example, do you pronounce the word *epitome* as *i-PIT-i-me* (correct) or *I-pi-tome* (incorrect)? Another common mispronunciation is *aks* (incorrect) instead of *ask* (correct).

Using Incorrect Words

For example, for the verb form of orientation, do you say *orient* (correct) or *orientate* (incorrect)?

Voice Modulation

When speaking, it is important to change the emphasis of words by raising and lowering your voice. This is called **modulation.** You can stress a word to make it stand out from the others by simply raising the volume of your voice. You can also provide emphasis by raising or lowering the pitch of your voice. **Pitch** describes the highness or lowness of a sound. **Intonation** is the rise and fall in the pitch of your voice.

Another effective technique for emphasizing words is simply to pause so that the word or phrase following the pause receive extra emphasis. You can also introduce the words you want to emphasize. The words preceding the pause prepare listeners for the important information to follow.

> Now, here is the key to increasing profits. [pause] We must all sell 10 percent more product each quarter.

The pause lets the listener know that what is to follow is related to increasing profits.

When speaking, you cannot emphasize everything you say. The opposite—emphasizing nothing—is equally ineffective. Speech that is **monotone** is delivered with the same intonation, stress, pitch, and volume. A monotone speech offers no variety and, worse, no emphasis.

Control Body Language

Body language is how gestures and facial expressions communicate feelings. Effective communicators control their body language to coincide with and complement their messages.

When preparing for your presentation, close your eyes and visualize yourself making the presentation. See yourself as a confident presenter in front of a friendly, receptive audience. Visualize how you would handle problems—a difficult question, for example.

Remember, in most cases, the audience is rooting for you. They want you to succeed as much as you want to succeed. The following sections provide information about body language that will be helpful as you prepare your presentation.

Make Eye Contact

As you begin to speak, make eye contact with someone in front, then someone to the left, someone to the right, and so on. This engages the audience and makes them feel as if you are talking directly to each person.

Connecting with the friendly face of a colleague or a listener who gives you a look of interest or a nod of agreement will bolster your confidence. This can help you settle in and feel comfortable in front of the group.

Avoid Unnecessary Movement

Any movements outside of normal hand gestures, facial expressions, and motioning toward your visuals could distract the audience. If you have water, do not drink excessively. Do not play with materials, such as a pen, your papers, or a pointer; do not fiddle with jewelry, clothing, or hair; avoid tapping the podium or walking around a great deal. Too much of any of these and your audience will start paying more attention to what you are doing than what you are saying.

Stand Up Straight

You should stand erect with your feet comfortably apart. Slouching is distracting and good posture heightens your professionalism. Avoid shifting your weight from foot to foot, but do not lock your knees. Shifting from foot to foot shows discomfort and nervousness.

TEAMWORK

Record yourself for 10 to 15 minutes giving a presentation or reading a passage from an article, essay, or from this textbook. Trade recordings with at least two other classmates and evaluate each other's speaking skills based on the speaking checklist in Figure 12-7. Discuss the comments and make sure you understand them. Use this feedback to improve your speaking skills.

Smile

Unless the topic is too serious, display a friendly, at-ease smile as you introduce your topic. Show some enthusiasm for what you have to say and it is likely to be contagious.

Dress Appropriately

Clothing can be a loud communicator to the audience. Avoid being too dressy or too casual. Business attire that is understated, yet flattering, is the best choice. However, be sure to dress for the environment. If your presentation is demonstrating a piece of manufacturing equipment, you will dress much more casually than if you are presenting sales figures to the board of directors of a large corporation.

Practice, Practice, Practice

Effective presentations are the result of careful planning, preparation, and plenty of practice. You need to become familiar with the sequence of topics in the presentation. When practicing, present the key points over and over. Experiment with pausing, emphasizing a word, lowering or raising your voice, using visual aids and handouts, looking at the audience, and standing straight. As you practice, you refine, revise, and improve both the content and delivery of your message. Figure 12-9 provides some guidelines for practicing.

Practice in front of a mirror as if you were in front of your audience. Dress professionally when you practice so you can project confidence.

If possible, practice your presentation at least once in the room where you will actually deliver it so you can make adjustments if necessary. For example, you may decide you do not want a podium or you might want to change where the podium is placed. Other elements like lighting and placement of the audience might help you in your preparations.

Rehearse operating equipment for your presentation until you are comfortable. You want the audience to stay focused on what you are saying, not what you are doing.

Use friends or family can be a practice audience. They can provide feedback about your volume, rate, clarity, tone, rhythm, pronunciation, eye

Figure 12-9.   **Follow these guidelines for effective practice of your presentation.**

Guidelines for Effective Practice

- Practice in front of a mirror.
- Practice in the place you will speak.
- Practice using all equipment you will need.
- Ask friends or family to be your "practice audience."
- Time yourself.
- Work on improving transitions.
- Get away from your notes.

contact, visuals, posture, and body language. If possible, select someone who is an effective, experienced speaker. Review the suggestions and criticisms and use them to improve your talk.

It is essential to control the length of your presentation, so time your practice presentation. If you are allotted 20 minutes, but in practice you are running 30 minutes, you need to figure out a way to trim about one-third of your presentation. This can be done by removing content or by speeding up your delivery.

Practice your transitions between points. Use your voice, body movements, or visual aids in addition to words to tell the audience you are introducing a new thought.

Practice presenting by only minimally referring to your notes or not at all. Commit some of your presentation to memory so that you can look at your audience and move with ease. Remember, you should not read your presentation. Your presentation notes are for reference only if needed.

Handle Questions

Plan how you will handle questions from the audience. This is important to keep your presentation on topic and on time. If someone interrupts with a question that is on topic, you might choose to answer briefly and move. If the question is off topic, you could ask the person to wait if the information is covered later in the presentation or to see you at the end of your talk if it is not. Avoid letting questions throw you off stride. Instead, ask the audience to save questions for the end of your talk. In a situation where you do not know the answer, just say so. Offer to find the information later and get back to the individual.

Remember that audience participation is a valuable tool for a presenter. But, as you think about handling questions, keep your allotted timeframe in mind. Shorten the presentation if you feel that questions will be time-consuming.

If someone else is speaking before you, consider what you will do if that person runs over the allotted time. If this occurs and another speaker follows you, be courteous and try to shorten your presentation. However, if a break or intermission follows your talk, you might be able to take a few minutes of that break time. If you are the last speaker at the end of the day, you may more comfortably go over your time limit. But, be aware that some people will leave.

Checkpoint

1. When learning to control your voice, what is the first thing you should do?
2. What are five things you can do to control you body language?
3. If a question is off topic, what can you do?

Chapter 12 Review

Chapter Summary

Oral Presentations

- An oral presentation is a speech, address, or presentation given to a group.
- Oral presentations vary greatly in length, topic, and audience and may be formal or informal.
- In almost any career, you will need to make some sort of presentation, if only on an infrequent basis.
- A presentation involves the same basic work as any other communication.

Planning a Presentation

- The secret to a successful presentation is planning.
- Planning a presentation begins with identifying purpose, audience, situation, main ideas, organization, and materials needed.
- Once you have gathered the needed information and analyzed the audience and time available, determine a delivery method for the presentation.

Preparing Content for a Presentation

- As you draft the presentation, begin with an introduction, identify the main points, identify subtopics, and end with a conclusion.
- Facts and humor can be used to enhance the presentation.
- Visual aids can make the presentation more interesting and informative.
- Presentation notes should be used to help you during the presentation, but you should not read directly from your notes.

Giving a Presentation

- You can improve your presentation skills by learning to control your voice.
- Control your body language to complement your speaking.
- Practice your presentation until you are comfortable with what you are going to say.
- Be sure to have a plan for handling questions.

Review
Your Knowledge

1. What is an oral presentation?
2. List the six things that need to be identified when planning a presentation.
3. What are demographics?
4. How are most oral presentations delivered?
5. What does the content of the presentation include?
6. What is the purpose of presentation notes?
7. Describe the difference between pronunciation and enunciation.
8. What is intonation?
9. Explain body language.
10. Why should you have a plan for handling audience questions during your presentation?

Apply
Your Knowledge

1. Write a one-page summary of oral reports. Include a definition along with descriptions of the different elements of an oral report.
2. Select a common product, such as an iPod or video game console. Create an outline for a 15-minute presentation in which you persuade your audience (your classmates) to purchase the product. Indicate where you will use visual aids and describe what they will be.
3. Develop the content for the presentation outline you developed in activity 2.

4. Give the presentation you developed in activity 3. Before giving the presentation to the class, practice delivering the content, using the visual aids, controlling your voice, and controlling your body language.

Practice
What You Have Learned

Access the *Fundamentals of Business Communication* Student Companion Web Site at www.g-wlearning.com/Communication. Download each data file for this chapter. Follow the instructions to complete a reading, writing, and grammar activity to practice what you have learned in this chapter.

Connections
Across the Curriculum

Math. Create a spreadsheet of tips for making a speech. On the X axis, create a rating system of Yes, No, and Sometimes. On the Y axis, list the positive attributes of a good speech, such as Proper Volume, Clear Pronunciation, etc. Use this list as both a self-evaluation tool as well as a tool to evaluate others when they are making a presentation.

Social Studies. Research the term rhetoric. What does it mean? Where did the term originate? Write several paragraphs on your findings.

Build
Your Business Portfolio

Not only are references an important part of a portfolio, but a letter of recommendation may also be requested in an interview. A letter of recommendation is written by someone for whom you have worked or someone who knows you personally. This letter will describe your competencies, skills, and other good characteristics about you. Ask several people to write a letter of recommendation.

1. Scan the letters of recommendation and save them in your ePortfolio. Create a subfolder named Recommendations. Save each scanned letter with the file names Recommendations 01, Recommendations 02, etc.
2. Place the original letters in your container for your print portfolio.

Careers
Agriculture, Food, and Natural Resources Careers and Communication

People who have jobs in this career cluster work with food products and processing, power, structural systems, and plants and animals. Careers in natural resources, environmental services, and agribusiness are also included. With the demands of an expanding population, globalization, and increasing public awareness of nutrition, careers in this cluster should provide strong opportunities in the future.

Communication skills are important in every aspect of employment to be successful in day-to-day interactions with both coworkers and the public. Working with the public demands strong listening skills as well as the ability to speak with a purpose. Describe a situation in which someone pursuing a career in this career cluster would need to speak to a client or audience.

Public Speaking

Public speaking is a competitive event you might enter with your organization. This event allows you to showcase your communication skills of speaking, organizing, and making an oral presentation. This is usually a timed event you can prepare for prior to the competition. You will have time to research, prepare, and practice before going to the competition. Review the specific guidelines and rules for this event for direction as to topics and props you will be allowed to use.

To prepare for the public speaking event, do the following.

1. Read the guidelines provided by your organization. Make certain you ask any questions about points you do not understand. It is important you follow each specific item that is outlined in the competition rules.

2. Read this chapter to help you prepare your speech.

3. Practice, practice, practice. Your speech will be judged by a panel of professionals. Practice your speech in front of your peers until you are comfortable.

4. Present your speech to your student organization prior to a meeting or local community service organization. This will help you to practice speaking in front of others.

13
Using Digital Media

The newest computer can merely compound, at speed, the oldest problem in the relations between human beings, and in the end the communicator will be confronted with the old problem, of what to say and how to say it.

—Edward R. Murrow, American broadcast journalist

Presentation software is readily available to business users and home users alike. A professional-looking presentation can be quickly created by using templates, themes, and styles provided with the software. If your needs go beyond what is provided by common software, high-end graphics, video, and audio software can be used, although these may require upgraded computer hardware. This chapter discusses digital media presentations and how to create them.

Objectives

When you complete Chapter 13, you will be able to:

○ **Explain** the role technology plays in effective presentations.

○ **Describe** the laws and licenses that govern use of technology and digital media.

○ **Identify** hardware that may be used to create and display digital media presentations.

○ **Explain** the role various digital media software programs play in effective presentations.

○ **Obtain** media (images, video, and audio) and use those items in a digital media presentation.

○ **Describe** the design principles of a digital media presentation and the steps involved in producing a presentation.

Terms

visual design
Electronic User's Bill of Rights
copyright
intellectual property
plagiarism
licensing agreement
end user licensing agreement (EULA)
digital media
graphic
animation
camera shots
lighting ratio
production
storyboard

Go Green

When you go to the office supply store to purchase paper, look for recycled paper. Find the package label that shows the maximum available recycled materials.

1. Does your school or work use recycled paper? If so, what does the label say about recycled materials?

2. If the paper products that you use are not recycled, is there any message about the company and what they are doing to save trees while making their paper products?

Role of Technology in Effective Presentations

The business world expects slick and well-put-together presentations. Readily available presentation software makes creating these presentations easy. Most businesses, large and small, invest in software packages, such as Microsoft Office, that contain relatively easy-to-use presentation programs, like Microsoft PowerPoint. Easy access to the presentation software does not, however, automatically lead to *effective* presentations.

Technology, including presentation software, animation tools, digital images, video, and audio, along with applications for editing all of these media put the power to create an effective presentation at your fingertips. In order for the presentation to convey your message and persuade the audience, the message must be clear, not lost in the technology. Basic design principles must be adhered to along with all you learned about giving presentations in Chapter 12.

Components of Effective and Persuasive Digital Media Presentations

Remember the goal of a presentation: to convey a message or persuade the audience. If you have mastered all of the basic skills of giving an effective presentation, what remains to be considered for a digital media presentation are the actual elements of the presentation. You need to consider content and technique.

The content, as with any presentation, is the *what.* In the case of a digital media presentation, however, the *what* does not just mean what words will you use, but also what images and sounds will be a component of the message you are delivering.

The technique is the *how.* How will you deliver your presentation? You may make the presentation in person and control the advancement of the elements. In some cases, you will not be present and the viewer will control

Reading Prep

Before reading this chapter, go to the Review Your Knowledge section at the end of the chapter and read the questions. This will prepare you for the content that will be presented. Review questions at the end of the chapter serve as a self assessment to help you evaluate your comprehension of the material.

the advancement of the presentation. The presentation may be delivered at a standalone kiosk with no human interaction. The audience may be one person or many. Will the presentation be delivered on a laptop computer or in a large auditorium with an LCD projector and a sound system? The way in which the presentation will be packaged and delivered is important to know when making decisions about the digital media techniques you will use.

Ultimately, the content and technique should be driven by the purpose of the presentation. Who is the audience and what do you want the listeners to think or feel when your presentation is complete? You should always consider that the purpose of a presentation is not only to have a message and to impress, but also to impact and influence the audience.

Design Principles in a Digital Media Production

The visual design of a digital media presentation can be just as important as the content. The **visual design** is the arrangement of the visual, artistic elements used to accomplish a goal or communicate an idea. Understanding the principles of visual design will help you to better express your idea. An effective visual design will:

- improve the clarity of the message; and
- be visually appealing.

The basic elements of art are lines, shapes, forms, space, color, and texture. These basic elements are governed by the design principles shown in Figure 13-1. To create an effective presentation, you need to utilize the design elements just as an artist would in creating artwork. Instead of pencils and paints, you will apply the design elements using digital media tools and computer software.

Proportion is the relationship of the size of elements to the whole and to each other. In general, if you want to call attention to or emphasize an item, you make it larger.

Balance is an arrangement of elements to create a feeling of equality across the product. No one part commands all of the viewer's attention. An imbalanced digital media presentation might have too many elements in one section of the screen and not enough in another. **Symmetry** is used to create formal balance so that what appears on one side of the screen is mirrored on the other. Keep in mind, however, that it is not necessarily the number of elements, but sometimes their color, darkness, or thickness that can be used to create an informal balance.

A presentation without variety may be viewed as uninteresting, which means that the message of the

Figure 13-1. All presentations, including digital media presentations, must follow basic design principles.

Design Principles

Proportion
- Creates size relationships.

Balance and Symmetry
- Creates equality and stability.

Variety
- Creates visual interest.

Emphasis
- Creates a focal point and draws attention.

Harmony
- Creates unity.

Repetition
- Creates consistency and pattern.

presentation may seem uninteresting as well. Using different digital media components, such as animation, images, and art, increases the visual interest.

You can use emphasis to draw attention to the element you want viewers to see first. Emphasis can be created in a variety of ways, including size, color, weight, and location of an element.

Harmony is a design principle that creates unity in a presentation. Harmony in a presentation can be created with color, patterns, or common shapes and images. Harmony must be balanced with variety. For variety to be used effectively, certain elements in the presentation still need to have something in common. The similarities in the visual design elements are the harmony.

Likewise, repetition of colors, lines, shapes, or textures, can be used to create a pattern within a digital media presentation. Patterns are also used to create visual design consistency. They can carry a theme throughout a presentation, highlight similar types of information, and show connections between different parts of the presentation.

In addition to these basic design elements, digital media is governed by additional design principles that are not part of a static layout.

- Movement creates action and a sense of perspective within space.
- Rhythm creates a visual or auditory tempo or pace.

Movement in a digital media presentation may be real action (a video clip) or just the appearance of action (wavy lines in a presentation about waves in the ocean). There are also many ways to create movement within a presentation, such as animating the movement of text and images.

Rhythm is the regular repetition of objects or sound to show movement or activity. Rhythm can also be used to create a sense of energy or urgency. Used strategically, rhythm can dramatically add to the impact of your message.

Perspective is an artistic technique that creates the illusion of depth on a two-dimensional surface. It is created by varying the sizes of objects (scale) within a field and overlapping the objects. The objects to be viewed as closer are made larger and placed in front of the objects that are to be viewed as farther away. Converging lines also create perspective.

Checkpoint

1. In regard to the elements of a digital media presentation, what two things need to be considered?
2. What is the visual design of a digital media production?

Laws and Licenses Governing Digital Media

The Internet provides countless sources for obtaining text, images, and audio. Additionally, you can use your own equipment, such as a cell phone or digital camera, to capture your own media. However, just because all of this media is readily available, it does not mean that it is free for you to use in whatever way you choose. There are laws that govern the use of media and the creators of the original media retain certain rights.

Copyright violations are serious and can result in legal action.

Shutterstock

Electronic User's Bill of Rights

The **Electronic User's Bill of Rights,** originally proposed by Frank W. Connolly of American University in 1993, is modeled after the original United States Bill of Rights, although it contains only four articles. The Electronic User's Bill of Rights details the rights and responsibilities of both individuals and institutions regarding the treatment of digital information. It is not legally binding, but rather guidelines for appropriate usage. There are four articles in the Electronic User's Bill of Rights.

- Article I: Individual Rights
- Article II: Individual Responsibilities
- Article III: Rights of Educational Institutions
- Article IV: Institutional Responsibilities

Article I focuses on the rights and freedoms of the users of computers and the World Wide Web. Article I states that "citizens of the electronic community of learners" have the right to access computers and informational resources, should be informed when their personal information is being collected, have the right to review and correct personal information that has been collected, should have freedom of speech, and have rights of ownership for their intellectual property.

Article II focuses on the responsibilities that come along with those freedoms outlined in Article I. It is the responsibility of a citizen of the electronic community to seek out the information he or she needs and use it effectively. It is also the individual's responsibility to honor the intellectual property of others, to verify the accuracy of information obtained from the electronic community, to respect the privacy of others, and to use electronic resources wisely.

Article III provides for the right of educational institutions to access computers and informational resources. Like individuals, an educational institution retains ownership of its intellectual property. Each institution has the right to use its resources as it sees fit.

Article IV focuses on the responsibilities that come along with the rights and freedoms granted in Article III. Educational institutions, in the electronic community of learners, are held accountable for the information that they use as well as what they provide. Institutions are responsible for creating and maintaining "an environment wherein trust and intellectual freedom are the foundation for individual and institutional growth and success."

Copyright Laws

A **copyright** acknowledges ownership of a work and specifies that only the owner has the right to sell or use the work or to give permission for someone else to sell or use it, Figure 13-2. Copyright laws are in place to protect the creators of original work, known as **intellectual property.** The laws cover all original work, whether it is in print, on the Internet, or in any other form or media. You cannot claim work as your own or use it without permission.

Scanned Media

Scanners are a common piece of equipment in many business and home offices. A scanner is used to create an electronic (digital) version of printed material. The fact that you have scanned something, however, does not make the content yours. Whether it is text, artwork, or a photograph, all rights of that material remain with the owner. In order to use scanned material, permission must be obtained from the owner of that material.

Internet

Most information on the Internet is copyrighted, whether it is text, informational graphics, illustrations, or digital media. This means you cannot reuse it without first obtaining permission from the owner. Sometimes, the owner of the material has placed the material on the Internet for others to reuse, but if this is not explicitly stated, assume the material is copyrighted.

Many Web sites list rules, called the terms of use, that you must follow for downloaded files. The agreement may come up automatically, for example, if you are downloading an entire file or software application. If, however, you are copying an image or a portion of text from a Web site, you will need to look for the terms of use information.

Figure 13-2.	Copyrights, patents, and trademarks are similar, but cover distinctly different aspects of intellectual property.

Copyright, Patent, or Trademark?

- Copyrights apply original works of authorship (writing, artwork, music, digital media, etc.) fixed in any tangible expressive form. An idea cannot be copyrighted.
- Patents apply to inventions.
- Trademarks apply to words, names, or symbols identifying goods made or sold.

Copyrights are automatically granted and can be registered, but this is not necessary. Patents and trademarks must be registered to secure your rights. The registration process can be long and difficult, and your ideas may have to be disclosed in the process. So, often, intellectual property is further protected by trade-secret laws that protect internally guarded ideas, codes, and formulas forming a competitive edge for the company.

Unless the terms of use specifically state that you are free to copy and use the material provided on a Web site, it must be assumed the material is copyrighted. You cannot reuse the material without permission. If you claim somebody else's material as your own, you are guilty of **plagiarism,** which is not only unethical, but also illegal.

Licensing Agreements

A **licensing agreement** is a contract that gives one party permission to market or produce the product or service owned by another party. The agreement grants a license in return for a fee or royalty payment. Licensed items may be copyrights, patents, trademarks, techniques, designs, or expertise, among other things.

A licensing agreement may be personal or commercial. It may be *nonexclusive*, meaning the owner may sell licenses to many people. On the other hand, the license may be *exclusive*, meaning that only one entity has the right to use the product for a specified amount of time.

BUSINESS ETHICS

Using Social Networking Media

Social networking media is commonly used by organizations to reach out to existing customers and to find new ones. Because it is so available and easy to use, those who are writing communication for the organization must be ethical when using Web sites such as Facebook or Twitter for business purposes. Remember that it is unethical to send e-mail to customers who have not requested to be on an organization's mailing list. Doing so is considered spam. Keep your messages honest and return messages from those who have taken time to respond to your communication. Use good judgment and represent the organization in a professional manner.

Audio and Video

Audio and video files are typically controlled with an **end user license agreement (EULA),** which defines how the material can be used. These licenses usually grant the purchaser the right to use the audio or video file on a personal or corporate Web site, in television and radio broadcasts, in films and videos, on compact discs and DVDs, in software, as ringtones, and in podcasts. Every EULA, however, is different. Before you purchase a license for specific audio or video media, you should carefully read the details of the licensing agreement.

Software programs are also governed by EULAs. Be sure to understand the agreement. Some allow the software to be installed only once on one machine. Other agreements may allow the software to be installed multiple times on the same machine to allow for reinstallation after a hard drive failure. Yet other agreements may allow the software to be installed on any machine owned by the company who purchased the software. This is called a **site license.**

Digital Media Presentations

Licenses to use digital media presentations, which may incorporate movies, animations, and videos, can also be purchased. Depending on the content, however, there may be more restrictions on the use of a digital media presentation than what is typically found for individual audio or video files.

For example, you may purchase the license for a ready-made digital media presentation on proper netiquette. The license may allow you to use the presentation within your company for viewing by all employees. However, that license may not allow you to place the presentation on your corporate Web site for anyone to view for free.

Electronic Communication

EULAs for electronic communication typically provide the rights to download, install, and use the software necessary to communicate electronically using either a computer, phone, personal digital assistant (PDA), or smartphone. These agreements are usually personal, noncommercial, and nonexclusive, though you are usually permitted to use the devices for business correspondence. As with any legal agreement, it is important you read the EULA so you clearly understand what you are and are not permitted to do.

CASE

What Rights?

Josh Hanneken is an employee of a nationwide hardware store chain. He has been placed in charge of creating a presentation about a new set of benefits that will take effect in the coming year. Once it is ready, employees across the nation will log into the corporate intranet and view the presentation.

Josh has started planning the presentation and has done some preliminary research as well. He has found some media on the Internet that he would like to use, including sounds, graphics, and photographs. He is thinking that copyright laws would not be in effect since he is using the media for educational purposes— educating the employees.

1. Do you think that Josh has a clear understanding of copyright law?

2. Would a typical EULA allow Josh to use the media in the manner that he plans?

3. Are there any other considerations?

Checkpoint
1. What does the Electronic User's Bill of Rights cover?
2. What does a copyright do?
3. What does a licensing agreement allow?

Presentation Hardware

All digital media presentations are developed and presented using computers, such as a desktop computer, laptop computer, tablet PC, iPad, or smartphone. The computer, used in conjunction with various input and output devices, allows you to pull together images, sounds, and text and integrate them in a presentation exactly as you want.

Computer equipment may vary greatly in the office, from desktop units to laptops and smartphones.

Shutterstock

Computer Hardware

The basic components for a computer system are the computer, a monitor, a keyboard, and an input devices such as a mouse or a touch screen. These components may be separate, as with a desktop unit, or integrated in one device, as with a laptop computer or smartphone.

Computers purchased within the last few years typically have sufficient processing power to run most standard presentation software. If you intend to do high-end graphics work, however, check the system requirements of the graphics software against your computer. The software may require an advanced graphics card, increased RAM, or other computer enhancements in order to run on your system.

Other hardware that is useful for obtaining and working with digital media include a graphics tablet, scanner, and webcam or video capture board. Adding these components can be extremely useful for accomplishing specific tasks.

Digital Media Equipment

Beyond the computer hardware discussed above, there are a number of other devices that are used to produce a digital media presentation.

- A digital camera or digital video recorder is used to capture photos and videos.
- A digital sound recorder is used to capture speech, music, or other sounds.
- A synthesizer or music keyboard is used to create music.

The above hardware items are input devices. There are many options for output devices to display a digital media presentation. The presentation could be displayed on anything from a smartphone and to a theater-size screen. Other possibilities for display include a touch screen, interactive whiteboard, overhead projector, and a video or home theater–style projector.

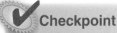

Checkpoint

1. What is used to create and present all digital media presentations?
2. What are the four basic components of a computer system.
3. List three computer input devices that may be used to help produce a digital media presentation.

Presentation Software

Powerful application software is used to combine various elements into a digital media presentation. Unlike in the past, this software is available to the average user. Some common applications that may have a role in a digital media project include the following.

- Spreadsheet applications, such as Microsoft Excel or IBM Lotus 1-2-3, are used to make calculations and create tables, graphs, and charts.

- E-mail applications, such as Microsoft Outlook and Gmail, are used to exchange messages pertaining to the project as well as project files.

- Web browsers, such as Mozilla Firefox, Safari, or Google Chrome, are used to browse the Internet for research or to obtain required files.

- Databases, such as Oracle, Microsoft Access, or FileMaker Pro, are used to organize large amounts of information.

- Project management applications, such as Microsoft Project, Gantt Project, or Basecamp, are used to develop and maintain a schedule for the work to be done.

TEAMWORK

You need to buy a projector for the meeting room in your office. The meeting room is 20′ × 35′ and people will be seated anywhere from 10′ to 30′ from the display screen. Form a team with two to three classmates to determine the best projector for the room.

A. Work together to find an online calculator that will allow you to determine the recommended resolution and lumens for a room of those dimensions.

B. Knowing the specifications for the equipment you need, have each person on the team research a different manufacturer of projectors (for example InFocus or BenQ). Each person should record information about the projector chosen, including the price.

C. As a team, review the information obtained individually. Based on the requirements and the specifications of the projectors researched, which would be the best fit for the desired application? Make a decision as a team.

Each of these applications provides the basic tools needed to develop a digital media presentation or to assist in its development. Software applications that are more specific to digital media development itself are discussed in the following section.

Popular Digital Media Software

Digital media–development software can be divided into five main types: text, audio, video, graphics, and Web site development. You should note that some software works with multiple file types, such as Microsoft Expression Media, which works with both audio and video files and allows you to integrate and overlay them. Other application software is part of a suite of applications designed to be used together. These programs, like the Adobe Creative Suite, allow for the seamless transfer of content from one application to another.

Text Editor Software Applications

Text editors are used to write documents or other types of text-based files. A common use in digital media would be keying XHTML commands into a document that can then be imported or copied and pasted into a Web site development application. Examples of text editors include Microsoft Word, Microsoft Wordpad, and Macromedia HomeSite. However, there are many from which to choose, including some that are free or inexpensive.

Audio Software Applications

Audio software is used to create and edit audio files. Audio software allows you to filter out background noise, increase or decrease the volume, and change the speed at which the audio is played. You can also trim the audio to just the portion you need to use. Microsoft Expression Media, Adobe Audition, and Apple GarageBand are a few examples of audio applications.

The many available presentation software packages allow professional presentations to be quickly created.

Shutterstock

Video Software Applications

Video software is used to create, edit, and manipulate video files. Commonly used applications are Adobe Premiere, Microsoft Expression Media, Apple Quicktime, Apple iMovie, and Apple Final Cut Pro.

Graphics Software Applications

Graphics software is used to resize, crop, and change the color of existing images. Additionally, you can use the software to alter images. The software can also be used to create original artwork from scratch. Examples of graphics application software include Corel Paint Shop Pro, Adobe Fireworks, Adobe Photoshop, Microsoft Paint, and Microsoft Expression Design.

Web Site Development Software Applications

Web site development software is used to create the pages on a Web site. Several commonly used applications are Microsoft Expression Web and Adobe Dreamweaver. Many people use online Web site development in place of application software, particularly for simpler Web sites.

Emerging Digital Media Software

At present, the emerging software that will impact digital media presentations the most seems to be in the arena of three-dimensional (3D) graphics and virtual reality (VR) software. Three-dimensional models are created using graphics modeling programs, such as 3ds max or Maya. These models are then integrated to build a virtual reality world. A virtual world allows you to experience events, circumstances, and places as if they were real. Virtual home tours are an example of a digital media presentation using 3D models and virtual reality technology.

Today, spatial sensors can be used to interact with a 3D virtual world. Think about the Xbox Kinect. Unlike the Nintendo Wii or Playstation 3 Motion, the user does not hold a controller to interact with the game. It is only a matter of time before this technology filters into the business world. Even now, there are virtual reality rooms (sometimes called *caves*) in which you become fully immersed in the virtual experience; not too far removed from the holodeck experiences seen on the *Star Trek* franchise of movies and television series. Far more than just fun and games, however, these rooms can allow for advanced training in jobs that would be difficult or impossible to train for without risk to human life.

The Microsoft Xbox Kinect controller detects the user's body movements and translates them into game action. No handheld controllers are required.

Microsoft Corp.

Selecting the Right Tools for the Job

Despite all of the new, high-tech equipment and software, the old adage remains true: having the right tool for the job makes all the difference. When considering which software to use for a digital media project, first look at the project as a whole. Determine what the desired end product is and which components the product will need to incorporate. The timeline and monetary and time budgets are also important.

If the end product is a presentation with text, some clipart, and a few charts to be given to fellow employees, a presentation using Microsoft PowerPoint will adequately meet the needs of you and the audience. You would likely speak directly to your coworkers while manually controlling the advancement of the presentation.

However, if the end product is a presentation that will broadcast worldwide to your corporation, a high production value is generally expected. The audio and video must be synchronized and all part of a single source file. So, an application that integrates the various components of a digital media presentation, such as Adobe Creative Suite, would be the preferred tool for such a job.

 Checkpoint

1. What are the five general categories for software used in creating a digital media presentation?
2. List two emerging technologies that can be used in digital media presentations.
3. When considering which software to select for creating a digital media presentation, what is the first thing to look at?

Digital Media

The term **digital media** refers to an integration of graphics, videos, and audio files. The files can be inserted into the presentation, linked to the presentation, or embedded. Object linking and embedding (OLE) is a way to reference the source file from within another file, such as a presentation.

In a general sense, a medium is any means of conveying information. *Media,* the plural of *medium,* has the same purpose: to convey information. Careful placement of digital media in the presentation is important.

Graphics

A **graphic** is any visual aid—any informational graphic or illustration (see Chapter 18). This may be a drawing, diagram, painting, photograph, logo, table, map, chart, etc. Graphics (visual aids) are used to attract attention, provide visual interest, illustrate, entertain, or inform. Digital media projects almost always contain graphics because the medium is visual by nature. Within the project, a single graphic may serve multiple roles, such as a logo that both promotes a company brand while also adding visual interest.

While graphics can add visual interest and emphasis, care must be taken to avoid overuse. Too many graphics in a presentation will become distracting and the presentation will lose its effectiveness. If your presentation is cluttered with graphics, your message can be lost. While planning a presentation, the role and placement of graphics should be carefully considered. It is important that each graphic have a purpose and support the goal of the presentation, as shown in Figure 13-3.

Animation

Often, graphics within a presentation are animated. **Animation** is the representation of motion with graphics or in text. An animation may be as simple as an object that blinks on and off or that slides onto or off of the edge of the screen. However, an animation may be more complex, such as a 3D model that shows the movement of a machine, and saved as an animated GIF, AVI, or MPEG file.

The illusion of motion is created in an animation by displaying in rapid succession animation frames that each contain a small difference. The small differences are interpreted by the brain as motion. Think of the stick figure cartoons you can create on the edge of notebook paper. By fanning the pages, you can see motion in the animation.

Figure 13-3. Evaluate each graphic before using it in a digital media presentation.

Evaluating Graphics

Ask the following questions about a specific graphic before using it in a digital media presentation to determine if the graphic is appropriate.

- Does the graphic support the goals of the project?
- Do the colors in the graphic contrast with the background of the presentation?
- Will the graphic be distracting to viewers?

Likewise, the following overriding questions should be asked about the presentation as a whole.

- Are there too many graphics in the presentation?
- Are the graphics an appropriate size for use in this type of digital media project?
- Have necessary permissions been obtained to use the graphics?

Digital Photography

Even though there are vast resources available on the Web, there will be times when the image you need cannot be found. In these situations, you may need to take a photograph. If you take a picture with a digital camera, the picture can then be directly downloaded to the computer where your digital media presentation is being created.

Cameras

The quality and sophistication of cameras can vary greatly. They range from simple point-and-shoot cameras up through high-end SLR cameras with multiple, interchangeable lenses. Which camera you use depends on your needs and the funds available for the camera's purchase.

Every camera has its own set of features, so review the user's guide. There are, however, some common features on most cameras. In addition to the obvious power switch, there are usually options to allow for automatic or manual flash operation, a way to zoom in and out, and the ability to preview the image before you take it as well as to review it afterward. Even the simplest cameras usually have a selection of automatic settings that provide the best choices for obtaining a good picture in different scenarios. For example, if you are taking pictures at a gymnastics meet, you would choose a setting appropriate for sports.

Resolution

Most cameras also allow you to select the number of **pixels** (picture elements) with which the image will be recorded. This is referred to as the **resolution** of the image. The greater the number of pixels, or the higher the resolution, the crisper and clearer the picture will be. Higher resolution, however, also means a larger file. So consideration must be given to exactly where and how the image will be used to determine what is necessary. An image that will be in print generally should be a minimum of 300 dots per inch (dpi). For a 3 × 5 image, this is 900 pixels × 1500 pixels. The best approach is to take the photograph at a high resolution and then use photo editing software to adjust the size and resolution as needed. Be aware, you can easily adjust the image to a lower resolution, but adjusting the image to a higher resolution causes problems. This is because the software must interpolate the pixels to fill "blank spaces" when increasing the resolution.

Photo Editing

Rarely is a photograph perfect. An image that may work well in one circumstance may need to be altered to be appropriate in another. Fortunately, there are many software applications that allow you to edit an image. Some photo-editing software includes Adobe Fireworks, Adobe Photoshop, Corel Paint Shop Pro, Mac iPhoto, Microsoft Expression Design, Microsoft Paint, Serif DrawPlus, and Serif PhotoPlus.

Sometimes you may need to take your own photographs to include in a digital media presentation.

Shutterstock

Photo-editing software can be very simple and easy-to-use. On the other hand, high-end programs can be complex, but allow more-advanced editing functions. Photo-editing software allows the manipulation of an image in many ways. An image can be cropped, rotated, or resized. The contrast of the image, along with the brightness and the color, can be altered. The image itself can also be altered.

Filtering is a technique by which a special effect is applied to an image. The concept comes from photography. A photographer may place a filter (a special lens) over the camera lens to alter the look of the scene being photographed. In the case of photo-editing software, the filter is being applied during the editing stage instead of the creation stage. There are hundreds of filters from which to choose. Common filters include blur, feather, sharpen, mosaic, cracked paint, distort, watercolor, pastel, and painting.

Layering is the process of building an image by putting different parts of the image on different levels. Think of each layer as a sheet of tracing paper that is stacked on the other layers. The benefit of this process is that you can turn on and off different layers. By using layers, you can compose a scene in the photo-editing software. The background can be one layer. Another layer can be created for each object or person in the scene. Then, the layers can be rearranged to bring one object in front of another, for example. The final composition can be flattened and saved in a common image file format, such as JPEG or TIFF, and then used in a document or presentation.

Masking is a way to give the appearance of change to an image without actually altering the original image. By covering up or selectively exposing only certain parts of an image, what is seen may look very different but the original image is not adversely impacted. One very common use for a mask is to outline an object or person in a photograph so the background is not seen.

Video

While graphics are stationary images, video refers to live-action movies. As with other digital media, videos can be files that you capture, create yourself, or obtain through online resources. If you obtain a video through an online source, you must get permission from the copyright holder in order to distribute it within your digital media presentation.

You can record your own video with a digital camera, digital video camera, or cell phone. However, a video of good enough production value to include in a digital media presentation requires planning and, typically, a little better equipment than your cell phone.

While a video can quickly and sometimes more accurately convey what might otherwise take many slides in a presentation, it is still important to make sure that the video being used is appropriate for the situation, Figure 13-4.

Planning a Video

Sometimes recording on the fly can produce interesting and stylistic results. Usually, however, a video for a digital media presentation has a specific purpose and specific requirements. The best way to make sure your video is to the point and contains all of the elements needed for your presentation is to write a script for your video. A **script** provides the outline and structure for the video. It details what will happen and when, what the scenes will look like, what will be said by any individuals, and what the

Figure 13-4. Evaluate each video clip before using it in a digital media presentation.

Evaluating Video

Ask the following questions about any video you are planning on using in your presentation.

- Does the video support the goals of the project?
- Will the video be distracting to viewers or helpful?

Likewise, the following overriding questions should be asked about the presentation as a whole.

- Are there too many videos in the presentation?
- Are the videos an appropriate size for use in this type of digital media project? For example, if the presentation is being delivered via the Web, will it take too long to download?
- Have necessary permissions been obtained to use any people appearing in the video?

actions of the individuals will be. It also makes clear the sequence of events. Following a detailed script helps ensure the finished video will meet the needs of the presentation.

Video Camera Features

There are essentially three types of cameras used for recording digital videos: studio camera, camcorder, and webcam. Digital video cameras are connected to a computer using a high-speed interface, such as FireWire (IEEE 1394) or USB.

A studio camera is a large piece of equipment, as you may have seen on a television news set. The camera only picks up a video feed, no audio. The video feed is sent to a recording device for storage or broadcast. The audio is picked up by a system of microphones placed in strategic locations. The audio feed is sent to the same recording device for storage or broadcast. At some point prior to the broadcast, the audio and video are mixed and synchronized.

A camcorder is smaller than a studio camera. Size varies, but the camcorder can be held in the hand or rested on the shoulder. There are two types of camcorders: professional and consumer. Both types simultaneously record audio and video. The professional version records audio and video on separate tracks that must be later mixed together. The consumer version records audio and video and mixes them at the same time.

A webcam is a low-resolution digital video camera, usually combined with a microphone for recording audio. Many computers now come with a webcam built into the monitor. Webcams are used to broadcast live, realtime video for video conferencing (teleconferencing), live chatting, and home security, among other things. The content from webcams can be recorded and saved as a file, but be aware that the quality is not very high. Additionally, the video recording function of most cell and smartphones is webcam resolution.

The quality of a video is determined by resolution, canvas size, and color depth. *Resolution* is determined by the pixel dimensions of the frame (just like a photograph). The number of frames per second (fps) is also important to the quality of the video. Smoother and sharper videos are created with higher frame rates (greater fps), but the file size also increases. Be aware, there are standard frame rates for playback devices. For example, a computer plays video at 30 fps. The **canvas size** is the area in which the video will be displayed. Another way to refer to this is frame size. The canvas size should match the output device for delivering the digital media presentation.

Color depth is the number of distinct colors that can be represented and is based on the number of bits used to define a color (24-bit color, 32-bit color, etc.). Color depth is important for the realistic appearance of a video. The greater the color depth, the more lifelike the images will appear, but the larger the file will be. However, the number of colors that can be seen in the video delivered is determined by the hardware in use. It is important, therefore, to consider the delivery method when determining the color depth setting.

Using a Video Camera

The features of video cameras vary by model and manufacturer. In general, there are usually options to zoom in and zoom out. There will be a way to view the video as you are recording it and usually an option to review it afterward. Studio cameras and professional camcorders allow for adjustment and fine-tuning of numerous settings, such as f-stop, focus, and focal length. Consumer camcorders usually have a selection of automatic settings that provide options for recording in different scenarios.

If video footage is not available for your digital media presentation, you may need to shoot it yourself.

Shutterstock

The basics of using a video camera are straightforward. Hold the camera steady; a tripod helps with this. Point the camera in the direction of the scene you are shooting. Frame the scene using the viewfinder. Then, activate the recording function. Remember, any movement of the video camera will appear in the recording. So, unless you want to use this as an effect, which is common, be sure the camera remains steady. The next section discusses basic principles of videography.

Videography Basics

When creating a video, you need to apply visual design basics to the scene, just as you would to any graphic element. There are countless choices for how you might record any given scene. The choices you make are dictated by what information you want to convey, the tone you want to set, and the limitations of the setting. The basic choices when recording (or *shooting*) a video lie in the following areas: camera shots, camera angles and moves, and lighting.

The common terms used to define **camera shots** are: wide shot, medium-wide shot, medium shot, bust or head shot, medium close-up, and close-up. Each of these types of shots has a different purpose in videography, such as establishing the scene or allowing for a more personal connection with, for example, the main character in the scene.

When taking a photograph or creating a graphic, a point of view is chosen and then the image is created from that viewpoint. When creating a video, however, you do not need to keep the camera still as the scene unfolds. You have some basic options for moving the camera while recording, which creates some effects unique to videography. You can **pan** the scene, showing what is to the left or the right of the current view, or tilt the camera to show what is above or below. The entire camera can also move in a circle around the scene, which is known as **trucking,** or it can **dolly** to move toward or away from the scene.

The four basic elements of **lighting** are direction, quality, lighting ratio, and control. Each of these lightning elements contributes to the overall effect of the lighting and needs to be considered when selecting the lighting for a video or a specific scene within a video.

The *direction* of light is related to the height and angle of the light source. *Height* is the location of the light source relative to the subject. Is it above, below, or even with the subject? **Lighting angle** refers to the slope of the light's beam. Together, height and angle dictate where the shadows and highlights fall on the subject of the video.

The hardness or softness of the light on the subject is the quality of the light. Hard light is created by strong beams of light, which cause sharp edges between light and shadow. In contrast, soft light is created with diffuse light. Consequently, the transition from light to shadow is soft, not sharp.

Lighting ratio is the difference in brightness between the lightest area of the shot and the darkest. This is quantified by a numerical ratio. The brightest area is compared to the darkest area in terms of how many times brighter it is. How great of a ratio can be captured in a video depends on the sensitivity of the video camera. The commonly used lighting ratios for videos are 2:1, 3:1, and 4:1. A ratio of 2:1 is probably most frequently used.

Various methods are used to shape and color the light emitted from light sources. For example, a piece of colored, translucent material may be placed in front of a beam of light to change the color of the light. Or, part of the beam could be blocked in order to create a shadow or reduce a highlight in a specific area of the scene.

Editing Video Footage

Once you have recorded the video you need, called the **footage,** it will undoubtedly need to be edited before it is ready to be included in your digital media presentation. Depending on the editing software you are using, there are several modifications you can make.

- Create clips (short segments) from the video.
- Cut clips of video from one location and paste them in another.
- Overlay and synchronize audio, text, and voiceovers (narration).
- Add transitions between segments of video.
- Change the canvas size, color depth, and frame rate.
- Add informational graphics, illustrations, and animations.
- Save the video in different file formats for DVD, podcast, or the Web.

There are several outstanding video-editing programs available, including Adobe Premier Pro, Apple Final Cut Pro, Apple iMovie, Avid FreeDV, Avid Media Composer, and Microsoft Windows Movie Maker, among others. Some video-editing programs must be purchased, but there are many shareware and freeware options. Before purchasing software, you may wish to download a trial version to be sure the software contains the features that you need.

Audio

Audio in a digital media project can take many forms. A presentation can be enhanced by sound effects, music, or voiceovers. As with graphics and video, audio should not be overused in a digital media project. Figure 13-5 shows questions to ask when evaluating audio.

Sounds may be recorded, created with a computer or musical instrument, or obtained through online resources. Online resources allow you to search for specific sounds. Some "stock" sound and clipart sites offer sound effects and short audio files. Be sure to read and follow the terms and conditions for using any downloaded files. While many sounds can be obtained free of royalty, there may be a fee or you may need to obtain permission to use the audio files.

Figure 13-5. Evaluate each audio clip before using it in a digital media presentation.

Evaluating Audio

Ask the following questions about audio before using it in a digital media project.

- Does the audio support the goals of the project?
- Is the sound quality appropriate for this digital media project?
- Will the audio be distracting to viewers?

Likewise, the following overriding questions should be asked about the presentation as a whole.

- Are there too many sounds in the presentation?
- Are the audio files an appropriate size for using in this type of digital media project?
- Have necessary permissions been obtained to use the audio? Are the sources appropriately cited?

Checkpoint

1. What is a graphic?
2. What is the difference between a graphic and a video?
3. What are three ways in which a sound may be obtained?

Creating a Digital Media Presentation

Knowing what to do and how to do it is a good first step in creating a digital media presentation. This provides the general background you need to begin thinking about your specific presentation and how you will create it. After that, you will be ready to produce the presentation and, finally, to publish it for the audience.

Stages of Production

There are many elements involved in creating a digital media presentation, all of which need to be thought out, planned, and carefully evaluated. This entire process is known as the **production** of the digital media project. There are three main stages of production.

- Preproduction is the planning, scripting, storyboarding, etc., of the presentation.
- Production is the creating of the graphic, video, and audio elements.
- Postproduction is everything that occurs after production to create the final master copy.

Preproduction is all about planning. It is the work done before any video is recorded, pictures are taken, or sound is recorded. This includes planning the presentation, storyboarding the entire project; indicating what each component will look like or be comprised of; scripting any video segments; identifying any special effects, audio, graphics, etc., and preparing them; creating the production schedule and assigning tasks; and obtaining whatever resources are necessary (personnel, hardware, software, etc.). Exactly what is done at this stage depends on the situation and the desired end result.

Presentation Planning

There are many different methods for planning a digital media presentation. Each has its own advantages and some may work better for certain types of presentations than others. As you gain experience in presentation planning, you will learn which methods work best for you. You will also learn that some form of planning is crucial to the success of your project.

There are several basic elements involved in planning for a digital media presentation. The first is to figure out who your audience will be. Knowing that will often dictate what sort of presentation you put together, what the presentation contains, and how it will be delivered. Other key components of planning are outlining your presentation and storyboarding it. You will also need to carefully plan your time. Making sure that your project is completed on time requires a functional timeline and schedule.

Knowing Your Audience

Before you begin creating a presentation, you need to think about who the audience will be and research what is important to this group of people. Determine what message they need to hear. Also, decide the best way to convey a message to the group. This information will help you define your target audience, as shown in Figure 13-6.

Figure 13-6. When planning a digital media presentation, it is important to identify who is the target audience.

Who Is the Target?

The target audience is the group of people who will view or use your digital media presentation and, hopefully, receive the message you are sending. Ask the following questions to refine your understanding of the audience, which, in turn, will refine your understanding of what your presentation needs to be.

- What are the demographics of the audience?
- What does the audience already know about the topic?
- Is the audience there by choice or is attendance required?
- What does the audience need to get out of the presentation?
- What does the audience expect?
- How will the audience use the digital media project? Will it be a large audience in an auditorium or one or two people at a computer monitor?

Outlining

Outlining is simply creating a structure for the content of your presentation. The general information is the top-level items and the more detailed information is at the lower levels. Chapters 7 and 17 discuss in detail how to create an outline.

An outline allows you to determine exactly what topics will be covered and where they will be covered within the presentation. While outlining, you may find that a topic is missing or decide that coverage of the topic would be better in a different section of the presentation. Since you are still in the planning stages, this is not a problem. You can easily move things around at this stage.

Storyboarding

While an outline sets the topics to be covered, a **storyboard** illustrates the content of the digital media presentation, as shown in Figure 13-7. A storyboard contains a sketch of each important scene or event along with a brief description of what will happen. The description is not always included. The storyboard provides a visual representation for ideas. The team then has an opportunity to verify that everyone has the same understanding of what the presentation will be.

Storyboarding also provides the opportunity to work out the project's organization. The relationship between events or points of the presentation can be decided. Additionally, the way in which a user may navigate an interactive presentation will become apparent while you are storyboarding.

Time Management

A crucial component of any project is developing the schedule for the project. Once you know what the project will consist of (through outlining or storyboarding), you will know what tasks will be necessary to complete the project. A schedule needs to identify all required tasks for building, testing, and producing the project. For each task, **milestones,** important dates that need to be met to keep the project moving forward, are set so that progress can be checked. Milestone dates can be determined in one of two ways.

- Set milestone dates moving forward from the current date based on experience and an estimate of how long a given task will take.

- Set milestone dates starting with the final due date and working backward (known as backdating).

Determining Digital Media Presentation Type

How do you know which of the many presentation types to use? There is not a simple answer to this question. There are, however, some guidelines.

Part of determining what type of presentation to create may be conditions beyond your control. A limited amount of time or budget will dictate what you are able to do. Likewise, the equipment you have—recording devices, computer hardware, software—can limit what you are able to do.

The most significant factors to consider are the audience and the goal of the presentation. By working through the planning phase, you will determine exactly who the audience is and what it is expecting. You will determine what information you need to present in order to convey the message as well as the best media to use for that purpose.

Figure 13-7. Storyboards are an outlining tool based on frames or time codes for the presentation. A storyboard contains a sketch of the scene and a brief description of what will happen.

Presentation Design

No matter what type of digital media presentation you are creating, you need to consider the overall design of the presentation. It needs to be visually pleasing, not distracting, and the right vehicle to promote your message. The principles that apply to creating artwork or taking photographs are the same ones that apply to the layout and design of a digital media presentation.

The fundamental principles of design are balance, variety, harmony, emphasis, proportion, pattern, movement, and rhythm. These principles can be applied whether you are creating a slideshow presentation, Web site, DVD, or streaming video.

Using Master Slides

Once you have developed a design, it needs to be applied consistently across your presentation. You can easily establish consistency for a digital slideshow presentation, such as those created with Microsoft PowerPoint, through the use of master slides. A **master slide** is one containing design elements that are applied to a particular set of slides or all slides in a presentation. If you need to make a design change, simply change the master slide and it is reapplied to all associated slides.

Master slides typically contain a background design, image, or text, as shown in Figure 13-8. The master slides might also include headers and footers. Often there is a master slide for title slides and then another for all other slides. In a more complex presentation, there may be master slides for each type of slide. For example, a title-and-content slide is one with a title and an area for text or images. This type of slide may have a specific design that coordinates with, but is different from, a title-and-two-content slide, which has a title and two areas for text or images.

Figure 13-8. Master slides are an easy way to ensure each slide in a presentation has the same theme. This adds harmony to the presentation.

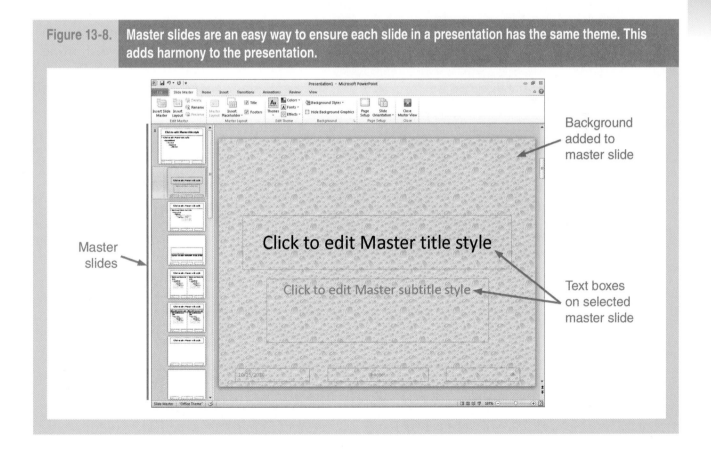

By publishing your digital media presentation as a standalone presentation, it can be viewed by individuals or small groups without you being there to display it.

Shutterstock

Transitions

Movement can be used to transition from one slide in a presentation to the next. This is considered a type of animation and can be used to add visual interest. Transitions make the movement from slide to slide far less static. For example, a slide can appear to flip and spin off of the screen while another slide spins into place. Or, a slide can fade away while the next slide fades into view.

Slideshow presentation software typically provides ready-made transitions from which to choose. These transitions can be independently set for each slide. However, while transitions can be fun and visually interesting, they can also be extremely distracting if they are overused. The audience may become focused on the variety of transitions and miss the message.

Creating a Standalone Presentation

A standalone presentation contains everything needed to view the digital media presentation. Most presentation software has a function that allows you to create a standalone presentation. For example, in PowerPoint 2010, you can create a video from a slide presentation that then can be distributed on CD/DVD, via the Web, or as an e-mail attachment. The video will include all animations, transitions, and other media, as well as incorporate all timing sequences and any recorded narrations.

Creating an Interactive Presentation

One of the keys to effectively delivering your message is holding audience interest. The audience needs to be engaged if you want them to receive the message. This is particularly important when the presentation is a standalone presentation. When you have a standalone presentation, such as one running at a kiosk, something needs to draw the audience in and hold its attention. Aside from having a visually interesting presentation, you can engage the audience by allowing interaction with the presentation.

Action buttons are available in most presentation software packages. These buttons allow you to give the viewer control of the presentation. Viewers can use buttons to move forward through the presentation, view the previous slide, return to the first page (home page), etc. Videos and animations can also be linked to buttons to allow the viewer to access additional content. When viewers interact with the presentation, they are more likely to take the time to consider the message.

TEAMWORK

Form a team with three to four classmates. Together, you will create a digital media presentation in the form of an infomercial for your school's foreign language department. The goal of the presentation is to make the audience aware of the languages that are available to learn, the real-world applications of these languages, and the opportunities to have experiences beyond the traditional academic setting. As a team, work through the planning stages, determine what form the presentation will take, create or obtain all components of the presentation, create the presentation, and package and deliver the presentation.

Checkpoint

1. What are the three stages of production?
2. What is the first step in planning a digital media presentation?
3. What are the eight basic principles of design?
4. What is a standalone presentation?

Chapter 13 Review

Chapter Summary

Role of Technology in Effective Presentations

- Effective digital media presentations can be quickly and easily created with commonly available presentation software.
- The visual design of a digital media presentation can be just as important as the content.

Laws and Licenses Governing Digital Media

- The Electronic Bill of Rights provides guidelines for using digital media.
- Intellectual property is protected by specific copyright laws.
- A licensing agreement allows intellectual property to be copied in exchange for a fee or royalty.

Presentation Hardware

- Most computers purchased within the last few years can easily run presentation software.
- In addition to a basic computer system, you may need an upgraded video card or RAM if you will be doing high-end graphics work.
- Additional hardware, such as a scanner or video capture card, may be needed.
- You may also need digital media equipment such as a digital camera, video recorder, and synthesizer or music keyboard.

Presentation Software

- A variety of software packages are available to create digital media presentations.
- Digital media–development software ranges from free to expensive, so review your presentation requirements before purchasing a program.

- There are several emerging technologies that are finding their way into digital media presentations, such as 3D graphics and virtual reality.
- Once you define the goal of your digital media presentation, you will be able to compare the software options and which program will work for you.

Digital Media

- A graphic is any visual aid.
- Animation is a representation of motion in graphics or text.
- Even with readily available stock photos, there may be times when you need to create your own.
- Video can be purchased from a stock footage house or shot yourself.
- Audio in a digital media presentation may be narration (voiceovers), sound effects, or music.

Creating a Digital Media Presentation

- The three stages of production for a digital media presentation are preproduction, production, and postproduction.
- A digital media presentation must be planned, just like any other document you write.
- The design of a digital media presentation must adhere to the fundamentals of design: balance, variety, harmony, emphasis, proportion, pattern, movement, and rhythm.
- A standalone digital media presentation can be displayed without the author present to show it.
- An interactive digital media presentation allows the viewer to control the presentation.

Review
Your Knowledge

1. What are the two possible goals of a presentation?
2. What two things will an effective visual design achieve?
3. List the four articles in the Electronic User's Bill of Rights.
4. What is the role of a EULA in purchasing software?
5. What are the five types of software that may be needed for digital media presentations?
6. Define digital media.
7. If a 3 × 5 photograph is 300 dpi, what are the pixel dimensions?
8. What is a video?
9. Describe the three stages of production.
10. Describe a standalone digital media presentation.

Apply
Your Knowledge

1. Research the role of technology in giving effective presentations. Write several paragraphs explaining your findings.
2. Using the Internet, locate a copy of the Electronic Users Bill of Rights. Read it, and then rewrite it in your own words. Write an answer to each of the following questions.
   A. As a student, how might you contribute to the body of work that is shared via the Internet?
   B. Does the educational institution you attend contribute to the resources that are discussed in this Bill of Rights?
   C. When you move into the corporate world, how might you or your company contribute to these resources?
   D. In what way might individuals or institutions abuse the rights outlined in these guidelines?
3. Search the Internet or store advertisements for a SLR digital camera that costs less than $150.
   A. What are the specifications for the camera? What are its zoom capabilities? What is the pixel density?
   B. What are the specifications for the camera on a typical cell phone?
   C. Are there any differences between an SLR digital camera and the one on a cell phone?
4. Locate an online stock photo house that offers a monthly subscription. Read the End Users License Agreement. Are there any restrictions or limitations on where the photos could be used? List three business documents in which the photos could be used based on the EULA. Cite the URL of the online stock photo house.
5. Research video editing software. Identify software that will allow you to do basic editing, such as cutting/trimming clips, adding voiceovers, and adding graphics to the video. List your top five choices for both freeware and pay software. If you are going to share the finished video with friends, are there any copyright issues to consider?
6. Use slideshow software, such as PowerPoint, to create a master slide or a template for a presentation on your favorite hobby or sport. Consider the following.
   A. What image or graphic would be an effective addition to all slides in the presentation?
   B. What color scheme would go well with the topic and the image/graphic you have chosen?
   C. How can you apply the basic visual design principles to your master slide?

Practice
What You Have Learned

Access the *Fundamentals of Business Communication* Student Companion Web Site at www.g-wlearning.com/Communication. Download each data file for this chapter. Follow the instructions to complete a reading, writing, and grammar activity to practice what you have learned in this chapter.

Connections
Across the Curriculum

Social Studies. Research the history of storyboarding. Write a short paragraph on where it began. Then write another paragraph explaining how you feel it can help in creating a digital media presentation.

Math. Create a spreadsheet to show digital media software that is available for creating presentations. On the Y axis, list several available software packages. On the X axis, list tasks such as animation, graphing, etc. This chart will help you decide which type of software you will need as you create digital media presentations.

Build
Your Business Portfolio

When you apply for a job, college, or community service position, you will be asked to complete an application. The application will have your contact information, education, and other items of interest for the interviewer. You may be asked to complete the application while on site, which means you will have to fill it out by hand. This takes patience and time, so you should practice filling out several different applications.

1. Download several applications from the Internet or obtain them from other sources. Practice completing the applications by hand until you have one that has a clean, neat appearance.
2. Scan the two best applications for your ePortfolio. Create a subfolder named Applications. Save each application with the file names Application01 and Application02.
3. Place the original applications in your container for your print portfolio.

Careers
Marketing, Sales, and Service Careers and Communication

If you crave variety and enjoy a fast-paced environment, a career in marketing, sales, and service may be perfect for you. Careers in this cluster include all of the jobs involved in buying, distributing, marketing, and selling products and providing follow-up service to customers. Related jobs include finding new customers and tracking marketing data.

Strong, outgoing personalities and good communication skills are key qualities for these workers. Describe situations in which a person in a career in this cluster would need good presentation skills.

Marketing Presentation

Making a marketing presentation is a team event you might enter with your organization. This event will demonstrate your team's knowledge of marketing techniques as well as written persuasive skills and oral presentation abilities. To prepare for this event, do the following.

1. Work with your team to create the marketing presentation. Read the guidelines provided by your organization. Make certain you ask any questions about points you do not understand. It is important you follow each specific item that is outlined in the competition rules.

2. Apply persuasive written skills that you learned as your team revises the presentation.

3. Use your proofreading and editing skills to complete a final document. Review Chapter 7 for proofreading and editing direction.

4. Make the presentation professional by using the digital media presentation techniques described in this chapter.

5. Practice, practice, practice.

Unit 5

Listening and Reading for Successful Communication

In This Unit

Listening and reading are two very important skills in business. From reading a job application to listening to instructions from your manager, these skills will be applied every day in your career. This unit explains how to be an effective, active listener and an effective, active reader. Completing this unit will help you meet college and career readiness (CCR) anchor standards for reading, as outlined by the **Common Core State Standards**.

14
Listening with a Purpose

I like to listen. I have learned a great deal from listening carefully. Most people never listen.
—Ernest Hemingway, American author and winner of the Nobel Prize in Literature

Good listening skills are critical to business. Experts in communication at the University of Minnesota have estimated that 80 percent of on-the-job tasks depend on listening skills. Being a good listener requires understanding the difference between "listening" and "hearing." Good listeners know when to take notes, when to comment, and when to remain quiet. They also continuously evaluate what they hear to check their understanding and stay focused on the topic.

Objectives

When you complete Chapter 14, you will be able to:

Differentiate between hearing and listening.

Identify the criteria for becoming an active listener.

Demonstrate how to apply active listening in formal situations.

Terms

hearing

listening

passive listening

active listening

complex response

evasive

prior knowledge

literal

inferential

bias

skepticism

rapport

Go Green

When is the last time you looked up a telephone number in a printed phone book? Encourage your school and place of employment to opt out of receiving printed phone books, which often end up in landfills. Instead of a printed phone book, use your computer or other electronic devices to find current phone listings.

1. Research white-page listings on the Internet. Which Web sites offer this service?

2. How do you find phone numbers for business and personal calls?

Listening Is a Skill

Think about how much time you spend listening. In any given week, you may listen to your favorite music, get directions from someone, or receive feedback from others. But are you really listening? When you *listen*, you make an effort to process what you *hear*. To process what you hear, you need to consider the speaker's purpose, relate what you already know to what you hear, and show attention.

Hearing is a physical process. When sound waves reach your ears, which send signals to your brain, you are hearing. Listening is an intellectual process. **Listening** combines hearing with evaluating. In addition, listening often leads to follow-up. Just because you think you are listening does not mean you are really hearing what the speaker is saying.

Few people would argue against the importance of listening, yet listening skills are often ignored. Children and students are expected to listen, but are not always taught to listen as they are taught to read, write, and speak. Listening skills are hard to observe and measure. In most cases, listening is assumed. How effectively someone is listening, therefore, is often unknown.

A salesperson or customer service representative, for example, must carefully listen to what the customer says and does not say in order to improve sales and customer satisfaction. Also, your attention and understanding in meetings, as well as your ability to carry out instructions, can influence your success in significant ways. Managers must listen in order to know what their customers want, what their employees and coworkers think and feel, what problems their supervisors are facing, and what their top executives expect. Therefore, listening is a critical management skill.

If you are like most people, you take listening for granted. Listening is not something you think about and probably not something you would choose to study. There is no question that, however, good listening is a critical skill for career success. Your attention to what a supervisor or a client says can make the difference between successful and unsuccessful performance at work. These characteristics—being clear, courteous, concise, and correct—are known as the *four C's* in English instruction. Remember the four C's and use them as a checklist for quality whenever you prepare and review written communication and oral presentations.

Reading Prep

Before reading this chapter, preview the special, "boxed" features so that you may relate the information as you read the content. Special features focus on topics of interest that relate the material that is presented in the chapter.

When you listen, you evaluate what you hear. It is important in business to *listen*, not *hear*.

Shutterstock

Passive Listening

Passive listening is casually listening to the speaker. You may or may not hear everything that is said, and you are not actively trying to *listen* and understand. When you are watching a movie, you are a passive listener. You are not involved with the speaker and you may not hear every word that is spoken. Passive listening is appropriate when you do not have the need to interact with the speaker. Passive listeners are more interested in *hearing* and less interested in *listening*.

Active Listening

Active listening is fully participating as you process what other people say. Active listening is used to get information, respond to requests, receive directions, and critically respond to something. Active listeners consider the purpose of the speaker, relate what they already know to what they hear, and show attention through body language and words. Active listeners know when to take notes, when to follow directions, when to comment, and when to remain quiet. To be a good active listener, it is important to continuously evaluate what you hear. This helps you check your understanding of what you hear. It also helps keep you focused on the topic and aids your memory of what you hear.

Listening for Specific Information

The purpose for active listening will vary according to the situation and the needs you bring to that situation. You will be a more effective listener if you can identify your purpose and adapt your listening behavior accordingly. When you are aware of the specific information needed from a speaker, you are better prepared to receive that information. There are some things you can do as an active listener to make sure you collect information in an efficient and accurate manner.

If you must listen for a great deal of data, prepare in advance whenever possible. Before you go to a meeting, attend a conference, or make a telephone call, decide what information you hope to take away with you. If you initiate the contact when you have a number of issues to discuss, questions to ask, or items of information to provide, develop a list before making contact. If someone contacts you, have a pad and pen or your computer in front of you to take notes. Apply this principle to e-mails, phone calls, and meetings and you will find that you save a great deal of time—not just your own, but other people's, too.

When someone responds to your request or question, you probably need no special motivation to listen carefully. After all, the response should interest you since you requested it. If the response is complex, however, you may miss part of it. This is especially true if part of the response is unexpected. A **complex response** is one that is hard to understand. It might be very long or the person may speak in language that is not clear. Always make sure you understand all parts of the response and its details. Write notes and ask questions to clarify any points that are confusing.

In some situations, speakers may provide *non-answers*. That is, the speaker may say something that is off-topic or **evasive,** which means avoiding giving you a direct answer. In some situations, the speaker may not know the answer and try to hide the uncertainty. In other situations, it may be uncomfortable to give an answer because the issue may be sensitive and not appropriate for all members of the audience. Whenever you recognize that the speaker does not know an answer, be gracious. Pressing people for information they do not have can result in embarrassment for everyone. Nonetheless, it is extremely important to listen attentively to whatever information the speaker does provide.

CASE

Detour to a Deadline

At a press conference, Tyrone Brooks, the press secretary for a large auto parts company, was taking questions about the company's downsizing. Tara Blixen, a reporter, asked if the company will lay off any additional employees within the next year. Mr. Brooks replied:

> As I said earlier, we have been studying our operations very closely nationwide. We are doing all that we can to keep layoffs to a minimum. At this point, we expect the next quarter to turn sales around as some of our new green technology divisions get up and running. That's the last question, folks. Thank you for your time.

Tara completed her news story and e-mailed it to her editor. Tara's story began:

> Franklin Enterprises plans no more layoffs in the coming year, according to spokesperson Tyrone Brooks.

Later the same day, Tara's editor was surprised to hear a radio news report that presented the story quite differently. The rival story began:

> Are more layoffs in store at Franklin Enterprises? At a press conference today, company spokesperson Tyrone Brooks skirted the question, leaving hundreds of employees and subcontractors hanging in the balance.

1. Did Tara use active listening skills when gathering information?

2. How well did Tara evaluate the message before she e-mailed her news story?

Actively Listening to Requests

Requests come in all shapes and sizes. Some are simple and need only a brief response. Others are tedious and time-consuming. In many cases, your first decision must be whether you can or should perform whatever is being asked. Your second decision may be whether you can do so in the allotted time.

To be helpful and cooperative, you might be tempted to try to fill every request, including unreasonable requests. It is wise to always question and evaluate the requests you receive. You must decide whether the request is reasonable or consider the time required to do something that is not one of your assigned job tasks.

- Listen to be sure you understand the *what, where, when, why,* and *how* of the request.
- Ask follow-up questions to clarify complex issues.
- Make comments that summarize what you are to do.
- Do not rely on your memory; take notes, especially for numbers, dates, and other details.
- Summarizing is an active listening technique that can help to ensure you omit nothing. When you summarize, you write or think through all of the main points you just heard.

Each listening situation has a unique set of circumstances. In addition to listening skills, your judgment and decision-making abilities may play a role. Sometimes people are clear, but still omit important information. Picking up on what is not said is known as reading between the lines. This is a crucial skill to develop.

Actively Listening to Directions

When others are directing you, help them out by *actively listening* to what they are saying. Accept the responsibility for what you must do, when you must do it, where, why, and how.

If you can predict that you will be given directions and know what they relate to, be prepared. Find out as much as you can about what you are

When listening to a speaker, think about what is being said. Evaluate the information and decide what action to take.

Shutterstock

to hear at the meeting or the presentation. Bring the catalog, report, manual, budget, or whatever other materials will be discussed. Having this **prior knowledge**—experience and information you already possess—will give you something to which you can relate your new knowledge.

At the meeting or presentation, apply all of the techniques you learned earlier. Evaluate and summarize your notes, ask follow-up questions, and give feedback to the speaker. If you are listening to a complex process, take notes that clearly define and differentiate each step. Review the steps to make sure you understand each point and that you have not overlooked any detail. If necessary, politely ask the speaker to slow down or repeat a point.

In short, make sure you have the information before leaving. Write a brief summary of the information you learned. This written summary will also help you retain the content. Ask questions and make comments to clarify and confirm the information.

- You said this software can be networked, but does that apply to all operating systems?
- In other words, our ten percent discount is on the wholesale, not the retail, price. Now I understand.
- Must we submit both forms to human resources?

Also, as you listen to directions, try to anticipate your future needs. Will you need any help or further directions later, after the meeting? Find out when and where you can get help if a problem should arise and make note of it.

When possible, give feedback to the speaker to show you understand the information that is being presented. Sometimes, simply making eye contact tells the speaker you are listening. If there is an opportunity to give comments or ask questions at the end of the presentation, your feedback will be appreciated by the speaker.

Listening to Persuasive Talk

When a speaker is trying to persuade you to do something, that speaker has a purpose: to influence your attitude or behavior. When you know what the speaker wants, you will be better able to analyze what is being said.

Sometimes you can recognize persuasive talk, but the speaker's motives may not be obvious. In this type of situation, try to determine the speaker's purpose by asking yourself questions.

- What is in it for the speaker?
- Whom does the speaker represent?
- What does the speaker want me to do or believe?
- What are the pros and cons on this issue?

A speaker's statements may be interpreted as **literal;** that is, the speaker means exactly what the words indicate. Or, the statements may be interpreted as **inferential,** which means you are to draw a conclusion from what is said. For example, consider the following statement from a salesperson trying to sell a maintenance-service contract for a laptop computer.

❏ With the contract, complete computer repair is a telephone call away!

Is this a literal (actual possibility) or inferential statement? Since the process of repairing the defect begins with a telephone call to request that your computer be serviced, the statement is inferential. If the statement were literal, the telephone call would repair the computer, which, of course, is not correct.

It is also useful to be aware of your own needs and motivations when listening to persuasive talk. Persuasive speakers often try to predict your objections and argue against them in advance. A savvy person might direct arguments using *prior knowledge* of any weaknesses you may have.

For example, if you are a cost-conscious manager, an employee proposing a new technology application may emphasize its cost-saving features and downplay other characteristics, such as the need for training. However, without evaluating these other characteristics, you might agree to a program that is inappropriate because all you have thought about is how it will save your department money. Active listeners recognize when their own needs and motivations get in the way of the whole picture. Active listeners try to listen *above* their preferences so they make rational, rather than emotional, decisions.

Evaluating as you listen means weighing the validity of the information you hear. A touch of skepticism is a good thing. It is not always wise to automatically accept information as accurate. Use silent self-talk to question incoming information. If you doubt the accuracy of what you hear, you may politely ask the speaker to support questionable statements.

Do not make the mistake of being a passive listener. Recognize that effective persuasive speakers carefully prepare and adjust their presentations to obtain the results they want. As a listener, you should prepare your mind to analyze incoming information. Take into consideration the speaker's purpose and your own needs and motivations so that you come away from the interaction with results you can live with as well.

A good active listener asks questions to clarify information. Always be an active listener.

Shutterstock

Identifying Types of Active Listening

There are several types of active listening: informative, evaluative, empathetic, and reflective. Each type of listening serves a specific purpose. You may engage in more than one type of active listening at one time.

Informative listening occurs when you need to learn specific information or instructions. For example, a customer service representative must use informative listening to determine what the customer needs.

Evaluative listening occurs when you must determine the quality or validity of what is being said. For example, if a salesperson tells you that by purchasing a piece of equipment you will save thousands of dollars each year, you must evaluate this statement to determine if it is valid.

Empathetic listening occurs when you attempt to put yourself in the speaker's place and understand how he or she feels. Customer service representatives very frequently must use empathetic listening to understand why a customer is upset. By understanding why the customer is upset, the customer service representative may be better able to assist the customer.

Reflective listening occurs when you consider what the speaker says. All active listening involves reflective listening.

Checkpoint

1. What is the difference between hearing and listening?
2. What is the difference between passive listening and active listening?

Becoming an Active Listener

In any listening situation, active listening requires your complete engagement in the situation. Here are some of the things you can do to become an active listener.

- Think about the speaker's purpose before, during, and after the presentation.
- Evaluate what you hear by relating the information to what you already know—your prior knowledge—and experience and information you already possess.
- Make eye contact with the speaker to show attention.
- Take notes when necessary.
- Ask questions and make comments when appropriate.
- Adopt good listening habits, such as sitting in front of the room.
- Fight distractions; never engage in texting or answer your cell phone when listening to a speaker.
- Concentrate on the presentation.

Recognize the Speaker's Purpose

Whenever you speak, you have a purpose or reason for delivering the message. Likewise, whenever you listen, you are listening to someone who has a purpose or reason for delivering the message. Your job as listener starts by recognizing the speaker's purpose.

Recognizing the speaker's purpose is often easy. In many situations, the general purpose seems clear before the speaker even begins.

- The agenda for your national sales conference shows that the chief financial officer is speaking on *The Need to Cut Sales Costs*. Is there any doubt about the purpose of this presentation?

- You have a message from a good customer who calls every time a rush order is needed. Your prior knowledge of this customer gives you a good idea of the purpose of the call.

However, sometimes the speaker's purpose is not readily apparent. For example, a small, employee-owned company will be purchased by one of two buyers. The president of the company knows that one buyer will bring a new president, while the other buyer will not. When the president speaks with the employees, one of the companies is presented favorably—the one that will keep the president—and the other is presented unfavorably. The employees believe the president is simply passing on information, yet the real purpose is quite different—to sway employees in favor of the buyer who will retain the president. This is an example of the president showing bias. A **bias** is a prejudice—a personal or unreasoned distortion of judgment.

When listening to persuasive talk, it is important to determine what the speaker is trying to get you to do. You may need to infer some things from what the speaker says.

Shutterstock

Use Prior Knowledge

The better you know the speaker and the situation, of course, the better you can detect a speaker's real purpose. For example, if you know a speaker has a history of being honest and following through on promises, then you are probably safe to assume the speaker will be forthright in speaking to you. In contrast, if you know a speaker frequently hides information, you should be more careful when detecting the purpose of the communication.

Keep in mind that a touch of skepticism can help you interpret the real meaning of a message. **Skepticism** means you have a degree of doubt. People often speak of a *healthy dose of skepticism*. It is not useful to doubt everyone all of the time, but balancing belief with skepticism is smart. A time for skepticism is when you know the speaker stands to benefit from what is being said. Your skepticism should go into full gear if the statements seem exaggerated.

CASE

What Are the Facts?

Roland Pelzer was recently assigned to manage all promotional materials for Classic Works Theater Company. He still has much to learn about this new area, but a coworker, Suzanne Varnas, provided some helpful information. Yesterday, a representative from Allied Printing stopped by Roland's office to talk about his company's services. The rep told Roland:

Allied Printing is an agent for independent printers. That means we can guarantee you the lowest cost and the fastest deliveries. For example, we would charge you only 29 cents a copy for this brochure. Other printers would charge you more.

As Roland listened, he thought to himself:

Suzanne said you get the best prices when you deal directly with the printer. When you deal with an agent, the agent gets a commission. That must cost more. But I know we paid more than 29 cents a copy for the *Death of a Salesman* brochure. I'd better ask Suzanne about that.

1. How did prior information help Roland evaluate what the Allied rep had to say?

2. What other prior knowledge came in to play here?

3. How can Roland's active listening affect his company's bottom line?

Evaluate What You Hear

As you learned earlier, active listening means combining hearing with evaluation. Throughout any conversation, meeting, or presentation you must assign meaning to and evaluate what you hear, as shown in Figure 14-1. Often assigning meaning to what you hear is simple. When your boss says, "We're doing so well this week, we can close early on Friday," the meaning is obvious. Or, is it? The problem with assigning meaning to words arises because people do not always say what they mean. However, you can derive meaning from more than just the speaker's words.

Note Body Language and Other Nonverbal Cues

Body language and other nonverbal cues will help you interpret speakers' messages. Body language is nonverbal communication based on your facial expression, hand gestures, and body position. When you watch as well as listen to someone speak, you often understand more than when you only listen. Seeing someone speak provides more information about the meaning of the words than simply hearing the person speak.

Figure 14-1. There are a number of questions you can ask yourself as you evaluate a speaker. Silently research the topic in your mind to uncover what you already know.

Tips for Evaluating What You Hear

- Do the speaker's facts support what you have heard, read, or seen from other sources?
- Do the speaker's facts agree with or contradict facts earlier presented by the same speaker?
- Do the speaker's conclusions agree with your experience?
- Do the speaker's suggestions and recommendations have substance?
- Does the speaker meet the test of common sense?

  > This type of questioning can help you to actively listen and respond appropriately. Once you begin evaluating what you hear by relating old information to new information, your evaluations will take various forms, such as those listed below.

- You recognize misunderstandings or deceptions.

  > He isn't really answering the question, is he?

  > He knows a lot about our trading relationship with Asian countries, but hasn't said one word about Europe.

- You recognize discrepancies between old information and new.

  > Did she say 20 percent? I've heard estimates much, much higher. I wonder which number is accurate.

  > Wait a minute. Didn't he say just the opposite of that last week?

- You check your own understanding.

  > Oh, I get it. To speed up the approval process, from now on I could…

  > I guess this means the budget cut will affect us sooner rather than later.

- You clarify information.

  > Oh, I thought she said 70 before. She must have said 17.

  > That graph sure helps. Now I see the sales growth he's talking about.

- You recognize similarities between old and new information.

  > Hmm, this agrees with what I read yesterday in the newspaper. There must be some truth in this.

  > The problems he's reporting about this project are just like those that surfaced on the earlier project. Maybe we need to examine how we handled the earlier project.

Consider the numerous interpretations possible for this simple statement: "I must thank Bob for all of his hard work." Reading this comment, you may assign the most obvious meaning, assuming the speaker has sincere thanks to give Bob. However, *watching* the speaker say this might lead you to another interpretation.

What if the speaker rolls her eyes when she says thanks to Bob? This probably means she is being sarcastic and Bob did not do enough work. Furthermore, Bob's presence will affect how you interpret the statement. If Bob is in the room watching the speaker role her eyes, the speaker could be teasing Bob, but she could be openly insulting or reprimanding him.

Other nonverbal cues, such as tone of voice, also help you assign meaning to a speaker's words. Which words does the speaker emphasize when she announces her gratitude to Bob? Emphasizing certain words affects the meaning of the sentence. What is the speaker doing when she makes the announcement? If she is shuffling through papers, the message can be interpreted as less sincere than if she delivers the message while sitting upright and looking Bob in the eyes.

Consider Personality

The speaker's personality is another factor to consider when assigning meaning to what a person says. Consider the example presented earlier: "We're doing so well this week, we can close early on Friday." How can the boss's words be interpreted in any way other than literally? Well, if he is being sarcastic, the real meaning may be, "We're way behind and will have to work late on Friday," or, "Just because it is Friday doesn't mean we're closing any earlier than normal."

Employees who know this person well may fully understand what he means even though he has said just the opposite. If he is a joker, his comment may mean nothing. He may simply have made the remark to get a chuckle from employees who know better. The more you know about a speaker, the easier it will be to assign meaning accurately to that person's words.

The personality of the speaker can be an important part of the message. If the person has a serious personality, you can probably assume anything said is not done so in a joking manner.

Shutterstock

Evaluate the Message

Knowledge of speakers not only helps you assign meaning to their words but also helps you evaluate their messages. Evaluating the message means judging the accuracy and truthfulness of what you hear.

- Does the message make sense?
- Does the message match the nonverbal cues given by the speaker?
- Does the message fit with other information you have; can you think of any reason not to believe it?

All of the above are important questions, but the only way to answer them is to use your prior knowledge. Relate the new information to information you already have and believe. If new and old information match or agree, you may choose to believe what you hear. However, when new and old information contradict each other, you must question what you hear.

For example, when you listen to candidates for political office, you know their purpose is to convince you they will do the things you want done. Candidates may say, for example, that they will reduce taxes, create jobs, increase access to health care, and reduce crime. Do you believe them? The only way to answer this question is to compare their claims with what you already know about the situation. Your knowledge of and opinion on all the issues will help you determine whether you believe the claims of political candidates.

Evaluating messages based on prior knowledge has at least three general benefits.

- Improved memory.
- Improved focus.
- Improved understanding.

Research shows that people remember information better when they can personalize it. To personalize it means to directly relate it to you. By relating new information to what you already know, you are, in effect, personalizing it. You will remember more of that information. When information has no personal connection, the mind is more likely to wander. People begin thinking about other things if they do not connect with what is being said. By relating new information to old, you personalize the information. Your ability to pay attention to that information increases.

Checkpoint
1. What is bias?
2. How can skepticism be useful to the listening process?
3. What can be used in addition to the words to understand the meaning of a message?

Active Listening in Formal Situations

Routine business situations require that you listen carefully and evaluate what you hear. More formal situations, such as job interviews, meetings with managers or other executives, business lunches with clients, or as an audience member listening to a speaker, require extra attention as to how you are coming across as a listener. Through your actions, you must show that you are listening carefully. Show attention, take notes, ask questions, and make comments as appropriate.

Show Attention

One way in which you can participate as a listener during face-to-face communication is to convey through body language that you are paying attention. This is true in all situations, but can be especially important to your career in formal situations. Here are some key ways to show attention.

- Face the speaker and give him or her your full attention.

- Engage in enough eye contact to signal that you are focused, but avoid staring, which can be intimidating and distracting.

- Lean toward, rather than away from, the speaker to indicate you are paying attention.

- Be appropriately responsive; smile or laugh at a humorous anecdote and frown at bad news.

- Nod your head when you understand a point. If you are puzzled by something, let the speaker know by furrowing your brow or asking a question.

Apply these suggestions as they fit the circumstances. Be mindful that the speaker will be evaluating your body language. Nonverbal cues such as roving eyes, a flat affect, and inappropriate facial expressions communicate indifference and even rudeness. *Affect* is the feeling or emotion communicated by your facial expression and body posture.

BUSINESS PROTOCOL

Business Dining

When business requires you have a meal with your manager or customers, observe the commonly accepted rules of behavior. Dress appropriately, arrive on time, and turn off your cell phone. Refrain from placing personal items on the table. If you are dining with people from other cultures, be aware that their eating customs may differ from yours. If you are unsure of how to properly use utensils, search the Internet for dining etiquette before you arrive at the event. Remember that the meeting, even though over a meal, is for business purposes, so avoid personal topics.

In order to show attention, you actually need to be paying attention to the message. Your attention builds positive rapport with the speaker. **Rapport** is a feeling of harmony and accord in a relationship that encourages further communication. The discipline of showing attention makes it easier to ignore distractions. By committing yourself physically to the task of listening, you are less likely to stray from the object of your attention.

Take Notes

Jot down the speaker's points that are meaningful to your purpose for listening, as shown in Figure 14-2. To do this effectively requires careful, active listening. Consider the thought process you must go through to take good notes. You must not only *hear* what is said, but you must also comprehend, evaluate, and translate or summarize the information; you must *listen*. Then, you must determine if the information is important enough to write down. Next, you must quickly record it. While writing, you must continue listening unless the speaker stops while you write.

Figure 14-2.   **Consider these tips for taking good notes and use them as appropriate.**

Tips for Taking Good Notes

- Be selective. Write down only what is important or you may not remember.
- Organize your notes as you write, if possible. Let the format of your notes correspond to the speaker's message.
- Use abbreviations and symbols. If the notes are for you only, cut as many corners as you like as long as the notes remain useful.
- Avoid noting information that appears in a handout. Highlight or put a check mark in the margin of the hand out to remind yourself of key points.
- Write down the main point of a visual aid. If it contains data you need later, write down the source or ask the speaker afterward for a copy of the graphic.
- Often speakers summarize the most important points in the closing. This is a good time to be listening carefully with pen ready, if necessary.

Do *not* use note-taking as a substitute for active listening. However, it is important to always write down things you must do following a discussion or meeting. Relying on memory is not a good idea. Carefully listen for any such directions, whether directly stated or implied, and write them down. You will often leave meetings with many things on your mind, some of which you will forget if you do not take notes.

TEAMWORK

Form a team with two classmates to practice active listening as your instructor delivers a 15 to 20 minute lecture. During the lecture, each team member will work independently. Take notes summarizing the main idea, the main points made, and the conclusion of the lecture. After the lecture, meet as a team and discuss each member's notes as well as what mental activities you engaged in to minimize distractions and barriers. Prepare a team report for your instructor.

Provide Feedback

Clearly, some situations call for quiet listening. However, when possible, provide feedback by asking questions and making comments. Be aware that the tone of questions and comments can influence the communication process. Friendly questions that ask for clarification or further information are welcomed by a speaker. Figure 14-3 for examples of questions. Such feedback will put the speaker at ease and provide an opportunity to repeat or elaborate on a point. By asking friendly questions and making friendly comments, you show that you are listening, interested, and confident enough in the speaker to seek more information.

Figure 14-3.   **Friendly questions can help establish a rapport with the speaker.**

Friendly Questions

These questions can be considered friendly questions. Friendly questions are usually welcomed by the speaker.

- Did your marketing questionnaire elicit any information on family income?
- This summary sheet says the year's sales goal is ten percent higher than last year's. Is that ten percent over last year's actual sales or ten percent over budgeted sales?
- How expensive is this new technology for fuel conservation?
- I agree we must get our budget back on track, but do we have some specific ways to get around the higher prices in the marketplace?
- If we give them a copy of the appendix, will it answer all of their questions?

If spoken in an unfriendly tone, questions and comments can put a speaker on the defensive and create communication barriers, as shown in Figure 14-4. Challenging questions or comments are *not* a form of constructive feedback. Even if the speaker has a good response to an unfriendly question or comment, the challenge may create an uncomfortable atmosphere.

You can avoid the pitfalls of friendly versus unfriendly by carefully phrasing your question or comment. Pay attention to the following points.

- Ask questions at the appropriate time.
- Be sure the question is relevant.
- Limit the length of your question.
- Observe good diplomacy.
- Avoid nitpicking.
- Never get personal.

Avoid interrupting a speaker in group meetings or a presentation. In meetings, jot down your question or comment and wait until the speaker finishes. A presenter may invite questions during a presentation or indicate that questions and comments will be taken at the end. If you have more than one question or comment, pause between them to give others a chance to participate.

Avoid questions or comments that do not relate to the topic. The speaker may not be able to answer and other listeners will probably become impatient. If you need to discuss an unrelated topic, approach the speaker after the formal session concludes.

Keep your questions and comments short. Also, avoid getting into a long, one-on-one discussion. This is inconsiderate of the group. If you need to pursue a discussion beyond a follow-up question or comment, do so at the end of the session.

Figure 14-4.	Unfriendly questions can damage the relationship between you and the speaker. Be sure to avoid unfriendly questions.

Unfriendly Questions

These questions may be considered unfriendly questions. Unfriendly questions can put up a barrier between you and the speaker.

- Last week you said last month's sales were up ten percent, but today you say they were down five percent; which is it?
- You claim there are no problems with clear-cutting forests, but how do you account for the article in last week's *Forestry Magazine*, which listed several problems with clear-cutting?
- That sounds like a very high number; do you have empirical evidence to support that claim?
- You always talk about participative management, but have you really implemented it in this department?

No matter how much you disagree or how wrong you think a speaker is, always maintain a professional tone. If you ask a good question or make a good comment in an unprofessional or sarcastic manner, your lack of professionalism is what people will remember. If the speaker appears to have given incorrect information, give the speaker the benefit of the doubt and carefully phrase your question or comment.

Do not allow a small detail to become a distraction. Sometimes a speaker makes a general point with which you agree, but supports it with a detail or two with which you disagree. Do not challenge the detail unless you foresee it being misused later. In most cases, the general point is the more important aspect and the rest can be disregarded.

If a speaker says something with which you disagree on principle or that you find offensive, consider letting it go by. As a listener, it is not your role to challenge a speaker on behalf of your beliefs. If your disagreement is intense, consider approaching the speaker in private. However, your goal should be to share a different perspective with the speaker, not to embarrass or argue with him or her.

Arrive Early

Arriving early is not merely a courtesy to the speaker and other meeting participants, but it is also an aid to your listening. By arriving early, you have time to settle in, familiarize yourself with your surroundings, greet people you know, and shuffle any necessary paperwork before the speaker begins. The beginning and end of any speaking situation are often crucial. Speakers often introduce and summarize main points both at the beginning and the end. By missing the first few minutes of a presentation, you cannot benefit from the speaker's attempt to focus the discussion and introduce main ideas. Finally, arriving late is simply disruptive to all other participants.

Sit in the Front

The front of the room usually provides fewer distractions. You are less likely to be distracted by those sitting between you and the speaker. From the front, you can hear the speaker better and see any visuals with less effort. By sitting in the front of the room, you will more easily be able to participate in the communication process.

Fight Distractions and Barriers

Good listeners fight external distractions so they can give all of their attention to the task of listening. Good listeners are also aware of the barriers, both internal and external, that might interfere with good listening. You can learn to concentrate on the message and ignore outside distractions. The power to concentrate also helps to keep internal distractions—those created by one's own mind—in check as well.

Do not be a lazy, passive listener. Passive listeners stop paying attention when the information becomes too long or complex.

Remain open-minded when listening. Closed-minded listeners tune out a speaker because they are not interested in learning from the speaker or in helping maintain an environment conducive to open communication.

Be flexible as a listener. Inflexible listeners refuse to listen to a speaker who has said or implied

TEAMWORK

Choose a social or political issue that is controversial. Find a classmate who disagrees with you on the issue. Ask your classmate to explain his or her position to you. Paraphrase each point your classmate makes using neutral language. Then, trade places. When you and your classmate have both objectively paraphrased each other's arguments, discuss any difficulties you had doing so.

something they disagree with, especially if the speaker has said something that contradicts their value and belief systems.

Be sincere when listening. Insincere listeners are those who hear the words, but do not listen to the message. They often avoid eye contact with the speaker and, therefore, cannot benefit from the speaker's body language.

Stay interested in the topic. Bored listeners are those who find no interest in the subject. They either become impatient and hostile with the speaker or preoccupy themselves with something else.

Be an attentive listener. Inattentive listeners pay little attention to the speaker's message, but may concentrate on the speaker's body language and mannerisms. They become distracted by text messaging, conversing with others when they should be listening, and by other outside noise.

Technology makes it easy to do more than one thing at a time, which is called multitasking. Think twice, however, before you decide to multitask when you are engaged in listening. Anything that takes your mind away from what the speaker is saying will present a barrier to active listening.

Make sure the environment is conducive to listening. If you are in a noisy environment, do not make a telephone call to discuss something important. If you are in a meeting, close the door if there is noise in the hallway. Be aware that noise and other distractions affect concentration, even when you think you are not noticing them.

Jumping ahead is a barrier to actively listening. This may take the form of thinking about what you want to say next. It may also be thinking about the fact that the speaker is running over the allotted time and you will be late for your next meeting. Remain focused on the speaker, not on what you have to do next.

If you bring biases to the situation, they will interfere with your ability to listen. Do not decide in advance that a speaker lacks credibility or does not deserve your attention. Personal biases and preconceived ideas are a strong filter that can distort your ability to be a good listener. Actively listen and give the person a chance.

 Checkpoint

1. In face-to-face communication, how can you indicate you are paying attention without saying anything?
2. When taking notes, which points should you write down?
3. What are the two best ways of providing feedback?
4. What are the two ways to classify barriers to listening?

Chapter 14 Review

Chapter Summary

Listening Is a Skill

- Hearing is the physical process of sound waves reaching your ears and being processed by the brain.
- Listening involves evaluating what you hear.
- Passive listening is casually listening to a speaker without evaluation.
- Active listening is fully participating in what the speaker is saying.
- The types of active listening include informative, evaluative, empathetic, and reflective.

Becoming an Active Listener

- You can become an active listener with practice.
- An active listener recognizes the speaker's purpose by using prior knowledge.
- Active listeners evaluate not only what is heard, but body language and other nonverbal cues.

Active Listening in Formal Situations

- Formal business situations, such as interviews or meetings with a manager, require extra attention to show you are an active listener.
- Show attention through your body language.
- Take notes regarding what is meaningful to your purpose or something you must do after the meeting.
- Provide feedback through friendly questions and comments.
- Arrive early for the meeting.
- While listening, fight any distractions and barriers.

Review Your Knowledge

1. What is the difference between hearing and listening?
2. What is the difference between passive listening and active listening?
3. Name four reasons for active listening.
4. Explain what it means to be evasive.
5. Explain the difference between a literal and inferential statement.
6. How can you use prior knowledge to help you be a better listener?
7. What is body language?
8. How can personality be important in listening to a speaker?
9. What does evaluating the message mean?
10. How can you become an active listener in formal situations?

Apply Your Knowledge

1. Consider the four types of active listening: informative, evaluative, empathetic, and reflective. Think about three situations in which these types of active listening can be used. Try to have at least two situations in which three of the types are used. Write several paragraphs describing each of your three situations.
2. Observe two speeches or presentations (live, on video, streaming on the Web, or on television). For one, be a passive listener. For the other, be an active listener. The day after observing each speech, write down as much as you can recall. Which one could you better recall? Write several paragraphs describing what you did differently when listening to each speech.

3. During a class lecture or discussion, write down any questions your classmates ask or comments they make. After class, categorize these questions and comments as friendly or unfriendly. For each that appears in the unfriendly category, write a note next to it that describes the point you believe the question or comment was intended to make.

 ## Practice
What You Have Learned

Access the *Fundamentals of Business Communication* Student Companion Web Site at www.g-wlearning.com/Communication. Download each data file for this chapter. Follow the instructions to complete a reading, writing, and grammar activity to practice what you have learned in this chapter.

 ## Connections
Across the Curriculum

Math. Create a grid to record your daily listening habits. On the X axis, enter the four types of active listening. On the Y axis, list each person to whom you listen in a day's time. Check the appropriate type of listening that you did each time.

Language Arts. Based on your findings in the math activity, write several paragraphs to analyze your listening habits. Could you identify the type of listening you were doing each time? Identify what you did well, where you could improve, and what your goals are to becoming a better listener.

 # Build
Your Business Portfolio

In the portfolio activity for the previous chapter, you completed an application by hand. However, you may be asked to complete an application on a Web site. Practice filling out several online forms so you have a feel for how it is done.

1. Locate several applications on the Internet. These may be job applications, college applications, or applications for volunteer service.

2. Practice completing the applications until you have one with a clean, neat appearance.

3. Create a screen capture of the two best applications (use the [Print Screen] button and then paste into Word) and save them in your ePortfolio. In the Applications subfolder, save each application with the file names Application 03 and Application 04.

4. Place a printed copy of each screen capture in your container for your print portfolio.

 # Careers
Law, Public Safety, Corrections, and Security Careers and Communication

With strong interest in public safety and national security, careers in law, public safety, and corrections are increasingly in demand. Keeping citizens and the country safe is the core mission of careers in this cluster. Career pathways include working in corrections, emergency and fire management, security and protection, law enforcement, and legal services.

Good communication skills are crucial for someone pursuing a career in this cluster. One important communication skill is the art of listening. Why is listening important in this field of service?

Event Prep

Help Desk

Help desk is a competitive event you might enter with your organization. This event allows you to demonstrate good communication and listening skills. There is an objective part of the event as well as an oral presentation. You will be evaluated on your verbal and nonverbal skills as well as the tone and projection of your voice. The judges will present you with a help desk scenario and ask you to interact with them. Review the specific guidelines and rules for this event for direction as to topics and props that you will be allowed to use.

To prepare for the help desk event, do the following.

1. Read the guidelines provided by your organization. Make certain you ask any questions about points you do not understand. It is important you follow each specific item that is outlined in the competition rules.

2. Review this chapter for information on how to be an active listener. One of the performance competencies is listening, so it is important for you to focus on listening skills.

3. Practice speaking in front of your peers until you are comfortable. Your speech will be judged by a panel of professionals.

15
Reading with a Purpose

To read without reflecting is like eating without digesting.
—*Edmund Burke,*
18th century Irish statesman
and philosopher

Much of what goes on in the business world is centered on reading: e-mails, letters, reports, manuals, brochures, pamphlets, flyers, reference guides. These are just a few examples of the communication that a busy worker comes in contact with on any given day. Some communication will be unimportant, some will be important, and some will be critical to your success. In this chapter, you will learn about various purposes for reading. You will also examine your own reading skills.

Objectives

When you complete Chapter 15, you will be able to:

Describe the importance of reading skills.

Apply techniques that will enable you to master the skill of active reading.

Use specific reading approaches that contribute to productive use of reading materials.

Explain general reading techniques.

Describe tips that will help you improve your reading skills.

Terms

active reading

protocol

boilerplate

presumption

skimming

prioritize

scanning

reading for detail

Go Green

As the need arises to purchase new computers for your home or office, look for computers made of environmentally-friendly materials. Many manufacturers of technology equipment are doing their part to make equipment with more ecofriendly materials. You can now find mercury-free computers and electronic devices built with components that have reduced amounts of brominated fire retardants (BFR) and polyvinyl chloride (PVC).

1. Find an advertisement in your local paper or on the Web for computers and monitors. Can you find a manufacturer who produces environmentally-friendly equipment?
2. Use the Internet to research PVC and BFR. What impact do these materials have on the environment?

Reading Is a Skill

Reading is something you may take for granted, but, like speaking and listening, reading is a skill that needs to be used with precision in the business world. When reading skillfully, you get meaning from written words and symbols and evaluate their accuracy and validity. No matter what type of job you have, you will have to read communication related to employment, benefits, policies, and procedures. In addition, much of your business may be conducted through e-mails, reports, and forms. You might also use the Internet to research and access information related to your work, much of which must be read. Finally, you can continue learning through reading on your own, which is a key to growing in your chosen career.

Active reading involves concentration. Have you ever read something and found yourself halfway down the page, wondering how you got there and what you missed along the way? Your eyes moved across the text, but your mind did not actively process the words, phrases, and sentences. This experience tells you that reading is more than a passive activity. Active reading requires you to be involved and to do something in response to the words.

Reading Prep

Before reading this chapter, think about the chapter title. What does the title tell you about what you will be learning? How does this chapter relate to information you already know?

Checkpoint

1. What occurs when you read skillfully?
2. What two things are required in active reading?

Active Reading

Active reading is a complex task. To actively read, you must:

- consider the writer's purpose for writing;
- consider your purpose for reading;
- relate what you read to your prior knowledge; and
- evaluate reading material both as you read and after you read to ensure understanding and form judgments.

Reading for detail relies heavily on knowing your purpose for reading, using prior knowledge, evaluating through listening to your thoughts, and taking note of information in and out. Without these efforts, you cannot hope to make a solid judgment about the material's accuracy or validity.

Consider the Writer's Purpose

Knowing the writer's purpose before you begin to read helps you to absorb the message and understand how and when you need to respond. In most cases, you can determine the writer's purpose before you start reading. Seeing an e-mail with a subject line of *Horizon Industries Estimate* tells you the writer's purpose at a glance. In other cases, you may need to read only the return address or the first sentence of a letter.

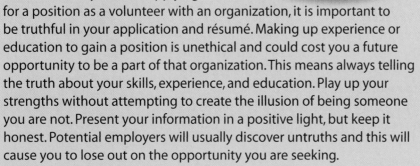

BUSINESS ETHICS

Truthful Applications

When applying for a job, submitting an application for acceptance into a university, or even applying for a position as a volunteer with an organization, it is important to be truthful in your application and résumé. Making up experience or education to gain a position is unethical and could cost you a future opportunity to be a part of that organization. This means always telling the truth about your skills, experience, and education. Play up your strengths without attempting to create the illusion of being someone you are not. Present your information in a positive light, but keep it honest. Potential employers will usually discover untruths and this will cause you to lose out on the opportunity you are seeking.

For example, the return address on an envelope says *Automobile Club of America*. Since you requested information about membership benefits and dues, you can predict what message is contained inside.

Suppose an interoffice envelope is addressed to you and it is from the person managing the United Way campaign. You collected for United Way in your department last year. What do you think this envelope contains?

In another example, you have received a memo and clipped to it is a small booklet. The subject line on the memo reads *Training Courses for Fall.* You immediately know the booklet is a catalog from human resources listing all of the upcoming training programs.

Suppose you have a letter in your inbox from Glendale Mail Services. You have not heard of that company, but the handwritten note on the letter is from your manager indicating the firm is the one discussed with you. That is your purpose for reading the letter.

How can you identify the writer's purpose before reading much, if any, of the message? Your prior knowledge of the writer and of the specific situation allows you to make sense of whatever written material is before you. You can ask yourself these questions.

- Who is the writer?
- What is the writer's purpose?
- Does the writer expect something from me? If so, what is it?
- Is the writer trying to persuade me to do something? If so, what?
- Does the writer have a bias regarding the subject? If so, how might that have influenced what was written?

Of course, these questions are almost automatic when you read a sales letter, advertisement, or marketing brochure. Whenever the writer has a financial motive, remember that the goal is to persuade you to make a purchase. In other situations, a motive may be less obvious.

A bias is a prejudice that influences someone's thinking. Biases may be purposeful or accidental, conscious or unconscious. The more you know about the writer, the better you will be able to identify a bias and assess motive. As with listening, it helps to have a touch of skepticism as you interpret a message.

Consider Your Purpose for Reading

Knowing what you are looking for helps you focus. If your expectations are correct, you will have a head start on comprehending the written material. If your expectations are incorrect, you can quickly identify your error and adjust to the new information, provided you actively read. Always concentrate to be sure you read what is actually on the page and not just what you expect to see. Be aware that the writer's purpose for writing is not necessarily the same as your purpose for reading. The three primary reasons for reading are reading for information, reading to follow directions, and reading persuasive writing.

To be an active reader, you must understand why you are reading.

Shutterstock

Reading for Information

When reading for specific information, combine skimming, scanning, and reading for detail. First, *skim* until you find the portion of the document that is likely to contain the information. Then, *scan* to locate the specific piece of information. When you find the information you are looking for, *read for detail.* These approaches to reading are discussed later in this chapter.

For example, unless you work in the legal department, you might not need to read contracts word for word. However, if the contract is for your project, you might want to skim it to make sure the names are correctly spelled, the dates are correct, and all information is accurate.

Many times, business communication contains words and phrases—even entire paragraphs—that are there for reasons of protocol. **Protocol** is a custom or rule of etiquette based on a tradition. Strict adherence to protocol often requires standard language, also known as **boilerplate** wording or paragraphs. If you need to read documents containing boilerplate material, it is unlikely you will read word for word. Over time, you will learn to recognize what you can overlook when you read familiar types of communication at work, particularly when your purpose is to find specific information.

CASE

Consider the Source

Mark Brandenberg is a new marketing manager for a magazine publishing company. A coworker gave him a photocopy of a news article with the following paragraph flagged.

> The current status of the pulp industry, affected by developments in the environmental protection area and the scarcity of natural resources worldwide, leads to the conclusion that paper prices must rise by up to 32 percent next year alone.

Mark's company purchases millions of dollars of paper each year. The projected increase would be a financial disaster for the magazine. Somewhat frantic, Mark rushed to see Elena Mateo, Director of Purchasing, and told her about the price increase.

Looking worried, Elena reached for the clipping and scanned the article. Then, her face relaxed. "Ah, look at this, Mark. The source is a spokesperson for the Federal Lumber Association. I'm not ready to get too worried yet. When environmental protection groups talk about stopping a logging operation, the lumber companies and paper manufacturers have to react. They often consider a worst-case scenario, and that often gets presented in the scariest terms possible."

1. Was this article for persuasion or information?

2. Did Mark have any biases as he read the article?

3. Did Mark use active reading skills?

Reading to Follow Directions

Reading to follow directions is a common workplace reading task. This often calls for reading for detail. When reading to follow directions, you:

- complete forms, such as a job application;
- follow step-by-step processes, such as instructions for assembling a piece of furniture;
- follow a general process or procedure, such as using a style guide when writing; or
- learn to operate a piece of equipment by reading a manual.

When reading to follow directions, you must pay attention to the sequence and combine reading approaches.

Directions (unlike instructions) must be followed in sequential order to obtain the desired result. A set of directions might also call for use of specific materials or may be quite complex. Therefore, it is best to read through a set of directions at least once before starting to complete them. You might also need to reread items within the directions several times to fully understand what must be done.

Reading Persuasive Writing

Persuasive reading materials try to convince the reader to take some course of action. Reading persuasive materials, whether print or online, has a direct impact on the reader's decision-making process. Some examples of persuasive reading materials include the following.

- e-mail blast from a travel agency wanting you to use its services
- letter of application written by candidates for an open position
- report concluding the company must modify its brand to sell to a different target market

The marketing material a real estate agent shows you is an example of persuasive writing. When reading this material, be aware that the agent is trying to sell you a house.

Shutterstock

- form letter from a charitable organization asking you to donate time or money

- sales letter or a marketing brochure

- e-mail from a colleague asking you to be on a committee to plan a company event

- e-mail from a manager encouraging you to apply for a new position in that manager's department

To evaluate the merit of persuasive writing usually requires reading for detail. Often persuasive writing requires the highest degree of detailed reading because of the need to constantly evaluate as you read. A wise reader does not presume the writer's information is accurate or the opinions valid. A **presumption** is something believed based on probable or assumed reliability.

Use Prior Knowledge

If you walk in at the end of a movie, you do not know the characters or the plot. As a result, understanding who is doing what to whom and why it is being done are difficult. However, if you catch the end of a television show that you watch often, it will not take you long to figure out what is going on. The same is true when you read business communication and documents in the course of the workday. Your prior knowledge allows you to quickly make sense of the new information. Consciously or unconsciously, you run through the answers to these questions in your mind.

- What do I already know about the writer?

- What do I already know about the situation?

- What do I already know about this subject in general?

- Did I request this information?

- Have I said or done something recently that prompted this information?

- Am I receiving this information because it relates to my job? How does it relate?

- How can I use this information?

This recall of prior knowledge to aid reading works at all levels of your thought process. As you think about the situation, you must attach new knowledge to prior knowledge and act accordingly.

A similar use of prior knowledge in reading takes place at the word or concept level. If you come across words or groups of words that are unfamiliar, you can often figure out a meaning by recalling usage in other contexts. Having the skill of applying prior knowledge to new words and concepts is important to your success as a reader.

TEAMWORK

Collaborate with the team assigned by your instructor. Make a list of the various types of reading materials that you regularly read to find specific information (for example, bus schedule, onscreen TV guide, blogs, text messages, newspaper, magazines). For each type of medium, list the information you are reading to find and discuss strategies for finding it quickly.

Evaluate What You Read

Evaluation should take place both as you read and after you read. The need to evaluate *after* you read should come as no surprise. Common sense tells you this must be done in many cases. To evaluate something *as* you read is also natural, even though you might not be aware you are doing so most of the time. Consider the questions and comments that you think about as you read. These are likely to be an evaluation of either the message or your own understanding of the information.

Think of evaluation as interaction with the written word. Evaluation is one of the most important factors in being an active reader. Evaluate after reading by asking questions such as these.

- Do the facts support what I already know or have heard, read, or seen elsewhere about this topic?

- Do the facts support the writer's conclusions?

- Do I accept what the writer is saying or do I need to find another source?

- Does the writer's tone match the words?

- Are there unwritten messages here that I should think about?

- Are there questions I need to have answered before I act?

The evaluation process is simple in the course of everyday reading related to routine job tasks. Most of the time, the evaluation takes place unconsciously. However, many job tasks require a more conscious analysis. Just as you would analyze and critique the content of your own written drafts, you will often need to analyze and critique what others have written.

 Checkpoint

1. What are four things you must do when actively reading?
2. What is boilerplate material?
3. What is a presumption?

Reading Approaches

All reading tasks do not require the same level of focus. How you approach a given task is determined by the type of communication, the writer's purpose, your purpose for reading, and your prior knowledge of the topic or situation. Three basic approaches can be used, depending on these factors. The approaches are *skimming, scanning,* and *reading for detail*.

The more you read on the job and understand your purpose for reading, the more you will be able to easily select and sometimes combine these approaches. The approaches of skimming, scanning, and reading for detail will help you become a more efficient reader.

Skim to Get an Overview

Skimming means to quickly glance through an entire document. In doing so, you will notice headings, key words, phrases, and elements such as boxes, informational graphics, and illustrations. The goal of skimming is to get a sense of the main ideas and scope of the content. When you skim, you combine new information with prior knowledge to determine your next step. For example, you might decide to read for detail, read and make notes for a response, or conclude that your purpose is satisfied. Skimming is especially useful when you want to:

- read for general information;
- read simple responses and requests;
- review the general coverage or content;
- preview something you must read in greater detail; and
- locate a specific section of a long document, such as a report.

Skimming is a fast process. For busy people, it is a good skill to have. However, you need to be aware of when it is appropriate to skim and when it is not. For example, material for an important project may be skimmed at first, but it would probably be wise to thoroughly read the material at a later time. On the other hand, a brochure for a new product may be skimmed for key points on features and benefits and filed or recycled.

Be especially careful in the workplace when skimming e-mails and letters. Many busy workers make the mistake of skimming only the beginning of a communication and drawing conclusions without further reading. This can create problems because business writers often place important information at the end of a document. The intent is to have the reader read the most important information last. Miscommunication and problems can occur when readers do not skim each paragraph.

CASE

The Bottom Line

Reuben Patrikas purchased a color printer from Deluxe Products for his employer's graphic design business. Reuben traded the old printer because it kept breaking down as the repairs were expensive and inconvenient. With this in mind, Ron Ahola, the Deluxe sales representative, gave Reuben a sales brochure on service contracts:

> This service and maintenance contract covers you for a full year. If anything goes wrong with the printer, just pick up the phone and we'll be here in no time at all. Plus the maintenance schedule keeps the machine in optimum shape.

Reuben thought about it only briefly. He knew how important it was to have a reliable printer. "That sounds great, Ron," he said. "Where do I sign?" A few days later, the bill for the printer and service contract arrived. Reuben's boss was surprised by the service contract, questioning its need when the printer has a one-year manufacturer warranty.

1. Do you think that Ruben read the brochure for detail or just scanned it?

2. What is the appropriate reading approach to take for reading a contract?

One of the most important reasons for skimming is to help you prioritize your work. To **prioritize** means to rank items in order from most to least important. Prioritizing is an important skill that will help you manage and organize your work. Workers who receive a lot of reading material use skimming to determine how to prioritize further detailed reading and writing responses. Tips for skimming are given in Figure 15-1.

Scan for Specific Information

Scanning means to quickly glance through a message to find something specific. Skimming is done when you are not sure what is in the communication. Scanning is done when you know the information you need is in the communication, you just have to find it. You scan when you want to find a:

- phone number in a listing on your cell phone;
- word in a dictionary or index;
- date for an event in an e-mail you previously read;
- number within a table; or
- quotation from the transcript of a speech you heard.

However, if you scan too quickly, you are likely to miss what you are looking for. Tips for scanning are shown in Figure 15-2.

Figure 15-1. Follow these tips for skimming a document to get an overview of the information.

Tips for Skimming

E-mails and Letters

- In e-mails, the SUBJECT line should tell you the purpose of the message.
- Check the letterhead or e-mail address to see if you know the company.
- Check the signature block to see if you know the writer.
- Check to see if others were copied on the e-mail or letter.
- Check for attachments.
- Skim the body of the message.
- Look for words that are underlined, italicized, boldfaced, or in all uppercase letters.
- Look for information that is called out, such as a bulleted list.

Reports, Proposals, Brochures, Articles, Online Information

- Read the title.
- Skim section titles and headings; use the table of contents if there is one.
- Flip through pages, spending no more than 10 to 15 seconds on each page.
- Look at informational graphics and illustrations; skim their captions.
- Read the headings and note sections that are boxed, bulleted, numbered, or set in different typefaces.

Figure 15-2. Follow these tips for scanning a document for specific information.

Tips for Scanning

- Identify as specifically as possible the information you must find.
- Determine clues or characteristics that will help you locate the information.
- Look briefly each time you see an item with characteristics that match your search to see if it is what you need. If it is not, continue scanning.
- If necessary to determine whether you found the exact information you are looking for, you may have to quickly read surrounding material.

Read for Detail

Reading for detail involves reading all words and phrases, considering their meaning, and determining how they combine with other elements (sentences, paragraphs, headings, graphics, etc.) to convey ideas. Reading for detail is what most people think of when they hear the word *reading*. Reading for detail is necessary in many situations, such as when you read a textbook chapter to learn the concepts being taught. You also read for detail when you read a proposal to determine whether to work with an outside source on a project.

The process of reading for detail can be complex and may be different for each reader. Consider the words and the way those words are used by the writer to evoke a response from the reader. This involves many factors, including:

- prior knowledge of words and other language symbols, such as spacing and punctuation;
- interpretation of aspects of the text, such as the purpose, writer's tone, truthfulness, and information in/out;
- prior knowledge of the situation/topic and whatever this knowledge suggests to the reader, including related emotions and biases; and
- general prior knowledge—that is, the life experiences the reader brings to the situation/topic.

Generally, the process of reading for detail involves using the approaches shown in Figure 15-3. Notice how the process of reading incorporates elements of active reading introduced earlier in the chapter.

Checkpoint

1. What are the three approaches to reading?
2. What is the difference between skimming and scanning?
3. What is the type of reading most people think of when they hear the word *reading?*

Figure 15-3. Follow these tips for reading a document for detail.

Tips for Reading for Detail

- Anticipate content and the purpose for reading based on prior knowledge.
- Be aware of the purpose for reading.
- Read word by word or phrase by phrase, connecting concepts to form larger concepts.
- Question and comment on the writer's statements, while checking your understanding and comprehension of the material.
- Reread until you understand or read ahead to see if later text provides clarity.
- If you get stuck on words or concepts, use prior knowledge to work through the problem areas or seek help from a coworker or reference materials.
- When you finish your detailed reading, evaluate what you have read considering the purpose and analyze.
- Draw conclusions about the reading based on the purpose and situation, putting biases and emotions aside.

General Reading Techniques

Your reading skills and habits, good or bad, were probably set years ago. If your skills are good, you should have no problem applying them on the job. You can get even better by applying some of the strategies in this chapter. If your reading skills are weak, you can strengthen them by practicing. Read as much as you can and challenge yourself to apply the principles of active reading. If you strive to actively read, the more you read, the better you will get.

Prioritize Your Reading

Every day, business workers spend a lot of time reading: e-mails, reports, spreadsheets, online information, and other communication. One of the first orders of business, then, is to prioritize. To prioritize, think through your tasks and make decisions about the level of importance of each. Prioritizing will probably start with opening your e-mail application and skimming the names of the senders and the subjects. If you have printed documents in your inbox, skim each one. For

TEAMWORK

Collaborate with a partner on the following activity. Do the steps in the order listed. Start by selecting a newspaper or magazine article that interests you.

A. Individually, skim the article and write one sentence that states its general subject and main idea. Write down the elements in the article (headlines, words, phrases, etc.) that were most helpful to you in your conclusions. Do not tell each other what you have written.

B. Compare notes and discuss the similarities and differences. Then read the article in detail and discuss the accuracy of your conclusions.

Always practice good reading habits. Doing so will help you to be a better active listener.

Shutterstock

each e-mail or document, decide if you need to read it immediately, if you can wait and read it later, or if you need to read it at all. Separate the material into three groups.

- Read now: important to your job duties and current priorities; read as soon as possible.
- Read later: material you do not have to read today.
- File or discard: information you do not need now (file) or will never need (discard).

Prioritizing ensures that you do not take time away from doing other important tasks. Most business e-mail systems have automated features that help with prioritizing. Learn to use these tools to make your task easier.

Making a daily "to do" list in order of importance is also a good habit to form. Assign due dates for reading materials and other tasks, including items that do not have a formal deadline. This will help avoid having low-level items stay on the list too long as new, more important ones come along.

Mark Reading Materials

Always read printed documents with a pen, highlighter, or self-stick notes ready to use. These tools help you focus on and mark key information. For complex e-mails, printing and marking can be helpful.

- Write notes, questions, or comments in the margins.
- Highlight or underline important text.
- Attach self-stick notes to important pages.
- Use stick-on tabs to mark pages you will use repeatedly.

Highlighting information helps you focus while reading and also to remember what you read. It will help when you need to refer to the materials in the future.

Read Phrases, Not Words

Active readers read groups of words, rather than individual words. Reading word by word is slow, reduces your concentration, and reduces your ability to connect concepts to form meaning. Many words have significant meaning only when combined with other words to form phrases. Some words acquire new meaning when attached to other words. Words combine to make meaningful phrases.

Read the following sentence one word at a time.

> One of the companies that submitted a bid for this project is Dean & Brown Contracting.

Now read the same sentence in meaningful phrases:

> One of the companies / that submitted a bid / for this project / is Dean & Brown Contracting.

Reading in phrases requires concentration and steady practice. If you find that you do not already read in phrases, practice this technique. This change in the way you read will help you read faster and improve understanding at the same time.

Build Your Vocabulary

To build your vocabulary, make a point of looking up words you do not understand. If it is inconvenient to check a dictionary while reading, write down unknown words and look them up later. You will, of course, need to reread the document once you learn the meanings of the words. Work especially hard at understanding words and terms that are commonly used in your industry or business. Consider buying a vocabulary-building book, either in print or electronic form.

Use the Internet to research names you do not recognize. Is there a piece of legislation in the news that affects your life or your business? Use the Internet to research things like this as well, especially if there is vocabulary you do not understand.

Highlighting key phrases can help you find the information later.

Shutterstock

The best way to improve your vocabulary and reading in general is to read more and to read a variety of materials. A large vocabulary not only makes your reading easier and your writing more exact, it also makes you a better thinker. Reading on your own is a form of self-education. Develop the habit of supplementing the information you receive in school or on the job with reading selections of your own. By expanding your knowledge through reading, you will increase your self-confidence and become more comfortable with new challenges.

Control Your Reading Environment

Is your place of work or school a noisy environment? Are you interrupted often as you read? If your answer to either question is yes, consider what you can do to reduce or eliminate these interruptions. It is important that you are comfortable and able to focus so that you are able to retain what you read and can use your time efficiently.

You may need to take reading home or get to work early in the morning before others arrive so you can have quiet time to catch up on your reading materials. Some people who work in very busy or noisy environments form the habit of arriving early at work so they can address the day's reading before the distractions begin. It is also possible that you can form the habit of blocking out distractions.

Be Ready to Read

If you have a job where it is hard to find the time to read, plan your reading time, for example while everyone else is at lunch. Put it on your daily schedule. Print reading materials and organize them in a folder so they can easily be accessed. This way, you will be able to take the materials with you to read during your commute or while waiting for a meeting to start.

Checkpoint
1. What are the three groups for prioritizing reading material?
2. What is the best way to improve your vocabulary?

Improving Your Reading Skills

If you know you are a slow reader or have insufficient reading skills in general, now is the time to try to correct that. Reading more and using a dictionary are the best ways to improve your reading skills. By reviewing your reading habits, you can look for those areas where your skills need improvement. Here are tips for improving how effectively you read.

- Time yourself. How long does it take you to read and understand a section of text or a chapter of a book? If it takes you too long, read more to practice.

- Pay attention to how often you interrupt yourself before finishing reading something. If frequent, look for the factors that might be the cause and work on staying focused.

- Assess your reading environment. Find ways to make it quiet and comfortable.

- Pay attention to your thoughts as you read. If you think about something other than what you are reading, you are not concentrating and will not remember what you have just read.

- Consider whether you use different reading approaches for different kinds of reading. If not, review the techniques discussed here and practice using them to suit various reading needs.

- Try to recognize whether you read word by word or phrase by phrase. Practice reading in phrases.

- Keep track of the number of times you read a page and find that you do not really know what you just read. Analyze why this is happening and use the information in this chapter to try to correct it.

If you feel that you need professional help, a class on reading comprehension or time management might be the answer for you. Libraries and schools offer classes for reading improvement.

When reading for detail, your environment may have a big impact on how much you retain. Reading outside where a lot of people are passing by you may present too much of a distraction.

Shutterstock

Checkpoint

1. What are the two best ways to improve your reading skills?
2. What are two classes that may help improve your reading skills?

Chapter 15 Review

Chapter Summary

Reading Is a Skill

- Active reading is a skill that can be learned and improved, even if you are already a good reader.
- Active reading involves concentration; you must be involved and do something in response to the words.

Active Reading

- To engage in active reading, you must consider the writer's purpose, consider your purpose, relate what you read to prior knowledge, and evaluate the reading material.
- Knowing the writer's purpose helps you understand the message.
- Knowing why you are reading helps you focus.
- Applying prior knowledge helps you quickly understand the message.
- Evaluation should take place both as you read and after you read.

Reading Approaches

- The three basic approaches to reading are skimming, scanning, and reading for detail.
- Skimming means to quickly glance through the document to get an overview of the information.
- Scanning means to quickly glance through the document in search of specific information.
- Reading for detail involves reading all of the words and phrases, considering their meaning.

General Reading Techniques

- Prioritize your reading.
- Mark reading material to help you focus on key information.

- Read phrases, not words.
- Look up words you do not understand to help build your vocabulary.
- Control your reading environment and be ready to read.

Improving Your Reading Skills

- Reading more and using a dictionary are the surest way to improve your reading skills.
- By reviewing your reading habits, you can look for those areas where your skills are weakest and then work to improve those particular areas.

 **Review**
Your Knowledge

1. What two things are required of you for active reading?
2. Explain why it is important to consider the writer's purpose for writing.
3. What is a bias?
4. What are the three primary reasons for reading?
5. What is a protocol?
6. What does using prior knowledge enable the reader to do with information?
7. What are three questions you can ask yourself to help evaluate what you read?
8. What are the three reading approaches?
9. List the three general groups that can be used to prioritize your reading tasks.
10. List two things you can do to improve your reading skills.

Apply
Your Knowledge

1. Read a news or magazine article online or in print from beginning to end. Answer the following questions.

   A. What is the main point of the article?

   B. Were any statistics or facts cited to support the information in the article?

   C. Was anyone quoted in the article to support the story? How did the quotes help you understand the topic more clearly? In what way did the quotes help you judge the credibility of the information?

   D. Did you have to reread all or part of the article to answer the questions? If so, what approach did you use to find the information? How did that reading differ from the way in which you first approached the article?

2. Select a marketing or sales brochure that you have received in the mail. Read the entire brochure and determine the writer's purpose.

3. Select a news or magazine article or some other two- or three-page piece of writing. Do the following.

   A. Imagine you have to scan the material for these five items: numbers, proper names, quotations, questions, and the word *you*. What characteristic of each item will you look for to help you locate it? Hint: The characteristic should be something you can quickly spot that also distinguishes the item from other text as much as possible.

   B. Scan for each of the items (one at a time) and write down the number you find.

   C. Consider whether you used characteristics of these items other than those you listed (in point A) to find the items. If so, write down those other characteristics as well.

4. Select a magazine or journal related to a topic unfamiliar to you. For example, if you do not know much about science, you may select an article from *Scientific American* or *Science*. You will use this article to help build your vocabulary.

   A. Read the article, making note of any words you do not understand.

   B. For each word you did not understand, look up a definition in a dictionary.

   C. Write one sentence for each word you looked up.

5. Locate a business or organization in your community that offers reading-skills workshops. Write a summary of the objectives of the workshop, when the workshop is offered, and how much the workshop costs.

Practice
What You Have Learned

Access the *Fundamentals of Business Communication* Student Companion Web Site at www.g-wlearning.com/Communication. Download each data file for this chapter. Follow the instructions to complete a reading, writing, and grammar activity to practice what you have learned in this chapter.

Connections
Across the Curriculum

Math. Create a grid for one week to record the reading you do each day. On the X axis, enter the labels Item Read, Purpose, Time, Approach Used (Skim, Scan, Read for Detail), and Purpose Achieved (Yes or No). On the Y axis, list each reading activity that you have for the day. As you finish each activity, check the appropriate columns to see how you did for each assignment. At the end of the day, analyze your grid and check whether your purpose for each reading assignment was achieved.

Language Arts. Based on your findings in the math activity, write several paragraphs to analyze your reading habits. Identify what you did well, where you could improve, and what your goals are to become a better reader.

Build
Your Business Portfolio

Applying for a position may require you to mail or e-mail your application to the interviewer. When sending your application information, you will need to include a cover letter to introduce yourself and your qualifications for the open position.

1. Select a job for which you would like to apply. Use an online source such as CareerBuilder or Monster to select an advertisement for employment.
2. Create a cover letter for this position.
3. Save the document file in your ePortfolio folder. Create a subfolder named CoverLetters. Save the file with the name CoverLetter01.

You will be creating other cover letters in the future, so this will be the first one.

4. Place a printed copy of the cover letter in your container for your print portfolio.

Careers
Manufacturing
Careers and Communication

Careers in the manufacturing cluster involve skills in planning, managing, and making raw materials into quality products. The cluster pathways involve production, process development, equipment maintenance and installation, and inventory control. Other pathways include quality, health, safety, and environmental assurance.

Strong interpersonal and communication skills are key qualities for these workers. One skill that is necessary for this career is the ability to actively read. Describe a situation in which someone pursuing a career in this cluster would need to read and understand technical documents.

Event Prep

Business Communication

The business communication competitive event consists of an objective test that covers multiple topics. Participants are usually allowed one hour to complete the event. One of the topics that will be included is reading comprehension. Reading comprehension is an important skill that good communicators practice and apply in everyday life. By participating in the business communication event, you will be able to demonstrate that you are an active reader and are able to apply good technique when listening.

To prepare for the objective business communication test, do the following.

1. Study this chapter and review the concepts for improving your reading skills.
2. Make sure you understand the reading approaches of skimming, scanning, and reading for detail.
3. Review the tips in this chapter for reading to follow directions and practice the techniques. Participants sometimes forget to carefully read the directions and understand what is needed to successfully complete a competitive activity.

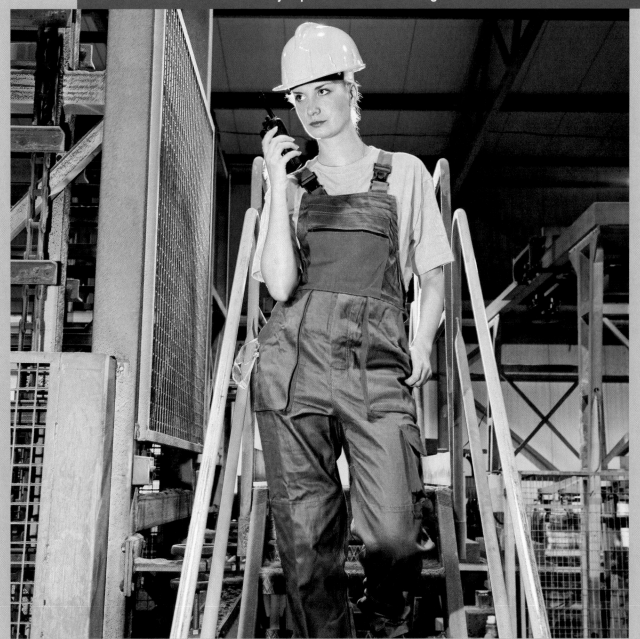

Good communication skills are very important in manufacturing careers.

Shutterstock

Unit 6
Writing for Successful Business Purposes

In This Unit

Your first step in the business world is to find employment. This unit shows you how to prepare for and conduct a career search. Once you have started down the road to a successful career, you will likely need to write some form of reports as part of your career. As part of your reports, you may need to include visual aids to help communicate data or information. This unit covers writing business reports, both formal and informal, and discusses using visual aids. Completing this unit will help you meet college and career readiness (CCR) anchor standards for writing, as outlined by the **Common Core State Standards**.

16
Writing and Interviewing for Employment

There is no substitute for hard work.

—Thomas Edison, American inventor

When you are seeking employment, the communication you prepare—cover messages, résumés, application forms, and follow-up communication—are all selling tools. You must persuade the reader that your skills and experience fit the position. When you interview, you have the opportunity to personally sell your knowledge, skills, and experience and to present an appropriate and appealing impression of who you are. This chapter guides you through the aspects of the employment-communication process.

Objectives

When you complete Chapter 16, you will be able to:

- **Organize** information about your work experience and education to plan and write an effective résumé.
- **Describe** the parts of a résumé.
- **Explain** the two basic formats of a résumé.
- **List** different ways in which you can publish your résumé.
- **Write** a persuasive cover letter that expresses your job goals and qualifications.
- **Identify** the steps to prepare for a job interview.
- **Explain** the importance of evaluating your performance in an interview.
- **Write** follow-up messages after a job interview.
- **Describe** the employment process.
- **Discuss** how to research and plan for a career.

Terms

résumé	job interview
keywords	thank-you message
reference	application form
chronological résumé	employment verification
functional résumé	background check
scannable résumé	
cover message	

Go Green

Computers that are always on consume a lot of energy. To remedy this situation, software companies are creating new applications for computers that monitor how much energy and money can be saved when you take advantage of a computer's sleep and shutdown schedules. Taking advantage of these applications can save energy and extend the life of your equipment

1. Search the Internet and find an application that will monitor your computer. What does the application monitor and what controls does it offer?

2. What kind of energy-saving applications are available for your MP3 player?

Writing a Résumé

A **résumé** (pronounced rez-uh-may) gives an employer a profile of your career goals, education, and work history. The chief purpose is to sell yourself to a potential employer by showing how your experiences and skills match the qualifications of the job you are seeking. Think of a résumé as a snapshot that tells the employer who you are and why you would be an asset as an employee. Fortunately, word processor technology makes it easy to tailor your résumé to each person and company you contact.

A résumé is the first impression that most employers will have of who you are. It must be well written and error free. Good writing is important, but the writing is different from other types of business messages. You need to use words and phrases that match the words and phrases in the job description. You also need to organize the information in a way that highlights your qualifications you think the employer is seeking.

Always use the writing process as a guide to developing the selling tools you need for each job. Figure 16-1 shows the steps to follow in the prewriting process.

Reading Prep

As you read this chapter, think about what you are learning. How can this information apply to the other classes you are taking?

**Checkpoint**

1. What is the chief purpose of a résumé?
2. What words and phrases should you match in a résumé?

Parts of the Résumé

Résumés have standard parts that employers expect to see. Including these parts with headings helps the employer skim and scan to evaluate your qualifications. The following sections describe standard résumé parts in the order in which they usually appear. Some parts are optional and should be included only if they apply to you and the position you are seeking.

Figure 16-1. **The process of creating a résumé begins with the prewriting stage.**

Prewriting

Use the prewriting steps to plan your résumé:

- **Think.** What information about yourself will present the best case for the specific position you want?
- **Plan.** What organization is best suited to present the information?
- **Read.** What skills or qualifications is the employer looking for according to the advertisement for the position?
- **Research.** What do you know about the company and the job duties that will help you present your information in the best light?

When deciding on how to format each part, consider the overall length of the résumé. Will it be one page or two? A general rule of thumb is a recent graduate should have a one-page résumé, while somebody with several years of experience may have a two-page résumé. Remember to allow adequate white space on the page for readability. Also, consider how the résumé will be presented or sent to the employer—printed, e-mailed, or uploaded to an online job-application system.

Name and Personal Information

Include your name, address, telephone number, and e-mail address at the top of the résumé. You may also include a fax number if you wish. Place the information at the top of the page in a style that balances the general layout and assists with fitting the résumé in the available space with adequate spacing between parts. Figure 16-2 shows various ways to format personal information.

When applying for a job, be sure to use an e-mail address that is your real name or at least a portion of it. E-mails with nicknames or screen names do not make a professional impression. Before you begin applying for jobs by e-mail, set up an e-mail address that you will use for professional communication. There are several free e-mail providers that can be used for this purpose.

Summary and Career Objective

The summary section is optional. It may be labeled *Summary* or *Profile*. A summary is an opportunity to highlight qualifications specific to the job. Introductory summaries are especially valuable for people who have considerable experience and expertise in a particular field. The opening summary can include experience gained outside of a paying job. You can list skills and accomplishments acquired through volunteer work, extracurricular activities, hobbies, or other unpaid activities. Include items in the summary that are relevant to your career objective or to the job for which you are applying. These two examples point out specific information:

SUMMARY
Experienced electronics sales professional with annual sales of $100,000+.

SUMMARY
High school graduate with business major and fluency in German and Spanish.

The objective section is also optional. It may be labeled *Career Objective* or *Career Goal*. The objective or goal can be a general or specific description of the position you are seeking.

Specific
CAREER OBJECTIVE
Seeking a position as an administrative assistant to a senior executive.

General
CAREER OBJECTIVE
Seeking an entry-level marketing/sales position with opportunity for training and career growth.

Figure 16-2.   **Personal information can be presented on a résumé in several different ways. There is no one right way.**

Karen Gomez
32 Ultra Vista Avenue
San Bernardino, CA 82408
909-555-2323
kgomez@e-mail.com

Karen Gomez
32 Ultra Vista Avenue   909-555-2323
San Bernardino, CA 82408   kgomez@e-mail.com

Karen Gomez
32 Ultra Vista Avenue
San Bernardino, CA 82408
909-555-2323
kgomez@e-mail.com

A summary statement and career objective can be combined and either heading may be used. Following are two examples of a combined statement.

SUMMARY
Electronics sales professional with five years retail experience and annual sales of $100,000+ seeking managerial position with large retailer.

CAREER OBJECTIVE
High school graduate with business major and fluency in German and Spanish, seeking entry-level position with a multinational firm.

Work Experience

The work experience section contains details about your work history. The labels *Experience* or *Work History* may be used instead of *Work Experience*. Obviously, this section will be the main focus of the employer's attention, and it should be given careful attention as you develop your résumé. Complete as many drafts as necessary until you are satisfied that each item is relevant to the position you are seeking. This section should show an employer what you have to offer. Following are the steps that go into preparing this

Be sure to bring several copies of your résumé and references to your job interview. You may be meeting with several people.

Shutterstock

section. However, the format you select will dictate the final order. Formats are discussed later.

1. Begin with your most current employer.

2. List the positions you held, the dates of employment, and names and locations of employers.

3. Describe work experience with each employer.

4. Use action verbs.

List your current or most recent employer first. Continue listing employers in reverse chronological order to the earliest job you held. If there are any gaps in employment, be prepared to explain why in an interview.

For each employer, list the details of the position you held. Do not list the addresses or telephone numbers of employers. You will provide these to the potential employer when you complete a job application form.

The best résumés use the work experience section to do more than list the duties, tasks, or job functions. Instead, think about how to describe your job functions in terms that point out your skills and achievements on the job.

Use phrases such as *responsibilities included* or *responsible for* instead of expressions like *duties included*. This communicates responsibility on your part. Take the time to analyze what you have done and find the aspects of your experience that say something positive about you to a potential employer.

Note that volunteer work may also be listed in the work experience category of your résumé. When first entering the job market, consider whether experience you have acquired through unpaid activities can be presented in terms of skills that are relevant to the job you are seeking. If so, list this information and use the heading *Experience* instead of *Work Experience*.

Describe your work experience with emphatic words that communicate an action or achievement. Usually, action verbs such as assisted, sold, built, organized, processed are good words to choose. You want the potential employer to perceive you as an achiever—someone who contributed to the business or organization. A dull listing of job duties and responsibilities will not highlight your achievements. Consider these two examples:

Part-time stock clerk during the holiday season.

Maintained continuing supply of merchandise during the busy holiday season, ensuring that products were available to hundreds of additional shoppers.

These two people are describing the same work experience. Which one would you contact for an interview?

In the following example, the applicant describes duties as a stock clerk. Instead of being a dry list of mundane tasks, the message communicates hard and conscientious work and a willingness to put in extra time to help the boss make the business a success.

EXPERIENCE
2010 to present: Stock Clerk, Jefferson Market, Detroit, MI

- Worked after school three nights per week stocking shelves and assisting the manager with preparing the store for the following day's business.

- Accurately recorded inventory levels using an electronic system, contributing to the manager's ability to ensure that goods were kept in stock for customers.

- Often worked extra hours to ensure that shelves were fully stocked, aisles were cleared, and displays were properly set up for the next day's opening.

This is where the writing process comes in. Draft and revise the descriptive statements until you have a list of concise statements that accurately describe what you have contributed to past employers.

Use Keywords and Concrete Terms

Employers often scan résumés for **keywords,** words and terms that specifically relate to the functions of the position for which they are hiring. Carefully review the advertisement for the job you are seeking and underline the keywords. If you have the relevant experience, use the same words to describe it. Remember, do not stretch the truth. Only use the keywords if they fit your background.

Also, describe your skills and achievements as specifically as possible. It is easy to fall into general statements, but look for where you can express something general in a more concrete way. Consider these examples:

General

Sold and oversaw installation of computer hardware and software to large corporate customers.

Specific

- Achieved an average of $5 million in annual sales of computer systems to local businesses, including the Manning Hardware chain, Sun Sports Clubs, and WXYZ Television.

- Managed the installation of systems for these clients, including signing of service contracts and oversight of delivery and setup.

The following description is from a résumé responding to an advertisement for an office manager. The employer is looking for someone experienced with managing both staff and office operations in a large legal or real estate office. Notice how the applicant managed to pack action words, keywords, and concrete terms into three short sentences.

- More than 10 years experience managing the daily operations of a 30-person real estate firm with annual sales of $7.5 million.

- Hired, trained, and supervised five full-time office support staff, including a receptionist, administrative assistants, and junior agents.

- Scheduled appointments, managed contracts, and maintained financial records for legal work that was outsourced to a firm handling our transactions.

Use Words That Reflect the Latest Language in the Field

The fast pace of change in our society is reflected in constantly changing language and terminology throughout all fields. Buzzwords reflect the latest technology, ideas, equipment, and issues in a given industry or business. Technology is especially fast-paced and it impacts every field. For example, new terms are constantly being created in the healthcare field. The same is true of the entertainment field, which is trendy and always changing. Read trade magazines, job advertisements, and information on company and industry Web sites before tailoring your résumé to a specific job. Use the latest industry buzzwords when possible, but also be aware that overusing buzzwords can distract a potential employer from focusing on your skills.

Education

If you are still in school, list the courses you have taken that are most relevant to the job. If you are out of school, list your education beginning with the most recent diploma or degree earned. Include high school, colleges, and business or technical schools. If currently enrolled in high school, give your expected graduation date. If currently enrolled in college, indicate the number of years you have attended. Graduates should indicate the year a degree or diploma was earned, the type of degree received in college, and major subject and minor subject (if any). Also, list any certifications you earned, special courses or training programs completed, or any other educational achievements related to the job you are seeking.

Healthcare is one of the fields constantly changing and developing new terminology. Be sure to use current language for the field in which you are seeking a job.

Shutterstock

EDUCATION

- Associate of Arts degree in Computer Science, 20--, College of San Mateo, Redwood City, CA

- High school diploma, 20--, Redwood City High School, Redwood City, CA

Honors/Awards/ Publications

Employers look for well-rounded individuals, so list any relevant information that shows your involvement in activities outside of work or school. Include honors, awards, or publications that are relevant and the corresponding year. Employers are especially interested in applicants who are community oriented and who do volunteer work, so be certain to list any such activities and the years of service.

HONORS, AWARDS, PUBLICATIONS
- National Honor Society in high school, 20--

- Outstanding Leadership Award, 20--, honor received for service as vice president of the school's student business organization, Redwood City Chapter

- Published 14 articles in the school newspaper

Memberships and Professional Affiliations

If you are a member of professional and business associations, include them if they are related to the job for which you are applying. List these in the order of relevance to the position, with most relevant listed first. This section is optional, but should be included if the organizations are related to the job you are seeking.

Special Skills or Additional Training

List any specialized skills you have that are relevant to the position. For example, if you are fluent in a language other than English or have taken courses or received training from employers in addition to your formal education, you may add a category for this information if it does not fit elsewhere.

References

A **reference** is a person who knows you well and can comment on your qualifications, work ethic, personal qualities, and work-related aspects of your character. It has become customary for references to be provided only on request, so this does not need to be indicated on the résumé. Employers who require references in advance usually indicate this in the job advertisement. Otherwise, you will be told during the interview process when references are needed.

To be prepared, put together a list of three or four people for whom you have worked and someone who knows you socially. Do not list relatives. Get permission from the people who you intend to use as references. Format the reference list similarly to the résumé. Be sure to bring copies of your references to the job interview.

Checkpoint

1. Which section of the résumé is the main focus for an employer?
2. Why would you list any activities outside of school or work?
3. When are references typically provided to an employer?

Résumé Formats

After you have finished the writing process for your résumé, as outlined in Figure 16-3, you need to decide on the appropriate format. Two aspects need to be considered when formatting a résumé: how the information pertaining to work history is organized and how information is visually presented in terms of layout and formatting. The two basic résumé formats are chronological and functional.

Chronological Résumé

The most popular format is the **chronological résumé,** which emphasizes employers and work experience with each. The order of presentation is reverse chronological order, with the most recent employer listed first, as shown in Figure 16-4. In the chronological résumé, employers expect to see company name, dates of employment, job title, and a list describing the work experience.

Figure 16-3. Follow the steps in the writing process to ensure that your résumé is well written and error free.

Drafting, Revising, Editing, and Proofreading Your Résumé

- **Draft.** Select the standard parts or categories of information that best fit your situation. Follow the guidelines given in this chapter for writing descriptions of your job duties and achievements.

- **Revise.** Résumés should be one page for applicants with shorter work histories and two pages for more experienced applicants. A great deal of the revision work involves making the information fit the one- or two-page format.

- **Edit.** Be sure to use the keywords for which the employer will be looking. Describe your past work duties and achievements in language that represents current usage in the field. Use words and phrases that appear in the job description so your résumé can be scanned for these words.

- **Format.** Select the format that best suits your information and the job for which you are applying.

- **Review.** Whenever possible, enlist the opinion of someone who is a good writer and who has experience with résumés.

- **Check spelling/grammar and proofread.** An error-free résumé is essential. Errors in a résumé give the employer a poor impression of you and your attention to detail.

Functional Résumé

Another common résumé format is the **functional résumé.** A functional résumé lists work experience according to categories of skills or achievements, rather than by employer. In this format, work experience is emphasized, as shown in Figure 16-5. The advantage of this format is that it highlights your best skills, some of which may not have been used in your most recent job. If you have not had much work experience and want to emphasize skills used in other capacities, a functional résumé works well.

The résumé in Figure 16-5 presents Jeanette's important achievements and skills first, followed by a list of her employers in reverse chronological order. Jeanette had a lot of material to work with and had to decide what aspects of her previous jobs to emphasize. She selected her strengths and briefly described them to demonstrate why she would be a good choice for an employer to select for a job with management responsibility.

Jeanette took a risk in stating that she wants a managerial position, since her résumé does not reflect any actual experience in managing a staff. However, she wants recruiters to know that is her goal. She wants them to look at her achievements in working with others and her steady progress up the career ladder. Each time she changed jobs she took on more responsibility and handled it well. More than likely she will be considered for a high-level editorial position, but some companies might be willing to give her the opportunity for which she is looking.

Figure 16-4.   This is an example of a chronological résumé.

ROBERT R. JEFFRIES
518 Burnett Road
Randallstown, MD 21123
Home: 301-555-1234
Mobile: 301-555-4321
E-mail: rjeffries@e-mail.com

OBJECTIVE
To obtain an administrative position as assistant to a senior-level executive in an institution of higher education, private industry, or large government agency.

EXPERIENCE
August, 2009–present
Administrative Assistant to the Director of Education, College of San Mateo, Redwood City, CA
Develop Correspondence
- Screen the director's correspondence and assist with preparation of responses
- Prepare e-mails, memorandums, and letters to ensure accuracy and timely response
- Assist with research, editing, and final preparation of reports

Assist with Staff Management
- Manage the calendars of five staff members and the director
- Write meeting notifications, agendas, and minutes
- Schedule meetings and make special arrangements, such as catering and A/V equipment
- Maintain up-to-date personnel data for staff members
- Supervise two student clerks

June, 2008–August, 2009
Receptionist and Administrative Assistant, Principal's Office, Jefferson High School
- Scheduled appointments for student, faculty, and parents
- Answered telephones, screened, and directed calls
- Greeted visitors, faculty, and students and provided assistance as needed
- Prepared letters and documents
- Scheduled appointments and maintained the calendars of the principal and vice principals

EDUCATION
Associate's Degree, June, 2008, Essex Community College, Baltimore, MD
Major: Office Administration

SPECIAL SKILLS
Computer: Microsoft Office Suite, Adobe InDesign, HTML
General: Excellent speaking and written-communication skills, highly organized, and able to prioritize organizing and planning of multiple projects.

Figure 16-5.	**This is an example of a functional résumé.**

Jeanette Evans
121 East 66th Street
New York, NY 10021
212-555-5678
jevans@e-mail.com

CAREER OBJECTIVE
Executive or managerial position in the field of environmental sciences publishing.

KEY ACHIEVEMENTS
- Managed the Long, North, & Greenhouse and Goldberg & Thomas lists of scientific and environmental titles, including reference books, monographs, texts, and collections of historical papers. Representative titles include *Conservation of Inland Wetlands, Animals of the Great Lakes Regions, Marine Sources of Organic Fuels,* and *The Role of Light in Evolution.*
- Delivered more than 30 presentations to sales staff and to company management describing new books and editorial plans.
- Recruited authors from leading faculty of major universities and from technical, research, and engineering staffs in industry and signed close to 100 new titles.

SPECIAL SKILLS
- Knowledgeable about editorial development, copy editing, production, photo research, and artwork preparation for scientific and technical books.
- Familiar with promotion methods for scientific and technical books, including direct mail, space advertising, mailing list selection, catalog accounts, bookstore and professional association sales.

EMPLOYMENT HISTORY
2008–present
Long, North, & Greenhouse, New York, NY. Executive Editor

2004–2008
Moss & Wallace Book Company, New York, NY. Senior Editor

2000–2003
Eldridge Press, Boston, MA. Special Projects Editor

1998–2000
Lawford Book Company, Cambridge, MA. Production Editor

EDUCATION
B.A. in Art History in 1996, Smith College, Northampton, MA

CASE

Honesty Is the Best Policy

Karen Gomez is an avid sports enthusiast. She played soccer and volleyball in high school and college and has won several major swimming championships. She is in training for the US Olympic swim team and is looking for employment that will help support her expenses. Her friend Jackie said, "I have a friend who works at a sporting goods store downtown. She told me they're opening a new store at the mall. Why don't you apply? I bet they'd hire you in a heartbeat."

Karen thought that was a great idea and went right to the mall and applied for the job. As she was completing the form, she noticed that the application asked for references. Since this was an unexpected opportunity to apply for a job, Karen was not prepared and had not asked permission to use several colleagues as a reference. She really wanted this opportunity to interview, so she put down their information anyway.

The HR manager said Karen applied just in time as the interviewing was going to start in two days. The HR manager told her that the references would be checked later in the afternoon.

Karen became flustered but did not reveal that she did not have permissions for these references. She assumed that the people she listed would be okay with her listing them as references. At least she hoped that would be the case.

1. Was it okay for Karen to list these people as references without their permission?

2. Do you think the HR department would consider Karen for this job if the references say they were not willing to give her a reference? Could this cost Karen an opportunity to interview?

Electronic and Scannable Résumés

The process of applying for a job is often completed online, either through a company's Web site or an online job-search site. You may need to send your résumé as an e-mail attachment or uploaded file. In these cases, your résumé should be formatted in the word-processing file just as if it were printed. However, be aware that the reader may not have any unusual fonts you have used, so only use common fonts such as Arial, Times New Roman, or Calibri. If you use a font that the reader does not have, a font substitution will occur when the file is opened and this may drastically change your formatting.

In some cases, you will need to cut and paste your résumé into an online application form. This process usually strips out formatting such as bold, tabs, and indentations. You may need to make adjustments to the layout of your résumé after it is pasted into the online application.

In some cases, you may create your résumé as a Web page on your own Web site. You will need to set up the résumé using HTML or other programming language, then upload the page to your Web site. Refer to books on programming Web sites for information on how to do this. After your résumé Web page is live, you can then provide the URL to employers when you apply for a job.

Some employers also scan résumés that they receive in printed form and enter the data into a database. A **scannable résumé** is formatted so as not to use typographical elements, such as boldface, bullets, and indentations. Here are some guidelines to follow:

- Use a one-column format.
- Avoid horizontal lines, boxes, or shading to set off sections.
- Avoid asterisks, dashes, parentheses, and brackets.
- Use all capital letters for headings.
- Do not use italics, underlining, or graphics.
- Double-space between items in each section.

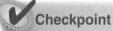

Checkpoint

1. What are the two basic formats for a résumé?
2. Why should you use only common fonts in a résumé that is to be submitted electronically?

Publishing Your Résumé

After you have completed writing and formatting your résumé, you will need to publish it. This is the process of making the document available to the person who needs to receive it. The next sections outline options for publishing your résumé.

Printed Copy

The traditional way to publish a résumé is by printing. A printed copy is usually mailed, but may be hand delivered instead. Print your résumé using a laser printer, not an inkjet printer. Print on good-quality paper, not standard bulk printer paper. The paper should be white or off-white. Colored and patterned paper should not be used.

Fax

To fax your résumé, you must first print it, unless your computer has a direct faxing option. Select the fine resolution option on the fax machine. Always include a cover sheet with the name of the person who will be receiving the fax to ensure it does not get lost. Follow up the fax with a mailed copy of your résumé. Usually, a résumé is faxed to ensure the employer receives it as soon as possible, not as a substitute for a mailed copy.

Often, your job search will be conducted online. Many times, you will be submitting a résumé and job application through a Web site or via e-mail.

Shutterstock

E-mail

When sending a résumé as an e-mail attachment, find out which format the prospective employer prefers. Depending on the employer, you may need to send a PDF or text-only file. However, most companies can accept a file from any word processor. If sending a file from a word processor, it may be a good idea to open the file on another computer to see if the formatting changes.

Online

There are many Web sites, like CareerBuilder, Hotjobs, and Monster, where recruiters can access résumé-type information on potential applicants. These sites are also good locations for finding posted jobs. Using these sites, you can provide your résumé to an employer who has posted a job offering. Most of these sites also offer the option of posting your résumé.

You can also post your résumé on social networking sites, such as LinkedIn and Facebook. Be careful regarding what other personal information you post on these sites. Be sure to view anything you post through a potential employer's eyes. Ask yourself, "how will this reflect on me in a job interview?"

Checkpoint

1. What is the traditional way in which a résumé is published?
2. List two ways a résumé may be published electronically.

Cover Messages

A **cover message** is a letter or e-mail sent with a résumé to introduce yourself and summarize your reasons for applying for a job. This is a sales message written to persuade the reader to grant you an interview. It provides an opportunity to focus a potential employer's attention on the aspects of your background, skills, and work experience that match the job you are seeking.

TEAMWORK

Meet with a group of your classmates and take turns describing skills that you have acquired in the workplace or elsewhere, such as doing volunteer work, babysitting, or hobbies. On a whiteboard or flip chart, list one or two skills for each team member. Work together to write descriptions to impress an employer. Practice using action verbs and keywords.

The cover message should not repeat the details in your résumé, but provide a summary highlighting your key qualifications that fit the job for which you are applying. The message should also explain why you are submitting your résumé. For example, you might be responding to an advertisement or you might have a special interest in working for a particular company. If someone gave you the name of the employer to contact, be sure to provide information on that person's connection to the company.

Figure 16-6 shows an example of a cover message that the reader should find persuasive. This is a letter that will be printed and placed in the mail. Figure 16-7 is an example of a request for an interview that is being sent by e-mail.

Writing a cover message is an important part of the process. It sets the tone for the résumé that follows. Use a positive tone, but do not be boastful. Convince the employer you are the best person to hire for the job by presenting those personal qualifications and characteristics that attest to your ability to be a good employee. You can express confidence in your ability to adapt your training to meet the employer's needs. You should also show genuine interest in the business. If it seems appropriate, suggest your ultimate career goal, as well as your immediate objective. For example:

> I maintained a 3.0 GPA and have taken business education courses in marketing, communication, and accounting. I have also worked part-time as a restaurant crew member, a frontline customer-service job that helped me develop a strong work ethic as well as excellent interpersonal communication skills. In my senior year, I participated in our school's co-op program. Through this special program, I acquired on-the-job experience as an assistant sales correspondent for the Value Insurance Company. I believe my retail experience would be an excellent match for the position of marketing trainee in your organization.

Make sure the cover message is perfect. Whether you send a printed letter or e-mail, follow the standard business standards shown in Chapter 9 and the writing process outlined in Chapter 7. Make sure to check for correct grammar, punctuation, and spelling. A cover message, like all business communication, must be completely error free.

Figure 16-6.   This is an example of a cover message that will be sent as a letter.

Jennifer S. Fitzpatrick
204 West Pickford Road
Jefferson City, MO 65001
(Home) 573-555-1234
(Cell) 573-555-4321

June 5, 20--

Ms. Cheryl Lynn Sebastian
Director of Administration
Jefferson City Convention & Visitors Bureau, Inc.
100 E. High Street
Jefferson City, MO 65101

Dear Ms. Sebastian:

Introduction → The position you advertised in the *Network Journal* on March 14 for a customer service trainee is exactly the kind of job I am seeking. According to your ad, this position requires good business communication skills. As you can see by my résumé, my educational background and experience working at a travel agency prepare me for this position.

Body → For the past two years, I worked as a part-time receptionist at the Barcelona Travel Agency. While working there, I gained experience dealing with customers on the telephone, as well as greeting walk-in customers and handling their requests for information. I also had the opportunity to observe the full-time staff at work and attend department meetings. At these meetings, I learned the importance of satisfying customer needs and meeting the challenges of working with the general public.

As the enclosed résumé shows, I will graduate from Southeast High School in early June. I took several business courses, including a business communication class. These classes helped me develop good English and verbal communication skills. In addition to my education and work experience, I can offer your organization a strong work ethic and the ability to fluently speak Spanish.

Conclusion → I would like very much to meet you and hope that you will contact me by phone or e-mail to schedule an interview for the position. If I do not hear from you within the next couple of weeks, I hope you will not mind if I follow up with a phone call.

Sincerely yours,

Jennifer S. Fitzpatrick

Enclosure

Figure 16-7. **This cover message is an e-mail. Notice that the résumé is included as an attachment.**

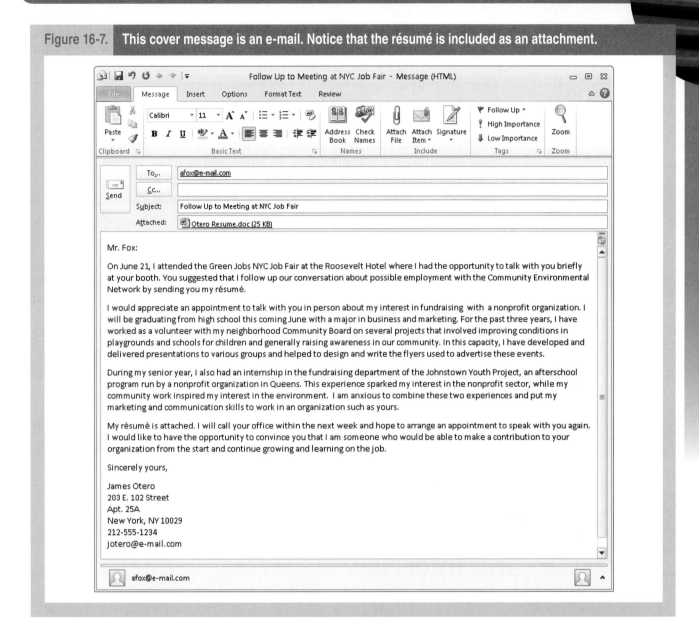

Introduction

Begin the cover message with an introduction that tells the employer who you are and why you are applying for the position you are seeking. If you are responding to an advertisement, mention the position title and where you found the ad. If you are sending a general letter of application, explain in specific terms how you identified the company and why you are interested in it.

Body

In the body of the cover message, demonstrate your ambition, determination, and abilities. Highlight the positive traits and skills that the employer seeks, as highlighted in the job description. Explain why you are qualified and how your skills and experience make you the best candidate for the job. Do not expect the reader to infer why you are the right person to hire—point it out.

Remember that your résumé is attached to the letter, so do not repeat all of the facts on it. Present enough to encourage the reader to look at the résumé for the facts about you. You should also make reference to the résumé.

Describe your ability to meet the employer's needs. Reassure the employer that you do not want just work, but the chance to tackle a problem and help solve it. For example:

> During my senior year, I was elected vice president of our student professional business organization. By working to gain the support of my peers and to stimulate team effort, I have become aware of the importance of good interpersonal relations. This awareness will help me relate to and better serve the needs of your customers.

Conclusion

The conclusion has a twofold purpose: to request an interview and to make it easy for the reader to grant that interview. Leave no doubt in the reader's mind about your desire to be contacted for an interview. State how and when you can be reached or indicate how and when you will make a follow-up contact. Supply the employer with the information necessary to arrange an interview.

> I will contact your office to request an appointment to discuss the position. If you prefer to contact me, I can be reached after 4:00 p.m. at 214-555-4321.

Checkpoint

1. What is the purpose of a cover message?
2. What are the three basic parts of a cover message?

Job Interview

The **job interview** is the employer's opportunity to probe the details contained in your résumé and to assess you as an individual. This is your opportunity to sell yourself in person. Ultimately, the evaluation will be based on a number of factors in addition to your qualifications. The answers to the interviewer's questions, of course, are important in the interviewer's decision-making process. However, your body language, how well you express yourself, and the image you present all play a part in the evaluation.

Many people get nervous before an interview. That may interfere with your ability to come across well. However, you can make the interview something positive to anticipate. The way to do this is through research, preparation, and practice.

Research

The first step in preparing for a job interview is to learn as much as you can about the job and the company. There are several ways to do this.

If the company has a Web site, thoroughly browse it. Pay special attention to the About Us section to get an overview of the company. Look for press releases, annual reports, and information on products or services offered by the company. Many companies also post information specifically directed to the interests of job applicants.

While a company Web site can be a valuable source of information, do not limit your research to it. Use your network of friends and relatives to find people who are familiar with the company, industry, type of product, or type of position. Get as much information as you can from them.

Check with local organizations, such as the chamber of commerce and library or city directories. These resources might provide information about the company and its officers.

Call the company's human resources department. Indicate you are interested in employment opportunities at the company and would like to know more about working for the company. The human resource department often has materials designed specifically for potential employees.

Come to the job interview prepared. Be sure to dress appropriately to help make a good impression.

Shutterstock

If you are applying for a job in a field or industry that is unfamiliar to you, it is especially important to educate yourself. Use the Internet or your local library to find industry trade journals, trade associations, newspaper articles, and other publications. Read about different aspects of the field. Try to find examples of contributions the company you are applying to has made to the field.

Preparing for the Interview

Interview questions are intended to assess your skills and abilities and explore your personality. Your answers to the questions help to determine whether you will fit in with the company team and with the manager's leadership style. Interviewers also want to assess your critical thinking skills. They may ask you to cite specific examples of projects you have completed or problems you have solved.

Questions Likely to Be Asked

Spend some time trying to anticipate questions the interviewer is likely to ask you. Prepare suitable answers and memorize them. Following are ten common interview questions.

- What makes you a good employee?
- What are your strengths?
- What are your weaknesses?
- Tell me something about yourself.
- Describe the experience you have that relates to the position.
- What type of position are you interested in?
- What do you plan to be doing five years from now?
- In what type of work environment do you function well?
- Why do you want to work for this organization?
- Are you willing to work overtime?

Write down your answers to these questions and practice them in front of a mirror or with a friend or relative. Practice until you can give your planned responses naturally and without reading. The more prepared you are with the answers, the more relaxed, organized, competent, and professional you will appear to the interviewer.

Hypothetical Questions

Interviewers may also ask hypothetical questions. These are questions that require you to imagine a situation and describe how you would behave. Frequent topics of hypothetical questions relate to customer care, handling a heavy workload and setting priorities, and getting along with coworkers. For example, the interviewer may ask, "what would you do if you were working to meet a deadline and a coworker was constantly interrupting you to discuss things other than work-related issues?" You cannot prepare specific answers to these questions, so you will need to rely on your ability to think on your feet.

Remember, however, the interviewer is aware that you are being put on the spot. Therefore, he or she will give weight to other aspects of your answer, in addition to what you say. Body language is first and foremost. Work with a friend or relative to practice making eye contact and speaking with confidence. Avoid fidgeting or looking at the ceiling while thinking of your answer. Instead, keep looking at the interviewer and calmly take a moment to compose your thoughts. Keep your answer brief, as running on too long risks losing your train of thought. Try to relate the question to something

Be prepared to answer questions in a job interview, including hypothetical questions designed to see how you can think on your feet.

Shutterstock

that is familiar to you and answer honestly. Do not try to figure out what the interviewer wants you to say. Showing that you can remain poised and project confidence will carry a lot of weight, even if your answer is not ideal.

Questions to Ask

Write down the questions you have about the job, salary, benefits, and company policies. Check job Web sites to find out what the standards are in the industry for the position you are seeking. Be prepared to discuss these issues with the potential employer. The interviewer will probably answer many of your questions before you need to ask, but you will be prepared so that no important items are left unanswered.

One particularly tough question to ask relates to salary. Usually, the interviewer will tell you what the company expects to pay for the position. Sometimes, however, an interviewer will ask you what salary you want or expect. Prepare for questions about salary through research of the industry. If you are unsure, you can simply tell the interviewer that the salary is negotiable. In these cases, it is common to state your current salary and indicate you expect an appropriate increase.

Keep in mind that the questions you ask reveal something about your personality. Asking questions can make a good impression. Questions show that you are interested and aware. Good questions cover the duties and responsibilities of the position, to whom you will report, what a typical day is like, and how many people are in the department. While the company is deciding if you are right for the position, you are deciding if the position is right for you. Ask questions that help you understand more about the job and the company.

Be aware of how you word your questions. Some questions are not appropriate until after you have been offered the job. At that point, the answers will help you to determine whether or not you will accept the position. In the early stages of the interview process, your questions should show you are interested in learning about the company so you would be a valuable employee.

Here are some questions you may want to ask.

- What are the specific duties for this position?
- To whom will I report in this position?
- Do you have a policy of promoting employees and of providing on-the-job training?
- What are the working hours?
- Is travel, weekend work, or extensive overtime required?
- What is the salary you are offering?
- What are you anticipating as the start date if I am hired?
- When do you expect to make your hiring decision?

Other questions that might be appropriate may concern commuting time, provision for equipment required to perform the job, the size of the company or department, and the potential for career growth in the organization. Figure 16-8 shows questions to ask when deciding whether or not to accept the job.

Figure 16-8. Once you are offered the job, ask specific questions to help you decide whether or not to accept it.

- What is the policy regarding overtime work?
- May I expect to have a written job description so that I will know exactly what is expected of me?
- When will I be eligible for a vacation, and how much vacation time will I receive each year?
- Will I be required to join a union or professional association as a condition of employment?
- What is the salary range for the job, and how often could I expect to receive a raise?
- What is the company's policy regarding sick days, personal leave days, and holidays?
- What health benefits will I receive; medical, dental, and vision insurance?
- Does the company have a retirement plan?
- Does the company have a deferred compensation plan, such as 401(K)?
- Does the company have an employee credit union?
- Does the company have a stock purchase or profit-sharing plan?
- Does the company pay bonuses, and how does an employee earn a bonus?
- Will the company pay tuition for employees who take job-related courses and are any in-service training or seminars offered?
- Does the company provide free parking for employees?

Dressing for the Interview

The interview is a meeting in which you and the company discuss the job and your skills. Interviews are usually in person, but sometimes an initial interview is conducted by phone. Usually, the face-to-face interview is the first time you are seen by a company representative. First impressions are important, so dress appropriately, be well groomed, and be on time. Your appearance communicates certain qualities about yourself to the interviewer. When dressing for an interview, consider what you wish to communicate about yourself.

The easiest rule to follow is to dress in a way that shows you understand the work environment you will be entering and know the appropriate attire, as the person in Figure 16-9 demonstrates. If your interview is with a large corporation, a suit and tie is appropriate for a man and a solid-colored pantsuit or dress is appropriate for a woman. On the other hand, if you are interviewing for a job in fashion, it may be appropriate to wear a trendy outfit that is in good taste.

It is better to dress more conservatively than more trendy. Use the information in Figure 16-10 as a guide. Employers understand that interviewees want to put their best foot forward. Dressing more conservatively than needed is not likely to be viewed as a disadvantage. However, dressing too casual or trendy or wearing inappropriate clothing is likely to cost you the job.

Checkpoint

1. What is the first step in preparing for a job interview?
2. Why should you practice answering questions that are likely to be asked in a job interview?
3. Why is it better to dress more conservatively for a job interview rather than more trendy?

Evaluating the Interview

Evaluate your performance as soon as you can after the interview. Make a list of the things you feel you did right and the things you would do differently next time. Every job interview is an opportunity to practice, so do not feel your time was wasted if you discover you are not interested in the job. Here are some questions to ask yourself.

- Was I adequately prepared with knowledge about the company and the position?
- Did I remember to bring copies of my résumé, work samples, and any other requested documents to the interview?
- Was I on time for the interview?
- Did I talk too much or too little?
- Did I honestly and completely answer the interviewer's questions?
- Did I dress appropriately?
- Did I display nervous behavior such as fidgeting, giggling, or forgetting things I wanted to say?
- Did I come across as composed and confident?
- How was my handshake, and did I make eye contact during the handshake?

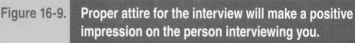

Figure 16-9.   Proper attire for the interview will make a positive impression on the person interviewing you.

Shutterstock

✔ Checkpoint

1. When should you evaluate your performance in a job interview?
2. Why is it important to evaluate your performance in a job interview?

Figure 16-10.   **Be sure to dress appropriately for a job interview. This will be the first time the employer sees you in person, so make a good first impression.**

Appropriate Attire for a Job Interview

Women

- Wear a suit or dress with a conservative length.
- Choose solid colors over prints or flowers.
- Wear pumps with a moderate heel or flats.
- Keep any jewelry small.
- Have a well-groomed hairstyle.
- Use little makeup.
- Avoid perfume or apply it very lightly.
- Nails should be manicured and of moderate length without decals.

Men

- Wear a conservative suit of a solid color.
- Wear a long-sleeved shirt, either white or a light color.
- Tie should be a solid color or a conservative print.
- Wear loafers or lace-up shoes with dark socks.
- Avoid wearing jewelry.
- Have a well-groomed haircut.
- Avoid cologne.
- Nails should be neatly trimmed.

Interview Follow-Up Messages

After a job interview, follow up is an important tool you can use to keep your name in front of the employer. It also shows that you are a professional who understands business protocol. There are several categories of messages you might send after an interview, as discussed in the following sections.

BUSINESS PROTOCOL

Arriving on Time

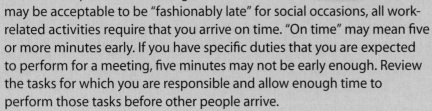

Arrive on time for business meetings and work every day. Tardiness is rude and not acceptable. Even though it may be acceptable to be "fashionably late" for social occasions, all work-related activities require that you arrive on time. "On time" may mean five or more minutes early. If you have specific duties that you are expected to perform for a meeting, five minutes may not be early enough. Review the tasks for which you are responsible and allow enough time to perform those tasks before other people arrive.

Thank-You Message

Immediately after the interview, write a short **thank-you message** to the person who interviewed you. It is surprising how many people do not follow up. This means when you send your thank-you message, you will stand out as someone with good manners and a genuine interest in the position. A thank-you message is an easy way to keep your name active during the selection process.

Thank the interviewer for taking the time to talk with you about the job and your career interests. Restate any important point that was made and reinforce your strong interest in the job (if you are still interested). This thank-you may be in the form of a printed letter sent through the mail or an e-mail. While handwritten thank-you notes are best in social situations, business thank-you letters should always be keyed and formatted in business style.

Keep the letter brief and to the point. You want to remind the interviewer of your name and reiterate your enthusiasm, but remember your reader is very busy. Also, you do not want to seem too pushy. A good balance is achieved in the example shown in Figure 16-11.

In some cases, you might feel that you need to further convince the interviewer that you can do the job. If you sensed hesitancy on the interviewer's part related to a particular skill or area of experience, use the follow-up letter to shore up your chances. The message in Figure 16-12 was written by an applicant who felt that confronting a deficiency in her qualifications might improve her chances of getting the job.

Figure 16-11. **This is a standard interview follow-up message.**

Dear Mr. Ahmad:

Thank you for the opportunity to discuss the position of marketing trainee last Thursday.

I am very excited about the possibility of working for Ellsworth Technologies. The job is exactly the sort of challenging opportunity I had hoped to find. I believe my educational background will enable me to make a contribution while learning and growing on the job.

Please contact me if you need any additional information. I look forward to hearing from you.

Sincerely,

Figure 16-12. **This interview follow-up message reassures the employer of a willingness to learn new skills required for the job.**

Dear Mr. Lockwood:

Thank you for meeting with me on Monday to discuss the position as your executive assistant. I enjoyed becoming acquainted with you. I am very interested in the job, and I know I would find the work challenging and satisfying.

After learning more about the duties, I realize that my knowledge of advanced statistical methods may be light. The subject intrigues me, however, and I really want to learn more about statistical methods. I did well in the one course on statistics I completed at Mitchell College, and I know the school offers advanced programs in statistics. If given the opportunity to work for you, I would enroll for this training in the evening division.

Please express my appreciation to Mr. Cullen and Ms. Roh for giving me so much of their time.

Sincerely,

Employment decisions can take a long time. Some companies notify all applicants when a decision has been made, but some do not. If you have not heard anything after a week or two, it is appropriate to send another brief message to follow up. Be sure to maintain a positive tone. Avoid sounding impatient or demanding. Simply restate your interest in the job and politely inquire whether or not a decision has been made. See Figure 16-13 for an example that is short and to the point.

Acceptance and Withdrawal Messages

Accepting a job is one of the most fulfilling messages you will ever write. But, it still requires your attention and the use of the skills you have learned. Think of this as your first official act as a new employee. It remains important to present an image of intelligence, organization, courtesy, and cooperation.

In writing the acceptance message, let your natural enthusiasm show. Be positive and thank the person who has been the bearer of good news. Say that you look forward to the job. The example in Figure 16-14 is short and to the point. The message expresses enthusiasm without going overboard. The writer also uses the opportunity to confirm her understanding of the employment process going forward.

If you must decline a job offer, write a short message that states the facts. It is not necessary to try to justify or explain your decision. Be positive; never say anything that might come across as negative about the job you are declining. You never know, you may end up looking for work with the employer again in the future. Also, do not try to make the employer feel better by giving objective reasons, such as, "I have been offered a job closer to where I live." Just positively state your decision to accept another offer.

If you decide to withdraw an application, simply write that you have reconsidered your intentions and no longer wish to be considered an applicant. Close with a brief word of thanks for whatever consideration you may have received. Figure 16-15 shows a message to a company that has not followed up on the interview. Figure 16-16 shows a message to a company that has shown interest following the interview.

Figure 16-13. An interview follow-up message such as this can be sent if you have not heard from the employer after a couple of weeks.

Dear Mr. Sukarno:

Thank you for interviewing me for the position of Help Desk Associate in the IT Division of North Shore Medical Center. I am following up to let you know that I am still very interested in the position.

My past experience in customer care for Hartfield Electronics provided me the opportunity to become skillful at responding to the demands of meeting customer needs in a technology-driven enterprise. I strongly feel that my background would be an asset to a healthcare institution such as yours where quality service is essential to every worker at all times.

I hope you are still considering me for the position. Please let me know if I can provide any additional reassurance or information.

Thank you again for your consideration. I look forward to hearing from you as soon as a decision has been made.

Sincerely,

Checkpoint

1. When should you write a thank-you message for a job interview?
2. Why is it important to develop a well-crafted acceptance message?
3. When writing a message declining a job offer, why is it important to be positive in the message?

Figure 16-14.	This is a typical message for accepting a job offer.

Dear Mr. Upton:

I am delighted to accept the position of Research Assistant in the Research & Development Department of Universal Corporation. I am excited about working with you and cannot wait to meet the rest of the team and get started on the projects we discussed.

The list of references you requested is attached. As soon as I receive the formal offer letter and additional forms you mentioned, I will complete and return them. As we discussed, I will wait to hear from Molly Evans in Human Resources for further instructions about the medical exam and background check, which I understand must be completed before I can start work.

Thank you again for this wonderful opportunity. It is just what I was looking for.

Sincerely,

Figure 16-15.	This message is withdrawing an application to a company that has not made an offer.

Dear Mr. Ahmad:

This is to let you know that I have accepted a position with another company. Therefore, I am no longer an applicant for the position of Research Associate at Horton Laboratories.

I appreciate the consideration you gave my application.

Sincerely yours,

Figure 16-16.	Sometimes, you will need to write a message declining a job offer.

Dear Ms. Mabuto:

Thank you very much for offering me the position of Research Assistant at Uptown Research, Inc. I considered your offer, but have decided I must decline.

I am grateful for the opportunity you extended and appreciate your confidence in me.

Sincerely,

Employment Process

The employment process can take a substantial amount of time. From the time of your first inquiry about a position to the final hiring decision, you will complete various steps that will bring you closer to employment. The next sections cover some of the steps not discussed earlier in the chapter.

Application Form

At some point in the employment process, you will need to complete a job **application form,** as shown in Figure 16-17. Some companies require this in advance of interviews. In other cases, the application form is filled out by candidates only after they have been screened and gone through the interview process.

Some employers use printed forms and others accept applications only online. A typical scenario is for an applicant to go online to a company's employment page, open the job description, review it, and then proceed to apply online. The applicant is often asked to upload a résumé at the end of the form.

Figure 16-17.   At some point in the employment process, you will need to fill out a job application form.

Shutterstock

When you fill in an application form, you will need all of your personal data on hand—social security number, information about your citizenship status, and locations and names of past employers. If you are going to be completing an application in the offices of an employer, be sure to take all of this information with you. Like your résumé, an employment application needs to be free of spelling, grammar, and usage errors. Carefully check the form before submitting it. Also, use your best handwriting.

Employment Verification

Employment verification is a process through which the information you provided about your employment history is checked to verify it is correct. Most employers only verify dates of employment, position title, and other objective data. Most employers will not provide subjective information about their employees, such as whether or not the employer considered you a good employee.

Background Checks

A **background check** is a look into the personal data about you that is available from government records and other sources, including public information on the Internet. Such records as credit reports, driving records (if relevant to the job), and criminal records are usually part of the background check. The employer should disclose to you that such a check is being conducted and may ask for your permission to do so. You must give permission for the employer to conduct a credit check on you. Verifying your past employment, checking references, and educational background might all be conducted under the background check.

As part of the background check, many employers use Internet search engines, such as Google, to search for your name. Many also check social networking Web sites, such as Facebook and LinkedIn. Be aware of this before posting any personal information or photos. These checks might work for or against you, depending on what the employer finds. It is up to you to ensure that the image you project on social networking sites will not prove embarrassing or, worse, prevent you from achieving your career goals.

Checkpoint

1. What are two ways in which a job application form may be completed?
2. What is employment verification?
3. What are three things that may be part of a background check by an employer?

Career Planning

As you begin your search for a career, you should evaluate your goals and objectives. What type of job is best suited for you? There are many career research sources to help you evaluate which careers would make the most of your talents, skills, and interests.

- **Career aptitude tests.** A career counselor can administer career aptitude tests, which analyze personal interests, strengths, and weaknesses as the first step in choosing a career.

- **Internet.** Research on professions, demographic trends, industries, and prospective employers will give you insight to careers that may be of interest to you.

- **Career handbooks.** The Occupational Outlook Handbook and the Career Guide to Industries (both written by the US Bureau of Labor Statistics) describe training and education needed for various jobs. These handbooks can help you research career opportunities.

- **Organizations.** One example of an organization is the States' Career Clusters Initiative (SCCI), which gives information to prepare for the 16 career pathways. You can gain valuable information by reading requirements for these career pathways.

- **Networking.** Talking with people you know can help you evaluate career opportunities as well as lead to potential jobs.

Checkpoint

1. What do career aptitude test measure?
2. What is networking, as related to a career search?

Chapter 16 Review

Chapter Summary

Writing a Résumé

- Writing to advance your career goals is probably one of the most important writing tasks most people will ever do.
- A résumé is a document that provides potential employers a profile of your career goals, your work history, and your job qualifications.

Parts of the Résumé

- The most important part of your résumé is the listing of your work experience and achievements.
- Other parts of the résumé, however, are essential to presenting a complete profile of you for the employer.

Résumé Formats

- When choosing a résumé format, consider which format will best present your work experience and job goal from the perspective of the potential employer.
- The two basic formats of résumé are chronological and function.
- Often, you will submit a résumé in electronic form, in which case you need to use common fonts and be aware of other formatting issues related to sharing computer files.

Publishing Your Résumé

- Résumés are traditionally printed and mailed to an employer.
- A printed résumé should be on good-quality paper that is either white or off-white.
- Sometimes, you may fax a résumé to an employer.
- E-mail and online forms are other ways in which you may publish your résumé.

Cover Messages

- A cover message, either a letter or e-mail, is a selling or persuasive message.
- A cover message provides an introduction to who you are and why you are the right person for the position you are seeking, but should not repeat all of the information on your résumé.
- Writing a cover letter provides an opportunity to focus a potential employer's attention on what you want them to know—how you are perfect for the job.

Job Interview

- The job interview is your opportunity to impress upon the interviewer that you are the best person for the job.
- Before the interview, conduct research on the job and the company.
- Practice your answers to questions you think will likely be asked in the interview.
- Be sure to dress appropriately for the interview.

Evaluating the Interview

- As soon as possible after the interview, review your performance.
- Ask yourself critical questions and determine how you can perform better in the next interview.

Interview Follow-up Messages

- Immediately after your interview, it is important to follow up with a thank-you letter or e-mail to the person who interviewed you.
- A thank-you letter can be a deciding factor when the interviewer makes a decision about filling a position.
- When writing to accept a position, show enthusiasm for the opportunity, but remain professional.
- Sometimes you will need to write an employer to withdraw from consideration or to reject an offer of employment.

Employment Process

- At some point in the employment process, you will need to complete an application form for the Human Resources Department to keep on file.

- The company will also verify your previous employment and complete a background check to make certain that the information you have provided is correct.

Career Planning

- When beginning a career, analyze your goals and objectives.

- There are many resources available for evaluating possible career choices.

# Review
Your Knowledge

1. Why is a résumé important to your search for employment?

2. What are the prewriting steps to create a résumé?

3. List the parts of a résumé.

4. Describe the two basic résumé formats and why one might be selected over the other.

5. A résumé is traditionally printed and mailed. List three other ways in which a résumé may be published.

6. Explain the purpose of a cover message.

7. What is the purpose of a job interview?

8. Why is it important to review your performance in an interview?

9. What must you do immediately after an interview, which shows both professionalism and courtesy to the interviewer?

10. List three sources of information about you that an employer may consult during a background check.

Apply
Your Knowledge

1. List all of your past work experiences. Write a brief description of your job responsibilities. Also list your educational background and any other information you think should be included on your résumé.

2. Using the list you created in #1, organize the information according to the parts of a résumé. Write any additional descriptions or information that is needed to fill out the sections of your résumé.

3. Consider the two basic formats for résumés. Select a format for your résumé and write a short paragraph describing why you selected that format.

4. List different ways in which you can publish your résumé. Write a brief paragraph describing each method, then select which method you think is the best way to publish your résumé and explain why.

5. Using the Internet, local paper, or other appropriate source, identify a job for which you want to apply. Write a cover letter that will accompany your résumé.

6. Select an area of the United States in which you would like to live, other than your hometown. Research employers in that area and identify one for which you would like to work. Write a two-page summary of the company, what service or product it offers, what function you see yourself performing in the company, and the location in which the company is located.

7. Work in pairs or teams as assigned by your teacher. Take turns interviewing each other. Refer to the typical interview questions given in this chapter, but come up with your own questions as well. When all interviews are completed, write a brief summary evaluating how you performed in the interview. Describe what you could do better in the future.

8. You have recently been interviewed for the position of assistant manager at a local restaurant. Write the following two messages.

   A. A follow-up letter to the interview.

   B. A follow-up letter after you have been informed that another candidate was hired.

9. Research employment laws concerning background checks and what an employer is and is not allowed to do. Write a summary of your findings. Be sure to include information regarding federal, state, and local employment laws, if applicable.

10. Use the Internet to research at least three careers that interest you. Write a brief description of each career, including the educational requirements and current salary ranges for the career.

Practice
What You Have Learned

Access the *Fundamentals of Business Communication* Student Companion Web Site at www.g-wlearning.com/Communication. Download each data file for this chapter. Follow the instructions to complete a reading, writing, and grammar activity to practice what you have learned in this chapter.

Connection
Across the Curriculum

Math. Create a grid and print *Résumé* on the X axis. Add labels for the two basic types of résumés. Also, add a label for electronic/scannable résumés. On the Y axis, list each component of a résumé. Place check marks in the appropriate columns for each to show the similarities and differences. Write several paragraphs discussing the type of résumé you think would be more appropriate for your use.

Language Arts. Identify careers that are available in the communication and multimedia fields. Obtain an application for several of those positions and go through the process of completing them as if you were applying for a job. What did you learn about the specific skills and qualifications that these jobs require? How did this information differ from other jobs for which you have applied? Write several paragraphs on what you learned.

Build
Your Business Portfolio

When sending your application information, you will need to include a résumé that describes your background and your qualifications for the position.

1. Create a résumé that highlights your talents and skills. Write a résumé that you will be able to use for one of these purposes: employment application, school admission, or community service.

2. Save the document file in your ePortfolio folder. Create a subfolder named Resumes. Save the file with the name Resume01. You will be creating other résumés in the future, so this will be the first one.

3. Place a printed copy of the résumé in your container for your print portfolio.

Careers
Hospitality and Tourism Careers and Communication

With increasing leisure time and personal income, many people have more resources for dining out, travel, and recreation. Career options in the hospitality and tourism cluster focus on food and beverage services, lodging services, travel, and all types of recreation. Those who work in this industry must have exceptional customer-service skills and like demanding and diverse work. These workers must also have a solid foundation in math, science, and technical skills.

Careers in hospitality and tourism require correspondence to clients both verbally and in written communication. Writing must be presented in a professional manner. Give examples in which writing a letter to respond to a situation might be needed.

Event Prep

Job Interview

Job interviewing is an event you might enter with your organization. By participating in the job interview, you will be able to showcase your presentation skills, communication talents, and ability to actively listen to the questions asked by the interviewers. For this event, you will be expected to write a letter of application, create a résumé, and complete an application. You will also be interviewed by an individual or panel.

To prepare for the job interview, do the following.

1. Read the guidelines provided by your organization.
2. Review the interviewing techniques presented in this chapter.
3. Write your letter of application, résumé, and complete the application (if provided for this event).
4. Solicit feedback from your peers, teacher, and parents.
5. Make certain that each piece of communication is complete and free of errors.

17

Writing Reports

Information is a source of learning. But unless it is organized, processed, and available to the right people in a format for decision making, it is a burden, not a benefit.

—*William Pollard, Minister and Scholar*

Reports are used every day in business, from providing project status to informing shareholders about financial assets of a company. In this chapter, you will learn how to approach writing informal and formal business reports. You will also learn about the standard parts of those reports.

Objectives

When you complete Chapter 17, you will be able to:

- **Explain** what a report is.
- **Develop** plans for informal and formal reports.
- **Write** an informal report using standard guidelines for formatting.
- **Research** information for formal reports using primary and secondary research.
- **Write** a formal report using standard guidelines for formatting.
- **Describe** the parts of a formal report.

Terms

report
progress report
informal report
periodic report
informal study report
formal report
primary research
qualitative data
focus group
quantitative data
representative sampling
secondary research
plagiarism
copyright
public domain
table of contents
executive summary
conclusions
recommendations
citations

Go Green

Presentations typically consist of slideshows, Web site demonstrations, and handouts of important points for the audience. However, not everybody in the audience will take handouts with them. The unused handouts represent a waste of paper, ink, and energy. Savvy presenters are taking advantage of technology to post presentations on YouTube, Facebook, or a Web site where interested audience members can visit to review information about the presentation.

1. If you were making a presentation, what media would you select to use that would make your presentation more environmentally friendly?

2. How much time, paper, and ink do you think you would save by posting a presentation, rather than printing handouts for 30 people?

Reports

Reports are documents used to present information in a structured format. In general, reports are used to convey information that is used as the basis for making business decisions. Reports provide facts from which conclusions are drawn and discuss problems with recommended solutions. Reports are developed for use inside of an organization. But, they may be sent to people outside of the organization, such as government agencies, stockholders, members, investors, clients, customers, and to the media.

Some reports are **progress reports,** which are written in a specified format and periodically submitted (monthly, quarterly, annually). Progress reports are also known as *status reports*. These types of reports can be as simple as a one-page update using a template or as complex as an annual report from a corporation written for its stockholders. A typical business report is a lengthy narrative document that provides a detailed response to a request for information, ideas, explanations, or recommendations. Some reports require extensive research and analysis related to a particular proposal.

Reading Prep

After you read this chapter, draw a conclusion about what you learned. Did the material cover the information you expected? Do you have additional questions about the material?

Checkpoint

1. What is a report?
2. Describe a progress report.

Planning Reports

Planning is the most important stage of preparing any kind of report. Planning involves focusing on the subject and outlining the content. Begin with the first step in the writing process: identifying your purpose and audience. Next, outline the content of your report so that it flows logically and is easily understood. After writing the draft, edit and revise the report as many times as necessary to create a polished, well-written document. Many reports have a wide and important audience and any errors can greatly undermine the writer's credibility.

Focus and Organize Your Topic

Here are some steps to help you in the planning stage.

1. Identify and name the topic.

2. Plan your introduction.

3. Outline the main ideas.

4. Think ahead to your closing.

Each report you write will cover one main topic. Whether the report is simple or complex, you need to begin by organizing the topic into logical sections that clarify the content for the reader. When you are writing a report that contains a lot of information, find the central theme that binds all of the information into a meaningful whole. Use this theme as the title of your document and explain it in your introduction.

You will want to capture the reader's attention by giving an overview of the report's contents. The introduction explains the reasons for the report and the benefits of the ideas or recommendations you are presenting.

Review the ideas that support your purpose and discard the nonessential information. Once you have all of the facts you plan to use, arrange them in the order that will make your report effective. Figure 17-1 shows a basic outline for a long report. For a short report, your outline might consist of a list of topics without detailed subheads.

Your closing should summarize the key points. In some cases, you will want to close with solutions or recommendations based on your study or analysis.

Develop an Outline

As you outline the report, consider the best order in which to present the material. There are several approaches to organization that can be applied to reports. The one you use will depend on the type of material you are covering. You can choose to organize by chronological/sequential order, order of importance, cause and effect, or problem-solution.

Chronological/Sequential Order

When you are reporting on the history of a situation or discussing a process, the chronological/sequential order is a good choice. Chronological means "in order of time." In this order, start with the earliest events and proceed to the most recent. A variation is to use the reverse order, where the most recent events are presented first.

Order of Importance

When organizing by order of importance, present information from most to least important. Readers can easily follow this logic. In some cases, it is better to present information in the reverse order, from least to most important.

Figure 17-1. This is an outline for a report.

Outline

I. Job Requirements
   A. Executives
   B. Managers
   C. Supervisors
   D. Staff
      1. Senior Level
      2. Middle Level
      3. Entry Level
II. On-the-Job Training
   A. Establishing Objectives
   B. Organization Planning
   C. Delegation of Authority
   D. Job Counseling
III. Job Rotation
   A. Principles of Job Rotation
   B. Advantages
   C. Problems
IV. In-House Courses
   A. Supervision
   B. Psychology of Motivation
   C. Internal Communications
   D. External Communications
   E. Interpersonal Relationships
   F. Management Decisionmaking
   G. Organization Planning and Control
V. Job-Related Training
   A. Company Structure and Objectives
   B. Long-Range Planning Refresher Technical Training
VI. Outside Sources
   A. Universities and Colleges
      1. Cost of Typical Programs Available
      2. Course Overviews
   B. Management Education (Seminars)
      1. Types of Seminars Offered
      2. Locations

A well-written report is organized in a way that makes it easy for the reader to find the information.

Shutterstock

Cause and Effect

The cause-and-effect organization is useful when your report reflects an investigation. This approach lists facts or ideas followed by conclusions. You should report your opinions only after careful research and fact finding.

Problem-Solution

The problem-solution organization works well when you are going to describe a problem and then offer a solution or multiple solutions. By presenting the problem, you communicate to the reader why an action is needed. Then, give the reader options for solving the problem. This approach is very common in the business world when writing a report to a superior.

Select an Approach

As you prepare to write, select an approach that supports your material. As with other types of writing, the direct or indirect approach can be applied to present the content of a report.

When using the direct approach, start with a general statement of purpose. Follow this with supporting details. The direct approach works best when the message is positive or neutral.

When using the indirect approach, list supporting details to prepare the reader for your general statement of purpose or conclusions. Reserve the indirect approach for when you have a tough argument to make or if the message is negative.

Checkpoint

1. What is the first step in writing a report?
2. List four steps in the planning stage of a report.
3. What are the four basic types of organization?

Writing Informal Reports

Informal reports are documents that do not require formal research or documentation. Informal reports are typically short, no more than a few pages long, and are commonly a part of the regular work routine. Informal reports may be written in the first person, using *I* when the writer is reporting on his or her own actions, ideas, conclusions, and recommendations.

Parts of an Informal Report

Informal reports generally fall into two categories: those that are written in narrative form and those that lend themselves to standardized formats. In the next section, you will learn about some specific types of reports and look at examples of how they can be formatted to suit the information. In straightforward, narrative reports, you can generally expect to need at least three sections: introduction, body, and conclusion.

Introduction

The introduction states the purpose of the report. If the report is being written at the request of someone, you might mention that in the introduction. For example:

> Following is a report on my visit to the new conference facility we are considering for next month's meeting on digital media and advertising.

Body

The body contains the information of the report. For the body of the report, decide whether or not the content has subtopics that will help the reader scan and skim for information. A short report on a site visit to view a facility might be divided into these sections: location, description of the space, and cost. The body of the report should be of sufficient length to communicate the purpose of the document.

Conclusion

Reports should end with a brief summary of main points from the writer's point of view. If you use headings, this section might be labeled *Conclusion, Recommendations,* or *Summary.* If your report does not have headings, the conclusion is the last paragraph. In the above example, the writer would likely conclude with a recommendation about whether or not to use the facility.

BUSINESS ETHICS

Intellectual Property

Did you know you must cite any information you use that was written by someone else? Intellectual property is anything that belongs to someone else—copyrighted material, trademarks, music, just to name a few examples. If you quote material for a blog, Web site, or even a PowerPoint presentation, you must give the owner credit for that material. It is unethical to present information as your own when it is not and can be illegal. It is also unethical to misrepresent data. Search the Internet for the proper use of intellectual material. The following questions can be asked to make sure that your material is presented ethically.

- Have I referenced the source if the information was not collected by me?
- Is the material properly footnoted?
- Does the owner of the material allow for this information to be used?
- Does the graphic accurately represent the data?

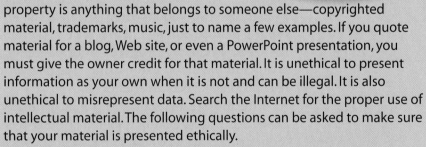

Types of Informal Reports

It is not possible to list the many types of informal reports used in business. However, this section describes a few types that are frequently used. Examples are also provided to give you an idea of how to approach writing and formatting. When writing informal reports, use the guidelines suggested in Figure 17-2.

Periodic Reports

Periodic reports are written according to a specified schedule: daily, weekly, monthly, quarterly, etc. A periodic report generally provides the status of a project, reports facts and figures over a specified period, or summarizes an ongoing activity. Examples are progress (status) reports, monthly sales reports, weekly reports on overtime worked by employees in various departments, and monthly reports on the status of a group of projects in a department. Such reports usually can be presented in a standard format.

Any report can be incorporated as part of an e-mail or created as a separate document and attached to an e-mail. In Figure 17-3, the report is incorporated in the body of the e-mail. While this format is not difficult to read, the layout makes it hard to make comparisons. Additionally, each quarter the report will have to be created from scratch. By contrast, Figure 17-4 shows an e-mail with the report as an attachment. The report is shown in Figure 17-5. It was created from a template that makes presentation of the numbers clear and easy to compare. This template can then be used each month, saving time and effort while creating a professional looking document to use as a handout.

Informal Study Reports

An **informal study report** provides information that is gathered by the writer through methods other than formal research, such as reading related documents, conducting informal interviews, reviewing competitive products, or making observations after visiting a site or attending a meeting. These reports may be initiated by the writer or prepared at the request of someone higher up in the organization. Informal reports on activities are sometimes written in the first person, using *I* to state your own actions, ideas, and conclusions or recommendations.

Informal study reports can be incorporated as part of a memo or e-mail or created as a separate document. Figure 17-6 is an example of a report based on an informal study. Note that this report uses appropriate headings to guide the reader.

- Method (describing the method used to obtain the data)
- Findings and Conclusions (including the procedure used)
- Recommendations

Figure 17-2. Follow these guidelines when writing an informal report.

Guidelines for Writing an Informal Report

State the purpose of the report.

This statement may be a reference to a request for the information or a general statement about the report's purpose.

Use suitable headings to guide the reader.

If your report covers more than one topic or if the topic can be divided into subtopics, use headings to help the reader scan and skim for information.

Make the report visibly appealing and readable.

Use informal language, such as abbreviations for company names, products, and projects, and visual elements, such as bulleted and numbered lists, to aid in readability.

Summarize, if appropriate.

Your summary might include action steps, open issues to be resolved, recommendations, or conclusions.

Figure 17-3. This is an example of a quarterly report sent as an e-mail. The report is in the body of the e-mail and is hard to use for comparisons.

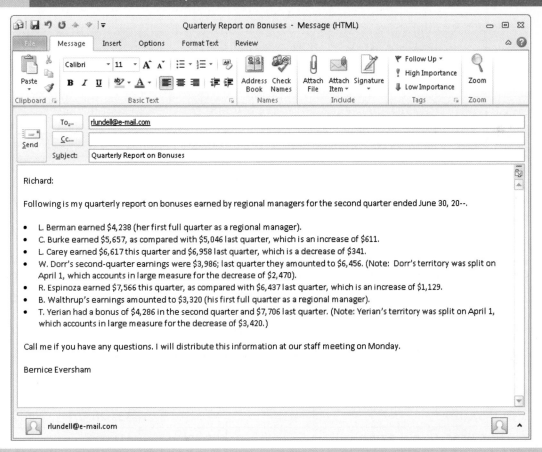

Figure 17-4. The quarterly report in this example has been included as an attachment to the e-mail. The attached report, shown in Figure 17-5, is easier to read.

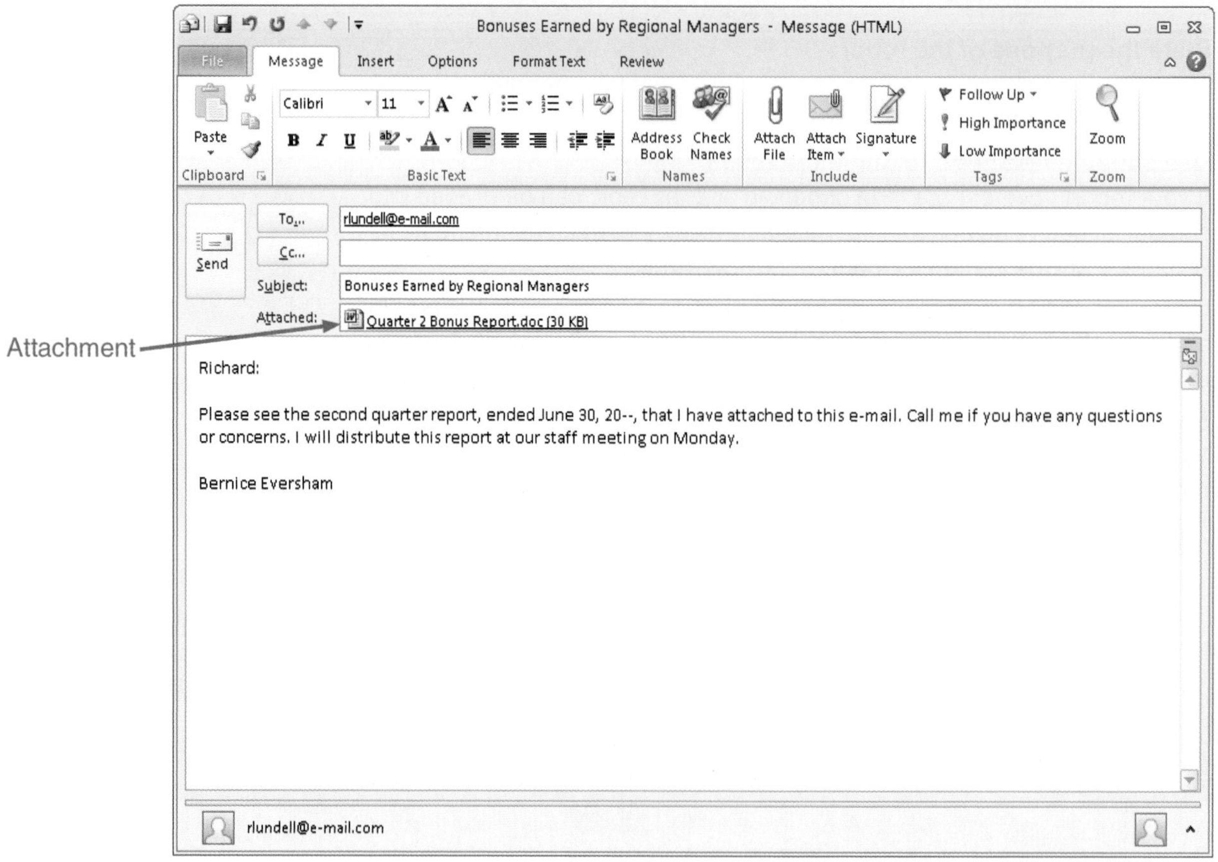

Attachment

Figure 17-5. This is the quarterly report sent as an attachment to the e-mail shown in Figure 17-4.

Martindale Sound Equipment
Bonuses Earned by Regional Managers
Quarterly Report

Second Quarter, 20--						
Manager	**2nd Quarter**	**1st Quarter**	**Increase**	**Decrease**	**Year to Date**	**Comments**
Berman, L.	$4,238	—	—	—	$4,238	Hired in April
Burke, C.	$5,657	$5,046	$611	—	$10,703	
Carey, L.	$6,617	$6,958	—	$341	$13,575	
Dorr, W.	$3,986	$6,456	—	$2,470	$10,442	
Espinoza, R.	$7,566	$6,437	$1,129	—	$14,003	
Walthrup, B.	$3,320	—	—	—	$3,320	Hired in April
Yerian, T.	$4,286	$7,706		$3,420	$11,992	
Total	$35,670	$32,603			$68,273	

Figure 17-6.	**This is an example of a report based on an informal study.**

Review of Customer Correspondence

I have completed the review of customer correspondence you requested on December 16 for the period of November 1 through December 15, 20--. As you suggested, I read all outgoing letters and e-mails written by the six Customer Care Specialists. During this period, 64 pieces of communication (18 letters and 46 e-mails) were written and mailed to customers on issues not covered by our form letters.

Method

As I read each letter, I assigned a grade to it:
- A (excellent)
- B (good)
- C (passable)
- D (poor)

The elements considered in assigning these grades were: tone (friendliness), helpfulness, accuracy of information, organization, and correct mechanics (grammar, spelling, and punctuation).

Findings and Conclusions

Number of Letters and E-mails	Grade Assigned
14	A
13	B
25	C
12	D

My evaluations were subjective; however, the distribution of grades I assigned supports the types of criticisms we have been hearing from the sales staff. As they mentioned to us at the last meeting, there are many examples of indifference, carelessness with facts, lack of clarity, and negativism. It seems apparent, based on the 64 pieces of correspondence that were examined, that the standard of customer correspondence is much lower than it should be.

Recommendations

Based on this informal study, I recommend we set up a written communications course for all Customer Care Specialists. I have contacted Dorothy Fairchild in Human Resources Training about setting up and teaching the course. Last year, she organized and taught a course for the Credit Department and, according to the credit manager, Clark Pinson, it was a great success. I will be happy to assist in setting up the course and will help the instructor in any way I can, if you think this is a feasible solution.

Idea and Suggestion Reports

Employees are often asked for ideas and suggestions for making improvements in the company. Some of the areas where input is often requested include improving employee morale, saving time and effort, and cutting costs. In responding to such requests, follow these guidelines.

- Be assertive in offering your opinion. You would not have received an invitation to contribute your ideas if they were not considered valuable.

- If appropriate, try to begin with positive remarks about the present situation and then tactfully proceed with your suggestions for change.

- Be specific; the reader should not have to guess at what you have in mind.

- When appropriate, group your ideas according to subject. Prominently display the subjects.

Look at the example shown in Figure 17-7. Rahima Dohani is responding to a request for suggestions on improving the company's Facebook page.

 Checkpoint

1. What are the three basic parts of an informal report?
2. List three types of informal reports.

CASE

Suggestions, Anyone?

Juanita Ortega is on the Operations Committee of GreenHomes Corporation. The committee was discussing the feasibility of establishing a recycling plan for the company. The committee chairperson, Wayne Crier, asked Juanita to study the matter and present a brief report, including specific recommendations concerning how a recycling program could be implemented.

Juanita decided to create a survey for employees to get feedback. Because she was pressed for time, she selected ten people she ate lunch with everyday. Juanita created a survey with the following questions.

- Would you be in favor of recycling?

- Why or why not?

Juanita tallied the responses and began to create a report. However, she found herself struggling for information, so decided not to create a written document. She went to the committee chairperson and gave her report verbally. When asked her for her report, she told him there was not enough information to put in writing. The chairperson told her that her findings were not adequate and to start the project over.

1. Was Juanita's survey adequate?

2. Did she have a representative sampling of the employees?

3. How could she have gathered more information so that a detailed report could be written?

Figure 17-7. This memo is a report that presents ideas and suggestions regarding a company Facebook page.

MEMO

TO: Jay Sanchez
FROM: Rahima Dohani
DATE: September 30, 20--
SUBJECT: Suggestions for Facebook Page

I am pleased to respond to your invitation to offer suggestions for our company's Facebook page. First, let me say that there are many good things about our current page. I like the informal style and the editorial quality is excellent. I think we've hit homeruns with the "Let's Get Going" and "Been There, Done That" features. But, I know you want suggestions rather than praise, so here are my ideas.

Design
Replace the old design with a new logo and a layout that looks less traditional. We are competing with new firms that are attracting travelers seeking adventure. To keep up with them, we need to move toward brighter colors, larger fonts, and bolder graphics that depict our more exotic and unique packages. I suggest that we hire a designer to give a new look to the entire page.

Photographs and Stories
People like to see photographs of themselves. Let's encourage our customers to send us shots that depict highlights of visiting our most exciting locations and prominently post them. We can also encourage these customers to share stories of their fun and adventures on the travel packages we've put together for them.

Features
1. A "Tours" column could be especially popular. Such a column would have good readership and, at the same time, give customers a chance to "sound off' on their personal likes and dislikes.
2. After studying the postings for the past year, I feel that we have too many management postings and too few postings about individuals. It seems to me that this should be principally a form for promoting our travel packages—not a management PR magazine.
3. I recommend that the page establish an "Employee of the Month" column to help customers identify with the staff members who have special expertise in various locales and types of packages. A committee of employees could select a person to be featured monthly on the basis of recommendations of supervisors and department heads. We might run the employee's picture with a brief biographical sketch and story about that person's special knowledge of the travel planning experience.
4. Finally, I suggest that a monthly "Celebrity Sightings" column be added where we publish photos and reports of celebrities who have visited a destination we feature. This column would appeal to customers who like to follow what their favorite celebrities are doing and hang out in the places where they might rub shoulders with the rich and famous.

If you wish, I would be glad to further discuss these recommendations with you. Certainly, Facebook is an excellent instrument for communicating with customers and I'm all for experimenting with ideas that will help to make it even better.

Researching Formal Reports

A **formal report** focuses on a main topic that is broad enough to be divided into subtopics for complete and clear coverage. Formal reports are often supported by formal research or information gathering.

Research techniques include conducting surveys, focus groups, or interviews and studying written information on the topic. Information gathering might include collaboration with other departments, consulting outside experts, or convening a taskforce or committee to work on different aspects of the report.

Whatever the length or purpose of the formal report, the goal is to prepare a valid, useful, and informative document. Here are some examples of general topics that require a formal report.

- Explain the reorganization of one or more departments in a company.

- Describe a plan for expanding a business, such as acquiring a smaller company and fitting it within the present organization.

- Outline the development of a new product or entry into a new market and strategies for a successful venture.

- Re-examine the company's objectives, which may represent a sweeping change in personnel, managerial responsibilities, and methods of operation.

- Study current products being marketed.

- Study customer preferences as to product and method of distribution.

- Describe the overhaul of the company's policy in an area that affects employee morale.

Consider the type of information needed to support the credibility of your report. If the report requires research, consider the two categories of research: primary research and secondary research.

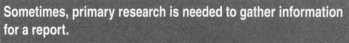
Sometimes, primary research is needed to gather information for a report.

Shutterstock

Primary Research

Primary research is conducted by the writer in preparation for writing a report. The most common types of primary research for a business report are interviews, surveys, and experiments.

Interviews

Interviews are an effective method of gathering **qualitative data,** which are information that provides insight into how people think about a particular topic. If your report topics and recommendations can use the support of information about customer attitudes, behaviors, value systems, motivations, or cultural background, interviews are a good means for primary research. Use the guidelines in Figure 17-8 when you are preparing for an interview.

Interviews may be conducted individually or in groups. A **focus group** is a small group of people with which the interviewer conducts a discussion to gather answers to a prepared set of questions. Focus groups are a good way to evaluate services or test new ideas. Typically, participants are asked about their perceptions, opinions, beliefs, and attitudes by responding to questions, demonstrations, or concepts for products and services. The focus group leader asks questions and encourages input from all of the participants. In addition to talking to the facilitator, focus group participants interact with each other at times during the discussion.

One-on-one interviews may be used to gather the same type of information collected in a focus group. Depending on the topic, individual interviews might yield better information. For example, if you wish to know whether a group of workers is getting adequate on-the-job training, workers may be more likely to give straightforward answers in a one-on-one interview.

Surveys

Surveys are used to obtain **quantitative data,** which are facts and figures from which conclusions can be drawn. Before spending time to study or research a topic, find out if the data you need already exist. If you want facts that will support conclusions about large populations, find authoritative sources that collect this kind of information.

Figure 17-8. Follow these guidelines when preparing for interviews.

Preparing for Personal Interviews

Interviewing to obtain information is a skill that requires preparation and practice. These guidelines will help you conduct successful interviews.

- Identify the topic of the interview and the information needed.
- Develop objective questions and maintain your objectivity during the interview.
- Explain the purpose of the interview when setting up the appointment.
- Establish the time, place, and duration of the interview.
- Indicate how long the interview will take.
- Choose a comfortable setting where you will not be interrupted.
- Explain the purpose again at the beginning of the interview and ask the interviewee if there are any questions before getting started.
- If you are going to record the interview, ask for permission to do so in advance.
- If you take notes, use abbreviations and record key phrases. Do not attempt to create a word-for-word record. If necessary, stop at the end of each question and answer to summarize and confirm what you have written.
- Follow up the interview with a thank-you note.

A survey can be conducted through personal interviews, over the telephone, or through a questionnaire. Your success will depend on identifying a representative sampling. A **representative sampling** is a group that includes a cross section of the entire population you are targeting. Surveys conducted by professionals in the field, such as political polls and product marketers, use complex formulas and methods for sampling. In a business setting, groups that represent a subset of respondents, such as customers or employees, can be identified through the use of company data.

Surveys are often used to collect data on which to base a report.

Shutterstock

A written survey is highly structured and contains multiple items for response. Some items to consider before deciding to use a written survey include the following.

- Is a questionnaire the best method for getting the information?

- Who is the target audience?

- How many people should receive the survey in order for you to get an adequate number of responses?

- How will you go about selecting a representative sampling?

After you have answered these questions, you are ready to start drafting the actual survey. When constructing a survey, it is important to develop questions in a format that encourages responses, as suggested in Figure 17-9. A survey is shown in Figure 17-10.

If a survey is mailed, it should be accompanied by a cover letter that identifies the purpose of the questionnaire, how the response will be used, and a deadline for returning the form. It is important for the recipient to understand that his or her time is respected and that timely responses are valuable to the success of the survey. In some cases, an incentive, such as a gift, a copy of the final report, or some other motivational item, is used to increase the number of returned surveys. Always make it easy to return the questionnaire by enclosing a postage-paid envelope or creating a document that can be complete and returned by e-mail.

Figure 17-9. Follow these guidelines when creating a survey.

Creating a Survey

Make the questions easy to answer.
Write questions that have a choice of answers, such as yes/no, multiple choice, or agree/disagree/strongly agree/strongly disagree. These are known as *closed-ended questions* and make it easy for the responder to give an answer. *Open-ended questions*, those that are subjective, take more time to answer and tally.

Write objective questions.
Write questions that do not lead respondents to a particular answer. Biased questions produce biased data.

Put the questions in a logical sequence.
Group items and, when possible, give them headings.

Keep the survey short.
If you ask too many questions, the respondent may not want to take the time to complete the survey.

Include space for comments.
Often the best information comes from unstructured responses.

Experiments

Depending on your topic and the circumstances, an experiment can provide support for the topic of a business report. Testing a new process or doing a trial run of a new marketing strategy can provide convincing support for an idea or recommendation. Data can be gathered for a report by direct observation of the experiment.

An example of an experiment is a type of research conducted by retailers. Retailers often use secret shoppers to observe and report on the behavior of sales staff. The secret shoppers record their experiences and the retailers use the information to identify areas where sales consultants need additional training.

When collecting data by observation, objectivity is important. The observer needs to accurately record data and remain unbiased. If you are enlisting the assistance of others to be observers, develop a checklist or series of questions so each assistant records consistent data.

Secondary Research

Secondary research is data and information already assembled and recorded by someone else. This might include published materials or resources available to you on the job. In many cases, you will conduct secondary research first to find credible information to support your ideas, then conduct primary research if data are not found.

There are many sources available as you research a report, so take advantage of the opportunities to gather information. A wealth of information is available in print and online. Good sources include articles published in

Figure 17-10. **Surveys are useful tools when you want to collect a large amount of data from a group of individuals.**

SEMINAR SPECIALISTS INC.
QUESTIONNAIRE FOR POTENTIAL CLIENTS

Your completed questionnaire will help us know you better as we work cooperatively to determine your training and/or seminar needs. Please answer all questions thoughtfully; each is designed to address one particular area of training.

1. Do you have an immediate training need within your organization?
    ☐   Yes
    ☐   No
    If yes, briefly describe it on the lines below.
    _____
    _____
    _____

2. Do you have an immediate seminar need for your employees?
    ☐   Yes
    ☐   No
    If yes, briefly describe it on the lines below.
    _____
    _____
    _____

3. Would you be interested in attending a session on Assessing Training Needs in Today's Business Environment?
    ☐   Yes
    ☐   No

4. Have you ever contracted the services of a training seminar specialist?
    ☐   Yes
    ☐   No

5. Would you be interested in meeting an individual training specialist from SSI?
    ☐   Yes
    ☐   No

    If yes, what is the best time of day to contact you? _____

Thank you for your assistance.

If you would like to schedule an appointment, please e-mail us at ssiconsult@e-mail.com well-respected magazines, journals, and newspapers. Books written by experts are good sources, as are collections of information, such as encyclopedias, yearbooks, almanacs, business manuals, and libraries. Government data, reports, and publications are widely available and the information can be freely used. Industry and trade association Web sites and publications provide specific information, as do Web sites, blogs, and databases devoted to specific topics.

When you conduct secondary research, consider the reliability and credibility of the sources you use. Ask yourself these questions.

Information collected from research conducted by somebody else is secondary research.

Shutterstock

- What are the author's credentials?
- What is the reputation of the publication in which the source material appears?
- Is the source a mainstream publication or an unknown?
- Is the information current?
- What is the copyright date?
- Are more current sources available?
- If data are presented, how were they collected and what is the source?
- Can the information be validated through other sources?

Researching Online

When conducting research online, use search engines such as Google to identify major publications, trade and industry organizations, and government agencies related to your topic, Figure 17-11. Since there are so many Web sites available, it is important to start by narrowing your search. Decide what specific information you need to find out. It helps to write this down. Then, determine keywords to use in your search. It is usually best to be very specific first, then expand the search by being less specific if the search does not turn up enough hits.

Another way to search is to look for a source of information. Try to think of sources familiar to you because they are well-known or well-respected publications, authors, organizations, journalists, bloggers, or news sources. These sources publish information by writers whose credentials you can check.

Figure 17-11.   Google and other Internet search engines are valuable tools for conducting online research.

However, it is a good idea to be skeptical about any research conducted online. There is much misinformation on the Internet and finding accurate information can be hard. Check to see if the argument is logical and based on facts from reliable sources. If the writer makes sweeping generalizations or draws unsupported conclusions, the information may not be reliable.

Trade organizations and government Web sites are usually sources for reliable statistics and reports. Educational institutions, private industry organizations, and news outlets are also generally reliable sources on the Web. As you search Web sites, you will find links to additional sources of information. Be careful not to get sidetracked by these links. Each time you move to a new link, consider the reliability of the source.

Crediting Sources

Writers can reference material from other writers provided proper credit is given. This is done by summarizing the work in your own words or by directly quoting a small part of the work. However, if you *copy* the work of others without permission, even if you credit the source, you are committing plagiarism. **Plagiarism** is use of another's work without permission and is illegal. Figure 17-12 gives tips to avoid plagiarizing when writing a document.

Figure 17-12.	Follow these tips for avoiding plagiarism. Plagiarism is illegal.

Avoiding Plagiarism

You can avoid plagiarism when referencing the work of others by using the following guidelines. Keep in mind, there is a difference between *referencing* and *copying* the work of others. Referencing the work by paraphrasing it or even making a direct quotation from it is acceptable if the source is credited. However, copying the work of others is illegal, unless the owner has given you permission to do so.

- Place material that is directly quoted inside of quotation marks.

- When quoting, paraphrasing, or summarizing information from any source, use a consistent system for crediting these sources. Depending on the number and types of sources, you may choose to use footnotes, a bibliography, or text references to a works-cited list.

- Consult a style manual, such as *The Chicago Manual of Style* or the Modern Language Association (MLA) handbook, for guidance and examples of various styles for footnotes, bibliographies, and other methods of listing sources.

- Always look for copyright information on the sources you use.

- If you plan to rely on or quote an extensive amount of the source material, you must obtain permission from the copyright holder to do so.

- Never cut and paste material from any electronic source, such as the Internet or electronic books. This is a bad habit that can easily lead to accidental plagiarism (it is still plagiarism whether or not you intended to plagiarize).

- Most information on the Internet is copyrighted and, therefore, you cannot use the material without permission. You may, however, reference the material.

- Be aware that material does not have to bear a copyright notice to be copyrighted. Any material is automatically copyrighted as soon as it is in tangible form.

A **copyright** legally protects the material's owner from the distribution of his or her work without permission. Pick up any book or magazine and you will find a copyright notice someplace in the publication. A copyright notice has a symbol and date, ©2012, and is usually followed by the copyright holder's name and statement of ownership. However, it is very important to understand that all material is automatically copyrighted as soon as it is in tangible form, regardless of whether or not a copyright statement appears on the work. This means that almost everything you read or any image you see is copyrighted, including material on the Internet. You will usually find a copyright notice at the bottom of a Web site home page, but lack of one does not mean the information can be copied.

Materials published by the US government are usually in the **public domain.** This means the material is not owned by anybody and can be used without permission. However, many government reports and studies are conducted by private institutions with government funding. But, if taxpayer money is used to fund the report, then the material belongs to the taxpayers (meaning it is in the public domain).

When you find information you want to use, be sure to keep careful notes. Organize your notes by setting up folders for each topic or source. The following information is needed for footnotes or a listing of sources at the end of your report.

- author's name
- publication title (article, magazine, journal, book)
- name and location of the publisher
- publication year
- if the source is online, the Web site name, URL, and date of information retrieval

When you put this information together in a footnote to cite a source, the footnote should appear at the bottom of the page. These examples follow the Modern Language Association (MLA) handbook:

Book
[1]Stephen R. Covey, *The Seven Habits of Highly Effective People: Powerful Lessons in Personal Change* (New York: Free Press, 2004) 91.

Online source
[2]Laura Fitzpatrick, Why Can't We Sleep? Time Magazine (17 May 2010) http://www.time.com/time/health/article/0,8599,1989451,00.html

Checkpoint

1. What is the difference between primary research and secondary research?
2. List three types of primary research.
3. What is plagiarism?
4. When is material copyrighted?

Writing Formal Reports

Once your research is finished and your sources are organized, you are ready to write the report. Because writing formally structured reports will probably be an infrequent task for most employees, it may take some time and effort to produce a finished product. Formal reports are written in the third person and follow a structured format that adheres to standards used by most businesses.

TEAMWORK

Work with your group to develop a survey that could be used in one of your classes to gather information about the buying pattern of high school students. Work cooperatively with your team to create the list of questions. Discuss how you would tabulate the data obtained from the questionnaire.

When you need to prepare a report, see if your organization has standards that must be followed. There may be templates that you will need to use to create a new report. If there are no standards that must be followed, it is up to the writer to determine the best approach for the report. In those situations, you may use the templates provided in your word processing software. You can also look for examples in your company library or by researching online. Find a variety of examples to help you get an idea of how to present the information.

Reports vary widely in terms of purpose, format, and content. However, these four basic guidelines pertain to all narrative business reports.

- Know the readers.
- Make the purpose clear.
- Make the report believable.
- Make the report readable.

Know the Readers

To a large extent, the readers determine the manner in which you write the report. You must take into account the reader's preferences as to language and style, biases regarding the subject (if any), knowledge of the subject, and familiarity with the terms the report contains.

Make the Purpose Clear

Have a clear purpose for the report and identify it for the readers. To make sure this important element is not overlooked, a formal report usually contains an introduction that discusses the purpose of the report.

Make the Report Believable

Provide supporting facts and figures from reliable sources for all information. Do not report your position based solely on opinion. In many formal reports, a conclusion must be drawn, but it should be based on facts you present in the report.

When writing a formal report, know the readers, make the purpose clear, make the report believable, and make the report readable. A formal report is bound to present a polished and professional package.

Shutterstock

Make the Report Readable

Organize ideas in a logical and sequential manner. Use graphic elements to clarify the report's organizational structure and make the document visually attractive. These include headings, numbered lists, indented paragraphs, and white space. Graphics may also include tables, illustrations, charts, graphs, and photographs. Making the report readable is essential and increases the chance that the reader will give your work the attention it deserves.

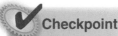

Checkpoint

1. List the four basic guidelines that pertain to all narrative business reports.
2. Identify three graphic elements that may make a report more readable.

Standard Parts of Formal Reports

The parts of a formal report vary according to the purpose and topic. The next sections cover several common parts that may appear in a formal report. You may choose to use the styles in Microsoft Word to create the headings of your report or follow the guidelines defined by your organization.

Title Page

All formal reports should have a title page designed for readability and visual appeal. These elements belong on the title page, as shown in Figure 17-13:

- name of the report
- name of the person or group for whom the report was written
- name of the author of the report
- date the report is distributed

Sometimes, other information, such as the location of the company, is also needed.

Table of Contents

A table of contents is necessary so the reader knows what is included in the report. This page may be labeled *Table of Contents* or *Contents*. The **table of contents** lists the major sections and subsections within the report with page numbers, as shown in Figure 17-14.

Executive Summary

The **executive summary** summarizes the main points in the report, as shown in Figure 17-15. It is sometimes referred to as a *summary* or *abstract*. This summary should be thorough enough to provide an overview for some recipients who may not read the entire report. It appears at the beginning of the report, before the introduction.

Figure 17-13. This is an example of a title page. Notice the parts.

A MANAGEMENT DEVELOPMENT PROGRAM
FOR BOWDEN INDUSTRIES, INC.

Name of
the report

A Report to the

President's Advisory Committee

Who the
report is for

Prepared by

Author of
the report

Susan Chen
Director, Development & Training
Bowden Industries, Inc.

Date the report
was published

June 17, 20—

Figure 17-14.   This is an example of a table of contents.

Begin introduction
on page 1 and use
Roman numerals
for preceding pages

CONTENTS

Figure 17-15. An executive summary provides a brief overview of the main points and, when used, appears at the beginning of the report.

EXECUTIVE SUMMARY

The President's Advisory Committee of Bowden Industries, Inc., requested a study to determine the reasons the company has had difficulty filling management positions and to find solutions to the problem. If Bowden is to continue on a path to future expansion, a concerted effort must be made to hire and develop the necessary managerial expertise.

Research

A thorough examination of hiring, training and development, management, and promotion practices was conducted. The research looked at why vacancies occurred, how they were filled, and the success rate of these hirings. The data suggest that management positions at Bowden require a high level of training, experience, and education and that there is no established route to provide this combination of preparedness for those entering management.

Findings

Findings showed that the majority of openings had to be filled from the outside because current staff had not been prepared to accept the greater responsibilities of management. The studies also revealed that those hired from outside required extensive training once they came onboard. The lack of inside promotions had a negative impact on morale and the on-the-job adjustment period for employees recruited from outside was very expensive.

Recommendations

The attached report recommends that the company create a formal, well-rounded training program under the guidance of an appointed director and a Management Education Committee for the purpose of training candidates for managerial positions.

iii

Introduction

The introduction of the report often covers the following. Refer to Figure 17-16. However, the order may be different than what is shown here.

- History or background that led up to the preparation of the report.
- Purpose for which the report was written, including the need or justification for the report.
- Method of gathering information, facts, and figures for the report.
- Scope of the report: what is covered and, if necessary, what is not covered.
- Definition of terms that may present problems for certain readers.

Body

The body of the report contains all of the information, data, and statistics you assemble. It is the "meat" of the report. Report types, formats, contents, and wording vary from one company to another, even by departments within the same organization. However, the basic principle for all writing—know your audience—is vital in deciding on the appropriate style and presentation. Factors that will help you determine the appropriate tone, language, and presentation for a report and content are discussed in the following sections.

Subject of the Report

If the topic you are writing about is very high level, such as a detailed proposal that will cost a lot of money, a conversational tone could take away from the objectivity that the reader might expect. You want to convince the reader you have thoroughly studied the matter and that your facts and figures are highly trustworthy. A more formal tone is more likely to achieve this goal.

If, on the other hand, you are writing a report on employee activities that boost morale and create a sense of team, a conversational tone would be appropriate. This tone is friendlier and will help set the stage for the theme of the report (boosting morale).

Your Place in the Organization

A report addressed to the company president is likely to be formal in tone. If you have a friendly relationship with your supervisor, a report you write for her or him may be more conversational.

Reader Bias

Sometimes bias on the part of the reader will influence your handling of the subject. Consider biases the reader might bring to the subject matter and develop content to address those. For example, if the reader is known to be very timid about innovations, your recommendation of new designs for existing products and packaging should concentrate on hard facts, rather than appealing to trends or popularity.

Figure 17-16. An introduction states the purpose of the report. A page number does not appear on the first page of the introduction.

INTRODUCTION

Bowden Industries, Inc., is often referred to as "a family that keeps outgrowing its home." This implies little planning, innovation, and management leadership in the company's twelve years of existence, which is simply not true. Product diversification, innovative marketing and manufacturing, and sound financial management all attest to the effective leadership with which the company has been blessed.

At the May 9 meeting of the President's Advisory Committee, the question was asked, "where will the managerial expertise needed for future growth and expansion come from?" The purpose of this report is to provide possible answers to that vital question.

History

In the past, Bowden has depended largely on universities and executive placement agencies for sources of managerial talent—and, of course, on its own promotion-from-within policy. By and large, these have been good sources of talent and, no doubt, will continue to be used. However, training and developing those new management hires has been through hit-or-miss, largely unstructured, on-the-job supervision. The results are mixed. Some people were well trained and quickly moved up when positions became available. Others languished and, seeing no opportunity for growth, left the company.

Scope

The term "management" in this report refers to all positions from first-line supervisors (classified as Levels 13 and 14 by the Human Resources Department) right on up to the top executive positions. No attention has been given to lower-level jobs in this report, although this is obviously a subject that deserves full exploration later.

Statement of Problem

During the past year, 44 vacancies occurred in management positions. Of that number, 22 were the result of retirement because of age or health, 13 resigned to accept positions in other companies, and the remaining nine were the result of newly created positions within the company.

It is interesting to find that 27 of the 44 openings had to be filled from the outside. In other words, only 17 employees were considered ready to accept the greater responsibilities of management. Actually, few of the people recruited from the outside were actually ready either (the unknown often looks better than the known); many required a long break-in period. Besides having a negative effect on employees who were denied promotion, outside recruiting and on-the-job adjustment are very expensive.

Reader Knowledge

Assess the level of knowledge the readers will bring and if there is variation within the audience. The amount of background information or explanation of the problem and the need to define terms depends on your assessment of the audience's prior knowledge. The higher the reader knowledge in the area covered by the report, the less explanation is needed.

Readability

Another aspect of preparing the body of your report is readability. Most reports contain several main sections and subsections. Select fonts and styles for these headings to guide the reader and make it easy to skim or scan the report for specific information. Headings are levels, beginning with the section opener title and continuing with the main heading and subheadings. Most narrative text can be divided into main and subtopics with no more than three levels of headings. Figure 17-17 shows examples of how to display these levels using the heading styles in Microsoft Word.

Conclusions and Recommendations

Conclusions or recommendations may come at the end of a formal report. **Conclusions** are the writer's summary of what the reader should take away from the report. **Recommendations** are actions the writer believes the reader should take. Both of these should follow logically from the information presented in the body of the report, as shown in Figure 17-18. If you make a leap in logic, you risk losing credibility with the reader.

Citations

If your report contains information from sources that you have researched, such as articles, books, Web sites, or reports or quotations from experts, these sources should be acknowledged in the report. **Citations** list the name of the author of the source, title, publisher, date of publication, and location of the publisher or online address. Citations may be listed in footnotes on the page where the reference occurs or in a bibliography at the end of the report, as shown in Figure 17-19. It is necessary to provide citations for both print and electronic sources.

Graphics

The text of a report can be greatly enhanced with the use of visuals in the form of tables, charts, graphs, drawings, or photographs. The choice of visuals depends on the subject matter. Always provide text references to graphics. Cite sources for graphics as well. Chapter 18 covers the development of graphics.

Other Elements

Complex reports may contain other elements that help the reader find information and understand the contents. These may include a list of illustrations or tables, glossary, and appendix.

5

JOB REQUIREMENTS

Job requirements for Bowden Industries are described in this document. Documentation follows for each level of career status.

Level 1 heading → **Senior Executives**

There are multiple levels of Senior Executives in the various departments of the company. The top senior position is the President, followed by the Chief Executive Officer and Chief Financial Officer.

Level 2 heading → **President**

The President leads the company and has multiple job responsibilities. Those responsibilities are as outlined in the following section.

Level 3 heading → **Responsibilities**

These responsibilities are extensive and not limited to the tasks listed in this document.

Figure 17-18. **Recommendations provide the writer's suggestions for a course of action.**

27

RECOMMENDATIONS

On the basis of this study, there would appear to be a definite need for a well-rounded education program at Bowden Industries, Inc. There are numerous possible methods of operating and conducting it. The following recommendations are offered.

1. Appoint a Director of Management Development, preferably a person with sound academic credentials (possibly a Ph.D.), teaching experience in management at the undergraduate and graduate levels, and broad business experience in supervision and management. The appointed person would report directly to the Executive Vice President or to the President.

2. Appoint a Management Education Committee, consisting of the top executive of each of the six divisions in the company and the Executive Vice President (ex officio). This committee would advise the Director of Management Development in planning and operating the program, using as many of the sources described in this report as feasible.

Figure 17-19.   Always cite works that are referenced in the report.

30

WORKS CITED

Arbor, Jonathan Cole, "Training That Works." *Train the Trainer (*March 20—) pp. 23–25.

Coletta, Nicole, *The Essentials of Performance Management*. New York: Future Publishing, 2010.

Newberg, Alexis, "Formal Training Programs at Bowden Industries," Report Submitted to the Executive Board, Bowden Training Department, 2009.

List of Illustrations or Tables

Your report may have numerous illustrations or tables. If this is the case, include a list at the front of the report with page references. This will aid readers in quickly finding information.

Glossary

If terminology in the report may be unfamiliar to some readers, a list at the end of the report to define important terms can be included. This list is called a glossary.

Appendix

Information that users might want to refer to, but is not integral to the body, may be included at the back of the report in an appendix. For example, if you conduct a written survey and report on its findings, you might provide the survey questionnaire in an appendix.

Binding

Formal reports are often bound to make the presentation polished and highly professional. Binding may be handled through a company's graphics department or an outside service. Office supply companies also sell a variety of binders that employees may use to bind their own reports. Very formal reports, particularly longer ones, might call for covers that are designed by graphics specialists and printed and bound by professional printing companies.

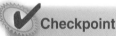 Checkpoint

1. What four elements appear on the title page?
2. What does the table of contents list?
3. What is an executive summary?
4. In which section is all of the information, data, and statistics presented?

Chapter 17 Review

Chapter Summary

Reports

- Reports are documents that communicate important information to individuals within or outside of the organization.
- Progress reports are completed on a periodic basis.

Planning Reports

- Planning a report is the most important stage of writing a report.
- Focus and organize your topic, develop an outline, and select an approach.

Writing Informal Reports

- Informal reports cover routine matters, are typically short, and generally do not require formal research.
- Informal reports can be written in the first person.
- An informal report generally has at least an introduction, body, and conclusion.
- There are several types of informal reports, including periodic, informal study, and idea and suggestion reports.

Researching Formal Reports

- Formal reports require gathering data and information through primary or secondary research.
- Primary research is data that you collect in preparation for the report.
- Secondary research is data and information already assembled and recorded by someone else.
- Sources must always be credited.
- Nearly all information is copyrighted and copying it without permission is called plagiarism.

Writing Formal Reports

- Formal reports are written in third person.
- Follow formatting directions as noted by your organization or requested by the person for whom you are writing the report.
- When creating a formal report, know the readers, make the purpose clear, make the report believable, and make the report readable.

Standard Parts of Formal Reports

- The parts of a formal report vary according to the purpose and topic.
- All formal reports should include a title page.
- A table of contents is needed to show the reader what is included in the report.
- An executive summary, also called a summary or abstract, is a summary of the main points.
- The body of the report contains all of the information, data, and statistics.
- Conclusions or recommendations may appear at the end of a report to suggest an outcome or course of action.
- Citations are the sources for information in the report.
- Many reports contain graphic elements, such as charts and tables.

 **Review**
Your Knowledge

1. What is a report?
2. List and describe the three major sections of an informal report.
3. What is a periodic report and how is it used?
4. What is the goal of a formal report?
5. What is primary research?
6. Define qualitative data.
7. What is secondary research and why is it important?

8. When conducting research online, why is it best to approach the information with skepticism?

9. Define plagiarism.

10. What is an executive summary?

 Apply
Your Knowledge

1. Research various types of business reports. Write a brief description of the general purpose for each type of report.

2. Design a report template based on the requirements of the situation below. Give the report a title and allow for other appropriate identification data.

> You are a marketing manager and have decided to ask the seven regional managers to keep a record of the expenses of each of their sales representatives and send you a report once a month. The information you want includes the name of the representative; car mileage, per-mile rate, and total cost; other transportation expenses (plane, bus, taxi); hotel and motel expenses; cost of meals; expenditures for the entertainment of customers; and miscellaneous expenses (telephone calls, postage, and tips).

3. Go to the library or use the Internet to locate a report produced by an agency of the US government, such as the Department of Transportation, Centers for Disease Control, US Census Bureau, or Department of Defense. Write a description of the report and its contents. Note how data are presented. Analyze the organization or the report and its effectiveness. Suggest any changes that you believe would make the report better.

4. Write an informal report based on the following situation. Use the three elements of an informal report to present the data and your recommendations.

> You are the general manager for Wiggins Stereo Outlet, a chain of six retail stores in and around Des Moines, Iowa. In the past six months there have been three burglaries and one fire. The president of the company, Amanda Wiggins, has asked you to evaluate three different alarm systems. Wiggins is concerned about cost, but primarily she wants a system with features that will make it an effective and efficient choice to protect the stores against both burglaries and fires. Each store is 5000 square feet, has two door entries, and two windows. None has a burglar alarm currently installed; all have battery-operated fire alarms. The data you gathered are shown in the table below.

	System Features	Cost
Allsafe	Window- and door-wired system, heat sensors, and fire sprinklers linked to an around-the-clock security service that automatically contacts police or fire	$24,000 for all six stores plus a monthly per-store service fee of $29.00
Prevention One	Window- and door-wired system and heat sensors that set off several loud alarms	$16,000 for all six stores
Strong Arm	Window- and door-wired system, heat sensors, and fire sprinklers linked to an around-the-clock security service that automatically contacts police or fire	$23,000 for all six stores plus a monthly per-store service fee of $39.00

5. Write a formal report for the following situation. Use all of the elements of a formal report to present the data and your conclusions or recommendations.

> You are an administrative assistant to the president of a company. The president has asked you to compare the sales, expenses, and profits for three competing companies and present the conclusions in a report. Select three similar companies, research each company's annual report, and gather the data needed for the report.

6. Write a description of each of the parts of a formal report. Describe the purpose of the part, where it appears in the report, and what information is typically included.

Practice
What You Have Learned

Access the *Fundamentals of Business Communication* Student Companion Web Site at www.g-wlearning.com/Communication. Download each data file for this chapter. Follow the instructions to complete a reading, writing, and grammar activity to practice what you have learned in this chapter.

Connections
Across the Curriculum

Social Studies. Research the history of copyright law. When did it begin? How has it changed over the years? Are copyrights necessary for social media? Write several paragraphs describing your findings.

Language Arts. Make a list of the various organizations or teams to which you belong. Can you suggest ideas that would help the group operate more efficiently? Ideas may include starting meetings on time, suggestions to do a fund-raiser for a good cause, or a campaign to recruit new members. Select an idea that appeals to you and present your ideas in a written report using the formatting standards presented in this chapter.

Build
Your Business Portfolio

After you have completed the portfolio activities in this class, you will have a solid start for your final portfolio. Remember, you will be adding and removing documents until you are ready to submit your portfolio for employment, school admission, or community service. If you are creating a print portfolio, you will need to organize your materials in an orderly and professional manner. Consult your instructor or another professional for guidance on assembling your materials.

1. Make certain all documents are error free.

2. Each document should be on clean, white, high-quality paper.

3. Provide a table of contents so that the person reviewing the portfolio will know what is included and where to find specific information.

4. If all of your pages are 8 1/2 × 11, you may want to place them in a binder or other type of notebook that will showcase your work. If your pages are of various sizes, find an appropriate container in which to place the documents.

Careers
Law, Public Safety, Corrections, and Security Careers and Communication

With strong interest in public safety and national security, careers in law, public safety, and corrections are increasingly in demand.

Keeping citizens and the country safe is the core mission of careers in this cluster. Career pathways include working in corrections, emergency and fire management, security, and protection, law enforcement, and legal services.

Good communication skills are crucial for someone pursuing a career in this cluster. One important communication skill is the art of conveying information through reports. Why is report writing important in this field of service?

Economic Research Project

The economic research project consists of writing a research paper and making an oral presentation of the paper. Good writing and communication skills are very important to present the research completed on the assigned topic. The research paper will be written and submitted before the actual event takes place. At the competition, the paper will be presented before a panel of judges. Review the specific guidelines and rules for this event for direction as to topics and props you will be allowed to use.

To prepare for the economic research project event, do the following.

1. Complete the research required for the topic. After the research is completed, apply your written persuasive skills that you learned in Chapter 10 as you write the paper.

2. Use your proofreading and editing skills to complete a final document. Review Chapter 7 for proofreading and editing direction.

3. Make the presentation professional by using the presentation techniques described in Chapter 10.

4. Review Chapter 12 for information on presentation skills to help you prepare your speech.

5. Practice, practice, practice. Practice speaking in front of your peers until you are comfortable.

Firefighters must have communication skills in order to maintain safety and effectively perform their duties.

Shutterstock

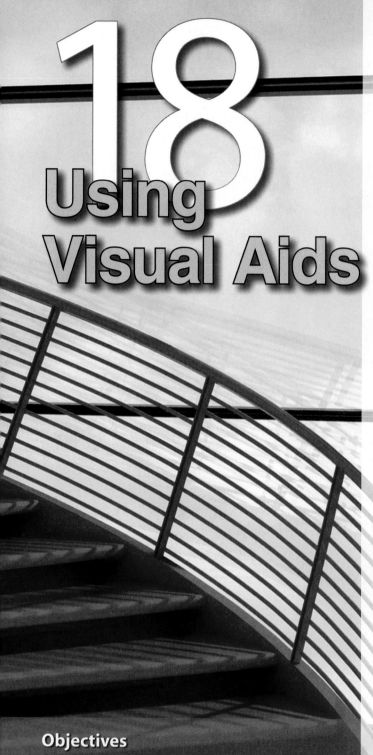

18
Using Visual Aids

One picture is worth a thousand words.

—Fred Barnard,
19th Century British illustrator

Everywhere, you can see visual aids that provide information. When you look up the statistics of your favorite athlete, the data are provided in a graphic form. If you are looking for driving directions, you will probably use a map or GPS display to guide you to your destination. These are visual aids.

As you create presentations, proposals, letters, reports, and other published documents, take advantage of opportunities to include visual aids to add clarity to the information. The recipients of the message will appreciate well-designed visual aids that help them understand the information you are presenting.

Objectives

When you complete Chapter 18, you will be able to:

Explain the importance of using visual aids.

Differentiate between types of informational graphics and when they are used.

Identify types of illustrations.

Describe techniques for properly using visual aids.

Terms

informational
  graphics
bar chart
line chart
pie chart
tables
organization chart
flowchart
illustrations
captions

Go Green

Have you noticed the Energy Star label that appears on products such as computers and other electronic devices? The EPA and the Department of Energy have created the Energy Star program to rate products. The Energy Star label guarantees the product meets a certain level of energy efficiency.

1. Go to the www.energystar.gov Web site. How does a product earn the Energy Star label?
2. Find the listing of Energy Star products on the Web site. Are there any products on this list that you currently own?

Types of Visual Aids

Visual aids are generally considered as either *informational graphics* or *illustrations*. These terms can be confusing to define because in common usage they are often applied interchangeably. In this textbook, an informational graphic presents data and may be referred to as a *table, chart,* and *graph*. Illustrations show images and may be referred to as *photos* or *drawings* (also called *line drawings*).

Visual aids add character to your documents and help illustrate important points that the reader might overlook or not understand. Therefore, it is important to carefully select the type and number of visual aids to create a proper balance. Generally, visual aids that are clear and to the point are better than more complex versions. If your document calls for presentation of data, informational graphics are a good choice as they depict facts and numbers in an easy-to-understand format. If your message describes objects, locations, or other tangible items, colorful photos and other illustrations may be more appropriate.

Clipart is available in most word processing and presentation software. Additionally, there are thousands of sources for freeware and for-purchase clipart on the Internet. However, just because these items are readily available does not mean you should use them. Visual aids should be relevant to your message. Clipart is a visual aid generally used to improve the visual appeal of the design of your document or presentation. Overuse of clipart quickly becomes distracting to the reader and can overpower the message of your communication.

Reading Prep

As you read this chapter, take notes on the important points you want to remember. Is this helpful in understanding the material?

Checkpoint

1. What are the two general types of visual aids?
2. What is the difference between informational graphics and illustrations?

Informational Graphics

There are a variety of informational graphics used in communication to present data. **Informational graphics** include graphs and charts (bar, line, pie, organizational, etc.), tables, and flowcharts, to name a few. The most commonly used informational graphics are bar, line, and pie charts. Professional-looking informational graphics can be easily created using various software, such as Microsoft Office. Refer to the help function of your software for specific directions.

Visual aids can improve written documents and presentations. Generally, visual aids are either informational graphics or illustrations.

Shutterstock

When you are creating a report or other written communication, carefully selected graphs or charts can be used to emphasize specific details that need attention or to visually break up a large block of text on a page. For example, if you are sending a printed or e-mailed newsletter that highlights growth in membership for the year, you might decide to include a graph that shows membership numbers. The graph can clearly show the growth and may be better understood than words. Or, you may choose to create visual interest within a report by breaking up the page with graphs showing specific details needing special attention. The graphs will help direct readers to the important details you want noted.

Informational graphics add character to your documents and help illustrate important points that the reader might overlook or not understand. It is important to carefully select the type and the number of informational graphics to create a proper balance. Too many informational graphics can be distracting rather than helpful, so careful planning is important.

Bar Chart

Bar charts are effective for showing a comparison of data. Generalizations about the data can be made just by looking at the size of the bars. Always provide enough information in your narrative to guide the reader in understanding the graph. Make sure the reader can understand if a tall bar is a positive or a negative.

When presenting data in a time series, such as years, months, hours, or minutes, a *vertical bar chart* is a good choice. The vertical bar chart in Figure 18-1 shows a comparison of computer sales during a four-month period. This chart makes it easy to visualize and understand the information.

Figure 18-1. **An example of a vertical bar chart.**

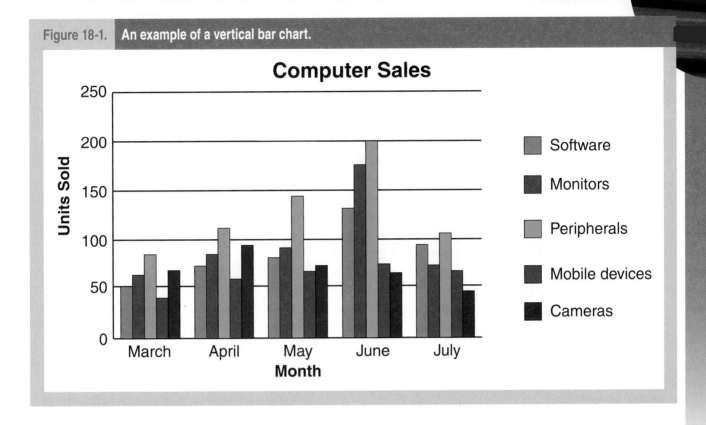

However, sometimes a *horizontal bar chart* is used because the information can be presented more clearly on the Y axis. The horizontal bar graph in Figure 18-2 makes it easy to compare the popularity of each movie over a three-month period.

Line Chart

A **line chart** is especially effective to show patterns, trends, and changes over time. Line charts show a series of points, representing measurements, that are connected by lines. The line chart in Figure 18-3 shows the fluctuation of the number of boys and girls participating in a sports program. Newspapers commonly use line charts to show the rise and fall of financial markets.

BUSINESS PROTOCOL

Office Behavior

Acceptable office behavior is required when working in a professional environment. Entire books have been written on this subject, but here are a few tips to keep in mind.

- Use your "inside voice."
- Be aware of your appearance and dress professionally.
- Keep personal calls and visits brief.
- If you bring food to your desk at lunch, be considerate about those around. Be aware of odors and clean up after yourself.

Make notes of other ideas on how to be a professional in an office situation.

Line charts are perhaps the most commonly used type of informational graphic. They are the best type of informational graphic to represent a trend or pattern. For example, you could collect data on the growth of your community's population over several years. A line chart can then be used to show the pattern of growth, either increasing or decreasing population.

Figure 18-2. An example of a horizontal bar chart.

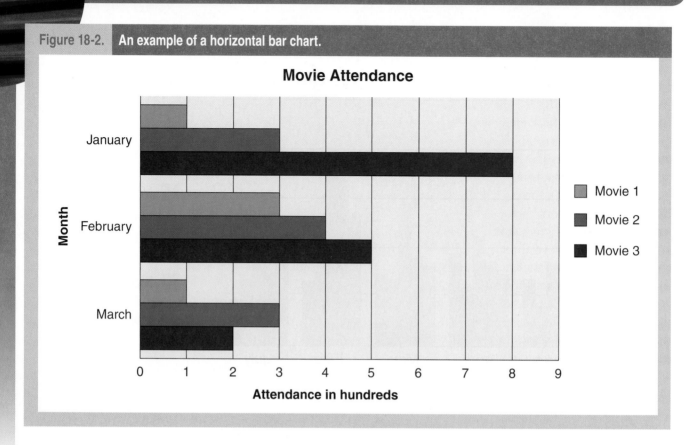

Figure 18-3. A line chart shows points of data connected by lines.

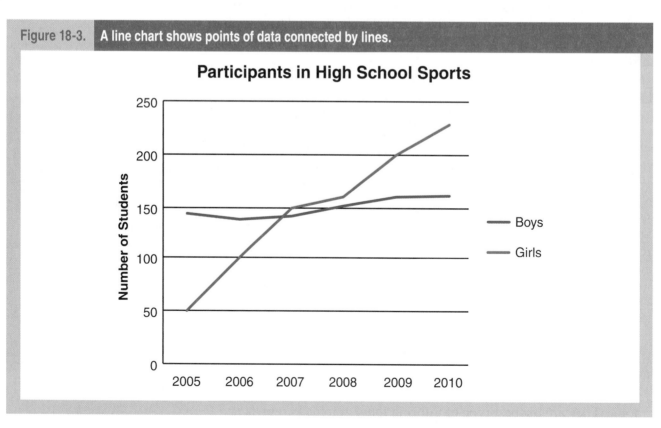

Pie Chart

A **pie chart** is most useful for showing the relationship of parts of something to the whole, Figure 18-4. For example, if you are looking at how your money is spent (food, car, gasoline, entertainment, etc.), the best way to represent this information is in a pie chart. A pie chart will show all of the parts (expenses) that make up the whole (your take-home salary) and will allow you to see where the bulk of your money is being spent.

Pie charts are attractive, but should be used only when appropriate for the example. Pie charts show a limited representation of information. They are only effective if there are fewer than seven pieces of the pie. Pie charts cannot show exact data and are difficult to use for comparing multiple data sets.

TEAMWORK

Form a team with two classmates. Discuss the type of informational graphics that would be useful for a business presentation on sales statistics. You will be showing sales for the year, increase or decrease from last year, and projected sales for the coming year. There are ten sales regions that will be represented in the report. Which type of informational graphic would be the best choice for presenting this information?

Table

A **table** presents detailed information in a series of columns and rows, as shown in Figure 18-5. Rows are horizontal and columns are vertical. Tables can communicate data in simple or complex form.

Tables are relatively easy to create in most software, such as Microsoft Office. Various formats may be used for a table, but always use a heading that is clear and descriptive. Design and layout are important for readability of a table, so be certain not to use too many rows or columns. Too many rows or columns may crowd the page. Label each column and row. Align the information in each column so that it is appealing to the eye.

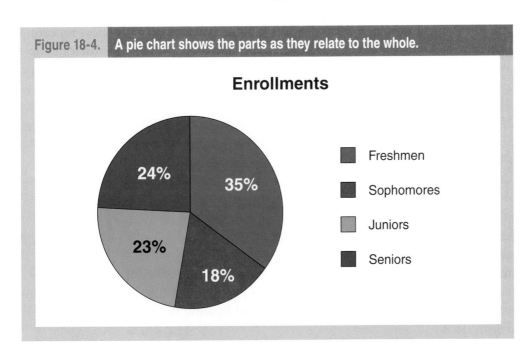

Figure 18-4. A pie chart shows the parts as they relate to the whole.

Enrollments

- 24%
- 35%
- 23%
- 18%

Freshmen
Sophomores
Juniors
Seniors

Figure 18-5.   An example of a table. This was created using a template from Microsoft Office.

Table 1: Projected Changes in Enrollments

Daycare Facility	New Students	Students Not Returning	Change in Enrollment
Ages 6–10			
Jack & Jill Daycare	110	103	+7
Sunset Daycare	223	214	+9
Cord Academy	197	120	+77
Montessori Academy	134	121	+13
The Child's Place	202	210	−8
Ages 0–5			
Jack & Jill Daycare	24	20	+4
Sunset Daycare	43	53	−10
Cord Academy	3	11	−8
Montessori Academy	9	4	+5
The Child's Place	53	52	+1
Total	998	908	90

Organizational Chart

Organizational charts show the communication protocol or structure within a company or organization. Most companies use organizational charts, or *org charts,* to show the chain of command. See Figure 18-6 for an example of an organizational chart. These charts show the reporting relationship between each level of manager and subordinate. Organizational charts only show reporting structure and employee titles. Organization charts are especially helpful for people who are new to the company to become acquainted with the organization.

There is no one set design or structure, but it is important to update the charts each time someone joins or leaves the organization or the organization structure changes. If organization charts are allowed to become outdated, they quickly lose their value. Regularly updating the charts is the best way to ensure the charts remain valuable.

Flowchart

Flowcharts are used to show steps or processes. They are helpful when step-by-step directions are needed. Flowcharts are commonly used in technical writing to provide directions for assembly of a product, such as how to put together a bookshelf or install software. Sometimes flowcharts are used in a company to show simple tasks, such as how to report a customer order. Various software can be used to create a professional-looking flowchart, as shown in Figure 18-7.

Figure 18-6. An organizational chart shows the structure of a company or organization.

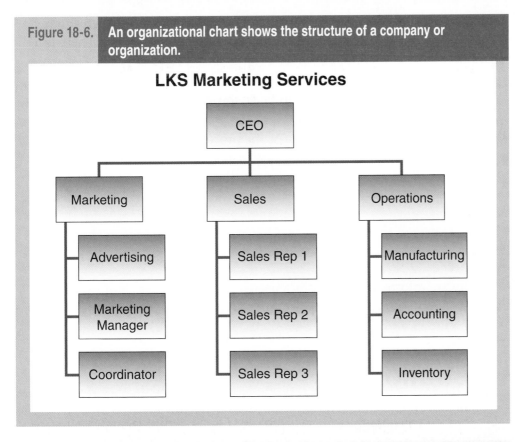

LKS Marketing Services

Figure 18-7. A flowchart shows a sequence of operation or logic.

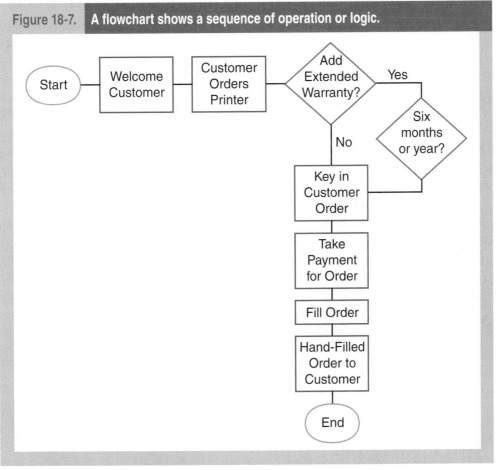

Flowcharts are commonly created using standard symbols. Each symbol is connected with at least one other symbol by directional arrows. There is a variety of symbols used in flowcharts.

- Circle, ovals, or rounded rectangles are used to start or end a process. These usually have words that indicate the start, such as "places order," or the end, such as "received order."

- Arrows indicate the flow of data or the process.

- Rectangles indicate processing steps, such as "order filled."

- Diamonds represent an IF-THEN decision. This includes "yes/no" or "true/false."

Checkpoint

1. Why are informational graphics used?
2. What are the three most commonly used informational graphics?

Illustrations

Some documents may require visual aids that show ideas as images instead of data. **Illustrations** include photos, drawings (line drawings), maps, and clipart. Illustrations can be used to enhance your writing or presentation.

- Photos show real life.
- Drawings are useful when describing buildings, layouts, and other situations where the reader needs to see how the narrative would appear in real life.
- Maps show geography or destinations.

As with informational graphics, use judgment when adding illustrations. Illustrations should be both clear and useful. Remember, if you use illustrations created by someone else, obtain permission to use the illustration and cite the source.

Illustrations can be used in many types of documents, from formal reports to handouts used in an informal presentation.

Shutterstock

In some cases, digital media, such as video or animation, can be used as an illustration. In order to use digital media, the information must be delivered electronically or in a presentation. See Chapter 13 for information on using digital media.

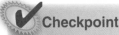

Checkpoint

1. When would an illustration be used instead of an informational graphic?
2. List four common types of illustrations.

CASE

Communicating Data

Suzette serves as historian of her local student organization. She has the responsibility of keeping an accurate report of awards that members have earned throughout the year. After the last competition, she put all of the information in a table to show the chapter's accomplishments.

Tomas, president of the student organization, asked her for the information. Tomas has asked Ms. Farley, the school principal, for funding so that members of the organization might go to National competition. She would like to see data showing the success of the student organization over the last three years at district, state, and national competitions. Suzette gave Tomas this table.

Chapter Awards (20-- through 20--)

	District	State	National
Individual	9	5	3
Team	6	4	2
Chapter	3	3	3

1. Is the information presented well? If not, how could Suzette have better represented it?

2. If Tomas presents this report to Ms. Farley, what could he do with the data to support his request to attend the National competition?

Techniques That Work

You need to plan which type of visual aid will enhance your message and communicate what is important for the reader to understand. Should you use an informational graphic or an illustration and which type? See Figure 18-8 for examples of when different types of visual aids are used. Planning will help you decide how to select and organize the visual aids to complement the text. It will also help you determine the level of detail to include within the informational graphic or illustration.

Remember, not all information lends itself to the use of a visual aid. Always look at the information and decide if a visual aid will add value to the communication or more clearly represent the information. To help you decide if your information should be represented in a visual aid, ask the following questions.

- Will the visual aid help to quickly and directly present the data?

- Will the visual aid highlight the most important facts?

- Will the visual aid help the reader understand the data?
- Will the visual aid help to convince the audience?
- Will the visual aid help the audience to remember the data?

Good visual aids will accurately represent information and get the attention of the audience. Visual aids should never take away from the message. They should complement or enhance the message being communicated.

Creating the Plan

As you are creating your document, make notes about which points would benefit from a visual aid. Keep a list of your ideas by topic and type of visual aid that would be appropriate. These notes will help you save time selecting visual aids when your writing is complete.

The steps for selecting visual aids are similar to the steps in the writing process.

- Identify the purpose. What do you want to accomplish with the visual aids? Will the visual aids add clarity to the subject or add interest?
- Identify the audience. Does the reader prefer basic, no-frills information or flashy visual aids?
- Identify the situation. Are you preparing a report that contains a lot of numbers or a proposal that needs flair?
- Select the main ideas. What does the audience need to know?
- Determine the organization. What is the best order in which to present the visual aids?
- Determine what visual aids are needed. How is the material being delivered, in print, electronically, or as a presentation?

Figure 18-8.	This illustration describes how various visual aids are typically used.
Visual Aid	**Used to Show**
Bar chart	Comparison of data
Line chart	Patterns, trends, and changes over time
Pie chart	Relationship of the parts of a whole
Table	Detailed information in a series of columns and rows
Organizational chart	Communication protocol or structure within a company or organization
Flowchart	Steps or processes
Map	Geography or destinations
Drawing	Details
Photo	Real life

Keep in mind that too many visual aids can be distracting to the reader. It is important to strike the correct balance of visual aids and text so the message is clear, yet the visual aids have an impact.

Identifying Visual Aids

Each visual aid should be assigned a *figure number* to identify and reference it in the text. If you have more than one visual aid (table, figure, chart, etc.), number each one accordingly. For example, numbering may be Figure 1, Figure 2, etc., or Table 1, Table 2, etc. If there are multiple chapters, visual aids are typically numbered noting the chapter first and the position of the figure as the second number, such as Figure 1-2 and Figure 2-2.

Along with the figure number, accurate captions and titles are important to identify the visual in the text. A **caption** is descriptive text that appears with the visual aid to identify its purpose. The caption is usually preceded by the figure number. The captions should be able to answer *who, what, where, when, why,* and, sometimes, *how.* Titles are generally used as headings on informational graphics to identify the content.

Source lines, also called credit lines, are used to identify the owner of the visual aid, if it is other than the organization creating the document or presentation. A source line can appear as a note below the visual aid, as shown in Figure 18-9.

Figure 18-9. A source line indicates where the informational graphic or illustration originated.

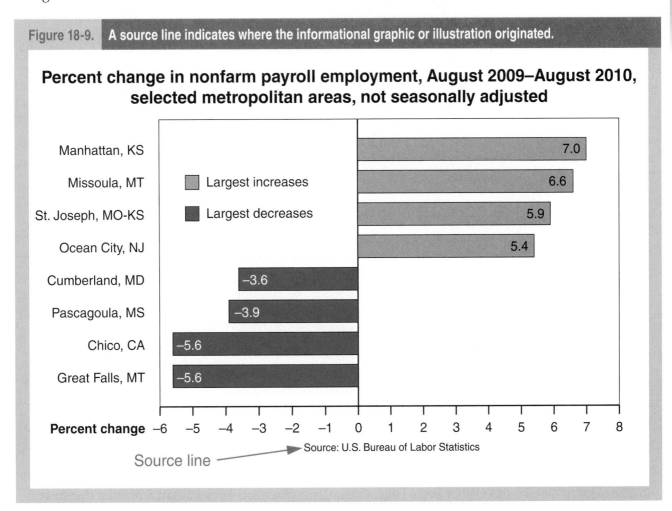

Percent change in nonfarm payroll employment, August 2009–August 2010, selected metropolitan areas, not seasonally adjusted

Be sure visual aids are used ethically. For example, it is easy to present data in a way that leads the reader to believe a larger or smaller difference exists between data.

Shutterstock

Creating and Placing Visual Aids

Professional-looking visual aids can be easily created within your document using your application software. While technology allows you to easily create visual aids, overuse of design elements will make the visual aid hard to read. This can lead to misinterpretation of the data or information. Avoid overuse of "bells and whistles," such as 3D effects and colors. Also, over-labeling the visual aid or trying to include too much data in one visual aid will detract from your message.

A visual aid within written communication should be placed as close as possible to the text that references it. This is the same rule whether the document is a report, newsletter, letter, or memo. The rule of thumb for placement of a visual aid within text is to be sure there is enough white space so that the page does not look crowded. Be sure to allow for white space around the visual aid (above, below, left, and right) so its content can be easily seen by the reader. See Figure 18-10 for an example of a well-placed visual aid.

Keeping Visual Aids Ethical

It is important to be aware of how you are presenting data so as not to be misleading. As you are deciding how to present your information, make sure the data are presented in a realistic and appropriate manner. It is unethical to present data in a way that leads the audience to misinterpret the details. Never distort or generalize information.

It is easy to make honest errors when you are creating informational graphics. As the creator, you sometimes lose track of objectivity. To make sure your data are accurately presented, ask for feedback from someone before publishing the message.

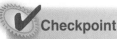

Checkpoint

1. What is the first step for selecting visual aids?
2. What is a caption?
3. What is the rule of thumb for placing a visual aid in a written document?

Figure 18-10. In a written document, the visual aid should be placed as close as possible to the text that references it.

5

Job Requirements

Job requirements for Bowden Industries are described in this document. Documentation follows for each level of career status.

Senior Executives

There are multiple levels of Senior Executives in the various departments of the company. The top senior position is the Chief Executive Officer, followed by the President and Chief Financial Officer, as shown in Figure 1-1.

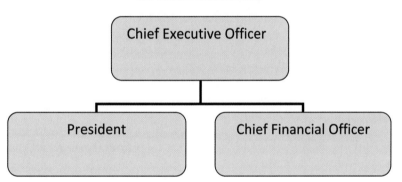

Bowden Industries

Figure 1-1
Organizational chart.

Chief Executive Officer

The Chief Executive Officer leads the company and has multiple job responsibilities. Those responsibilities are as outlined in this section.

Responsibilities

These responsibilities are extensive and not limited to the tasks listed in this document.

Chapter 18 Review

Chapter Summary

Types of Visual Aids

- There are two general types of visual aids: informational graphics and illustrations.
- Informational graphics are used to present data.
- Illustrations show images.

Informational Graphics

- Types of informational graphics include graphs and charts, tables, and flowcharts.
- The three most commonly used informational graphics are bar, line, and pie charts.

Illustrations

- Illustrations show images.
- In some cases, digital media can be used as an illustration.

Techniques That Work

- Choose a visual aid that will enhance your message and communicate what is important for the reader to understand.
- Using steps similar to the writing process will help you to plan your visual aids.
- Create visual aids that are simple and easy to read, but accurately depict the data or information.

Review
Your Knowledge

1. What are the two general types of visual aids?
2. Explain the importance of using visual aids to communicate.
3. Describe information graphics.
4. Explain the difference between a bar chart and a line chart.
5. What does a pie chart show the reader?
6. When is a table the appropriate visual aid?
7. What does an illustration present?
8. How should visual aids be numbered?
9. What is a rule of thumb for placing visual aids in a written document?
10. How do ethics play a role in deciding how to use visual aids?

Apply
Your Knowledge

1. Investigate the types of visual aids used in business. Identify several types of informational graphics (charts, graphs, etc.) and illustrations (photos, drawings, etc.). Write a paragraph about each describing how it is typically created.
2. For each situation below, identify which type of informational graphic should be used and explain why.
   A. statistical data showing the population growth for the last five years from the US Census Bureau
   B. concession stand sales for each home game throughout the football season
   C. personal expenses for the month of April
3. Identify three examples where an illustration may be used as a visual aid, one each for photo, drawing, and map. Write at least one paragraph for each describing what you would show in the visual aid, how it would be used, and why it would enhance the message.
4. The following visual aid shows the favorite colors of one elementary class in a neighboring community.
   A. Is this an appropriate representation of the data? Why or why not?
   B. Can the data be misinterpreted? Why or why not?

C. Are there ethical concerns with representing these data using this graphic? Why or why not?

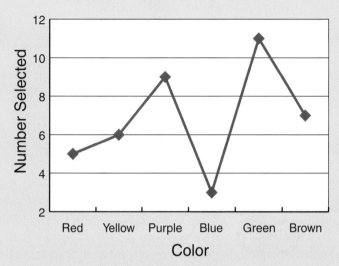

Language Arts. Prepare a written report of your findings from your research on sports teams. Include the informational graphic in the body of your report. Use an appropriate figure number and caption as you reference the informational graphic in your paragraphs.

Build
Your Business Portfolio

Your ePortfolio may be placed on a CD/DVD, your personal Web site, or other type of digital media. The important thing to remember is that you must organize the materials in an orderly and professional manner. You will need to create a structure on the digital media that will make it easy for the reader to find the information that is important to the position for which you are applying. Consult your instructor or another professional for guidance on assembling your materials. You may also find some helpful ideas by researching ePortfolio on the Web.

- Make certain that all documents are error free.

- Provide a table of contents so that the person reviewing the portfolio will know what is included and where to find specific information. For example, if your ePortfolio will be on your personal Web site, the home page can serve as the table of contents with links to each important piece of information.

- Create a structure for the information that is easy to follow and comprehensive. Remember, how you present the information in your ePortfolio also showcases your talents.

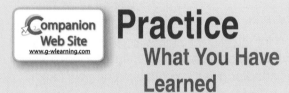

Practice
What You Have Learned

Access the *Fundamentals of Business Communication* Student Companion Web Site at www.g-wlearning.com/Communication. Download each data file for this chapter. Follow the instructions to complete a reading, writing, and grammar activity to practice what you have learned in this chapter.

Connections
Across the Curriculum

Math. Research three sports teams (baseball, basketball, football, soccer, etc.) for their wins and losses over the past five years. Use the Internet to help with your search. Collect the data and put the information into a spreadsheet. Create an informational graphic that shows your findings.

Careers
Finance Careers and Communication

Finance careers involve the management and use of money. The career pathways in this cluster include financial and investment planning, business financial management, banking, and insurance. Careers in finance exist in all parts of the economy.

Strong presentation skills, both written and oral, are key qualities for these workers. Professionals who work in finance present data to clients and colleagues on a regular basis. Describe a situation in which someone in finance would have a need to use graphics in a written report.

Event Prep

Graphic Design Promotion

The graphic design promotion competitive team will consist of specific tasks in completing a promotional flyer by a team. After your team has created the content for the flyer, the information must be edited and proofread so that it is grammatically correct and error free. Review the specific guidelines and rules for this event for each deliverable that will be required. This event will feature the creative abilities of your team to design a brochure as well as require strong written communication skills to convey the message.

To prepare the finished material for this event, do the following.

1. Review the section Writing Stage in Chapter 7. This chapter gives you direction on how to edit and revise the material.

2. Review the section Post-Writing Stage in Chapter 7. Techniques for proofreading are discussed in this section.

3. Study the proofreading checklist in Chapter 7. This will help you master the process and understand the techniques of proofreading.

Glossary

A

abbreviation: A shortened form of a word or letters used to stand for a word or term.

active listening: Fully participating as you process what other people say.

active reading: Actively processing the words, phrases, and sentences you read; requires you to be involved and to do something in response to the words.

active voice: Indicates the subject of the sentence performs the action when action verbs are used; the subject, or noun, of the sentence is doing the action.

adjective: Describes a noun or a pronoun and may provide details that give you a better understanding of the person or thing.

adjective pronoun: An adjective that acts as a pronoun.

adverb: A word that describes a verb, adjective, clause, or another adverb; adverbs tell how, when, or where something is done and can also limit or qualify a description.

analogy: A comparison of two unlike things based on a particular aspect each have in common.

animation: The representation of motion with graphics or in text.

antecedent: The word replaced by the pronoun.

apostrophe: A punctuation mark used to form possessive words and contractions.

application form: Typically printed or available online, it asks for personal and professional history that an applicant must submit in order to be considered for a job.

article: An adjective that limits the noun or pronoun it modifies.

autocratic: A leadership style in which the leader determines policy, procedures, tasks, and responsibility of each team member or employee within the company.

B

background check: A look into the personal data about you that are available from the government.

balance: An arrangement of elements to create a feeling of equality across the product.

bar chart: Effective means of expressing data; generalizations about the data can be made just by looking at the size of the bars.

barrier: Anything that prevents clear, effective communication.

bias: A prejudice or personal or unreasoned distortion of judgment.

bias-free words: Neutral words that impart neither a positive nor negative message.

blind copy: A notation used at the end of a memo or letter to indicate another recipient has received a copy without knowing the current recipient has a copy.

block-style letter: Formatted so all lines are flush with the left-hand margin; no indentions are used.

blogs: Web sites maintained by an individual who posts topics or opinions.

body: The message of a letter.

body language: The expression of nonverbal messages through gestures, facial expressions, and other body actions or posture.

boilerplate: Standard language developed by a company for correspondence as well as scripts for verbal communication by customer service departments.

C

camera shots: Different angles, sizes, and locations used in videography to serve various purposes.

canvas size: The area in which the video or image will be displayed.

capitalization: An uppercase letter (B) rather than lowercase (b); capital letters signal the beginning of a new sentence and identify important words in titles and headings.

captions: Descriptive text that appears with a visual aid to identify its purpose.

cell phones: Telephones that allow the user to move around and communicate without a landline.

chronological résumé: A résumé in which the order of presentation is reverse chronological order, with the most recent employer listed first.

citations: List the name of the author of the source, title, publisher, date of publication, and location of the publisher or online address; they may be listed in footnotes on the page where the reference occurs or in a bibliography at the end of the report.

clause: A group of words within a sentence that has a subject and a predicate.

cliché: Overused, commonplace, or trite phrases.

collective noun: Refers to a group or unit that contains more than one person, place, or thing.

colon: An internal punctuation mark that introduces an element in a sentence or paragraph.

color depth: The number of distinct colors that can be represented in a computer-based image and is based on the number of bits used to define a color.

comma: A punctuation mark used to separate elements in a sentence.

common noun: Describes a person, place, or thing in general terms.

communication: The process of sending and receiving messages that convey information, ideas, feelings, and beliefs.

communication process: A series of actions on the part of the sender and the receiver of the message; the parts include the sender, message, channel, receiver, translation, and feedback.

comparative adjectives: Compare two people or things.

comparative adverbs: Compare two actions, conditions, or qualities by adding *er* or more to the original adverb.

complete predicate: Includes the verb and other information that tells what the subject is or does.

complete subject: The simple subject and other words that describe it.

complex response: A response that is hard to understand because of length or language barriers.

complex sentence: A sentence that has an independent clause and one or more dependent clauses.

complimentary close: The sign-off for the letter in which only the first letter of the first word is capitalized.

compound-complex sentence: A sentence that has two independent clauses and one or more dependent clauses.

compound predicate: Contains two or more verbs joined by *and* or some other conjunction; both verbs describe action or state of being for the subject.

compound sentence: A sentence that has two independent clauses joined by a conjunction, such as *and* or *but*.

compound verb: A compound verb consists of two or more verbs in the same sentence; the verbs can be main verbs and helping verbs or contain two or more main verbs and no helping verbs.

compressed files: Computer files that may contain multiple native-format files, such as documents or photographs, and are much smaller in size than the uncompressed versions; they must be decompressed using extraction utility software to access the data they contain.

conclusions: The writer's summary of what the reader should take away from the report.

condescending: To assume an air of superiority.

conference calling: Verbal communication with three or more people on a telephone call.

confirmation message: A typical routine informational message written to confirm a verbal agreement made with a customer, client, or colleague.

conjunction: A word that connects other words, phrases, or sentences.

conjunctive adverbs: Words like *however* and *also* that connect or introduce clauses or phrases in a sentence.

connotation: A word's meaning apart from what it explicitly names or describes.

context: The environment or setting in which something occurs or is communicated; context is the other words or situation that surround a word, action, or idea and helps clarify meaning.

contraction: A shortened form of a word or term or a combined form of two separate words.

coordinate adjectives: Two or more related adjectives that appear before a noun or pronoun and equally modify it.

coordinating conjunctions: Join two or more sentence elements that are of equal importance; they include *and, or, not, but,* and *yet.*

copy notation: Appears below the signature on a letter to indicate that it has been sent to individuals other than the current recipient.

copyright: Acknowledges ownership of a work and specifies that only the owner has the right to sell or use the work or to give permission for someone else to sell or use it; the exclusive rights awarded to the author or creator of an original work.

correlative conjunctions: Two or more words that work together to connect words, phrases, or clauses in a sentence such as *neither/nor* or *rather/than.*

courtesy response: Written confirmation that a message was received and action was taken.

cover message: A letter or e-mail sent with a résumé to introduce yourself and summarize your reasons for applying for a job.

culture: Shared beliefs, customs, practices, and social behavior of a particular group or nation.

D

dangling participle: A writing error in which a participle phrase modifies nothing or the wrong person or object.

dash: A punctuation mark that separates elements in a sentence or signals an abrupt change in thought; also known as an em dash.

date: Consists of the month, day, and year; in a letter the month is spelled in full, the day is written in figures and followed by a comma, and the year is full and consists of numbers.

decoding: Translating the message once it has been received.

definite article: Refers to a specific person or thing; a common definite article is *the.*

democratic: A leadership style in which the leader encourages all members of a group participate and share ideas equally.

demographics: Information about a group of people.

demonstrations: Presenting an audience with visuals to explain how something works or is done.

demonstrative adjective: Typically refers to a person or thing in a general way such as *this, that,* or *those.*

demonstrative pronouns: Identify or direct attention to a noun or pronoun.

dependent clause: A clause that requires the rest of the sentence to provide a complete thought.

digital media: The integration of graphics, videos, and audio files.

diplomacy: Tactful handling of a situation to avoid offending the reader or arousing hostility.

direct: To give instruction or guidance.

direct approach: A method for organizing information in which the topic is followed by descriptive details; it is a very readable format often used in business writing.

directions: Routine business messages often presented in the form of a list; they must be carried out in a specific order so that the task may be completed successfully.

direct object: Someone or something that receives the action of the verb.

diversity: Difference or variety.

dolly: Moving the camera toward or away from the scene.

downloading: The process of saving files from a Web site or file transfer protocol (FTP) site.

E

editing: A form of revision that is focused on sentence construction, wording, and clarity of ideas.

Electronic User's Bill of Rights: Modeled after the United States Bill of Rights and originally proposed by Frank W. Connolly of American University in 1993, it details the rights and responsibilities of both individuals and institutions regarding the treatment of digital information; its four articles include Individual Rights, Individual Responsibilities, Rights of Educational Institutions, and Institutional Responsibilities; it is not legally binding, but rather guidelines for appropriate usage.

e-mail: A message that is created, sent, and received digitally (electronically).

employment verification: A process through which the information you provided about your employment history is checked to verify it is correct.

enclosure notation: Alerts the reader to materials that are included in the mailing along with the letter; the word *Enclosure* should be capitalized and italicized; list multiple enclosures or indicate the number of enclosures if there is more than one.

encoding: Putting the message into the format it will be sent to the receiver.

encourager: An informal team member role who is positive and influences others to be positive when challenges occur.

end user licensing agreement (EULA): Licenses that define how audio and visual material can be used.

enunciate: Clear pronunciation of words.

enunciation: Clearly and distinctly pronouncing syllables and sounds.

ethics: The principles of what is right and wrong that help people make decisions.

etiquette: The art of using good manners in any situation.

euphemisms: A word that expresses unpleasant ideas in more pleasant terms.

evasive: Avoiding giving a direct answer.

exclamation point: A punctuation mark used to express strong emotion and appears at the end of a sentence or after an interjection that stands alone.

executive summary: Summarizes the main points in the report.

F

facilitator: A team member role who helps the team work through each step of completing a task to come up with a solution.

fair use: A doctrine related to copyright law that allows for limited use of copyrighted material.

filtering: A technique by which a special effect is applied to an image.

first person: Refers to someone who is speaking or writing.

flowchart: Used to show steps or processes; they are helpful when step-by-step directions are needed.

focus group: A small group of people with which the interviewer conducts a discussion to gather answers to a prepared set of questions.

footage: Recorded video.

formal communication: Sharing of information in which specific protocol or rules of etiquette must be followed.

formal report: A report supported by formal research or information gathering that focuses on a main topic broad enough to be divided into subtopics for complete and clear coverage.

formal team: Teams created for a specific and organized purpose and have an appointed leader and members are chosen based on talents and skills.

formatting: The placement and style of the type on the page.

for-purchase software: Software you must buy to use, although you can often download a timed or limited-use demo.

four C's of communication: Standards that apply to all writing processes that help to produce written work that achieves clear, concise, courteous, and correct communication.

freeware: Fully functional software that can be used forever without purchasing it.

frequently asked questions (FAQ): A component of a company's Web page that provides answers to common customer questions.

functional résumé: Lists work experience according to categories of skills or achievements, rather than by employer.

future perfect tense: Formed by adding *will have* to the past tense; it expresses that something will happen over or during a certain time.

future tense: Indicates that the action or state of being will occur at a later time.

G

gerund: A verb form used as a noun that is formed by adding *ing* to the present tense of a verb.

global society: A society in which goods and services are bought and sold both inside and outside of the country of origin.

graphic: Any visual aid, informational graphic, or illustration.

guide words: Words such as *DATE, TO, FROM,* and *SUBJECT* that appear at the top of memos.

H

handouts: Printed materials distributed to the audience; also called *leave-behinds.*

harmony: A design principle that creates unity in a presentation.

headings: Words and phrases that introduce and organize sections of text.

hearing: A physical process in which sound waves reach your ears and signals are sent to your brain.

helping verbs: Verbs that work with a main verb to show action.

homonym: A word that sounds the same as another word, but the meaning and spelling of the two words differ.

hyphen: A punctuation mark used to separate parts of compound words, numbers, or ranges.

I

identity theft: A form of fraud that occurs when somebody takes your personal information and pretends to be you in order to make credit card purchases, withdraw funds from your accounts, or obtain other benefits to which you are entitled.

illustrations: Photos, drawings (line drawings), maps, and clipart that can be used to enhance your writing or presentation.

imperative mood: Denoted by the speaker or writer, it states a command or direct request.

impromptu speaking: A situation in which you did not have advance notice to prepare your speech or presentation.

indefinite article: Typically refers to a person or thing in a general way such as *a* or *an.*

indefinite pronouns: Refer to an object or person that has been identified earlier or does not need specific identification.

independent clause: A clause that presents a complete thought and could stand alone as a separate sentence.

indicative mood: Denoted by the speaker or writer, it expresses a straightforward statement or poses a question.

indirect approach: A method for organizing information in which details come before the main idea of the paragraph; often useful when one must present bad news to the reader.

indirect object: Names something or someone for whom the action of the verb is performed.

industry language: Language specific to a line of work or area of expertise.

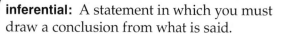

inferential: A statement in which you must draw a conclusion from what is said.

infinitive: Comprised of the word *to* and a verb in its simple present form, such as *to make;* an infinitive or infinitive phrase can serve as a noun, adjective, or adverb.

informal communication: Casual sharing of information with no customs or rules of etiquette involved.

informal report: Documents that do not require formal research or documentation; are typically short and commonly a part of the regular work routine.

informal study report: Provides information that is gathered by the writer through methods other than formal research, such as reading related documents, conducting informal interviews, reviewing competitive products, or making observations after visiting a site or attending a meeting.

informal team: Teams that come together usually for a social purpose.

informational graphic: Used in communication to present data, including graphs, charts, and tables.

inside address: The name, title, and address of the recipient.

instant messaging (IM): Participants conduct a conversation by keying and sending responses, rather than talking or using video; the conversation usually takes place in real time, but the messages can be stored and retrieved at a later time.

instructions: Routine business messages often presented in the form of a list; they may be carried out in any order.

intellectual property: All original work, whether it is in print, on the Internet, or in any other form or media, that is protected by copyright laws.

intercultural differences: Regional variations in culture; different regions of a country may have their own sets of values, behaviors, ideas, and even variations in language (known as *dialect*).

interjection: A word that expresses strong emotion, such as surprise, fear, anger, excitement, or shock; it can also be used as a command.

internal punctuation: Punctuation marks used within a sentence.

interrogative pronouns: Pronouns that are used to ask a question and typically do not have a known antecedent, such as *whose, what,* or *whom.*

intonation: The rise and fall in the pitch of your voice.

J

job interview: The employer's opportunity to probe the details contained in your résumé and to assess you as an individual.

K

keywords: Words and terms that specifically relate to a particular objective.

L

laissez-faire: French for "let do" or "let it be"; the leader using this leadership style allows each group member to complete his/her task without supervision.

layering: The process of building an image by putting different parts of the image on different levels.

layout: The relationship of the text to white space.

leader: People who can motivate and direct others and who can improve a process or situation.

leadership: The ability to motivate or guide others.

leadership style: The way in which a manager or team leader leads employees or team members; there are three basic leadership styles: laissez-faire, democratic (or participatory), and autocratic.

licensing agreement: A contract that gives one party permission to market or produce the product or service owned by another party in return for a fee or royalty.

lighting: Illuminating a scene for photography or videography.

lighting angle: The slope of a light's beam.

lighting ratio: The difference in brightness between the lightest area of a shot and the darkest.

line chart: Shows a series of points, representing measurements, that are connected by lines; are especially effective to show patterns, trends, and changes over time.

linking verbs: Verbs that show a state of being when they relate a subject to a subject complement.

listening: An intellectual process that combines hearing with evaluating.

literal: The speaker means exactly what the words indicate.

M

malware: A program intended to damage, destroy, or steal the data on a computer system.

masking: A way to give the appearance of change to an image without actually altering the original image.

master slide: A slide containing design elements that are applied to a particular set of slides or all slides in a presentation.

memos: Hardcopies used for intra-office communication.

milestones: Important dates that need to be met to keep the project moving forward.

mixed punctuation: A style in which a colon is placed after the salutation and a comma after the complimentary close.

modified-block-style letter: Places the date, complimentary close, and signature to the right of the center point of the letter; all other elements of the letter are flush with the left margin.

modulation: Changing the emphasis of words by raising and lowering your voice.

monotone: Speech that is delivered with the same intonation, stress, pitch, and volume.

movement: The appearance of action.

N

netiquette: A set of guidelines, or etiquette, for appropriate behavior on the Internet, including e-mail.

nominative case: Pronouns that are used as the subject in a sentence or as subject complements.

nonrestrictive clause: Provides information that may be helpful, but is not essential to the meaning of the sentence.

nonverbal communication: The expression or delivery of messages through actions, rather than words.

notations: Notes that appear at the bottom of the memo and are used to indicate specific things to the reader, such as additional recipients.

noun: A word that names a person, place, or thing.

O

objective case: Pronouns that are used as direct objects, indirect objects, or objects of prepositions.

objectivity: A point of view that is free of personal feelings, prejudices, or interpretations.

online meetings: A remote meeting conducted through desktop sharing and mark up tools; each participant can make suggestions and changes to presentations stored on the leader's computer.

open punctuation: A style in which there is no punctuation after the salutation or complimentary close.

oral presentation: A speech, address, or presentation given to a group.

organization chart: Shows the communication protocol or structure within a company or organization.

outline: A method of organizing information that helps clarify the relationship between ideas and sections of content; it helps to present the proper information and its sequence.

P

pagers: Electronic-communication devices that let the user know there is a message waiting.

pan: Showing what is to the left or the right of the current view.

paralanguage: The attitude you project with the tone and pitch of your voice.

parallel structure: A method of writing in which similar elements are expressed in a consistent way or using the same pattern.

parentheses: Punctuation marks used to enclose words or phrases that clarify meaning or give added information.

parliamentary procedures: Rules for conducting a meeting, where the majority rules, but the minority is respected.

passive listening: Casually listening to the speaker; you may not *hear* everything that is said.

passive voice: Indicates the subject of the sentence is acted upon when action verbs are used; the subject, or noun, of the sentence receives the action.

past participle: Indicates that action has been completed.

past perfect tense: Formed by adding *had* to the past tense, it expresses that something has happened over or during a certain time.

past tense: Indicates that the action or state of being has already occurred.

peers: Persons of equal standing or work position.

period: A punctuation mark used at the end of a declarative sentence, or a sentence that makes a statement.

periodic report: Generally provides the status of a project, reports facts and figures over a specified period, or summarizes an ongoing activity.

permanent compound: Compound words that always have a hyphen.

personal space: The physical space you place between yourself and others.

perspective: An artistic technique that creates the illusion of depth on a two-dimensional surface.

persuade: To convince a person to take the course of action you propose.

persuasive message: A message whose primary goal is to convince the reader to take a certain course of action.

phrase: A group of words that act together to convey meaning in a sentence.

pie chart: A chart that shows all of the parts that make up the whole; it is useful for showing the relationship of parts of something to the whole.

pitch: The highness or lowness of a sound.

pixels: Picture elements that record the image; a higher number of pixels will create a better quality image.

plagiarism: The illegal and unethical act of claiming somebody else's material as your own.

podcast: A series of digital media files, released at regular intervals, that contain information related to a specific topic; the files may be audio or video and can be retrieved by users at their convenience.

positive adjectives: Describe, but do not compare, people or things.

positive adverbs: Describe, but do not compare, actions or qualities.

possessive case: Pronouns that show ownership.

possessive nouns: Indicate ownership by the noun or an attribute of the noun.

postscript: Means "after writing" and is information included after the signature.

post-writing stage: The final edit of the document; after its final revision, the document is carefully proofread to detect any remaining errors.

predicate: Describes an action or state of being for the subject.

preposition: A word that connects or relates its object to the rest of the sentence; examples include *to, at, beside, during,* and *under.*

present participle: A verb form that indicates action is in progress or ongoing.

present perfect tense: Formed by adding *have* or *has* to the past tense, it expresses that something happens over or during a certain time.

present tense: Indicates that the action or state of being takes place now.

presentation notes: Used during presentations to keep track of where you are in the presentation and to remind yourself of points should you forget anything.

presumption: Something believed based on probable or assumed reliability.

prewriting stage: The time before one begins writing used to think about the topic and purpose, plan content, and conduct the necessary research.

primary readers: Readers directly involved in the purpose for writing.

primary research: Conducted by the writer in preparation for writing a report.

prior knowledge: Experience and information you already possess.

prioritize: To rank items in order from most to least important.

production: The entire process of creating a digital media presentation; there are three main stages: preproduction, production, and postproduction.

professional networking sites: Similar to social networking sites, they are used by professionals seeking to expand their career networks.

progress report: Reports written in a specified format and periodically submitted (monthly, quarterly, annually) to track the status of a project.

pronouns: Words that replace nouns in a sentence such as *he* or *she*.

proofreaders' marks: Specific symbols and notations universally used by writers and editors to note errors and changes.

proofreading: The process of checking the final copy for correct spelling, punctuation, and formatting and for typographical errors.

proper noun: A word that identifies a specific person, place, or thing.

proportion: The relationship of the size of elements to the whole and to each other.

protocol: A custom or rule of etiquette based on a tradition.

public domain: Material that is not owned by anybody and can be used without permission.

published: A document that has been made available to its receiver.

publishing stage: Printing the document and preparing it for submission.

punctuation: Marks used to show the structure of sentences.

Q

qualitative data: Information that provides insight into how people think about a particular topic.

quantitative data: Facts and figures from which conclusions can be drawn.

question mark: Punctuation used at the end of an interrogative sentence, or a sentence that asks a question.

quotation marks: Enclose short, direct quotes and titles of some artistic or written works; can also be used to show irony or non-standard use of words.

R

rapport: A feeling of harmony and accord in a relationship that encourages further communication.

readability: A measure of whether or not the document is easy to read.

reading for detail: Reading all words and phrases, considering their meaning, and determining how they combine with other elements to convey ideas.

receiving barriers: Occurs when the receiver says or does something that causes the sender's message not to be received.

recommendations: Actions the writer believes the reader should take.

recorder: Team member responsible for creating minutes, which is a written record of the meeting that can be used as reference for progress of completing the task.

redundancy: Repeating a message or saying the same thing more than once.

reference: A person who knows you well and can comment on your qualifications, work ethic, personal qualities, and work-related aspects of your character.

reference initials: Lowercase initials included at the end of a letter to indicate who keyed the document; only included if the typist differs from the writer.

relative pronouns: Pronouns used to begin dependent clauses in complex sentences.

report: Documents used to present information in a structured format.

representative sampling: A group that includes a cross section of the entire population you are targeting.

requests: Ask the reader for some type of action or response.

resolution: Selecting the number of pixels with which an image will be recorded with a camera.

restrictive clause: A type of dependent clause that identifies a particular person or thing and is essential to the meaning of the sentence.

résumé: A profile of your career goals, education, and work history to be given to prospective employers.

revising: Rewriting paragraphs and sentences to improve organization and content; it involves checking the structure of the document as a whole.

rhythm: The regular repetition of objects or sound to show movement or activity; it can also be used to create a sense of energy or urgency.

routine requests: Requests that are expected by the receiver.

S

sales message: A message that persuades the reader to spend money for a product or service, either immediately or later; an effective sales message attracts the attention of the reader, while selling the features and benefits of the product or service.

salutation: The greeting in a letter and always begins with *Dear* followed by the recipient's first name or, according to your relationship, title and last name.

scannable résumé: A résumé formatted so as not to use typographical elements, such as boldface, bullets, and indentations, for the purpose of allowing the document to be scanned into electronic format.

scanning: To quickly glance through a message to find something specific.

script: The outline and structure for the video detailing what will happen and when, what the scenes will look like, dialogue, and actions.

secondary readers: Readers who need to know the communication took place.

secondary research: Data and information already assembled and recorded by someone else.

second person: Refers to someone who is being addressed.

self-extracting compressed files: Compressed computer files that can be decompressed by simply double-clicking on the file.

semicolon: An internal punctuation mark used to separate clauses or some items in a series; it provides a stronger break than a comma.

sending barriers: Occur when the sender says or does something that causes the receiver to not receive the message.

sentence: A group of words that expresses a complete thought.

sentence fragment: A writing error, a sentence fragment is a dependent clause used alone.

shareware: Software that can be installed and used, then purchased if you decide to continue using it.

signature: Appears after the body of a letter and includes the writer's name and title.

signature block: Appears after the body of a letter and includes the writer's name, job title, and department; spaces are typically included between the complimentary close and signature block to allow for a handwritten signature.

simple predicate: Includes only the verbs that show action or state of being.

simple sentence: A sentence that has one independent clause and no dependent clauses and often contains one or more phrases.

simple subject: The nouns or pronouns about which the sentence gives information.

site license: Agreements that allow software to be installed on any machine owned by the company who purchased the software.

skeptic: An informal team member role who challenges the team to prove the solution is correct.

skepticism: A degree of doubt.

skimming: To quickly glance through an entire document.

smartphones: Advanced computerized devices that can be used to check e-mail, surf the Web, take pictures, and talk on the phone.

social bookmarking: A method of saving bookmarks to a public Web site so others may have access to them.

social media: An Internet-based tool that allows users to share information within a group.

social networking sites: Web sites that allow users to share information for the purpose of building relationships within their individual networks.

special requests: Requests that are not routine in nature and require planning an approach that will create a positive response.

split infinitive: Useful for emphasizing an adverb, it occurs when the adverb is placed between the word *to* and the verb.

Standard English: Word choice, sentence structure, paragraphs, and the layout or format of communication follow standard, accepted conventions used by those who speak English.

standard formatting: A generally accepted way to set up a document so its appearance follows a convention.

stereotyping: Classifying or generalizing about a group of people with a given set of characteristics.

storyboard: Illustrates the content of the digital media presentation and contains a sketch of each important scene or event along with a brief description of what will happen.

subject: The person speaking or the person, place, or thing the sentence describes.

subject complement: An adjective that describes the subject or a noun that renames or tells what the subject is.

subjective: An individual's interpretation that is dependent on personal views, experience, and background.

subjunctive mood: Expresses an idea, suggestion, or hypothetical situation.

subordinate clause: A dependent clause that is joined to the rest of the sentence with a subordinating conjunction, such as *since, because, when, if,* or *though.*

subordinating conjunctions: Connect dependent clauses to independent clauses; subordinating conjunctions introduce the dependent clause and include *although, because,* and *unless.*

superlative adjectives: Compare three or more people or things.

superlative adverbs: Compare three or more actions, conditions, or qualities; formed by adding *est* or *most* to the original adverb.

symmetry: A formal balance in which what appears on one side is mirrored on the other.

T

table of contents: Lists the major sections and subsections within a report or publication with page numbers.

tables: Presents detailed information in a series of columns and rows; rows are horizontal and columns are vertical.

team: Two or more people working together to reach a goal.

technical document: Provides the reader with technical information, often in the form of instructions or directions.

technical message: Provides the reader with technical information.

teleconferencing: Verbal communication with three or more people on a telephone call.

telephone etiquette: Using good manners on the telephone.

templates: Predesigned forms supplied in word processing software.

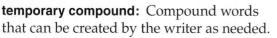

temporary compound: Compound words that can be created by the writer as needed.

terminal punctuation: Punctuation marks used at the end of a sentence.

text messaging: Participants conduct a conversation by keying and sending responses via cell phone, rather than talking or using video; the conversation usually takes place in real time, but the messages can be stored and retrieved at a later time.

texting: See *text messaging.*

thank-you message: A thank-you letter or note sent to the person who conducted your employment interview.

third person: Refers to someone being discussed.

timekeeper: Team member responsible for watching the clock to make sure meetings start and end on time.

tone: An impression of the overall content of the message.

transitions: Words, phrases, and sentences that connect ideas and clarify the relationship between sentences and paragraphs.

transmittal message: Routine communication accompanying documents or other materials attached to e-mails or sent by a delivery service.

trucking: Moving the camera in a circle around the scene.

U

uploading: Saving files to a Web or FTP site.

V

verb: A word that shows action or state of being.

verbal communication: Communicating with spoken words.

virtual team: A formal team whose members are in different locations.

visual cue: An element the reader sees and interprets to have a particular meaning.

visual design: The arrangement of the visual, artistic elements used to accomplish a goal or communicate an idea.

visual displays: Large graphic elements that accompany the presentation.

voice mail: Available with any landline or cell phone, it allows callers to leave voice messages that the phone's owner can access at a later time.

W

Web 2.0: Technology that allows users to collaborate and interact with each other on the World Wide Web.

Web seminars: Similar to teleconferencing, but with the added element of a video display; one computer display is shared over the Internet and the others attending the meeting can view the action onscreen; a Web seminar may consist of video, text, and voice communication.

white space: Margins, space between paragraphs, and any other blank space on the page.

wireless technology: Used to connect devices without the use of lines, cables, or other type of physical connection.

writer's block: A psychological condition that makes a writer feel unable to begin the writing tasks, therefore preventing a writer from proceeding with the writing process.

writing process: A set of sequential stages for each writing task that includes prewriting, writing, post writing, and publishing.

writing stage: Begun after the prewriting stage has been completed, it includes creating rough drafts, editing, and revising the piece.

writing style: The way in which a writer uses language to convey an idea.

written communication: Recording words through writing or keying to communicate.

Index

E

F